ESCAPE

from

THE AMERICAN CAGE

HOW TO REGAIN LIFE, LIBERTY, AND HAPPINESS

AND GAIN TRUTH, DIGNITY, AND LOVE

We pledge to build a safe, prosperous, united and happy society,
the United Societies of America
-- the best human-centered economy and superpower on earth.

KONRAD MILEWSKI

{Conrad Meelevskee}

Escape from the American Cage

How To Regain Life, Liberty, and Happiness

And Gain Truth, Dignity, and Love

Library of Congress Cataloging-in-Publication Data

Names: Milewski, Konrad, author.
Title: Escape from the American cage : How to regain life, liberty, and happiness and gain truth, dignity, and love / Konrad Milewski.
Description: First Edition. | Overland Park, KS, [2020] | Includes bibliographical references.
Identifiers: LCCN 2020922318 |
ISBN 978-1-7326073-1-6 (paperback) | ISBN 978-1-7326073-2-3 (Kindle ebook)

www.americancage.org
www.unitedsocietiesofamerica.org

You Love Mee

To the President of the United States of America,

To all past, present, and future presidential candidates,

To all past, present, and future government officials,

> *There is nothing in this book that you do not know.*
>
> *On the contrary, I believe you know so much more.*
>
> *I am desperately asking for your courage & leadership in seeking*
>
> *the highest truth.*

To the real heroes, our first responders and frontline workers,

> *During this tragic Covid-19 time, you gave your own lives for us.*
>
> *You have shown us true, selfless, and sacrificial love—the greatest*
>
> *possible Love. Thank you.*

To all Americans,

> *I wish you that you regain your right to life, liberty, happiness, and love,*
>
> *your true independence!*

To my American family & friends: Ann & Bill, Jennifer & Rolf, Leah & Steve, Bethani & Adam, Jessica & Valentin, Kelly & Tim, Sharon & Bill & Stefan,

Thank you for your trust, friendship, and inspiration.

To my wonderful wife Ola and fabulous children Paulina, Szymon, & Kornelia,

I love you beyond everything else! You are my deepest joy.

Contents

"When you see something that is not right, not fair, not just,

you have a moral obligation to say something, to do something."[*]

So, I am saying something and doing something right here, right now.

CHAPTER 1

Fake Independence

Locked in The American Cage

"In my country, I feel betrayed, helpless, and hopeless, as if I have been thrown into a cage."

"We don't live as if we were Independent."

      This book is about how to escape from our fake American Cage and regain our lost independence by living in accordance with The New Declaration. It is about how to escape from our mental cages and regain not only the right to life, liberty, and the pursuit of happiness but also to gain purpose, dignity, meaningful relationships and love. It is about truth, honesty, and courage. It is a dream about human-centered capitalism and democracy with a united, prosperous, and flourishing society. Finally, it is about a movement to revise, redesign, and implement our new American culture and economy, which will enable all Americans to be successful and happy. Although it is an extremely uncomfortable, embarrassing, dangerous, and painful journey, I encourage you to join me with an open, curious mind. Let us try to unmask our weaknesses, mistakes, injustices, meanness, and conflicting interests, unlock our homeland prison, fly away towards New America, and find true independence.

If you feel cheated, betrayed, and helpless (as if you have been thrown into a cage), it is time to do something about it. Based on all our virtues, characters, strengths, and beliefs, we Americans can escape from the cage and end the age of the cage for good. You are invited to join the movement. And please don't be offended by what you will see: the truth often hurts, but only the truth can set us free.

As per available studies, we can see that the vast majority of Americans are not experiencing the independence they were promised by The Declaration of Independence of The United States of America (from July 4, 1776).

"We hold these truths to be self-evident, that all men are created equal, that they are endowed by their Creator with certain unalienable Rights, that among these are Life, Liberty, and the pursuit of Happiness."

- **We don't** live as if we were created and endowed by our **Creator!**
- **We don't** live as if we were **all equal!**
- **We don't** live as if we respected our **lives!**
- **We don't** live as if we respected our **liberty!**
- **We don't** live as if we respected our **pursuit of happiness!**

To experience independence, first we must be able to experience anything. People must be given certain fundamental means to even start their journey toward becoming fully conscious individuals living meaningful lives as social human beings. Unfortunately, from the very beginning, the wild world does not give us any welcome package or any welcome hug. When we get to Earth, we are naked and defenseless, and immediately fully dependent on others. We will leave the Earth "internally alone," and in most cases, condemned to the grace of others. We are not able to survive without external help and without fundamental means. Isn't it frightening? Isn't it demotivating? Isn't it unfair? When we decide to stay on animal-like terms, life seems extremely brutal, unjust, cold, or pointless. But the whole world changes when we decide to live according to human qualities, such as the natural ability to use memory, to be aware of cause and effect phenomena in time, to bring order out of chaos, to understand things and solve problems, to accumulate knowledge and ultimately wisdom, to interact with other human beings and advance from relations into meaningful relationships, to surpass animal-like bonds or sexual impulses, and ultimately to live life, to be free, to grow and develop, to be healthy and happy, and even to go beyond ourselves seeking answers to existential questions such as why is there something rather than nothing? What or who caused all of it? Why we are here? What will happen after we die?

So, what kind of life qualities we are experiencing or not experiencing here in America?

The vast majority of Americans are not experiencing their right to life.

- We are **killing each other with firearms** more often than in any other developed country.
- We feel **unsafe and frightened** because we can easily be killed by anybody, anytime.
- We live in **great fear.**

The vast majority of Americans are not experiencing their freedom.

- We experience senseless acts of **violence**, **racism,** and **injustice.**
- We are a "**Mass-Addiction Society**" with the world's highest rates of **substance abuse**.
- We don't have enough **education** because we simply can't afford it.
- We are brainwashed and manipulated by over-invested **media and social media...**
- We don't have real **freedom of speech** anymore. Instead, we have **freedom of hatred.**
- We are enslaved by **debts,** controlled by banking, real estate, and other forces.
- We don't have **money,** and 80% of us own only 7% of the country's wealth.
- We don't have **time** because we simply can't afford it.
- We don't have our **American dreams** because we cannot sleep at night.

The vast majority of Americans are not experiencing happiness.

- We perform poorly and below comparably wealthy nations when it comes to **happiness.**

- We don't have enough **health coverage** because we simply can't afford it.
- We don't have healthy **lifestyles,** as we are on the edge of obesity or hunger.
- We are **stressed** and **depressed**.
- We commit **suicide** at an unprecedented level.
- We have the highest **income inequality** of all rich countries.
- We have no **social trust anymore.**
- We are **inundated with lawsuits**, as are our businesses.
- Confidence in the **government** has fallen.
- We don't have **meaningful relationships.** As a result, we are chronically **lonely**.
- We are a suffering nation.

The vast majority of Americans are not experiencing equality.

- We fail to ensure **dignity for all.**
- We don't have **decent living conditions** for all, like food, shelter, childcare, or education.
- We don't provide equal access to **life opportunities.**
- We have **socioeconomic inequality**.
- We don't fully **respect** and appreciate each other's **differences.**
- By contrast, we experience senseless acts of **violence, racism,** and **injustice.**

The vast majority of Americans are not living according to the Creator, who created and endowed us.

- We have forgotten that we have a **Creator** as mentioned in The Declaration.
- We have forgotten what real **love** is, and that it is one of the keys to happiness.
- We are **afraid**.
- We see **no hope**.
- We are in continuous and constant **fear.**

It also means that we are quite far from fulfilling the ambitions set out in the preamble to the U.S. Constitution:

"We the People of the United States, in Order to form a more perfect Union, establish Justice, insure domestic Tranquility, provide for the common defense, promote the general Welfare, and secure the Blessings of Liberty to ourselves and our Posterity, do ordain and establish this Constitution for the United States of America."

You could say "enough, it is not fair." It is easier to focus on negatives rather than positives, and on challenges rather than benefits. It is easier to destroy than to build, and ultimately, it is easier to list what we don't have versus what we already have. You are totally right. Let's see what we have and try to balance the overall picture.

The vast majority of Americans value, admire, and are ready to fight for our:

- **Liberty and freedom,**
- **Self-determination,**
- **Power (being in charge, deciding on our own)**
- **Entrepreneurship, inventiveness, and innovation**
- **Diversity**
- **Democracy and a free market**, our competitive advantages

The vast majority of Americans have the following strengths:

- We have a **"self-made"** mindset.
- We have a **strong work ethic,** a "badge of honor."
- We have **potential** and can work harder and longer, so we are more professional than others.
- We have the **American Dream**, coming from minimal personal means and rising to the top.
- We have a **competitive mindset**. Being #1 is winning, and being #2 is "losing."

- We have a **risk-taking mindset** of "nothing ventured, nothing gained."
- We have **confidence**, the ability to turn issues into opportunities (you better be optimistic).
- We have a **"work hard, play hard"** mentality.
- We have incredible **voluntarism** and we self-organize around major adversities quickly.
- We have an incredibly **giving** mindset and attitude. We gave $427.71 billion to charity in 2018.
- **We are effective and productive human beings.**

Isn't this an incredible foundation to build on? The sky is the limit, as we used to say.

It is a great foundation to begin with, no doubt about it. Now, sorry for being ironic, but you have even more strengths than those mentioned above.

You have "no time" to have more money, as you are struggling with everyday life. You are too busy to survive.

You have "no money" to have more time, as your debt commitments are counted in years.

You have "no education" to have more money and more time, and in the first place, you have no education, because you have no money and no time, or no time and no money.

You have "no dreams," including those American ones.

What is a prerequisite to have any dreams, even tiny ones? I think the most widespread and well-known approach is, to take a nap, or to start from very beginning – to have your eyes closed. As you are continually busy, worried, anxious, and tired, you are not in a position to do it right. Either you do not sleep at all, or you are unconscious or half-conscious – too tired to dream. If even by accident you have a dream, then you are too tired to reflect on it, or plan it. Forget about executing it.

Unfortunately, there are things even worse than those described above: you do not have the comfort of an emotional and social life.

You feel unsafe and frightened because you can easily be killed by almost anyone.

Although some people in the ivory tower have been telling you for ages that we are the most powerful and best armed nation on Earth, and in fact this may be true, the fact is that we are one of the most frightened nations on Earth. We are afraid of one another. How bad is that? While taking driving lessons, you are taught not to look into people's eyes while waiting at the intersection for the light to change. It can be your last red or green light, so you had better pretend to listen to music and not even dare to look around. As a society, we are not yet in a position to close important chapters in our history. Can you imagine us not having a gun or a whole set of guns at hand?

A few weeks ago, one car did hit another in a simple car accident at an intersection. Then two drivers got out from their slightly scratched vehicles and started shooting at each other. They both died, leaving devastated children and wives at the mercy of fate. What selfishness, and stupidity. In other civilized places, people would start arguing, screaming, or calling the police. In very rare and extreme cases, they would start a fist fight. No one would die. Life is too precious. Life is the only thing we have.

You feel insecure because you can be fired immediately, at any time, and left on the street with your box of staples, pens, and napkins. You know that you don't have any valuable savings that could give you some air to breathe and time to recover. According to one survey, close to 60 percent of Americans don't have enough cash to cover $500 worth of unexpected expenses.

You feel lost and hopeless, trapped by banks, insurance companies, and other dehumanizing systems.

You are lonely.

You are going through anxiety, stress, and depression.

You do not feel love anymore.

You are afraid.

This can be overwhelming, I know, but this is true for most of us Americans.

The great paradox is that we are not able to see this dysfunction as our problem. Our American lives are so perfectly faked that we believe everything is real. We are too close to the problem to see it right. We are the problem! We can have the impression that we act in someone else's theatre. "All the world's a stage, and all the men and women merely players" seems to be true. Good old William Shakespeare was right. To be fair in our judgments, let's not compare our dysfunctions to "the poorest in the world" or to "the weakest in the world." Let's compare ourselves according to our ambitions to be "the wealthiest in the world" and to be "the strongest in the world." Don't we want to be the best, the most competitive, and the most confident? Before proving that our dysfunction is real, I can already tell you that we are not the role model. We are not even among equals. We are far, far behind others.

"Stop, stop, stop. What are you talking about?!," you might shout with anger. We are the most advanced capitalistic system in the universe, and there are certain rules to be followed. We know what love and kindness are. But our currency is money. Through money, we communicate with one another, and appreciate people's value, efforts, outcomes, and lives. Through money, we build our power, security, and "prosperity." Through money we grow and develop, innovate, invent, and create. We bring money to the world. For us, time is money, so, by definition, we do not have time, and we had better accept it. Time turns into money. I would even venture that everything we touch turns into money. Our role model is the mythological King Midas, with his golden touch. We are the champions of the world in Midas-like football, with our brilliant golden touchdowns. Is anyone else playing this game? If you don't have money, you don't have value. If you don't have money, you don't matter. If you don't have money, we don't care. If you don't have money, you had better do something, you had better try harder, you had better earn some. I do not like my writing style, either. Forgive me this true analogy.

So how do we regain our Independence? How do we live according to the Declaration? How do we successfully escape from our fake American Cage? And how do we bring happiness to our lives?

In the next chapters of this book, I describe our fake American happiness based on reliable and credible sources. I describe our fake right to liberty and how enslaved we are by money, the media, and much more. I also describe our fake right to life, and how intimidated we are by guns, which terrorize us every day. I dare to rewrite the Declaration as our New Declaration. In more personal chapters, I share my view of my own happiness and how it was formed and is nurtured. Finally, I share my understanding of my Creator, which determines all aspects of my life. There are several places in this book where I define problems and propose solutions to the most critical ones. I suggest taking "what works best" from different societies and formulating the best solution of all, a "Made in the U.S.A." version. In this book, you will find suggestions on how to get started on your own journey, how to escape mental cages, what the transformative process of breaking with a false self looks like, what the role of personal responsibility is, what scientific research around happiness exists, including the miraculous impact of animals on us, how powerful giving is, what the fundamentals of human-oriented culture are, and how to establish bridges and partnerships. In addition, at the ends of some chapters, I make many recommendations for your personal use, including how to become more peaceful, more mindful, more intentional, more responsible for your own life, more educated on current socio-economic problems, more financially intelligent, and more independent from media, digitalization, gaming, filming, and other "addictions." The ultimate goal is for you to become a more joyful and happier person in a happier society. I encourage learning from many sources, especially conflicting ones that shake up your worldview, as well as thinking more and seeking the best possible solutions.

Why did I write a book about unhappiness in America?

Because I love you, the people of the United States, and I want you to flourish as others already do.

I feel your suffering, which is related to the hardships of everyday life, and I feel very sorry for you. Observing your struggles, exhaustion, enormous stress levels, how you get lost in your hard work, how you count each and every dollar to make ends meet, how you try to keep families together, how you try to find friends and maintain relationships, how you try to chase your own American dreams – I feel a deep sense of injustice, sadness, and frustration. There is so much energy, potential, good will, desire, and work that has been and will be done. There is a hope and belief in a better America in all of you Americans, but something is not functioning as it should be. Something is preventing you from living a truly joyful, prosperous life. There is so much waste happening. With all those enormous resources and the unstoppable drive you have, you permanently miss the target. That is sad, frustrating, and incomprehensible.

Why did I write this book about the American mental cage?

Because I care about you, the people of the United States, and want you to discover that there are ways that go beyond our current thinking and lead to happiness and prosperity.

Even having enormous amounts of energy, potential, good will, desire, a strong work ethic, and hope and belief in a great America does not guarantee individual or societal success. Regardless of one's good intentions, extraordinary enthusiasm, readiness to put in lots of effort, excellent strategies, deeply thought-through plans with well-defined milestones, well-allocated resources and well-controlled execution (WHAT to do), without a proper culture (HOW we do things and behave here) - nothing significant and sustainable will be achieved. Regardless of WHAT you do and deliver as a result, and regardless of HOW well you do it and how you behave, if there is no visible and clear purpose, values, or beliefs (WHY we exist? What is our PURPOSE?) – nothing valuable and relevant will be achieved. The PURPOSE example may look like this: "To preserve our lives and live as happily and joyfully as possible" because "human life is the most precious and the only thing we really have." Without my being alive, nothing matters. Nothing exists for me. I cannot experience it and know it. If I do not exist, I am not even able to know it and experience it. Again, although you are excellent in doing, performing, being highly productive, being highly creative, being highly motivated, and always winning, you are imprisoned in a unique American culture or variation of American cultures, that by design or by accident are not well calibrated with the PURPOSE defined above. Or those cultures are by design or by accident well calibrated with the purpose or variation of the purposes which are not the right ultimate purposes and do not consider human life as the most precious of all that is. There is a third possibility I can think of: you are sitting in your comfortable or uncomfortable version of your own American cage and have no clue that you are sitting there. You are not fully aware of life's purpose, or of the created or artificially evolved social norms, values, belief systems, codes of conduct, expected behaviors, behavioral patterns, social processes, and procedures of your cage. Most of the possible social systems of your cage were formed long before you were born.

There could be another variation of same third scenario: instead of sitting in your comfortable or uncomfortable cage, you are running around on autopilot before a serious crash happens. If you knew what was really happening around you, you would immediately try to escape from the cage. I say "try" because escaping the cage is very difficult. The individual is against the system, the inner self, his or her habits, schemas, or powerful ego – a fake incarnation of the historical self. Searching for the purified "self" requires going on a journey. No shortcuts are possible.

If our PURPOSE was "to preserve our lives and live as happily and joyfully as possible" because "human life is the most precious and the only thing we really have," would you really vote for the economic and social system that is not able to eliminate poverty for all, both "survival level" poverty (inability to satisfy basic needs for oneself and one's family, like food, clothing, and shelter, daily) as well as "human dignity level" poverty (inability to satisfy higher-level needs for oneself and one's family like belonging, acceptation, trust, inclusion, holistic development, proper physical, emotional, intellectual, spiritual growth, etc. to open the gate to more human-like life experience and flourishing)? Would you really vote for a lack of affordable education (with consequences: unconsciousness, "stupidity" of citizens, ease of steering the primitive masses by those with power and money, fake democracy because masses are easily brainwashed and manipulated, poverty, fear, lack of social trust, student debt, powerful and abusive media), a lack of affordable primary care (with consequences: poor health, poor performance, poor life satisfaction, early death), a lack of affordable housing (with consequences: homelessness, debts, people working long hours, no time for friends and family, no meaningful relations, loneliness, fear, stress, anxiety, ...), a lack of affordable maternity and paternity leaves (with consequences: poor parent-child bonds, poor self-esteem, mental and emotional instability, the inability to form healthy relationships in the future), guns on the streets (with consequences: mass murders, fear, feeling possessed by firearms, the inability to walk anywhere without feeling unsafe, lack of social trust), and so on and so forth? Please, think for yourself, what you would vote for and what you would vote against, to enable ultimate PURPOSE?

What if, while you are sitting, standing, or running in your cage, you expect something good to happen to you, but nothing good is really happening? What if you are spending your whole life in the wrong cage, the one that is not designed to be helpful or supportive? What if your cage is not designed to offer realistic opportunities or to give you the foundations for living a happy and joyful life? What if your attention is drawn away by motivational slogans like: "Dream big! Awaken a giant within you!" In case what you dreamed of is still not enough, "dream bigger dreams!" If you are failing, "be more creative, be more productive, work harder, and take more risks." If you are still failing, maybe something is wrong with you, as there is nothing wrong with the cage. After a while, in an ideal-normal situation, you would give up and stop banging your head against the wall. As your American DNA has no such "giving up" program that you can run, you keep trying to break the wall, although your head is already swollen, bleeding, and causing you enormous pain. The walls of the cage are unbreakable. You will give up sooner or later, but will never admit it. Giving up is not part of your vocabulary.

Bird in The Cage

What if you are like a **bird in a cage**, purchased at a flea market 40 years ago and kept locked up without any possibility of escaping? You stopped asking yourself questions like "What are my wings for? Are they a genetic mutation, or are they left over from an unfinished evolution process?" You also stopped asking yourself about your huge beak and strong claws, treating them as life's mysteries. "Life if simple. I just have to follow the food provided by the invisible hand of "My Master" who shows up usually every day, arriving from a distant outside world. I can get more luxurious, premium dishes any time I do something extraordinary – jump, rotate, stand on one leg, hang on my beak, or scream as loudly as possible, modulating my voice according to a desirable pattern. There are days when I really want to stretch my broad and lengthy wings, but the cage is too small to do it. It hurts, when I press against the cage's grills. There are nights when I dream about flying. Rising in the air, being high up there, close to the ceiling, and gliding down to the floor - I call it flying. I do not know if that is possible. I never seen anything like that, but I have such a strange intuition. Maybe I saw it when I was a baby, maybe I saw it on the wall of a big box (I call it a room, my visible world), or even behind its walls on a wonderful, blue canvas (I call it the sky) – something like me was dancing pirouettes high in the air – maybe flying. Maybe there is a different world out there, a different universe, a different life, a better life. I have to stop these unproductive speculations and this wishful thinking, and keep my both feet on the ground, waiting for the food to come. I had better behave well to avoid provoking The Highest Intelligence to punish me or forget about me.

One day, part of my cage disappeared. Some of the grills moved away, as if the door was open. After long hours of staring at this inexplicable phenomenon of nature, I moved closer and stuck out my beak. It was an unbelievable and amazing feeling, the enormity of fresh air in my nostrils and the enormous space ahead of me. But it was also terrifying. Too much space in front of me, and so much air. What if I could fly? No, no, no. What was I thinking? It was overwhelming. Nature is too large to control. I wish the invisible door would close again. Was this a dream or reality? Should I stay, or should I go?

What are your convictions, what are your thinking patterns, what are your life schemas, what is your worldview, what is your intuition, what are you dreaming of? What seems to be suspicious to you? Can you see the cage, or at least the contours of the cage in which you are trapped? What is it like? Can you see the door? Can you look outside? What if the door suddenly opens? Would you be interested in going and checking what's out there? Would you be willing to come closer to that door? Would you be brave enough to lean your head out of the cage? Would you be bold enough to conquer the unknown? Will there be less suffering? Will there be more happiness and joy? How do I know? How can I be sure?

What if you are like a sheep, as described by one of the Buddhist monks?

"What are you doing here in this life, on planet Earth? And of course, when we are born, we're not given that answer, we're just here, we've arrived not really understanding what we're supposed to do with our life. And of course, sometimes we just follow what other people do. But not many of you can stand just being sheep for a while. When it comes to sheep, I always remember the little story told me by one of our monks. He grew up on a farm [...], really was local boy. And he said, once, you know, he went out to check out on the sheep in the farm. And he saw the sheep, he didn't know how they started, but they had formed a circle around a thick lump of bushes. So, they could not see the other side of the bush, but they'd formed a circle and they were walking round and round and round, as sheep always do, following the one in front, and they didn't realize that they were going round and round and round in a circle which had no end. And if he hadn't [...] pulled one of the sheep out of line, they'd still be walking around that circle years later. And that's what sheep do. They follow the one in front not realizing they're getting nowhere, they're just going round and round. And of course, what we're doing here, we follow other people first of all. But then we are born with this wonderful mind which

will always question. And that's really important to develop that questioning mind... [...]

And that really attracted me, the questioning and not just being sheep. So, when it comes to what we're doing here, we don't just follow what other people say, we learn how to find out for ourselves."[ii]

I wonder which is better, being an eagle in a cage, or being a sheep in a circle. Which do you prefer? Does it really matter?

You can be the most powerful bird in the world,

but if you are locked in the cage, it is all for nothing.

Why did I write this book about unhappiness in America and the American mental cage?

Because I consider my life purposeful, happy, joyful, and prosperous so far – and wish the same for you. Why do I wish the same for you? Because I discovered and accepted my life's mission of contributing to the greater good by helping people to discover the true meaning of life and to find their own purpose, happiness, joy, and prosperity. Why do I think I am qualified to give recommendations? Because I am a first-hand witness to the experience of living a joyful life. But also because I intentionally spent hundreds of hours listening to, discussing, coaching, and mentoring thousands of people – trying to figure out what it really takes to live a purposeful, happy, joyful, and prosperous life. Because I spent hundreds of hours reading, analyzing, reflecting, meditating, engaging in discussions about the meaning and purposefulness of life, human suffering, human conditioning, and human potential, while touching on spiritual, religious, emotional, psychological, physiological, political, economic, social, and cultural aspects. Why do I dare to challenge or worse "laugh at" or "have mercy over" the American mental cage? "What the heck am I thinking?" I dare because I come from a different mental cage. I also have quite good insights into other existing mental cages of the world. I was born and raised in Poland, the Heart of Europe, and experienced many versions of socialism(s), capitalism(s), and transformational hybrids. I lived or worked in twenty-plus different countries with twenty-plus different nationalities, cultures, and worldviews, and experienced various levels of happiness or unhappiness in those places. I can see differences and similarities, detect analogies between the cages of the world and the American cage, and build reasonable bridges, cause-and-effect relationships, and comparisons. I have been deeply engaged in American life for years, working and living here as a student in my early 20s, graduating from an American business school in my 30s, becoming an immigrant in my 40s, and now living here with my family. I have hands-on experience. I have one leg, one arm and half of my head with an equal share of my senses in my American mental prison, and the rest in the other mental prisons simultaneously. Maintaining such a state of mind is a fascinating experience from a scientific or social point of view, but it is an exhausting one as well. Processing in parallel all the variables of different lifestyles and running real-time valuations of those takes lots of energy, time, and attention. I am doing my best to find the best formula for a "happy life.".

To broaden my understanding of the world, I have thrown myself into the mental cages of specific "interest groups" like global and local leadership groups, global and local business ecosystems, business consulting groups, churches, coaching associations, psychotherapeutic schools, mindfulness groups, volunteer groups and other groups, associations, schools, communities, and gatherings. I have observed their values, behaviors, cultures, patterns, lessons, best practices, conclusions, winning approaches and methods, losing approaches and methods, benefits, challenges, risks, and rewards. I also tried to go the extra mile by voluntarily imprisoning myself in monasteries, spending quality time with super wise monks or carefully studying the centuries-old wisdom of Hinduism, Buddhism, Taoism, Judaism, Christianity, and other religious and spiritual traditions. To further simulate the diversity and complexity of the world, I collected a variety of scholarly degrees and completion certificates, including an executive Master of Business Administration, a Master of Computer Science, leadership courses, change-, communication-, project-, innovation-management courses, coaching-, mentoring-, psychotherapist-, meditation- and you name it programs. On top of all of it, for about twenty years, I remained professionally active as a head of highly performing international teams within one of the largest life science companies on Earth – to be able to apply what was learned and to be in action, living a practical rather than a theoretical, illusory life. Those different worldviews, beliefs, values, different schools of thoughts, points of views, different areas of interest, research areas, knowledge bases, different starting points, maturity levels, capabilities, different motivations and ultimate goals, different tools, skills, and access to diversity allow me to look at things through different lenses, and at the same time see broader contexts. With intentional reflection, I was able to distance myself from specific mental prisons (of course not in a perfect, definite way), break my inherited and acquired thinking patterns, expose prejudices and habits, reveal internal contradictions, gain new perspectives, and get to know the powerful but hidden forces that shape and steer people's lives, as well as whole societies and nations. Of course, there is so much to learn, but so little time.

I wrote this book because I consider myself ready to contribute to the development of the future "human-oriented economy," "human-centered economy," or "happiness-oriented economy" of the United States of America. I wrote this book because I myself experienced the amazing effects of "human-centered economies." I wrote this book because I believe we can make progress in America toward a more purposeful and flourishing society, and finally achieve satisfactory levels of happiness, joy, peace, and unity. I have no doubt that this can be done here. Finally, I wrote this book because I was fascinated by the message of the Declaration of Independence. I promised myself that I would help the people of this land regain true independence by ensuring that "all men are created equal" is well understood and respected, by ensuring that "all men are born with certain unalienable Rights, that among these are Life, Liberty and the pursuit of Happiness" is well understood and respected. I dream an even bigger dream by hoping we can build a society that not only allows the "pursuit of Happiness" but also intentionally supports the achievement of happiness, joy, and prosperity by all of its citizens.

America is the place where the impossible becomes possible. I am ready to pledge myself to serve and support this noble movement, the Happy and United Societies of America.

When I say that I am living a happy and joyful life, that doesn't mean I am free of suffering and pain. Rather, it means I live a happy and joyful life despite suffering and pain, without which there would be no access to my deepest self and to humility. Without that, there would be no access to human unity. Suffering in life is inevitable regardless of the cage (especially when dealing with uncured diseases, aging, dying, and the loss of loved ones). Despite the material world limitations which cause existential and health-related suffering, the vast majority of suffering and pain is caused by people. We do it both intentionally and unintentionally (greed, selfishness, revenge, subjective worldviews, unawareness, unconsciousness, ignorance, and stupidity). There is so much of it that can be eliminated and lead to greater satisfaction in life.

Self-awareness, self-consciousness, and proper intellectual formation starting at the very early stages can lead to financial stability, an understanding of and appreciation for human dignity, learned self-trust and social trust, and love and the ability to love wisely. These are just a few examples of building blocks that heavily influence the quality and level of so-called culpable suffering.

Please allow me one important remark. Even though I am not an American citizen (I am a permanent resident), I use the phrase "we Americans" to identify more deeply with the life situations of Americans and to strengthen the narrative and my own ties with the reader.

Finally, I wrote this book because I fell in love with love years ago and decided to love others as best as I could. I have decided that you are the subject of my love as well.

It is time to begin

Please forgive me in advance if you will feel personally affected by my analysis and conclusions written in this book. My goal is not to accuse and blame anyone, but to show different truths seen through the eyes of someone coming from outside the system, from another world of values, beliefs, and cultures. That is how I perceive American reality. I try to confront it with other possible and already existing realities. My motivation is love for people and the world, and the deep desire to discover the truth. Let's be honest, the phenomena described in this work, like independence, equality, the right to life, liberty, happiness, love, dignity, responsibility, meaning in life, welfare, money, economy, capitalism, socialism, inequality, poverty, the right to bear arms, violence, homeland security, the army, culture, consciousness, the illusion of self, science, free will, ideals, the Creator, God, God in a human body, "new atheists," the afterlife, belief or disbelief, faith, hope and again love, are inherently complex, complicated, and interrelated phenomena. In many cases, they are burdened with historical factors and motives originating from many conflicted or less conflicted interest groups or burdened with present aspects and motives of people in power or those who desire to be in power. These are not one-dimensional matters; they are intricate constructs that require careful study and making wise choices, including sometimes choosing the lesser evil. Constant compromises and maintaining balance - that's what this is about. But before agreeing to general compromises, which most of the time lead to lose-lose situations, it is much better to put in additional effort and work out win-win solutions. Whenever there is a chance to see the bigger picture, to think long term, to spend more time investigating, better outcomes can be expected – much better than results from alignments, contracts, and pacts concluded in a hurry. Thinking about risks and benefits and anticipating consequences always helps.

As long as we stay loyal to the highest truth, contradictory ideas will sooner or later elect the best one, until another, more true idea emerges on the horizon of infinite possibilities, as part of the unstoppable cycle of progress, driven by human creativity and the desire to conquer, grow, and know the truth. "The truth will set us free," and in truth we must build our future. As long as we stay loyal to the highest love, conflicting parties will sooner or later unite and join efforts and forces.

I hope that I am able to discover at least some truth about America, discover some of America's lies – and offer you a fresh perspective, a fresh look at what is happening in your apparently awesome homeland.

But what is the highest truth? What is the highest love? I encourage you to face your own mental prison with full honesty, humility, courage, curiosity, and the attitude that you can change it, and remind yourself who is really thinking your thoughts, who is really experiencing your emotions, who are you, why are you here, what is the purpose of your life, what life mission do you recognize for yourself, what responsibility do you want and agree to take. I encourage you to think for yourself what the best possible life for you and the people around you could be.

I am not saying that the American people have given up on the American Dream. But they have been robbed of the critical means to pursue their happiness. How can you really dream when you can't sleep at night? How can you even think "outside the box" when the box is tightly closed and sealed and has no windows through which you can see the truth, a brighter future, and a better life? Do not get me wrong, you are continuously trying both consciously and unconsciously to open those "non-existing" windows as you feel intuitively that there is something out there – over the rainbow, beyond your box's ceiling. How can you really act on your dreams when you can't escape that box?

We live with the illusion of freedom, prosperity, and happiness. We live in a well-fabricated American cage and in the mini cages of our lives. We live in a house of cards, and even if there are more "ace of spades" cards in our deck – in comparison to other foreign houses of cards, those cards are played not by us, the American people, but only by a few lucky ones. As we are not holding any cards in our hands, maybe we are the cards in the American house of cards. Have we been played by someone all this time?

We are trapped in a golden cage which is obviously awesome, wonderful, beautiful, fantastic, amazing, and gorgeous, but only from the outside. "Everything is awesome" as in the LEGO world. In fact, the inside is grey, dirty, sad, frightening, depressing, and hopeless. We are living our lives in that shiny cage, very far from the promises made by the Declaration. It is hard to believe how far. Some of us agreed to live with such an illusion, but most of us have been cheated and trained without our conscious consent. Even when you realize that the cage is not the reality, it is almost too late or too hard to leave it and fly away freely. Having no resources or means to change the situation, we tend to give up, or worse, shift our thoughts and dreams to unconsciously accepting the cage as the norm, as the only world.

Midas-type capitalism, of course, is working, but only for 1-3% of us. If that is what the Declaration meant, we had better start from the very beginning, and learn how to read and comprehend it.

I am telling you, we have created the system that is clearly preventing us from flourishing. And paradoxically, the point is not that the economic system or the justice system are seriously broken. It works exactly the way it was designed to work. What if we live and work in a wonderful apple orchard, but the groundwater is poisoned, and penetrates the roots, leaves, and fruits of our trees? No matter how hard you try to optimize the process of collecting and processing fruit, no matter how hard you try to clean the fruit before eating, no matter how beautiful this fruit is on the surface or how good it tastes - the inside of this fruit is "contaminated." It is unhealthy, and sooner or later it will contribute to the disease and the breakdown of the whole organism or society. Obviously, to get rid of a problem, we need to change the water or at least introduce effective mechanisms to filter it and clean it. Although most of us would claim that we are living in the most powerful, most prosperous, "all-is-possible," amazing apple orchard, somehow those "Great American" trees produce bad and harmful fruit. The majority of us who sit in the shade of these spreading trees are in a continuous fight with our own existence, struggling with everyday life, whereas only a very small portion of us are living an awesome life. Even if someone argues, "I cannot see institutionalized, systemic inequity or racism in my country when I look at existing policies and procedures" (as we expect the laws should be promoting equality in today's America), it is still far from an appropriate judgment, it is far from the real root cause, it is an easy way out of a more fundamental problem. It doesn't take a genius to see the basic cause-and-effect relationship between things, especially between almighty capital and everything else. If you do not have enough capital, you will not have enough health coverage. You will have less of a chance to recover or defend yourself against the reality of sickness. If you do not have enough capital, you will not have enough education. You will have fewer opportunities to compete for better paid jobs. You will be easily manipulated by smarter, capital-hungry minds. You will not have enough legal support when you need it, so you will often be defeated, sentenced, or victimized. Will you be treated the same as someone giving millions of dollars to attorneys? In such a system, no. Is this inequality? Yes. Is this inequity? It depends. If everything is carried out in accordance with applicable law, all is just. Strength, agility, and bigger pockets win; that is the law of the jungle. Should we then change the overall logic of how our system works? Should we vote for more human-oriented capitalism? Should we take a look at wealth distribution? That is an enormous temptation. It is more complicated than it may sound. I dare to present in this book a so-called human dignity baseline, which gives us a good starting position to become real human beings before assembling the skeleton of a future human-centered and still effective economy. The equality of human dignity is going to form other socioeconomic layers and set us on the right course toward being a more flourishing, united nation.

Don't you think that the recent COVID-19 pandemic has shown us the painful truth about our economy and underlying systems? Don't you think that COVID-19 has proven to us that we are relatively poor people living in the richest country on Earth? Don't you think that COVID-19 has presented to us what wealth and social inequality really look like in our country? Don't you think COVID-19 has reminded us who our real HEROES are? Don't you think all those recent "George Floyd protests" against social injustice and racism that have happened in most American cities have shown us how dysfunctional and hypocritical our society is? Don't you think all those recent street protests against social injustice and racism that have happened in most American cities have shown us how angry, frustrated, and lost our society is? Don't you think all those recent protests have shown us what disagreement with the status quo is? We have learned that literally everything can be gone within a few weeks. We have learned what the most important thing in life is. We will not be able to bring happiness to America unless we balance our ego-driven desire for success with our desire for human joy and unity. American culture and social norms have to be rebuilt or reinvented. As we are dependent on one another, we cannot be happy without one another. We urgently need to regain our social trust, change how we look at each other, how we see each other, how we talk to each other, how we understand and appreciate our individual differences, and how we agree on important topics. We need to prioritize our new happiness-oriented economy. The truth is, to flourish as human beings, we have to be given favorable conditions. For example, newborns have no chance of surviving without other people's help. We are not talking about satisfying other higher needs. That is why we need one another. Those who came before us, those who are right here, right now, and those who will come after us – we all matter and contribute to every individual human life. We need to be connected, to share and learn from our own experiences and our wisdom, to act together to leverage our abilities and capabilities, and to ensure our nation's continuity and growing happiness.

Will we be able to sustain recently acquired knowledge? Will we be able to build a better future on this? Will we turn these lessons into wisdom? Our economy and culture require serious revision and intervention. We have to change our system to get the best out of it.

Isn't it a good moment to start all over, with new hope and a strong motivation, a will to change, and a "can-do attitude?" It is a very good moment to open and leave our cage right here, right now.

Are you willing to learn the truth about your cage?

Are you willing to open the cage?

Are you willing to escape from your cage?

Are you willing to fly away fearlessly?

The prize is great and monumental.

Your new home - your new America.

Your independence and our independence.

Your happiness and our happiness!

CHAPTER 2

Fake Happiness

Overwhelmed by fear, distrust, and purposelessness

"In my own country, I feel deprived of the possibility of chasing my happiness."

"We are a seriously suffering nation."

Have you ever heard that story?

Deborah and James, our middle class representatives, have 2 and a half children, 2 and a half pets, a 2 and a half bedroom house with a mortgage, 2 and a half yards (back, front, and side), 2 and a half cars, 2 and a half TV screens, 2 and a half other screens per person (smartphones, tablets, play stations, etc.). In addition to all the other 2 and a half stuff, they possess 2 and a half individual dreams – American dreams. They want to feel 2 and a half times better than other people from other nations, they smile 2 and a half times, 10 times more than people from other countries. They have been informed that they are supposed to be happy by design, with the potential to become even happier, at least 2 and a half times happier than others. O.K., that's too much math. To simplify, their lives are greater, bigger, wider, and cooler in every way.

As the pursuit of happiness is guaranteed by the Declaration, feeling good is the most important and desired state of being for Debbie and James. So they spend their non-existent time and fortunes on sports, food, self-improvement books, motivational events, and conventions, including "prosperity gospel" gatherings, psychotherapy, drugs, and feel-good pills. Debbie and James start their days very early, earlier than their neighbors, jog about five miles, and go to the gym at 5:00AM. They attend Zumba class, yoga, and weightlifting activities. There is nothing better than feeling alive and starting the day full of energy and speed, with a competitive mindset. One more bag of proteins and they are ready to conquer the world. Not yet – they are not ready yet. There is one more very important thing, and everything else will depend on it: brushing and whitening their teeth and styling their hair. They cannot imagine going out into the world without super straight, crystal clear, snow-white, shiny, exposed teeth - embedded in a captivating, smiling face. Also, they cannot face the world with bad hair. Having a "bad hair day" equals unhappiness. They cannot move forward without checking that item on a refrigerator TO DO list. A great appearance is a must. Now, they are ready to perform, achieve, and win. Winning and the willingness to win are key. Staying active all day long, without too many breaks or vacation days, is typical. Anything else will look and feel very un-American.

There are moments, moments that can last years, when our family is feeling tired, stressed, and overwhelmed. Indeed, there is an enormous pressure out there. The pressure is unbearable, especially when neighbors seem to be moving up the prosperity ladder much faster, introducing from time to time shiny new objects everyone desires: a new lawnmower, car (of course with a sunroof, self-parking features, an Artificial Intelligence steering system, and a hybrid power unit – not having those is embarrassing nowadays), motor boat (with a huge engine – to not risk embarrassment) and many more upgraded household items. The tragedy is when they learn that yet another neighbor just left the neighborhood for a better one without saying goodbye and joined a richer local community with much greener grass, much cleaner and warmer water in their community pools and a much safer environment - the "demilitarized zone" - patrolled and monitored 24/7 by a well-paid police department in a fancy and gadget-filled police cars. That "friendship" is probably gone. It will be quite a shame to show up at their "friends'" house in their 3-year-old, outdated mid-size SUV without any special features. Even worse, they will experience humiliation if they host reunions at their location. It is beyond their imagination to invite their "upper class friends" to their 20-year-old 2 and a half bedroom house, without an open floor plan, a spacious interior, a real, fashionable wooden floor, a fully equipped kitchen island, a fully furnished, illuminated terrace with a set of heaters or coolers depending on the weather, standard and infrared burners, stainless steel grates, and a smartphone-controlled, natural gas grill. Debbie and James decide not to invite their newly lost "friends" anymore. "We can always meet in a good restaurant."

There are moments when our family is feeling tired, stressed, and overwhelmed. But no one is going to see that, even themselves. They suffer quietly. They used to say, "our great country is about making money, competing, winning, facing and overcoming adversities, and chasing our dreams". Although it is painful and cannot be cured by regular painkillers, it can be addressed by different substances or more work. They are now fighting their darkest thoughts of not being wealthy, charming, influential, or powerful. But fortunately, every new day means new beginnings, new chances, new opportunities, and finally, happy endings. Dark thoughts are already repressed from consciousness – that is a brilliant self-defense mechanism or capability used by our heroes on a daily basis. "We are Americans – we never give up." Dreams will definitely come true.

There are moments when our family is feeling tired, stressed, and overwhelmed. But they never openly complain about their lives. No one has ever heard that they cannot make ends meet. On the contrary, they say, "we've just engaged in additional business, and it is going fantastically." They simply have no time for weakness, sickness, or whatever-ness – it is never in their schedule, never anticipated, and never talked about. Of course, weakness, sickness, or whatever-ness is clearly not economical. "We cannot afford that, and the moment we start dealing with the healthcare system, that will be our first step toward bankruptcy." They have their best friend - painkillers - nearby, ready to save the day. Nowadays, they do not even swallow the tablet. It melts directly in their mouths thanks to technological advancements. This is all for their convenience, for their peace of mind, for their own improvements. In case Debbie and James feel unmotivated, they immediately correct their course to stay positive – following the guidance of the "American Association of Positive Thinkers."[iii]

American minds need to be well programmed neurolinguistically to succeed. Debbie and James have their own everyday ritual, performed in front of their bathroom mirror or car's rearview mirror, saying out loud: "We are the best," "We are the first," "We are great, amazing, and cool," "We are the people with can-do attitudes," "We can achieve whatever we want," "God or Consciousness is on our side."

Debbie and James try to keep up to date with all of the contemporary teachings about positive psychology, positive thinking, positive parenting, and positive being, - and immediately bring them to life. Even so called "positive negativity" would be an acceptable alternative for their philosophy of life. There is nothing weird about it. They demand that school educators and their children's caretakers incorporate all possible techniques which make kids feel good and strong, emphasize their self-esteem, nurture their self-satisfaction, and make them proud of their own achievements. In case there are no noticeable results yet generated, obstacles have to be immediately eliminated to ensure that achievements occur no matter what. Lack of outcomes and then lack of immediate recognition may be very harmful to their pupils. "To be" is not as important as "to achieve" and "to have." They are always passionately cheering their children on: "You are doing great," "Great job," "You can do it," "You did it," "You did a great job," "You were doing great," "What a great catch, what a great pitch, what a great kick, what a great score, what a great win." "I love you so much." That is so nice to watch. That is so uplifting and inspiring. What a supportive and happy family. There is nothing to improve or correct. Everything is awesome and perfect already.

In case their own self-programming techniques are not enough, Debbie and James take anti-depressants. They know that everyone is taking some and Americans are the best in the world at taking them – so they must take them every day. After that, there is no mountain they cannot climb, no problem they cannot solve. They can really handle all possible adversities and achieve, achieve, and achieve. To compensate for their "work hard" mentality, they should "play hard" as well.

One of the pleasures for Debbie and James's souls is to worship presidents, Hollywood celebrities, entrepreneurs, and sportsmen. They do not worship the royal family, which of course they do not have. They make fundamental shifts in how they spend their leisure time. They spend more than 4 hours a day of their leisure time watching TV, scrolling through social media, surfing the Internet, and texting. Their kids are far more advanced and "modern," spending more than 6 hours a day in front of the screens (internet, social media, texting, and gaming). They love to dive into the news streams of conventional television networks every day. It is how they shape their understanding of the world, it is their democratic right and duty – to be informed of everything immediately. They love to dive into multi-episode TV series and engage emotionally with their favorite characters and their stories. They are always debating what to watch next, or how to watch things at the same time (e.g. "House of Cards" season 6, episode 4, or "Game of Thrones" season 8, episode 5, or "Sex and the City" season 6, episode 20, or NFL Chiefs game, or track the scores of college basketball teams, or monitor weather conditions), and ensure that there is always access to the news. However, James, Debbie and their children are not synchronized at all because they each have their own preferences and time constraints. That is why everyone needs his/her own media device – that is a no-brainer. Their whole day has its own structure: in the early morning, morning news and soap operas (although they hate calling them that), podcasts or radio news in the car on the way to work, school, or church, lunch news at lunch time, again podcasts or radio news in the car going back home, in the afternoon, entertaining reality shows, in the later afternoon good TV series, at night a good movie – most probably on-demand, and late at night talk shows or sports.

They love to be sucked into the stories, identifying themselves with those dealing with infidelity, family problems, medical problems, and tragedies. By watching dramas regularly, they guarantee their kids enough exposure to murders, making sure they will be ready for the real world. Kiddos will digest at least 15,000 murders before they leave their safe, warm, loving, sweet home. Debbie and James cannot imagine their existence without media. It makes them peaceful and hopeful.

When it comes to relationships, there is no time for serious ones. Debbie and James would be scared to death thinking about building any deep, long-term commitments. Their preference is for fleeting acquaintances. Anything else would be against their American individualism and focus on their own lives, properties, assets, belongings, and dreams. "We are self-made achievers." They are so lucky to having their "own" (mortgaged) house in a community of other "owned" (mortgaged) houses. Being locked in their own home prevents them from seeing anyone and being seen by anyone, except obvious exceptions like unknown dog-walkers passing by, birthday parties in the neighbor's backyard, or brief interactions when picking up their mail or mowing their lawn. Usually, they wave and shout "Hi" or "How are you doing?" Thanks God no one is walking in this country and everything is so "big" and "wide" that meeting anyone with the intention to talk is more or less impossible. Thank God they are not living in the city anymore. They could not stand the crowds.

When they approach a stranger, of course it has to be with a big smile. They ask "how are you doing?" but never spend too much time looking into anyone's eyes or entering into lengthy discussions. "If there is no business to talk about, what's the purpose of engaging in a dialogue?". Their ideal interactions are 5-minute meet and greets, without any commitments or in-depth debates. The algorithm is simple: smile, say hi, inform others about recent achievements, and leave. "A high-performing culture requires us to be efficient in everything we do," it goes without saying.

Time is money, and time is all we really have here on Earth, implying that money is also everything. They believe that to ensure equality and eliminate any prejudices, the common denominator, money, has to be applied. They used to think that money would make us equal. Everyone has the same chance to excel, only what's needed is hard work and clear goals built on personal dreams and if possible, on talent.

They usually ask 2-3 introductory yet critical questions: "What do you do for living?," "What do you do for work?," and again "What do you do for living?" If they have already met their conversation partners, they ask, "How is work?" Sometimes, so called "small talk" can expand into other adjacent areas, like what happened or will happen (based on statistics) in recent or forthcoming football, baseball, or basketball games." In case they have the luxury of speaking for one more minute, they discuss yard work, their kids' education, fitness, and yoga achievements, or weather, concluding their dialogue by discussing food, drinks, and barbecue tips and tricks.

Recently, Debbie and James were visited by old friends who arrived exactly as planned at 5pm and stayed exactly as planned till 6pm. All their time was spent standing and grabbing various types of nachos dipped in various types of sauces. In addition, Debbie and James offered their stunning meatballs, and for dessert they served their beloved cheesecake. Making the food themselves would have been a waste of time, so they bought everything. No one dared to sit and discuss anything at the table. It would be so "un-American" to sit and talk (except at Thanksgiving). "We better find the time for an annual gathering to express our gratitude to the New World." "We better do it quick-and-dirty and move on to the next item on our agenda." It would be quite rude to offer a seat at the table and engage in a deeper, longer exchange of opinions, knowing that people have other commitments. "Frivolous talk comes with no practical value. Who has hours to spend? We had better invest hours and not spend them." Debbie and James did not even notice when their guests left their house. Everything happened so quickly.

Debbie and James do not travel abroad. They really do not have any interest in finding out what's out there, outside of America. Sometimes they believe there is nothing beyond America's borders. That is actually proven by the National Football League and the Super Bowl Finals, as we are undefeated world champions, and no one is bold enough to compete. To be honest, they do not care, nor do they have enough time or money to double-check whether there is anybody there. Debbie and James know key facts about major "enemies" like Russia, China, North Korea, Pakistan, Afghanistan and others. They receive their education mainly from mainstream media, usually in the form of well-packaged military success stories. They have heard about Paris, Rome, Barcelona, London and other cities, mainly through myths or fairy tales that depict the good old Europe. Of course, they can point out their North American neighbors on a map. Like 65 percent of Americans, Debbie and James do not have passports. They always dream of visiting the U.K. and France, but with only ten to fifteen vacation days per year, there is no time to travel. What if they come back, and there is no work waiting for them? They could be out on the streets within hours. It is insane that in those European countries, people have so many days off. Can you imagine having more than thirty paid vacation days? How can they work like that? It would be hard to concentrate and achieve anything if they were always on leave. Crazy. No wonder we are the most prosperous power on the globe. So getting to know different cultures is definitely not for Debbie and James. The U.S.A. is big enough for them to spend their whole lives exploring so many cultures and diversities at home.

You may wonder if Debbie and James are happy? Let's find out together.

What is happiness?

Let's have a look at some definitions of happiness that can be found in various sources, like Wikipedia, *Psychology Today*, the Greater Good Science Center at UC Berkeley, or scientific and non-scientific "well-being" books or publications.

- Happiness is "the experience of joy, contentment, or positive well-being, combined with a sense that one's life is good, meaningful, and worthwhile."[iv]
- "More than simply positive mood, happiness is a state of well-being that encompasses living a good life—that is, with a sense of meaning and deep contentment."[v]
- "Happiness is used in the context of mental or emotional states, including positive or pleasant emotions ranging from contentment to intense joy. It is also used in the context of life satisfaction, subjective well-being, [...] flourishing and well-being."[vi]
- "It means the satisfaction with the way one's life is going. It's not primarily a measure of whether one laughed or smiled yesterday, but how one feels about the course of one's life."[vii]
- "Most of us probably don't believe we need a formal definition of happiness; we know it when we feel it, and we often use the term to describe a range of positive emotions, including joy, pride,

contentment, and gratitude. But to understand the causes and effects of happiness, researchers first need to define it. Many of them use the term interchangeably with "subjective well-being," which they measure by simply asking people to report how satisfied they feel with their own lives and how much positive and negative emotion they're experiencing."[viii]

As we could anticipate, happiness seems to be a strongly desirable state of human mind, emotions, and body where one experiences an individualized sense of meaning and overall satisfaction from one's own life. As per some definitions, happiness may be seen as external - externally triggered - influenced by situations, interactions with people, being in certain places, and using certain things, or determined by the fulfillment of one's own expectations. Happiness could also be seen as more future-oriented, linked to a specific day in the future that is grounded in hope. When current expectations will be met in the future, happiness will arise. Happiness is usually deepened by joy, or we could say, at deeper levels of happiness, joy exists. It may be worth recalling an interesting conversation between the 14th Dalai Lama and Archbishop Desmond Tutu, captured in the *The Book of Joy: Lasting Happiness in a Changing World*,[ix] where the gentlemen outlined eight pillars of joy, divided by mind (**perspective, humility, humor, and acceptance**) and heart (**forgiveness, gratitude, compassion, and generosity**). It seems that joy is not external, but rather spiritual and existential—it does not depend on anything in order to exist. Joy comes when you are at peace with who you are, experiencing the truth about yourself and the world and experiencing the power of love for yourself and all beings, including the Absolute. In addition, as we can learn from "The Science of Happiness" course from UC Berkeley, **social connections, kindness**, and **community** are the keys to happiness and joy.

Are we in a good position to measure our own happiness or the collective happiness of our fellow Americans? I bet we are. There are already lots of activities going on in that field and many researchers have published their outcomes. For instance, let's Google "happiness index" and have a quick look at the first page of search results. We can, of course, Google other closely related terms like "well-being index," "quality of life index," "better life index," "life satisfaction index" and many more. Here is what I got, surfing on the 4th of July, 2019.

The thing is, regardless of what report we pull out, we immediately notice an obvious problem we have at home.

- **The United States of America is performing poorly, and substantially below most comparably wealthy nations!**
- "the US [...is] found much further down the list."[x]
- "Nordic countries take four out of the five top spots, and are well known to be stable, safe and socially progressive. There is very little corruption, and the police and politicians are trusted."[xi]
- "Although the U.S. ranks highly for per capita income, it is only ranked 18th [...], substantially below most comparably wealthy nations."[xii]
- "That is because it performs poorly on social measures: life expectancy has declined, inequality has grown, and confidence in the government has fallen."[xiii]
- "Measured subjective well-being has declined [in the U.S.] during the past 10 years."[xiv]
- "The long-term rise in U.S. income per person has been accompanied by several trends adverse to 'subjective well-being': worsening health conditions for much of the population; declining social trust; and declining confidence in government"[xv]
- "U.S. society is in many ways under profound stress, even though the economy by traditional measures is doing fine." [...] "The trends are not good, and the comparative position of the U.S. relative to other high-income countries is nothing short of alarming."[xvi]

When we go deeper, it is getting worse. We can see at least three interrelated diseases that need immediate attention: obesity, substance abuse, and depression. If not cured, they will bring more and more tragic consequences to our society very soon.

- "The U.S. has one of the [...] highest rate of antidepressant use in the world."[xvii]
- "The U.S. has one of the highest rates of obesity [...] in the world."[xviii]
- "Major studies have documented the rising suicide rates [...]"[xix]
- The United States has been called "A Mass-Addiction Society".[xx]
- "The U.S. has among the world's highest rates of substance abuse.
- Among all 196 countries, the U.S. ranks 2nd overall in DALYs [disability-adjusted life years] lost to all drug use disorders; 1st in DALYs from cocaine use; 3rd in DALYs from opioid addiction; and 2nd in DALYs from amphetamine use."[xxi]
- "Psychologists have been decrying the apparently soaring rates of addictive disorders and seemingly associated mental disorders, including major depressive disorders and a range of anxiety disorders."[xxii]

As suggested by the World Happiness Report editors, there are hypotheses of possible causes of rising rates of addiction: rising stress levels associated with increased socioeconomic inequality, the market economy, mismatches between human nature and modern life.

- We experience increasing socioeconomic inequality. "High and rising income inequality in high-income societies leads to stress, which leads to addiction: 'As we have seen, trying to maintain self-esteem and status in a more unequal society can be highly stressful ... [...] The experience of stress can lead to an increased desire for anything which makes them feel better – whether alcohol, drugs, eating for comfort, retail therapy, or another crutch. It's a dysfunctional way of coping, of giving yourself a break from the relentlessness of the anxiety so many feel.'"[xxiii]
- We consume addictive products being stimulated by manipulative advertisements. "Addictive products boost the bottom line. Americans are being drugged, stimulated, and aroused by the work

of advertisers, marketers, app designers, and others who know how to hook people on brands and product lines."[xxiv]

- We eat badly. "35 percent of Americans are obese and have an increased risk of developing diabetes, heart disease, and even cancer." [xxv]
- In addition, we experience increasingly senseless acts of violence, racism, and injustice that continue to plague our nation. People of color and those of African descent have been experiencing systemic racism for years. The tragic deaths of George Floyd, Ahmaud Arbery and Breonna Taylor are just a few recent (2020) examples that provoked Americans to go out and protest.

Unfortunately, we are not talking here about individual well-being cases, we are talking about nation-wide epidemics. Let's repeat what we can see now in our country:

Declining life expectancy, increasing inequality, declining social trust and confidence in government, increasing obesity rates, rising depression, increasing substance abuse, increasing digital use (Internet, social media, gaming, smartphone) related addictions, rising suicide rates.

What is going on? Aren't you shocked? Aren't you disappointed? Aren't you sad?

Are we a role model nation for the world today or not? Are we really the leading power? Should others follow our lead? Are we the best – as we used to say and believe? Are we the first – as we used to dream and aspire to be? Are we fighting the right battles? Are we taking part in the right races?

Do we have the right purpose, goals, and ambitions?

What if we created our own world where we compared ourselves to ourselves, our own standards to our own standards? No corrective actions would be required or possible. Any direction we would take or any vision we would have would be fine. There would be no benchmarks for us.

Are we sitting on an island operating in a vacuum? To some degree, yes, as we are on the big continental island. Is that more of a cage than an island? Are we trapped in our own cage, without access to information about what is happening around us? And by the way, how can we navigate well throughout our lives without having any reference to externally located "reference points?" From basic physics courses, we know that without those reference points, we do not even know if we are moving, not to mention moving in a particular direction.

Shouldn't we treat those insights as a wake-up call? There is clear evidence of our declining well-being.

Let's have a closer look at available reports and analyze relevant charts and happiness categories. To make this book readable and not too scientific, let's reduce our scope to two reliable and credible sources: **"The World Happiness Report"** - an annual publication of the United Nations Sustainable Development Solutions Network and **"How's Life? Measuring Well-Being"** with the **"OECD Better Life Index,"** prepared and published by the Organization for Economic Co-operation and Development (OECD), an international organization that works to build better policies for better lives.

Before studying any graphs in detail, let's review what kinds of dimensions or aspects have been taken into consideration by researchers to ensure that the building blocks of overall "happiness indexes" are valid.

In the first report, the World Happiness Report, country rankings were built on three key happiness measures: **life evaluations, positive affect, and negative affect**, and then the variation of happiness across countries was explained by using the six main variables: **GDP per capita, social support, healthy life expectancy, freedom to make life choices, generosity, and freedom from corruption.**

To get estimates of key measures, so called Cantril ladder questions were asked and respondents valued their lives on a 0 to 10 scale, with the worst possible life as a 0 and the best possible life as a 10. Positive affect is based on the average frequency of happiness, laughter, and enjoyment on the previous day, and negative affect is based on the average frequency of worry, sadness, and anger on the previous day.

Did you experience the following feelings: happiness, laughter, and enjoyment during the day yesterday?

Did you experience the following feelings: worry, sadness, and anger during the day yesterday?

In the second report (OECD Better Life Index) we could see the following categories: **housing, income, jobs, community, education, environment, civic engagement, health, life satisfaction, safety, work-life balance** which builds up the overall index. At the next granular level, the following measures were used:

- Housing: Dwellings without basic facilities, housing expenditure, rooms per person
- Income: Household net adjusted disposable income, household net financial wealth
- Jobs: Labor market insecurity, employment rate, long-term unemployment rate, earnings
- Community: Quality of support network
- Education: Educational attainment, student skills, years of education
- Environment: Air pollution, water quality
- Civic engagement: Stakeholder engagement for developing regulations, voter turnout
- Health: Life expectancy, self-reported health
- Life Satisfaction: Life satisfaction
- Safety: Feeling safe walking alone at night, homicide rate

- Work-Life Balance: Working very long hours, time devoted to leisure and personal care

As per OECD data and analyses of 38 countries (including 3 non-OECD: Brazil, Russia, South Africa) the U.S.A. is performing extremely well (1st place!) in income/earnings categories: household net adjusted disposable income, household net financial wealth, personal earnings (2nd place), and rooms per person (3rd place). The U.S.A. is performing also very well in so called stakeholder engagement for the developing regulations category (2nd place). The self-reported health category also looks pretty good (3rd place) according to that particular study.

We should be proud. We are first, we are the best! We are the wealthiest citizens on Earth. We can buy anything we want and enjoy it as long as we want. O.K., where is the trick? How come such a successful nation with pockets full of money and endless possibilities receives such bad scores in other happiness-related categories? I know, you do not want to hear again that old saying that "Money won't bring you happiness" or "Money doesn't equal happiness." Even if that is true, many of us would argue that money at least makes life easier. Of course, we can always find someone who believes that money equals happiness. By the way, I like the saying, "Money does buy happiness if you spend it the right way." What do you think?

So, where is the trick? There is no trick, there is no magic. Maybe this is a misunderstanding, a misinterpretation, or a lie, whispered into our ears from birth till death that we are rich, wealthy, powerful, and full of unlimited potential.

As we are going to see in the Money chapter of this book, although we are the richest country on Earth, the majority of Americans never experience that richness. If you want to see the trick, here it is:

- **The wealthiest 1% possess close to 43% of the nation's wealth.**
- **Almost all wealth is in the hands of less than 20% of the U.S. population.**
- **More than 40 million Americans live below the poverty line.**

So, what is wrong with that? Even if we take those citizens living at the U.S. poverty line, which is around $12,000 per year, it is still better than tens of other countries. What can people from Madagascar, Afghanistan, or Ethiopia say, earning less than $100 per month, or less than $1,000 per year!? Or, what can people from Mexico, Brazil, China, or Russia say, earning less than $800 per year, or less than $10,000 per year. We are very wealthy by comparison. So, to solve that puzzle, it looks like there are other measures and aspects that need to be taken into consideration, like the "cost of living," "quality of life" of those whose income is at the poverty level, access to the healthcare system (is healthcare really available to those located on the poverty line?), access to education (is education really available to those located on the poverty line?), you name it. The poverty line is just a starting point. The above-mentioned systems are not available for most of those from lower or lower-middle class homes, unless they apply for substantial loans. There is more to analyze in the Money chapter.

Rank	Country	Average income Annually	Average income Monthly
9	United States	59,160 $	4,930 $
44	Russia	9,220 $	768 $
45	China	8,690 $	724 $
46	Brazil	8,610 $	718 $
47	Mexico	8,610 $	718 $
55	South Africa	5,430 $	453 $
68	Nigeria	2,100 $	175 $
69	India	1,790 $	149 $
72	Kenya	1,460 $	122 $
73	Ethiopia	740 $	62 $
74	Afghanistan	560 $	47 $
77	Madagascar	400 $	33 $

Table 1 Average income around the world, 2017, Selected countries vs. USA[xxvi]

Speaking of tricks, in an economy with huge wealth inequality like ours, using so called "average income" as a good measure to explain individual income may be very misleading. What is an average income of 1 million dollars and 30,000 dollars of income? It is, by the rules of math: ($1,000,000 + $30,000) DIVIDED BY 2 = $515,000. Who wouldn't like to earn half a million per year? Please, excuse me for this extreme example... But is it really extreme in our case? Let's try with another statistical measure, "median".

The median wage in the U.S. is around $30,000 per year, which yields about $2,500 per month.

That gives us a totally different picture. It is about 50% less than what is actually promoted as the average income. "Median" is understood as the middle value when a data set is ordered from least to greatest, meaning, we take all Americans' wages, order them from the smallest to the largest, and select the wage which is right in the middle of a whole set (for instance, about 160 million people were employed in the United States in 2018, we take the wage of the position numbered: 80 million, of course, under the assumption that all wages were ordered prior to the selection of this median).

So the ultimate trick is, we are all real millionaires when relocated to the poorest countries but not when we are at home. With all the costs of living that have to be paid and overwhelming inequality troubling us, we simply feel unsatisfied, frustrated, and unhappy. The other question is, how much pride, vanity, or thoughtlessness on our part cause such misery, and how much is real poverty. It would require an assessment of individual life situations, as well as insight into one's honesty, with an understanding of one's own values and belief system.

Let's come back to our happiness assessment. We can certainly see that although we are "the richest," we are not "the happiest."

Unfortunately, we are learning again that a purely GDP oriented country's socio-economy is not enough to guarantee its citizens a good life.

The United States strongly underperforms in the following dimensions: life expectancy, homicide rate, time devoted to leisure, and personal care, and is therefore located at the very bottom of the rankings.

In the remaining categories of the OECD report, our country is simply average: in labor market security, the employment rate, the quality of support networks, educational attainment, student skills, years of education, air pollution, water quality, voter turnout, life satisfaction, feeling safe walking alone at night, employees' hours.

Please take a look at self-explanatory charts based on the data coming from the World Happiness Report and the OECD data and its Better Life Index. I can only encourage you to study it further directly from the sources.

World Happiness Report

The fact is: we are not first on the list. We are not on the podium either. We are not among the top 10 or 15. We are in the top 20. What a relief that there are 100+ more countries analyzed in that report.

Instead of being the light of the world, we are somewhere there - against our own ambitions.

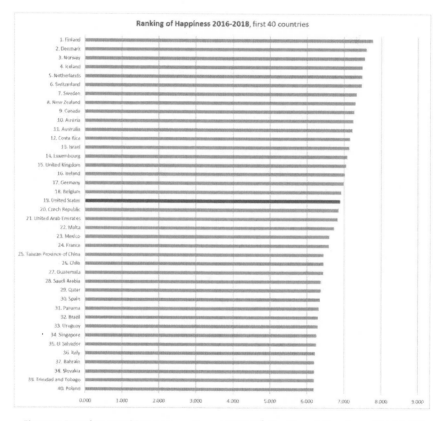

Figure 1 Based on World Happiness Report 2019[xxvii], Ranking of Happiness 2016-2018

How's Life: Measuring Well-Being[xxviii] and The Better Life Index[xxix]

"Your Better Life Index aims to involve citizens in the debate on measuring the well-being of societies, and to empower them to become more informed and engaged in the policy-making process that shapes all our lives."

Life Satisfaction

According to the latest OECD data, the United States' life satisfaction is somewhere in the middle of a ranking of the list of 38 OECD countries. It is not tragic that we are not the last. It is tragic that we are not the first. Shall we be satisfied with our "balanced" middle position? Balance is usually a golden rule in life, isn't it? Not when it comes to life satisfaction. We all want to live better lives. What if we move to the top? Do we all want to move up? What assumptions have to be changed? Are we brave enough to challenge the status quo? What are the forces that are going to pull us down right after we start climbing?

"Happiness or subjective well-being can be measured in terms of life satisfaction, the presence of positive experiences and feelings, and the absence of negative experiences and feelings. Such measures, while subjective, are a useful complement to objective data to compare the quality of life across countries. Life satisfaction measures how people evaluate their life as a whole rather than their current feelings."

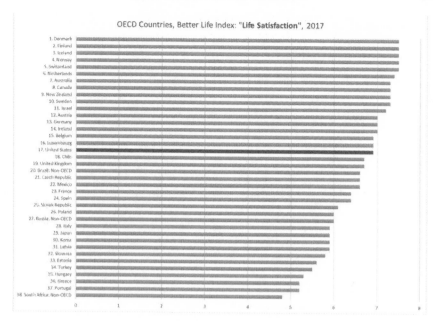

Figure 2 Based on OECD, Better Life Index: "Life Satisfaction" indicator[xx]

Safety, Homicide rate

According to the latest OECD data, the United States' homicide rate is much higher than that of peer countries. It is a shame. Look at the very bottom of the graph, where you can find us.

"Personal security is a core element for the well-being of individuals and includes the risks of people being physically assaulted or falling victim to other types of crime. Crime may lead to loss of life and property, as well as physical pain, post-traumatic stress and anxiety. One of the biggest impacts of crime on people's well-being appears to be through the feeling of vulnerability that it causes. […]

Homicide rates (the number of murders per 100,000 inhabitants) only represent the most extreme form of contact crime and thus do not provide information about more typical safety conditions. They are however a more reliable measure of a country's safety level because, unlike other crimes, murders are usually always reported to the police. […]

Social status also has an impact on victimization rates and perceptions of security. People with higher income and higher education usually report higher feelings of security and face lower risks of crime. This can be explained by the fact they can afford better security and are less exposed to criminal activities such as youth gangs or drug smuggling."[xxxi]

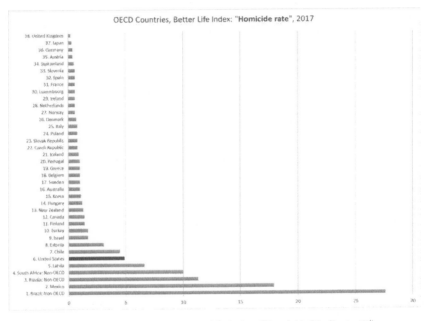

Figure 3 Based on OECD, Better Life Index: "Homicide" Indicator[xxxii]

Work-life balance, time devoted to leisure, and personal care

According to the latest OECD data, United States citizens spend far less time on leisure and personal care than citizens of other countries. So how do we recharge our batteries, how do we approach our problems anew, how can we spend some time with those we love – and in turn experience self-fulfillment and self-satisfaction and be touched by the healing power of intimacy? We know that the brain requires breaks to be effective. We know we should "work smarter, not harder." Of course, no one is talking about cheap shortcuts – still one has to put in an effort, even tremendous effort to excel and accomplish what's planned. We know that "quality counts at work, and quantity counts at home." To have quantity at home, we need time. Mastery would be when on top of quantity at home you invest quality time in family and friends. We know that the creative brain requires breaks but also intentional changes of context, sometimes intentional immersion in emptiness (as in the magic world of mindfulness), lack of analysis of thoughts, freedom from judgment or from chasing or triggering new thoughts, and "pure" awareness of what is. We start talking about consciousness, peace, and true rest. To play that new cultural game, to enjoy an awakening, we had better find time to find time, and then it will be much easier.

> "I think I am smarter than you think, I think" – I guarantee you, you will not grab the essence of this simple sentence unless you spend enough time on it. And you better start thinking in a new way as I think you are not thinking enough, as you think.

Now, take a look at the following graph, especially at the very bottom of it. Where is the U.S.A.?

"The ability to successfully combine work, family commitments, and personal life is important for the well-being of all members in a household. Governments can help to address the issue by encouraging supportive and flexible working practices, making it easier for parents to strike a better balance between work and home life. [...]

Furthermore, the more people work, the less time they have to spend on other activities, such as personal care or leisure. The amount and quality of leisure time is important for people's overall well-being, and can bring additional physical and mental health benefits."xxxiii

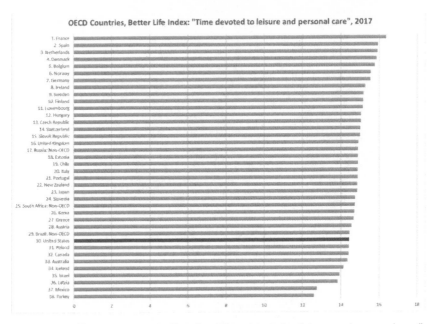

Changes in Happiness

You can say that we are the products of a history, we inherited the world in which we live, and most of the things are the results of the past because of the bad choices we made as humans, as American people. It is not our fault. We are trying our best. And this is a thing - are we really trying? Are we really changing for the better?

Let's be honest – we have not advanced in years, and we are getting worse. The U.S.A. is ranked as #112 on the happiness change list. That is mind-blowing. A negative index associated with a country (as presented in the following chart) means that the situation in that country is continuously worsening in the given period of time.

The average life satisfaction in the United States has declined during the past dozen years despite ongoing economic growth.

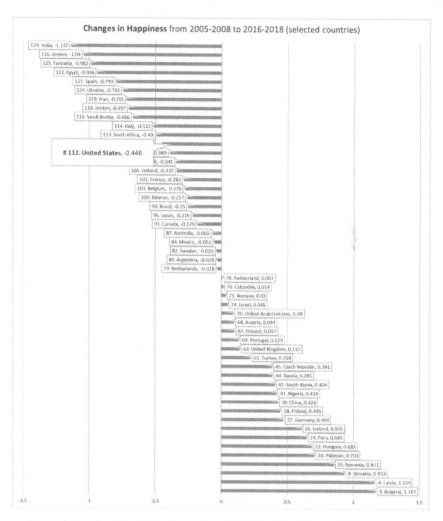

Figure 5 Based on World Happiness Report 2019[xxxv]*, "Changing World Happiness"*

This is indeed the very sad state of happiness in the United States. It is frightening to think what is going to happen next if we don't stop this negative trend.

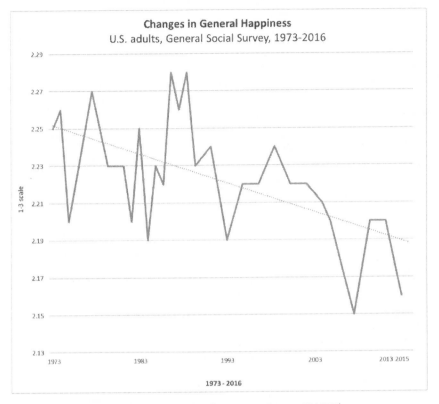

Figure 6 Based on World Happiness Report 2019[xxxvi],
"The Sad State of Happiness in the United States and the Role of Digital Media"

Addictions

Do you know that we are **"A Mass-Addiction Society,"**[xxxvii] as suggested by the World Happiness Report following dedicated studies? America is suffering an epidemic of multiple addictions and experiencing the rapid rise of adolescent depression, suicidal ideation, and suicide attempts. American "souls" are filled with discouragement, apathy, indifference, lack of internal motivation, confusion, lack of focus, lack of meaning, and lack of peace. There could be one major cause or set of interrelated causes that shape our individual and social mental health. We can already hear about dominating theories, best guesses, and speculations about excessive use of digital media and video games, the excess of available options due to general improvement of the quality of life, or the "irritating" inequality GAP in various dimensions (access to opportunities, education, wealth, health, …or even consciousness levels), the shift from physically lived life to mentally lived life during the information and knowledge era, the growth of individual freedom, social acceptance of self-determined identity and gender, new social norms and structures, and ever-present existential suffering viewed from the different contexts of the more conscious and less conscious minds (stretching towards extreme states of mind) of contemporary people. Of course, more causes can be found and claimed as root causes. But the complexity is coming from interconnectivities, individual conditioning, and systemic dynamics.

Digital revolution and happiness

It is not difficult to notice that we spend a huge amount of time using digital media, which has a great impact on how we communicate with each other every day. The use of screens (primarily smartphones and video games) is considered extremely heavy (in comparison to the non-digital era) and amounts for more than 6 hours per day per person – to make it even worse, per very young person (up to 18 years old). Yet the digital era is just starting.

Let me ask you the following rhetorical questions: what's the first thing you do when you wake up in the morning, and why is it checking your smartphone? Take a look at some supportive questions:

- Do you check your smartphone (short texts, chats, messengers, e-mails) immediately after you wake up, while you are still in bed?
- Do you check your smartphone immediately after you wake up, while sitting on the toilet?
- Do you check your smartphone immediately after you wake up, standing in front of a mirror (while brushing your teeth or styling your hair)?
- Do you check your smartphone immediately after you wake up, while you walk down the stairs to the kitchen?
- Or do you check your smartphone messages immediately after you wake up, while sitting at the breakfast table – keeping up silent conversations with your physical, loved ones?

Statistics are easy to predict. The vast majority of us grab our phones while in bed, or while sitting on the toilet. I wonder what the total number of smartphones dropped in the water while flushing is. This is the beauty of our times or the side effect of the technology revolution. We are simply at the beginning of that journey, learning together as a society how to engage with communication advancements in the most effective and hopefully healthy way.

But what is really wrong with digital communication and interconnectivity? In fact, it is quite easy to observe, looking at any randomly selected group of people that meets for lunch, dinner, birthday parties, trips to the theater, or movie nights. It is tragic and comic at the same time. It seems that according to animal instincts, we subconsciously attract one another, derive a certain pleasure from proximity, bodily warmth, or simple touch, but at the same time we exchange our thoughts using artificial, external media. Instead of direct conversations, we prefer to text, chat, and send video messages to our avatars – virtual representations of ourselves. We stare at each other through the windows of high definition cameras and touchable screens, we talk to each other through mics and portable speakers, we meet and greet with our augmented hands – carrying not yet implanted chips.

Why is this new form of co-existence so attractive? Building further on the social media research done by Mikołaj Piskorski,[xxxviii] Professor of Strategy and Innovation at IMD Business School, and a former professor at Stanford's Graduate School of Business and Harvard, who thoroughly studied the phenomenon of new media - it is about the fulfillment of our "primitive" needs, which were not fully met by pre-digital tools and methods. The digital revolution opens up new possibilities for us, offering totally new means of seamless, instant communication, and brings new dimensions of excitement, pleasure, satisfaction, the perception of multiplied group potential, the perception of knowing everything, the perception of being anywhere with anyone, and the perception of unity. In short, the deep human need to be admired (modeled by vanity and pride) is perfectly met in the virtual world of digital social media. Non-harmful exhibitionism is now possible – one can go and present in real time one's own achievements, championships, victories, prizes, and certificates without any false humility or guilt from showing off in front of the whole world. It is a new mechanism, a useful trampoline for our egos, allowing them to bounce higher and higher. Another deep human need (modeled by greed and curiosity) to observe others in hiding without any embarrassment, shame, or guilt - is perfectly met in a digital reality as well. You can simply stare at anyone, anytime, anywhere without any consequences (you think). You can watch them doing anything from routine to crazy, inappropriate, or dangerous activities. On top of that, you can be anyone you want, a small child who enters a virtual group of elementary school students working on coding and developing robots, an adult male interested in antique cars who joins a virtual car fanatics' group, a tall blond lady interested in getting a leading role in upcoming movies and who looks for new casting calls, or a crazy scientist who informs others of his or her discovery of a new particle by signing up for and publishing on a restricted scientific blog. You can also be "yourself" – but only if you want, as there is no pressure. Of course, these are just examples of unmet needs from the past that now can be satisfied in new, mind-blowing ways.

Of course, we can look at digitization from different angles and draw both negative and positive conclusions from it. As rightly observed by well-recognized American writer Nicholas Carr, the Internet has a direct impact on our brains - turning us into "The Shallows"[xxxix] – modern cavemen who without any deep reflection, thinking process, or decision-making process immediately and automatically react to external stimuli. Overreaction leads to a new situation, and that causes another spontaneous reaction. When the brain continually switches from one context to another, it is functioning in so-called unconditioned response mode most of the time. No major reasoning is employed. No evidence is gathered to properly assess the circumstances and proceed with adequate action. Memorization is not optimal because linear and longer learning are fully replaced by "hyper-text," non-linear and rapid learning. When we spend less than a couple of seconds on web pages, Facebook[xl] posts, tweets[xli], Instagram[xlii] graphics, or Snapchat[xliii] chats, information is simply not transferred from short-term memory to long-term memory. This happens because "consciousness" is not able to grab it so quickly and link it back to what's known, and also because the new information pushes older information further back in the memory queue. Short-term memory has fairly limited capacity: it can hold about seven items for not more than 20 or 30 seconds at a time. We are simply not learning (in a traditional sense). We are simply not thinking as deeply as we used to think. Are we getting dumber? I think it is too early to assess, but the consequences are visible, both in a positive and negative senses. For sure, the new intelligence we have acquired will give rise to new intelligence (just have a look at how kids interact with digital objects, how they search for information, how they orient themselves in space, how they link the dots of distant subjects and how they are able to build on the new building blocks of reality). On the other hand, we can see generations who suffer from lost wisdom, being left without memory, reflection, focus, patience, and perseverance. They struggle when solving complex problems as well as everyday roadblocks. They are also extremely lonely. Being in a constant consumption mode leaves our brains no time to rest. Instead of switching off devices, we become more addicted to them. New information is seen by the brain as a kind of instant gratification or suppression of drug-like cravings. Total consumption does not leave any space for creativity, self-realization, self-fulfillment, and joy. Life appears to be harder, less bearable, meaningless, and boring.

We communicate, but we do not connect.

We are created to be connected

"I think that technology is hijacking and exploiting that natural need for connection [...] It's really interesting to me that the more hyper-connected our kids are the more lonely and left out they feel. [We] have increases in depression, anxiety, suicidal thoughts, suicidal actions, loneliness, and feeling left out."

"Teens who spend five or more hours on social media are 70% more likely to have suicidal thoughts."

"I need you [...] to understand some things about how the brain works with connection. We have to touch or see or hear a loved one's voice to combat the stress in our bodies. [...] When we see, touch, or hear, our cortisol [often called the "stress hormone"] goes down and our oxytocin [known as the "cuddle hormone" or the "love hormone," because it is released when people snuggle up or bond socially] goes up. [...] That oxytocin is a little bit of a Pac-Man [maze arcade game developed and released in 1980] and then if you see or connect with somebody it becomes a big Pac-Man and it eats the cortisol - that's his job. But it does not work when you text. It doesn't happen if you read it. [...] If you need [...] to get encouragement from a parent or a loved one and you get a text - that's nice, but your brain will not change. The stress hormones will not go down. [...] We have to connect with our kids [or loved ones] at a different level."[xliv] - *Susan Dunaway, licensed and certified counselor*

Without meaningful and deep connections, we isolate ourselves from mankind, we move away from each other, we expand our own universe of loneliness, drifting alone toward the all-encompassing emptiness of space and time. We become more and more possessed by fear, we disconnect from the source of our identity, and we disconnect from the invisible but real unity of beings. We lose ground and fly away. We become more and more frightened by the perspective of getting sucked into black holes of nothingness or becoming dark matter. An unknown horizon is at our fingertips. It is happening now.

Some may ask, why is nothingness a bad thing? Maybe we are misinterpreting the whole evolutionary process. Isn't nothingness[xlv] at the core of some ancient spiritual traditions? Isn't it the destination of awakened minds? What if immersion in nothingness results in peace of mind, in release from existential suffering, must-haves, ambitions, commitments, and surrounding voices wanting something from us and demanding, ordering, and begging for attention and obedience? The reality of nothingness is terrifying, and at the same time, it tempts us with promises of blissful peace and nirvana. Sometimes one feels crushed and disappointed like a child being abandoned by one's own "loving" parents, while at other times, one feels powerful, like God, united with everything that exists, and endorsed by nature.

What else is so alarming when it comes to the digital revolution?

After a deeper dive into recent digital marketing and social media technologies, or more accurately, after reviewing and understanding the business models of leading digital companies, the overall picture becomes appalling. It turns out that on top of the information-sharing functionalities of well-known networks, they are designed to steer our attention and our thinking, to influence our decisions, and in the end, to ensure the collection of our money, bringing revenue streams into the pockets of networks' owners.

Facebook, Twitter, Google, Amazon and other similar platforms use sophisticated algorithms to capture data and information about their users to enrich those users' searching, sharing, or buying experiences. The personal details of surfing individuals can bring obvious advantages and benefits to those individuals, for instance, speeding up payments, giving recommendations while shopping based on personal preferences, or linking people based on their hobbies, locations, or interests. Unfortunately, recent investigations (including the story of Cambridge Analytica and how it used Facebook data to influence the 2016 presidential election) are bringing to light the dark side of social media's business models and companies' recent practices. Our personal data and all possible digital footprints we leave on the Internet are used by specialized algorithms to create our virtual profiles, including behavioral models of those profiles, with detailed needs and preferences. We exist in cyberspace as virtual avatars, whether we like it or not. Precious prospects or customers' data is then sold to interested parties who can afford it. In most cases, we don't know what has been collected and sold, but it can be used against us. The whole manipulation cycle continues.

There is a huge imbalance between the value that network participants and network owners receive. Business models are designed to increase company value at the expense of their platform's members. We can observe a wide stream of money flowing from consumers towards owners. This is a new era, with new magnates. Fair distribution of value is one problem that needs urgent resolution, but another big headache is true manipulation by design. It is not only disgusting but also very dangerous. Platforms are optimized to keep users' attention, to ensure users want more and spend more time and money, to make users feel better (how many likes and followers do you have?) and ultimately, to create addiction. I can imagine that that is hard to believe. Of course, it is getting more and more challenging. Platforms are programmed to keep you engaged, and guess what, through their evolution, platforms' owners have also discovered that to be more attractive and appealing to the audience and achieve greater engagement, they need to introduce fear in addition to the "entertainment and happiness" they initially offered. An army of psychologists and sociologists have been recruited to build the most effective models. When one is afraid, one is more willing to search, share, and react. Instinctively, when one shares one's fears, one immediately experiences some form of relief, a moment of greater peace. At the same time, fear created in our heads further isolates us from people even turning against one another. People search for revenge, react aggressively, or in social media terms, "micro-aggressively." We can already observe astronomical levels of fear triggered by that hate. The incorporated tactics of social platforms know what human evolutionary wiring is and what stimulus expected results will bring. The more you go into subconscious manipulation, the better.

Platforms are coded to filter the content before you see it. That is a powerful tool to escalate interest and excitement, but also hatred across the network, country, and globe. It is a powerful tool to shape people's opinions by presenting to them only the "right," fitting that to pre-existing criteria. When used for a long period of time, it is a powerful tool to shape people's mindsets, and in the end, to steer masses to act upon a given pattern or strategy. As a result, our society is becoming more and more polarized, vulnerable, and ready to explode when provoked by even tiny lies offered to it by well-trained algorithms – acting like agents who are at the service of an enemy. On an individual level, people are becoming more nervous while participating in contemporary public conversations. It is not too far away, going from fear and hate to violence. Isn't it humans' fault that we escalate bad news faster than good news, and that we tend to overreact to danger and underreact to luck? Of course, it is not always like that. Sometimes we are paralyzed in a life-threatening situation, and sometimes we are jumping for joy at hearing a success story, but in general we overreact and seek sensation most of the time. I would say it is more a bug than a fault. The fault is when we use human weaknesses or natural disabilities against ourselves. The fault is when knowing people's tendency to become addicts, we use sophisticated and hidden tactics to stoke that addiction. The fault is when people with high potential to contribute to the greater good and who already have the means decide to use those tactics against humanity for their particular, selfish gains. It could be because of stupidity, immaturity, greed, or desire for power – it doesn't really matter. What does matter is our lives, our quality of life, our preservation of and care for our lives. Social media may create value for all yet may destroy value and bring tragic results, from steered, manipulated conversations, to shaped, "fundamentalistic" opinions, to elevated and escalated hatred to individual or collective acts of violence. Are we really building the right foundations for our own future? Is this what we need?

Social distrust fueled by misleading lawsuit advertising

- "'Have you or a loved one been hurt? You deserve compensation! Call now to get $$$!' Everyone in America has seen some version of that TV ad. Usually, it comes with scary music, a dramatic voiceover, and some official-sounding language about a 'medical alert' or a 'drug alert.' The bombastic language and overdramatic visuals can mask the fact that these ads are often part of highly sophisticated campaigns that systematically target key moments in the litigation lifecycle to maximize profits for the plaintiffs' lawyers."[xlvi]

- Lawsuit advertising in the U.S. trends and drives the litigation lifecycle and influences public policy changes.

- While personal injury lawyers did not win a single trial, their firms will receive hundreds of millions of dollars in fees and costs from a single litigation—a significant return on their investment. [xlvii]

- "Plaintiffs' lawyers, companies that specialize in advertising and gathering claims (known as 'lead generators'), and third parties that finance the litigation spend about $1 billion on television advertising each year to seek plaintiffs for mass tort litigation."[xlviii]

- "[They] create mass tort litigation through misleading, fearmongering ads. Through these ads, call centers, and a network of law firms, businesses are inundated with lawsuits. As cases mount, they are pressured to settle due to the cost of never-ending litigation, the risk of liability (particularly in areas viewed as plaintiff-friendly), and damage to their reputations."[xlix]

- "Mass tort litigation is a profit-driven industry."[l]

- "The pervasiveness of [...] lawsuit ads poses a risk to public health and the ability to receive a fair trial."[li]

- The U.S. has the highest liability costs as a percentage of GDP of the Eurozone economies. Liability costs are 2.6 times higher than the average level.[lii]

- "U.S. liability costs are four times higher than those of the least costly European countries in the study." [liii]

- The U.S. has about three times as many judges and lawsuits per capita than other wealthy democracies like Canada, Australia, and

Japan. We have more than fifteen times as many lawyers per capita as Japan or Canada.[liv]

- **We are inundated with lawsuits, as are our businesses.**

We cannot trust those whom we ought to trust anymore. Can we even trust one another?

The Drug and Opioid Crisis

- "Recent data of the Institute of Health Metrics and Evaluation (IHME) show that the U.S. has among the world's highest rates of substance abuse."
- "Among all 196 countries, the U.S. ranks 2nd overall in DALYs [Disability-Adjusted Life Years] lost to all drug use disorders; 1st in DALYs from cocaine use; 3rd in DALYs from opioid addiction; and 2nd in DALYs from amphetamine use. The U.S. is moderate only for alcohol use disorders, ranking 39th. These very heavy burdens of substance disorders are matched by the high U.S. rankings on other mental disorders. The U.S. ranks 5th in the world in DALYs from anxiety disorders and 11th in the world from depressive disorders. Across all mental disorders, the U.S. ranks 4th in the world."[lv]

Allow me to repeat, **we Americans are:**

1st **in cocaine use**
2nd **in all drug use**
3rd **in opioid addiction**
4th **in all mental disorders**
5th **in anxiety disorders**

What's going on here? Asking questions about happiness in America may sound sarcastic or inappropriate. We are the nation that suffers! Let's face it.

We all know that drugs can be used to neutralize physical and emotional pain, to disconnect with the ego, and to temporarily minimize existential pain. On the surface, that can be seen as positive. Statistics may suggest that we are at least trying to reduce levels of suffering in our society with an increasing supply of narcotics, and figuring out a better starting point for many people hoping to recover. Is that really our conscious decision, our resilience strategy? We also know that most drugs are addictive, and if abused, caused terrible outcomes. When you correlate the increase in drug abuse with the increase in suicides in our country in the last decade, you will be surprised and saddened to see what's happening. The problem with drugs is subtle and very sly. It is tempting to offer quick relief to our crying souls. It is even more tempting to establish new "opioid-based" therapeutic, FDA approved, healthcare markets and capitalize on that new civilization's epidemics.

- "The opioid epidemic or opioid crisis is a term that generally refers to the rapid increase in the use of prescription and nonprescription opioid drugs in the United States beginning in the late 1990s.
- The increase in opioid overdose deaths has been dramatic: opioids were responsible for 47,600 of the 70,200 drug overdose deaths overall in the US in 2017. [...]
- Drug overdoses have become the leading cause of death of Americans under 50, with two-thirds of those deaths from opioids [...]
- What the U.S. Surgeon General dubbed "The Opioid Crisis" likely began with the over-prescription of opioids in the 1990s, which led to them become the most prescribed class of medications in the United States. Opioids initiated for post-surgery or pain management are one of the leading causes of opioid misuse, where approximately 6% of people continued opioid use after trauma or surgery [...]
- When people continue to use opioids beyond what a doctor prescribes, whether to minimize pain or induce euphoric feelings, it can mark the beginning stages of an opiate addiction."[lvi]

- Approximately 200 million prescriptions for opioids were written in America in 2017.
- Opioid companies misled sick people about how addictive their drugs were. Example:
  - OxyContin maker Purdue Pharma has reached a tentative agreement with 22 states and about 2,000 local governments over its role in a deadly epidemic. The deal will cost the company and its billionaire owners, the Sackler family, about $12 billion. [lvii]
  - Now, to see the whole craziness, we could listen to the interview with the former chairman and president of Purdue Pharma, Dr. Richard Sackler, who - to the question: "Do you know how much the Sackler family has made off the sale of OxyContin?" – answered: "I don't know." That is unconscionable, awful, insane and dangerous. This is our "reliable" and "credible" American billionaire businessman setting an example. He may pay about $3 billion in penalties and keep enjoying his carefree, non-addictive life. Why do we allow that to happen in our home cage?

Drugs and the Free Market

What about our brilliant free-market theory and model? Wasn't it designed to be self-healing, the best socio-economic system ever created? Customers know what they want, and businesses efficiently recognize and fulfill those needs. In other words, customers get products, services or experiences, in exchange for which businesses get economic value, measured in money. What if customers want dangerous products? What if they decide to entertain themselves to the extreme and are willing to pay for it? Both groups are maximizing their values: customers experience ecstasy, and businesses gain more cash and loyal customers. Where is the problem, then? Is our free economy a wonder drug? Let's ask one more question. In the long run, does the maximization of value work for both groups? For sure, business is going to leverage the potential of current, loyal customers but also can count on new customers' acquisitions. Without extensive promotion or aggressive mass communication, word of mouth will definitely help here (one cool pool party and the network of followers/addicts grows exponentially) as well as devoted physicians, who, in exchange for commissions, will be the products' evangelists. How can we not trust our doctors? What about customers? Customers, on top of the price they have already paid for products, may pay with their own lives. Due to free market transactions, customers will very soon enter the path of self-extermination, destroying step by step their quality of life, their friendships and families, degrading their dignity, falling into slavery to substances, substance providers, and their own primitive but powerful impulses. Having lost any sense of shame, they become completely powerless and senseless.

It is not hard to imagine that without other balancing forces, the free-market model may wreak havoc on our lives. Can we still trust that model? Should we be blindly enchanted by it? The argument that U.S. capitalism is so much better than anything else that exists or could possibly exist may not be valid any more. Model testing lasts at most two hundred years. Have we proven the model? Why don't we look at the results? We are looking at them in this book.

It is not hard to predict that if we allow hungry, purely profit-driven legal bodies to act without any limits on the market segments of vulnerable, susceptible prospects, they will sooner or later consume their own consumers who lack control of their own lives. The topic of "personal" consciousness is coming back. If we continue the simulation, we will most likely become emotional and physical slaves. Our free-market model may require urgent and constructive criticism with tangible adjustments.

Also, we may conclude that human beings can trade their independence and freedom for engagement in other risky activities like gambling, borrowing money, risky sexual behavior, sugar or artificial sugar consumption (corn sugar, sweeteners, and soda), gaming, shopping, extreme sports, and as elaborated earlier, the overconsumption of information.

"This whole country [U.S.A.] is a strip club. You got people tossing the money and people doing the dance." "Now that is the real truth." [lviii] *--Hustlers*

Our free economy is doing extremely well in some respects. Our GDP growth is outperforming every other economy's. The Amazons and Walmarts of the world are full of goods. Some extremely successful and happy demigods are proving that the American Dream is not just a dream but a reality. After all, the stadiums are filled to the brim with enthusiastic fans, proud and happy to participate in the games. The nation is playing and celebrating. But in other respects, such as household debt, student debt, obesity, gun violence, mental health issues, and suicide rates, we are doing poorly. What a miserable cage we are living in. Without any doubt, we live in a mass-addiction cage and are a "mass-addiction society".

Is the concept of a free market good or bad? Is capitalism the model that ought to be proposed to other countries, especially those of the Third World?

We can easily demonize the market economy, saying it is a home of a secret group of selfish people of great wealth who rule and control the whole society, or that it is a system of organized exploitation of poorer, not fully educated, lower-class members. But on the other hand, "it is simply empirically the case that no economic system has lifted more people out of real poverty than the vibrant market economy. [...] **The market economy is a great good, but it must be both legally and morally conditioned,"** [lix] Bishop Robert Barron, an influential American theologian, recently said, He echoed the point of view of Pope John Paul II, whom many considered a moral authority in his time.

"If 'capitalism' [refers to] an economic system which recognizes the fundamental and positive role of business, the market, private property and the resulting responsibility for the means of production, as well as human creativity in the economic sector, then the answer is certainly in the affirmative. But if 'capitalism' [refers to] a system in which freedom in the economic sector is not circumscribed within a strong juridical framework which places it at the service of human freedom in its totality, and which sees it as a particular aspect of that freedom, the core of which is ethical and religious, then the reply is certainly negative. [...]

...Society is not directed against the market, but demands that the market be controlled by the forces of society and by the State, so as to guarantee that the basic needs of the whole of society are satisfied." [lx] - Pope John Paul II

"We have already child labor law, minimum wage requirements, we have limitations to the work day, unionization, we have antitrust legislation, we have all these reforms of capitalism that represent legal constraint[s] upon the market," [lxi] continues Bishop Barron.

What about moral constraints upon possibly oppressive capitalism? Do we have some good examples? Sure, we have love of neighbors, caring for the poor, condemnation of greed, punishment for theft, punishment for fraud and killing, and many more. Our moral compass is already in place for years – hundreds of years - provided by religions or other non-religious schools of morality and ethics. It seems we had and still have access to ideals and perfect role models. All we need to do is to follow received wisdom. Because if not, then even the most brilliant social system will collapse sooner or later, turning against its own creators. If the only project that works is to live a simple life, then the basic rule of life is also simple: eat first, before you are eaten.

How do we escape our cages? Maybe by reflection on the status quo, by studying side effects, by taking the time to learn from our failures and successes, by applying changes, sometimes by experimentation, taking risks, going against the mainstream, going against common sense – which is usually not too common, but dominated by those who shout the most and the loudest. It will be a process of continuous improvement, with the goal of a better, human-centered economy. Are we motivated enough to start that journey? Let's define it in a more American way, as a race. Winning it is the only valid option. Let's put our cage on sale and start building the foundation of our newer, happier home.

If you are an entrepreneur, start building human-centered business models, profit-for-purpose business models, and value-driven business models. Start incentivizing correct behavior, creating legally and morally conditioned company cultures, policies, and codes of conduct, hiring and training people of integrity, and of course firing with integrity, as our cage has to be slightly different from others' cages. Even the firing process must always respect individuals. If you are not an entrepreneur yet, become one, and start building human-centered social models, family models, community models, and education models. Be inspired to influence and co-create human-centered, dignity-centered, and truth-centered government models. I will start with myself first, I promise. I write more on capitalism, socialism, and realizations of those "isms" in the Money chapter.

Suicides

- Suicide rates in America are up 33% since 2001.
- The highest rising group is age 15-24.
- Rates have risen 50% in last 10 years.
- Suicide is the second leading cause of death for young adults, after accidents.
- The Crude Death Rate per 100,000 was 14.48 in 2017 compared to 10.75 in 2001[lxii].
- We had almost 48,000 suicides in the US in 2018.[lxiii]
- In 2017, there were an estimated 1,300,000 suicide attempts.
- In 2017, firearms accounted for 50.57% of all suicide deaths.
- Suicide and self-injury cost U.S. $70 billion per year.

Let us pause here and honor Americans who have passed away. Words cannot express the magnitude of this tragedy. The most appropriate reaction is to keep silent.

What are the risk factors for suicide? It could be one dominant factor or a combination of factors, like individual, relationship, community, and societal factors. Let's have a look at selected ones:

- "History of mental disorders, particularly clinical **depression**
- History of alcohol and **substance abuse**
- Feelings of **hopelessness**
- **Isolation**, a feeling of being cut off from other people" [lxiv]
- **Lack of socialization and less time together - physical intimacy**
- "Family history of suicide
- Family history of child maltreatment
- Loss (relational, social, work, or financial)
- Physical illness" [lxv]

What are preventive measures for suicide? Some of our intuitions and initial research suggestions are:

- **More time together**
- **Meaningful relationships**
- **Deep sense of meaning**
- **Deep sense of self-value**
- "Family and community support (connectedness)
- Cultural and religious beliefs that discourage suicide and support instincts for self-preservation
- Effective clinical care for mental, physical, and substance abuse disorders
- Easy access to a variety of clinical interventions and support for help seekers
- Support from ongoing medical and mental health care relationships
- Skills in problem-solving, conflict resolution, and nonviolent ways of handling disputes"[lxvi]

To be fully honest, I think we are just beginning to understand what is really going on with our society and its suicidal tendencies. Having more digitized data and multiple digital touch points, we are facing a major data analysis project – to discover the true root causes, key patterns, and existing trends. We also have to acknowledge that current statistics are influenced by different numbers of registered cases and different levels of social awareness around the topic of depression and suicides. There is much more openness and acceptance in society than there was twenty-five or fifty years ago. Because of that, comparisons between time periods have to be adequately normalized or adjusted to show a more accurate picture. We did not talk about "these things" with such ease before, because shame and fear of social exclusion prevented us from talking to family, friends, teachers, and professional helpers. Let's do our best and be responsible adults. Let's examine this topic in depth, and help our brothers and sisters, who suffer today, to start experiencing hope and joy.

Consciousness & Mindfulness

Cutting connections with people undoubtedly leads to solitude and fear. However, it also allows for a better connection to oneself. One could discover one's own true self at the deepest possible level (if such a level exists). One could discover the nonexistence of self, or one formless consciousness, although that cannot be proven, and as such, must remain in the sphere of presumptions or form a belief system. As there are no satisfactory answers to the questions of what consciousness is and how and why it arises, consciousness becomes a new meta-object of faith and worship. Consciousness can be understood by a conscious "object" as a stunning awareness of being alive and knowing how to be oneself. It is also understood as the "nothingness" in which that awareness and every thought arises, in which matter and antimatter detected by the senses receive meaning through processes of interpretation. Without consciousness, nothing can be experienced or recognized. It is like being in a deep sleep, without knowing that we are dreaming and without knowing that we can wake up. Without consciousness nothing exists.

Consciousness is becoming trendy, especially among so-called "new atheists" who see it as the core of the final theory of everything. They think it is the single, all-encompassing framework of physics and metaphysics that fully explains the nature of the universe. Consciousness could bring a new understanding of immortality – as it exists beyond the dimension of time – and maybe beyond the space dimension as well. It is the origin of all that exists or at least all that can be "consciously" perceived. What if the cult of consciousness is an alternative to all other organized religions? All of us, regardless of labels: "New atheists," "Old atheists," "Religious people," or other "Identities," seems to have internal, natural desires to search for the truth. We are again trying to re-discover what constitutes human reasoning (or lack of it), morality, existence, or the best possible project for the best possible human life. If the best possible life for human beings is defined as a happy life, that is definitely counterintuitive to any "selfish gene" which emerged in the process of evolution. One could argue that we did not emerge to live pleasant lives (we would need a definition of a pleasant life), we emerged because we emerged and are now surfing on a wave of an ever-expanding universe, not because we decided to surf but because we were conditioned to surf. We are separate objects that sit on the wave of destiny, which could be seen as an aberration, an abnormality, an error in the natural ecosystems of randomly combined pixels glued together by electromagnetic and gravity forces. Maybe we should not know that we know that we know... But it seems we somehow know that we know that we know... – and that is why we have to deal with it. Knowing in its core makes us sad (although being sad is another unbelievable phenomenon we can be aware of) because we participate in an unstoppable life process where nothing really lasts. Nothing is stable, and sooner or later we will disintegrate into another form of possible forms. The beauty in this is that we are able to make a loop starting from nothingness, to "somethingness," to "somethingness" that knows it is something, something that knows that it will not be, to something that prefers to be, rather than not to be, to something that wants to counteract and slow down the process of becoming nothing, to something that is able to imagine (key word) that the end may not happen, knowing that it will happen, and find practical methods to ensure it will not, but it will happen.

Anyway, we are quite close to finding the method, or going more broadly, to find the new idol, called The Consciousness.

What if that is a revolutionary cure for loneliness? We can now see the sky-rocking trend of mindfulness, intentional living, living in the moment, yoga practices, stress-reduction techniques, meditation, and prayers. Although these mind-clearing methods have been around for thousands of years we rediscover them through advanced brain and anxiety studies, as well as through deceitful analysis of mass welfare and new communication patterns using digital media. Conscious living seems to be a very promising lifestyle proposal, or at least a complementary component of modern and good life.

As usual, wisdom will come from the proper use of all ingredients, with the aim of finding the ideal formulation. Using our collective wisdom, we know that going to extremes never brings optimal results. By contrast, it brings extreme and dangerous results. Let's assume someone decides to stay in a deep meditative state - almost 24/7, 365 days a year.

I would call it a "Zombie state" (special greetings to those who love zombie movies). Theoretically, this is possible with enormous amounts of practice (I am guessing 20 years of regular practice, but that depends on individual predispositions). Now, if this assumption is true, then any useful interaction with the outside world may not be possible. Your son comes home and says he was beaten up by some adults standing in front of the house. What would be the reaction of a deep, meditative mind hearing such a story? The meta-mind would likely say: "nothing matters," "let it go," "do not judge, observe, be in the moment." Any thought of revenge, any feeling of anger, any desire to solve the problem – would not be a valid meta-thought, motivation or valid scenario of a peaceful, non-existing self's mind – in an extreme case. Someone would say that this is a crazy exaggeration, that "you don't understand, it is not about being in a fully meditative state all the time, but sometimes, or as much as possible." Then the whole situation may in fact become a valid option for an attractive lifestyle. Mindfulness (in its practical definition, not an ultimate, spiritual one) is not meant to be the off switch, where nothing really matters as nothing really matters. Rather, mindfulness is seen as a state of mind "beyond" all thoughts, including meta thoughts = thoughts about the realized thoughts, including meta-meta thoughts = thoughts about meta-thoughts, including all possible levels of thoughts' hierarchy, sometimes referred to as the last floor of a building of thoughts, the roof of the mind plus the building and everything that surrounds it. In the most profound way, it refers to the entire mind. Mindfulness is seen as a peaceful state of mind that gives birth to a new evolutionary stage: seeing almost all - observers, sensing almost all - but not deeply feeling (because one is trying to not react to short and spontaneous emotional states), not judging anything, not following anything, not desiring anything – but simply being. Being involves staying still and at the same time surfing on the waves of consciousness – dabbling in everything that is and can be. In this state, there is no place for any identity created by personalized ego. There is no ego anymore. There is no tension between what is and what is expected to be the fake persona. There is no person that creates fake fantasies about the past (regretting) and about the future (dreaming). Existential tension dissolves in an undisturbed and controlled mind.

That is why it can be so appealing, and why it gives us hope that we can defeat anxiety, depression, and a willingness to depart the physical world before we do so naturally sooner or later.

Some would say that mindfulness practice - focusing on one's breath, scanning one's own body patiently while searching for connections with "every single" cell or tissue, observing one's own thoughts, and opening oneself up to all possible stimuli is the only way to experience a liberated internal life. What about reading a fascinating book? What about painting a stunning canvas? What about discovering a new divine particle or creating a new healing molecule? What about dancing with closed eyes, jumping into a pool, running on the shore of a lake, watching the sun rise, cuddling with a loved one, feeling the warmth of other bodies and hearing every beat of their hearts? Do these count? Isn't it already described as the so-called "flow state," in which time disappears, senses are sharpened, one feels in love with everything that arises, and identity melts and transcends itself? Many would say that these are indeed similar experiences. Curious people would ask, is steering our internal "well-being" all we can do? Unfortunately, not. Deep meditation states are sometimes compared to nirvana states caused by drugs. All the masks we wear, all the personalities we embody, all the emotions that enslave us, and all the personal and worldly worries and problems that overwhelm us are now gone. It is a kind of magic. Heaven on Earth. The Ego is gone. I am ashamed of nothing. I do not care about anything. It is the first time that "I am who I am," the state of being recommended by parents, teachers, motivational speakers, mentors, and good leaders. Finally, I am in the "be yourself" state. It seems that there is a certain logic here. We jump into the digital stream of information. We are totally immersed in it, leaving our physical bodies and starting parallel avatar-like lives. Those lives pull us in different directions. We are controlled by desires and shiny objects, and disconnected from each other. After a while, we feel like something is missing. We feel alone in the world. We alienate ourselves more and more. We feel abandoned, and too small to face a much bigger reality. We compete for a while to be heard and noticed. We are frustrated, as we don't control most things. We influence fewer people because our connection to other beings is looser. We harbor the illusion that hundreds of friends and followers are listening, but in fact no one is listening. Everyone shouts in all directions and flies away on the strings of the continuously expanding universe. We are in fact embedded in our own individual universes. We are lonely and abandoned, and feel paralyzing fear. We want that nightmare to end; we want to wake up. Can anyone set an alarm clock to spare us this suffering? Yes, there are prototypes of intergalactic alarm clocks that can start the waking-up process, or as we will call it in the future, the awakening process (we are already in the future, we just came "back to the future" from the past). There is one last thought that arises, or to be precise, the last meta-thought that arises—what if we stop thinking our thoughts? After a close look, we realize that that it is not possible. So what if we use a trick, and stop looking at thoughts as they arise? We discover mindfulness. In fact, we rediscover it, as history likes to repeat itself.

So where are we now? It seems we have multiple alarm clocks that can wake us up to the most optimal reality we can dream of, one in which we feel loved, understood, respected, needed, empowered, and free while living our lives here on Earth. Of course, we are not so blind or naive as to not realize that optimal reality is limited by the nature of our world, that existential and physical suffering is inevitable and that "properly" surviving requires smart survival strategies. Having our overgrown brains is a blessing and a curse at the same time. We are able to feel joy, experience beauty co-create new forms of life or forms, feel excitement and pride, live multiple lives in stories, and travel long distances, including to outer space. In essence, we are able to imagine and remember, learn and decide (at least on aggregated abstract levels – aside from whether the thought appears by itself or whether we still have the illusion of steering that process). Having overgrown brains, we accumulate all that has happened to us. We program our thinking patterns and our automated responses, and become what we "consume." We throw ourselves into subjective and collective prisons. We lock ourselves in our cages (cages of all possible shapes, qualities, and destinies). We predict the future, either the best possible one or the worst possible one. In so doing, we stress ourselves out. We worry, will I succeed? Will I be healthy? What if I fail? What if I get sick? Suffering is caused by imagination, and by the unstoppable force that demands that we satisfy most of our unconscious bodily and mental needs. Wouldn't it be better to be an Eagle or a Lion King, with no time, no planned desires, and no long-term stress, just quick episodes of pushing back the attack of other wildlife objects, or attacking to satisfy unconscious needs, mainly instincts of hunger and survival, always triggered by misunderstood stimuli? Do an Eagle and a Lion King know that they are going to die? Do they really care? Do they care about anything? What a wonderful life – a sky of nothingness, a savanna of nothingness. But would we want to live such a "perfect life" where we didn't realize that we were alive at all? It seems that there are no shortcuts that lead to the perfect life. To enjoy knowing that we are alive, we have to bear the consequences of that knowledge. It reminds me of the archetypical symbol and story of the tree of knowledge, good, and evil. There is a price that has to be paid in exchange for knowing more. Similarly, the more you invest in creating your own independent self, and differentiating it from others, the more you become distant from whatever is. After you follow the internal voice of the "false self" long enough, you realize you are alone, although unique, but on your own in this huge cosmos – one tiny star among billions in infinite amount of stardust. Excuse me for my pseudo-philosophical considerations and poetic reasoning; I am trying my best to survive my own suffering while typing.

So, coming back, what are the best examples of the strategies we have as human beings to cope with life's injustices: mindfulness, flow states, sleep, giving meaning to suffering itself, faith in certain worldviews, faith in something that always is and transforms, or faith in someone that always is, listens and influences. *And unfortunately, drugs.*

Meaningful Life

It has become very clear that we humans draw our strength from each other. Of course, toxic relationships will do the opposite, taking away our remaining strength. Being surrounded by those who care influences our ability to deal with difficult situations. Unfortunately, we are not good at making meaningful connections here in the United States. We are fabulous at making rapid, task- oriented, benefit- and profit- oriented connections. We do love networking, especially to leverage our business performance and maximize our individual success. The evidence we have from available happiness reports makes a powerful (for us, sad) case "that the large international differences in life evaluations are driven by the differences in how people connect with each other and with their shared institutions and social norms."[lxvii] And again, as we underperform in establishing quality connections – we underperform in our life evaluation scores.

- **Less than 10% of Americans have meaningful conversations.**
- **About 35% of American adults are chronically lonely.**
- **Only 30% of Americans trust their neighbors.**

Happiness comes from satisfying relationships.

"There are a lot of factors that impact happiness, everything from biology to income levels to the city one lives in. But I think the best predictor we see in the data of whether people are happy or not is whether they're satisfied or happy with their relationships. So, do we have somebody we can rely on in times of need? Do we have somebody we can share our hopes and worries with?"[lxviii] - Meik Wiking, happiness researcher and CEO of the Happiness Research Institute in Denmark

Beside the strength that comes from meaningful relationships, we can strengthen ourselves by defining, internalizing, and living purposefully. Finding meaning in life and finding meaning in suffering can be seen as an essential recipe for survival and a perfect recipe for a good life. As per Victor Frankl and his book *Man's Search for Meaning*,[lxix] finding meaning even in the most extreme and difficult circumstances (like being imprisoned in Nazi concentration camps, like Frankl, being tortured, or suffering from disabilities or from incurable disease) is an unbelievably effective strategy for people to survive. How can anyone find life worth living after being trapped in such imaginable conditions? Finding meaning in suffering seems to be the answer. Frankl would say that everything can be taken away from us except the freedom to make our own choices. Choosing our own response is life-changing, and in many cases, a life-saving ability. In the end, it is not about our situation, but rather our attitude towards our circumstances. Frankl also warned us that horrible life conditions are not the only traps into which humanity falls. Existential crises reach the "western world" despite its wealth and prosperity. Both living life in extreme poverty and living too comfortable a life can cause existential crises. It seems that nowadays we can easily be sucked into the black hole of existence by living fast-paced lifestyles, accepting demanding and stressful commitments, or simply being bored by having too many options on the table or no options at all as everything is already created, discovered, known, and available. "One day delivery" is already "delayed delivery." Paradoxically, reaching goals without any major effort can be very discouraging, demotivating, and destructive.

Person with nothing to live for subconsciously prefer death, but someone who has something to live for can endure almost anything, according to this famous saying by Friedrich Nietzsche:

"He who has a Why to live can bear almost any How."

Do you want to have a meaningful life? If so, "everything you do matters – that's the definition of a meaningful life," according to Jordan Peterson,[lxx] a Canadian clinical psychologist and professor of psychology at the University of Toronto. "Or do you want to forget about the whole meaning thing, then you do not have any responsibility.... [...] You can wander through life doing whatever you want, gratifying impulsive desires.... [...] You're stuck in meaninglessness, but you have no responsibility – which one do you want?"[lxxi] Peterson elaborates with honesty and passion.

At the same time, we know that life is suffering, life is not fair, people are dying, and we are going to die as well. So what's a reasonable strategy going forward?

"Get yourself together. Transcend your suffering. Make the suffering in the world less." lxxii

"Everything you do, matters – that's the definition of a meaningful life." lxxiii

What do you think? How do you feel about it?

Purpose is what gives true meaning, not money.

Following thousands of years of received wisdom, something is telling us that money is not the secret source of human wellness. There is much more to happiness out there. What if you have all the money you want, but do not find meaning in your life? Isn't it all for nothing? Isn't it true that when it comes to human beings as we all know them (or pretend we know), for them to really flourish, they need to find true meaning in life? What if we consider the teachings of professor Jordan Peterson, lxxiv who reminds us about the importance of purpose, meaning, and responsibility in our lives? Those aspects definitely bring whole new dimensions to our discussion of happiness.

"People need a differentiated and delineated purpose. It's way more important than the money. It isn't money that you need. I know you need money, for God's sake. I'm not ignorant, everybody needs money – that's not the point here. It's the provision of money without purpose [that] is not helpful and what people need is a purpose. [...]

And the reason they need that purpose is because that's what gives their life meaning. [...]

Do you really think that you would be satisfied if you had money without responsibility?"lxxv

For the people to find a meaning in their lives, they have to adopt responsibility and live it.

To be able to take responsibility, human beings need to have a purpose in life.

Hence, giving purpose to the people is of the highest importance.

Systematic provision of money to people is not a good idea...

We need to help people find their purpose and their place. [lxxvi]

Following Jordan Peterson, we learn that systematically providing money is not going to solve our problems in the long run. People must take responsibility for their own lives to have meaningful and happy ones. Although ensuring that people achieve "dignity income level" or "dignity net worth level" seems to be a noble idea, helping them to find their purpose and their place in the world should be one of the highest priorities of a wise and progressive society. Giving to those in need and at the same time influencing their positive growth, their positive destiny, and their self-reliance - is wisdom in itself. That requires certain capabilities on an individual citizen's level and on social, economic, and political levels as well.

On top of a "meaningful life," we should also aim for love. Love understood as a secret glue, as unity with everything, as the "multidimensional multi-verse, strings and membranes, gravity and quantum mechanics" of human flourishing. If the winning idea is to embed our life into the "universe of love" because it is so critical, why don't we set ourselves the goal of designing our social life and overarching systems around such an idea? I will come back to this in the My Creator chapter of this book.

Are we happy or not?

Are those statistics about the levels of happiness or unhappiness in our "happy cage," America, true? What if those have been manipulated? What if we still do not understand the science behind overall human happiness, and all those ratios, rankings, and ratings are simply presenting a false picture? We can be confused when hearing selected public figures - starting with the president, various government representatives, eloquent and experienced journalists, and smart graduates of the most prestigious universities – that the U.S.A. is definitely a country of happiness and happy people. It was designed to be a happy place and it is a happy place.

"Our country is free, beautiful, and very successful. If you hate our country, or

if you are not happy here, you can leave!"[lxxvii]

--The 45th President of the United States of America, Donald John Trump.

Also, analyzing one of the lectures that Ben Shapiro, a Harvard University alumnus and a *New York Times* bestselling author, gave at the University of California, Berkeley, we may start to believe in paradise here and now.

"America is an incredible place, it's the greatest place in the history of the world. It is... the most prosperous country... in the history of planet Earth. This country is an incredible place, full of opportunity...

Nobody by and large cares enough about you to stop you from achieving your dreams...

No one cares about you. Get over yourselves. I do not care about you. No one cares about you. No one is trying to stop you - because you are irrelevant to me...

That means in a free country, if you fail, it is probably your own fault...

It is a waste of time and energy blaming your failures on the system, unless you've got some evidence. [...]

Nobody rich is making you poor. Bill Gates did not make you poor. Bill Gates provided you a product, and if you bought it, that is your fault. The rich are not making you poor, they are paying your salary. [...]

You want to be rich in America? Here are three rules: You need to finish high school, you need to get married before you have babies, [and] you need to get a job." [lxxviii]

What if someone really feels bad and is unhappy with his or her own unique life situation? What if he or she suffers from the oppressive and toxic influence of the local community where he or she was born, from congenital disability and the inability to work effectively or for long hours, from the consequences of natural disasters or unexpected events like job loss in a rare specialty area or from violence, lack of trustworthy role models, warm friends, and a loving family or someone to lean on? What if he or she is living here among us? I think it is very easy to say what was just said from the position of a healthy, already wealthy, intellectually fit individual who has strong social support from a healthy, already wealthy, and intellectually fit environment. Of course, in certain circumstances such an argument could make sense. The whole picture suddenly changes when the individual struggles to satisfy basic human needs and his or her everyday life is like walking throughout a minefield. He or she continually faces trials and life-threatening conditions. Finishing high school, getting married, and getting a job sounds like an easy path to success. One could wonder, what could be the role of an author like Shapiro in a country like ours? Should we expect "happy citizens" of our paradise-like country to support those in need? Or should we just leave those in need to figure it out? Maybe we should look for best practices in the jungle. How is life organized there? What does nature suggest to us? The strongest and the most agile survive, regardless of whether they want to or not. But then, what if you get sick, what if you get in trouble, what if your life situation changes dramatically against your will and plans and overwhelms you so much that breathing alone (by yourself) is considered a great personal achievement? In the jungle, you will be eaten. To create and maintain paradise, should we proceed with a dedicated selection process, auditions and try-outs, allowing only "declared and diagnosed" happy people to join and to thrive, or should we put some effort into ensuring the growth of all citizens?

What about "**Hakuna Matata**"? Is there a place for it in our promised land, America? Is it our "problem-free philosophy"[lxxix]?

It seems that it is not only about how intellectually fit individuals are, or what reasoning methods they use, or what broad experiences they have, or how great a reservoir of capital they have or don't have. Rather, it is more about what fundamental beliefs, values, and worldviews they have, or in a broader sense, what social mindset and culture they inherit, cultivate, live, and shape. You can spend your entire life trying to climb the wall of your destiny, career, prosperity, and happiness, invest lots of energy in it, have very good intentions, and after you reach the coveted top and look at what's out there on the other side, suddenly realize sadly that in fact you have been climbing the wrong wall. That would be a tragic disappointment. The paradox here is that in the given moment everyone can be right on almost any given topic. "Everyone is right" usually means that nobody agrees with anyone. When wrestling with our own walls, we feel and are convinced that we are right and everyone else is wrong, and because of that, we need to correct other people's thinking and understanding. It would require a huge dose of humility, self-reflection, curiosity, risk-taking, trust, a do-it-yourself attitude, action, and courage to be able to accept other people's realities and make a conscious decision to start a new journey based on adjusted or new assumptions. How do we reflect on jungle-like thinking? How do we challenge jungle-like assumptions? How do we acknowledge that we are sitting in a jungle-like cage? How do we start seeing differently, recognize the available options, and try to do something new? How do we escape for a while? How do we escape for good? What would be your answer to the question: "Is it possible that I am always right?" or "Is it possible that due to my core biases, values, beliefs, and culture, I cannot easily see different dimensions, perspectives, approaches, solutions, and other life purposes?" I hope the answers to these questions are obvious. Nobody in their right mind would claim to be infallible and omniscient. And if so, by careful adjustments to our core assumptions about ourselves and the surrounding world, we can open a totally new chapter in our lives and truly aspire to make a better living. We could go even further, following Denzel Washington's recommendation:

"Do not just aspire to make a living. Aspire to make a difference."[lxxx]

Are we in America happy or not? Am I happy or not?

If not, am I going to do something about it? *E.g. take full responsibility for my own life, try as hard as possible to improve and reach out to good, helpful people?*

If I am happy, am I going to do something about it? *E.g. continue taking full responsibility for my own life, try as hard as possible to maintain that state, and reach out to those good people in need to help them?*

You can also say that that depends on what definition of happiness we are taking about. Coming back to the first chapter and the guarantee given by the Declaration of Independence, we certainly have certain unalienable rights, including *the pursuit of happiness*, but happiness itself is not clearly defined there. So we have a right to something, although we do not quite know what it means. And that itself can cause some social tensions. What if my understanding of *the pursuit of happiness* is having the right to chase my personal dreams no matter what, to meet any of my unmet needs no matter what, to fulfill my career aspirations no matter what, to grow my own business no matter what, to increase my own net worth (exponentially and indefinitely) no matter what (including the broadest range of assets, : current, non-current, physical, intangible, operating, and non-operating, cash and cash equivalent, real-estate properties, plants, equipment, vehicles, furniture, patents, stocks and other investments, business inventories...) all without jeopardizing or violating other coexisting rights such as life and liberty.

What if my understanding of *the pursuit of happiness* is having the right to live a peaceful life, to live life in harmony with all that exists, including myself and my internal, intimate life, as well as the world of nature and other human beings, to live the least stressful life possible, to live a balanced life, ensuring that the fulfillment of personal physical needs and goals is not in destructive opposition to personal social, emotional, and spiritual needs and goals, to live balanced life, ensuring that the fulfillment of overall personal needs and goals is not in destructive opposition to the needs and goals of my own society, finally, to live a joyful life?

These are just two examples out of 330.9 million possibilities for our pursuit of happiness - taking into consideration all of us, Americans. Now, it is not very hard to guess what would happen if we thought there was only one narrow definition of this right. Millions of other ones would then be wrong. If I believe that "capital no matter what" equals happiness, then I do not care about peace, harmony, balance, and joy. I can or sometimes have to align and cooperate with the external world simply to survive. I quickly learn that there are unwritten and powerful natural laws: the "law of good and evil," including the "economics of good and evil,"[lxxxi] the "law of attraction," the law that "what you give is what you get," the "law of hierarchy," the law that you had "better collaborate, otherwise you will be eaten'" and others. In general, I would not care about you as I would not need to for my happiness. On the other hand, if I believe that "my internal peace no matter what" equals happiness, then why should I care about any capital-dependent stuff or people? Minimal interactions with other people would work for me. Minimal engagement in any businesses or enterprises would be perfect. By contrast, as much exposure to peaceful and gorgeous (yet not brutal, but innocent) nature as possible would make me really happy. I would not care too much about you and the world of productivity to be happy. My own private cage is a happy one. I'm in Zombie mode. Considering just these two simple cases, we can immediately see that there is an obvious conflict between them. The last one would say, "why should I care about your greedy desire to own aggregate wealth, and fulfill your pleasures, which cannot be fulfilled using external means in the first place?" The first one would say, "you are a fool, as sitting alone in a mental prison with no connections to the real world is a fairy tale, an ideology created by the weak for the weak. How will you be able to eat anything, recover without sophisticated healthcare treatments or interventions, live in decent household conditions, including having clean drinking water and a waste water system, heating or cooling, trash collection, maintenance services, and so on and so forth?" Can we really treat these and other situations seriously and effectively extrapolate them (excuse the math jargon) to the whole population? As mentioned before, human beings are not able to survive on their own, especially at the beginnings and ends of their lives. Getting food, shelter, and clothing, ensuring protection from invisible, unfriendly viruses and bacteria, relocating from one place to another, escaping from floods, strong winds, lightning - even proceeding with basic "double P" activities with the obvious goal to not pee and poop in one's own nest – are just a few examples of our dependencies, required for our survival. Think about how successful you would be when attacked by foreign armies, not having support from those who decided to serve our country, defend and fight for our independence and freedom - your freedom.

We may want to agree on a joint definition of happiness and the right to pursue it. To simplify our terminology, why don't we call happiness the sum of externally driven happiness (personal success or just **success** – a very popular American word) and internally driven happiness (**joy**), both glued by **unity** with the external world, with ourselves, and with the origin – "the one Who/the one Which" caused it all? Personal success may come from individual achievements, accomplished projects, realized personal goals, advancements on a career ladder, local tournament wins, and championships in which your city or state football, basketball, baseball, or any-ball teams take part. "I am successful – I expanded myself." Joy, on the other hand, may come from inner peace, being present, breathing precisely, sitting still, listening carefully, touching gently, smelling deeply, or experiencing unity with all that is. It may come from getting lost in action based on my unique talents. It may also come from inspiring the success of others, and devoting oneself to others as a servant, patient listener, useful helper, or best friend. Joy may come from the understanding and acceptance of my current emotional state, body condition and state of mind, may come from appreciating my true self without any obligation to respond to the outside world's demands, which are in conflict with my true self. Joy may come from delight in the beauty of nature or the admiration of other humans' perfection, genius and creativity. "I am joyful – I deepened myself, I united myself with everything, I dissolved myself." For those who believe in the Creator (following the Founding Fathers' suggestion), joy is the result of God's blessing and grace – interactions with the ideal and its intervention. Joy is understood as coming not only from within (caused by the high quality of internal life), but also from engagement in meaningful relationships with people, in strong human-animal bonds, and in connectedness with all that exists, both visible and invisible. We can also come up with a totally different definition. Most importantly, we need one definition accepted by everyone to know what we are really aiming for.

Now, hearing about all those statistics, happiness report outcomes, the high percentage of chronic loneliness, the lack of meaningful relationships and conversations, the lack of trust between people, neighbors, co-workers, service providers, government institutions, and individuals, the higher amount of anxiety, depression, addictions, crimes, and suicides, and at the same time hearing everywhere how successful this country is, how successful and already happy American people are, one can be very confused. In those rare cases, if one does not yet consider him/herself successful or does not yet feel happy, it is a matter of time – "you can achieve anything," "you can make yourself happy," "you can unleash your full potential," "you can increase your value," – just awaken that giant within you. You can even do it without awakening any suspicious beast within you. Just increase your self-esteem by attaching to any "sexy" and shiny object of modern consumerism. Try it. You will be amazed at how quickly you'll gain additional value. It is so simple. Without any doubt a person with an iPhone 11 feels much better and is worth more than a person with iPhone X. Imagine how tragic the situation is for owners of iPhones 8, 7, 6, 5, 4, and 3. Being at the very end of the list, one can risk a nervous breakdown.

Let's not forget about a very powerful mental force: "comparing yourself to others" can be very destructive and can manipulate your sense of happiness in a very negative way.

"If you think you are having more sex than your neighbor, then you're happier. We are social beings. We compare ourselves to each other." [lxxxii]- *Meik Wiking*

Ultimately, it seems that such a happiness is relative.

We could continue cheating ourselves and call America the place of success, or the place for success, but in light of all that overwhelming evidence, we cannot call our country the place of happiness, or the place for happiness. That is clearly not the case. Personal success alone will not make you happy at all. Sooner or later you will feel alone, become too tired, burned out, anxious, frustrated and late for "incredible" new challenges. If you are really lucky, you will be able to celebrate your victories for very short moments, and after a while, all the successes will disappear, and the race to find new ones will start again.

We will not be able to bring happiness to America unless we balance our ego-driven desire for success with desires for joy and unity. American culture and social norms have to be rebuilt or reinvented.

As we are not self-sufficient, we cannot be happy without one another. We cannot pursue happiness without being well-connected. We urgently need to regain our social trust, change how we look at each other, how we see each other, how we talk to each other, how we understand and appreciate our individual differences, and how

we agree on important topics. We need to prioritize our new happiness-oriented economy.

We may want to form a new declaration, saying that in addition to life, liberty, and happiness, we can include love, dignity, and respect as the main building blocks of unity, and that we should pursue self-awareness and personal responsibility.

And empathy is part of love, dignity and respect.

"But right now, kids in this country are seeing what happens when we stop requiring empathy of one another. They're looking around wondering if we've been lying to them this whole time about who we are and what we truly value. They see people shouting in grocery stores, unwilling to wear a mask to keep us all safe. They see people calling the police on folks minding their own business just because of the color of their skin. They see an entitlement that says only certain people belong here, that greed is good, and winning is everything because as long as you come out on top, it doesn't matter what happens to everyone else. And they see what happens when that lack of empathy is ginned up into outright disdain. [...]

Not just feeling, but doing—that is the truest form of empathy; not just for ourselves or our kids, but for everyone, for all our kids."[lxxxiii]—Michelle Obama

You may ask me, "Are you happy?"

My answer is: "most of the time, yes, I am happy." I experience joy, satisfaction, and positive well-being most of the time. I try to find purpose in life. As such, I can see the goodness of life and the purpose of living most of the time. I try to achieve some of my personal goals, which are aligned with my life's mission and purpose, most of the time. I try my best to maintain meaningful relationships with my family members, friends, co-workers and every single person I meet along the way most of the time. Is it easy to maintain a happy status quo? No, it isn't. Is it joyful, despite the effort, invested time, and attention? Yes, it really is. Life is worth living while having this joy, this unity, and a healthy number of personal achievements. I describe my happiness in depth later in this book.

Problems and Solutions

So what can we do? I believe we can do a lot, and that we are only limited by our imagination. Take a look at spontaneous, unproven, unverified ideas. These are just ideas. You may come up with better ones, I have no doubt, and I encourage you to do so. What if we try to resolve the following problems?

<u>Significantly increase overall happiness in America to become one of the top 10 countries</u> per the World Happiness Report from 2019, the Ranking of Happiness from 2016-2018, or significantly increase life satisfaction in America to become one of the top 10 countries per the OECD's Better Life Index: "Life Satisfaction" indicator.

To do that we must draw on the brightest minds we have, and on the work done at the best science labs, colleges, and universities (Harvard University, California Institute of Technology, University of California, Berkeley, University of Chicago, Princeton University, Cornell University, Yale University, Columbia University, MIT, Stanford, University of Minnesota to just name a few). What a cool problem it would be for any ambitious student – making people happier. Of course, the problem of happiness is multi-layered and multi-dimensional, and finding the real root causes, relevant causes, and effects as well as the external and internal influencing forces with respective weights and directions would be crucial to the success of the mission. It is worth devoting one's career to solving such problems. It is worth devoting one's life to creating such a greater good. The individuals or groups that find solutions should earn respect from our nation, including lifetime scholarships to higher education institutions, and should be given prestigious and valuable prizes.

As mentioned, the happiness problem may be far too general and too broad to address in one step (or even multiple steps). What if we try to solve the following sub-problems first, and try to sort them out starting from the most fundamental ones (candidates for root causes of other causes) and ending at more syndrome-like ones. As there are so many layers, or hierarchies between root causes, problems, syndromes, or consequences – it should be an intellectual – scientific task to put those in the right order. Some of the sub-problems could be (maybe) managed in parallel, but usually the most effective approach is to find a master root cause. One of the most widespread "DIY methods" to find the cause-and-effect relationships underlying particular problems is the "5 Whys[lxxxiv]" iterative technique. By the "simple" repetition of the question "Why" (at least five times, per anecdotal evidence), one can determine the root cause. Each answer forms the basis of the next question. "Why aren't Americans happy?" "Because there is huge and increasing inequality." "Why is there huge inequality?" "Because (here multiple paths can emerge) the rich are getting richer reinvesting and multiplying their capital, and the poor are getting poorer (in relation to the richest) not having initial capital to invest." Or, "Because the rich are getting richer via access to the most sophisticated technologies and modern education, and the poor have no such access." "Why don't the poor have access to education?" "Because past generations of the poor were not educated as well," and so on and so forth. Reasoning like that can go in various directions (diving deep – down and again up on an argumentation tree, sometimes to the right, or suddenly to the left), but the intention is to deepen the topic as much as possible while maintaining logical relationships between causes and effects. It requires a certain mental discipline to not make counterproductive loops or misinterpret the outcome of what is the real root cause. It could be that there is more than one force acting simultaneously, making a significant impact on the overall problem.

―――――――

Also, to put our sub-problems in order, we could use proven and accepted reference models, criteria, or hierarchies, like Maslow's Hierarchy of Needs, or the Dilts Pyramid, which is a model of personal change that goes from one level to another or other socio-economic-psychological concepts.

Significantly increase our personal happiness and climb to a higher level on any credible happiness assessment scale

Can we understand happiness better?

Why don't we educate ourselves more about well-being, happiness, mindfulness, and emotional intelligence? There are already many schools of happiness, including dedicated happiness courses offered at renowned universities that are available for everyone. Below is generic advice to a person wanting to improve his/her sense of well-being, given by Laurie Santos, an Associate Professor in the Department of Psychology at Yale University who teaches popular course entitled "The Science of Well-Being:"

You can take some action and fix this
"The first piece of advice is just that the science suggests you can intervene [...] I think a lot of people who are not happy at a given time think that there's something about them. [...] There's some heritability to most well-being measures but there's a lot you can do to intervene in them. [...] Look, you can take some action and fix this."

Social connection
"One of the [biggest] effects on our own happiness is our social connection [...] Strong social relationships are necessary for happiness. [...] If you want to be like happy people you should focus on your social relationships and that means taking a hard look at your priorities [...] Are you making time for the people that you really care about in life?"

Be other-oriented
"Being other-oriented mean[s] the act of paying attention to other people over yourself; being the kind of person [who] gives to charity, volunteers time [and] is focused on other people generally seems to be a big one for your happiness and your health."

Healthy habits
"[Another one is...] just healthy habits and by that, I mean the stuff that we know is good for physical health like making sure you're getting enough sleep, making sure you're getting enough exercise, making sure you're eating right. Those physical things seem to have a huge impact on people's mental health much more than we think."

Be mindful

"[Another one is...] being a little bit more present, being mindful"

Be grateful and compassionate

"[...] Having a mindset that's a little bit more grateful and a little bit more compassionate generally"

Be religious

"[...] Being religious, it turns out, is actually pretty good for your happiness [...] not necessarily believing in religious doctrine, but actually taking part in religious practices [...] is correlated with happiness."[lxxxv]

Why don't we turn to our best friends, animals?

Based on various studies, we know that animals have an incredibly positive impact on people's health and well-being. Let's be surprised by the healing power of human-animal bonding.

- "According to the American Veterinary Medical Association (AVMA) the human-animal bond is defined as "...a mutually beneficial and dynamic relationship between people and animals." Indeed, humans have benefitted from this unique connection for thousands of years. Animals were so essential to the daily lives of early humans that there is evidence we may not have survived or thrived without them. How the Human-Animal Bond benefits us:
- **Stress reduction** – Petting an animal has been shown to reduce stress in humans. Lowered blood pressure is often the result of the extra exercise and lowered stress that can accompany pet ownership.
- **Increased healing and independence** – Service and therapeutic animals are invaluable to their handlers, providing help with daily tasks, emotional and mental support, and recovery from traumatic events.
- **Improved mood** – Studies show that the simple act of stroking a friendly animal increases dopamine and serotonin levels in the brain, two chemicals that are essential for happiness and relaxation.

- **More physical activity** – Caring for a pet involves some degree of physical activity and living with a pet that needs a daily walk or play session is an excellent way to get off the couch and out the door.
- **Immunity boost** – Children who grow up with animals in the home have been shown to have fewer allergies and are less likely to develop asthma than those who aren't raised with animals.
- **Social connections** – Thanks to their many needs, pets provide us with numerous opportunities to get out and interact with our friends and neighbors. This is especially helpful for seniors or others who may be less likely to incorporate a social activity into their daily lives.
- **Emotional support** – Your pet doesn't care how much money you make, what type of car you drive, what you look like, or whether or not you wear name-brand clothes. **Pets provide us with impartial, unconditional emotional support and love.**"[lxxxvi]
- "We believe animals are the x-factor the world has been looking for. They're that missing piece of the puzzle - the game-changing variable that will unlock solutions to these seemingly disconnected issues of physical, mental, and environmental health."[lxxxvii] – Jeff Simmons, President and CEO, Elanco
- "Pets can be a force to reverse the growing epidemic of social isolation."[lxxxviii]
- 74% of pet owners reported mental health improvements from pet ownership.[lxxxix]
- 40% of pet owners connect with neighbors through pets.[xc]
- 76% of cat owners felt that their cats helped them cope with daily stress much better.[xci]
- Dog owners decrease their risk of cardiovascular-related death by 36%.[xcii]
- Older adults who own a dog have a lower body mass index, make fewer visits to the doctor, and exercise more.[xciii]
- Preliminary findings of the research study on the emotional and health benefits people receive from service dogs indicate:
  - Recipients of a service dog showed a higher overall quality of life as well as better emotional, social, and work/school functioning than recipients who had not yet received a service dog.

- Family members with a service dog in the home exhibited better social and emotional functioning as well as decreased worry as a result of the recipient's health than family members on the waitlist.
- Family members with a service dog also exhibited better management of daily family activities than family members on the waitlist.[xciv] – Research led by Elanco in cooperation with the Purdue University College of Veterinary Medicine

- HABRI (Human Animal Bond Research Institute) has assembled scientific evidence that demonstrates how pets improve heart health; alleviate depression; increase well-being; support child health and development; and contribute to healthy aging. In addition, companion animals can assist in the treatment of a broad range of conditions from post-traumatic stress to Alzheimer's disease to autism spectrum disorder. Veterinarians are the professionals who keep pets healthy, so that in turn, they can positively impact our health and well-being.[xcv]

What if, when trying to solve the major problem of American happiness, we try to solve the following sub-problems?

- Increase American society's minimum basis for a dignified life
- Significantly decrease homicide rates to increase safety
- Increase access to education
- Increase social trust and quality of communities' support networks and confidence in government
- Decrease depression rates
- Decrease suicide rates
- Reduce the world's highest rates of substance abuse
- Reduce digital-related addictions
- Reduce the world's highest rates of obesity, in turn decreasing the risk of diabetes, heart disease, and even cancer
- Significantly increase time devoted to leisure and personal care to ensure healthy work-life balance

What if we try to solve the following problems?

Decrease the amount of time young people (age 1-18) spend on digital media *(to be even more specific, decrease it from the current six hours a day to one hour for 17-18-year-olds)* **AND increase physical social interactions between them.**

What a brilliant challenge to wrestle with. I am so curious, what would be your ideas, what would be your approaches? If you have them, make sure your family and friends get to know about them, make sure your local political representatives get to know about them, and make sure Washington gets to know about them. Let's try to find both "low-hanging fruit" solutions as well as "breakthrough" ones. Let's spend enough time on the root causes of the problem and respond with systemic solutions – those that will move the needle and have lasting effects. Here are, again, spontaneous ideas, all seen, heard, or invented, to start the ball rolling. I will share other suggestions in the next chapters. What about:

- **Keeping smartphones out of our bedrooms**
- **Keeping smartphones out of restrooms**
- **Not allowing smartphones at meals (including at restaurants or coffee shops)**
- **Not allowing smartphones at school**
- **Not allowing smartphones during sports or activities**

How do you like that? "Are you kidding me? I thought you were a reasonable person, but it seems you are another crazy fundamentalist not knowing how to really deal with the problem. You are recommending simple smartphone prohibition. We all know that such an approach is going to fail sooner or later. We have evidence from the past here in America. Why are you treating us as halfwits and taking away our freedom of choice? Wrong. Wrong. Wrong."

- "Do you know [you continue arguing] that when you are in the middle of a real-time multiplayer internet game, you cannot just simply put an action 'on hold,' pausing the whole world because you want a break? That would be ridiculous. Are you seriously playing or playing around? Decide." "Or, do you know that nowadays people communicate using technologies? Hello! We are not in a stone age anymore. Just because you can't keep up the pace doesn't immediately mean that everyone else has to slow down and adjust. Ridiculous, as I said before."

- "You cannot simply watch Facebook's walls or engage with Snapchat once a day [you still continue arguing] – it is like not existing at all, not knowing anything, not contributing to anything and not being with anything, with anyone and not being anywhere – being nowhere. In every single moment there is so much going on, so much is happening, and stepping out from this life-giving stream is like switching off the lights and risking oblivion and exclusion from a society or favorite groups.

- I cannot even imagine how embarrassing it would be to show up at school after one day (or even one hour) off social media."

"Snapchat - The fastest way to share a moment!"

"Snapchat lets you easily talk with friends, view Live Stories from around the world, and explore news in Discover. Life's more fun when you live in the moment!"[xcvi]

- "What if I am not invited to a party, and am not even able to see what is happening there while I am not present. I would freak out, I would explode, I would not be able to bear this tension. Even if it would be 24 hours of torture – I would prefer to stare at it and interact with it than passively wait in hiding, cut off from the world. I am not relevant if I am not participating in the virtual world. You cannot just simply disappear from social media – you have to defend yourself continuously [you may continue arguing on and on]."

What about:

- **Putting smartphones into a basket** immediately after entering one's home (kitchen, living room, dining room) or classroom

- **Activating the Screen Time** option to monitor time spent per mobile application and **setting up individual screen time** (beating America's average screen time record for teenagers, which is above six hours per day, and gradually beating one's own personal average). One can make a competition out of it and keep it like that.
- **Disable notifications** on any screen devices from all applications – except any emergency alerts – to keep you safe at all times. You decide when to engage with the content, rather than letting the content decide on your behalf.

All of those mentioned above will create an uncomfortable emptiness, an unbearable void. Yes, that is true. But it is a matter of time. When put on an information diet or detox, our minds will start fighting, firing back with reasons to retain the status-quo. Our hungry and angry brains will not be easy to live with. But it is a matter of time. Information addictions require special treatment: defining clear screen time targets, exact interaction moments during the day, exact durations per moment, alternative "addictions" to feed starving "main processing units" like scheduled board game time with family and friends, scheduled concerts, scheduled outdoor activities (kayaking, motor boating, tenting, climbing, picnicking or travelling to wired places), scheduled reading time, poetry readings, storytelling, or even movie-watching time. The desire for information can be satisfied as well but in a totally different form and on our terms. Information consumption has to be diligently scheduled and executed with discipline and honesty.

What about:

- **Schools introducing mandatory "SMARTphone handling classes** – how to handle smartphones in a smart way" with analyses of benefits and challenges, with practical use cases, with hands-on tools and techniques – and of course with gamification components. That class should be the most creative and crazy of all – and voted one of the best. Think about that!
- Workplaces introducing voluntary courses or web-based training on supporting younger generations in their handling of smartphones

- Telecom providers being obligated to initiate on all their subscribers' phones (for kids, teens, and adults) mandatory mobile-based training on "SMARTphone handling" once a year.

I know those are not revolutionary ideas. Some may already be in place here and there.

––––––––––––

What about:

- **Creating a Physical Human Advanced Communication Market (PHAC)** by bringing new products and services based on connected devices, wearables, human-brain interfaces, more general artificial intelligence, and human-loving new generation virtual assistants (Alexa's, Siri's and Hey-Google's of the world), having as the main (configuration) goal the amplification of meaningful, high quality, deep "physical human" to "physical human" communication. What if I am sitting with my 2 friends having a face-to-face conversation, and our experience is augmented by a microchip feelings detector, or by a virtual assistant's verbal moderation, walking us through the process of problem-solving, collecting intentions, aligning on objectives, marshaling facts to validate points of views, using voting tactics or ice-breaking games, by thought–steered connected physical gadgets, like self-refilling water cups, self-moving game pawns, self-drawing pens, self-rolling balls, self-jumping dices, and so on and so forth. At the center is always the goal of maximizing the quality of human to human interaction, where the happiness index of all participants is the key performance indicator worth measuring. What a dream. Do you think so? I am being realistic.
- **What about outdoor excursions with zero connectivity or electricity?** I can tell you, I spent my three most wonderful young adult years at such summer camps. Life was beautiful!

Significantly Increasing Social Trust

Define as clearly as possible our **American culture**: the way we do things and behave around here. So, it is less about our sentiments about the Founding Fathers, Washington, Franklin, Adams, Hamilton, Madison, Lincoln, Jefferson, the Statue of Liberty, New York, Las Vegas, the Golden Gate Bridge, the Grand Canyon, Hollywood, Silicon Valley, guns, American football, Thanksgiving turkey, Black Friday, Star Wars, Walmart, Apple, Google, Warren Buffett, the idea that we are all immigrants, or the American Dream. It's more about how we think, act, and interact. It is more about what our common system of values and beliefs is.

- Make it more visible that **integrity, personal happiness, trust, and personal and social responsibility** are key behaviors expected by American culture to shape a prosperous and flourishing society. Of course, we keep differentiating aspects of American Culture: **freedom, diversity, power, entrepreneurship, invention & innovation** – embedded in **democracy and a free market** – are our competitive advantage.
- Teach such American culture at the earliest stages of life as mandatory duties of citizens
- Expect American culture to be followed by public officials, business owners, investors and citizens – at least by any person in charge of others (so-called leaders). Acting according to key behaviors should be weighed at the same level as competency and should become official criteria while running for office or during recruitment processes.
- Find an answer to the question: "how do we compete for prosperity and happiness with strongly cohesive societies? or "how do we create even more value from our strongly diverse society? or "How do we aim for both a strongly cohesive society and a diverse one to maximize opportunities? - that would be phenomenal – our new American experiment.

Where are we right now? According to John Kasich[xcvii], 69th Governor of Ohio, our whole country is divided:

*"The whole country is divided, [...] totally divided. [...] We have to get out from our silos. We can't just absorb things that we agree with. It's one of the dangers in our country. And if we absorb only that which agrees with us, we do not grow as people and we have trouble finding the truth. One of my great concerns is that truth is at risk today. Because you've got your things that you believe, I believe other things and we don't even agree on the basics. That's how a country gets in deep trouble. **I'm worried about the culture. Not just short term but long term. We've got to listen to one another, respect one another.**"[xcviii]*

Increase social cohesiveness at the foundational level. Define that level. What unites us? What can unite us more, significantly more? Find ways to enable cohesiveness while keeping our diversity.

We should aim for the **United Societies of America** (U*S*A)[xcix].

Increase access to diversity and inclusion education for all. Review social, business, and organization theories and courses on effective collaboration, effective teams, like "Diversity and Inclusion Awareness" courses, "Fair and Effective Interviewing for Diversity and Inclusion" courses, "Exploring Unconscious Bias" courses[c], and "Boundary-Spanning Leadership."[ci]

"Diversity is being asked to the party. Inclusion is being asked to dance."[cii]- *Vernā Myers*

"Diversity" is like being asked to the party. It is a very nice gesture on the part of the host. You are there to watch, but after the initial excitement wears off, you want to actively participate as well. If not, you will feel like a stranger. You will feel jealous or unequal. That is why "Inclusion" is such an important complement to "Diversity". "Inclusion" is about being asked to dance while being at that party.

Increase the social responsibilities of investors and companies which have to create both financial and social value to exist. Review social, business, and organizational theories, promote profit for purpose[ciii] business models, dual-purpose businesses, and socially responsible companies with corporate social responsibility programs.

Increase the understanding of social capital in the United States and form tangible activities to increase value. As an example, take a look at The Social Capital Project by the Joint Economic Committee.

*"Hi, I'm Senator Mike Lee, Chairman of the Joint Economic Committee. At the JEC, we believe knowledge of social capital is essential to our understanding of our country's economic health and that it's vital to achieving **our goal of expanding economic opportunity for all Americans**.*

But what exactly is social capital? It's the value of things we do together - the value of our relationships with our families, our friends and neighbors, congregations and co-workers. Social capital is, of course, harder to measure than traditional economic indicators like GDP but it's arguably even more necessary to the success of our uniquely American way of life.

Americans simply cannot flourish in a free-market economy and voluntary civil society without the relationships that connect us to those very networks of opportunity.

Social capital is what empowers our communities to overcome challenges in our own lives and in the lives of the communities that surround us. [...]

*But over the last few decades, once strong American communities have been weakened by isolation and alienation. **The distribution of social capital*** *across the country is more unequal than it used to be and it's this very unevenness in social support and interpersonal connectedness that is a primary reason Americans endure unequal opportunities.*

For two years, the JEC's Social Capital Project has dug into the issues to better understand the state of social capital in the United States today...."[xciv]

Self-reflection time

Although it is not self-improvement, nor will it improve your happiness, I am still encouraging you to spend some time on self-reflection and make your own decisions. The process of getting out of an unhappy cage may be long and painful, but in the end, it may be very rewarding. Enjoy the process. If you don't believe in change, stay where you are, but please don't stay too long.

"Should I Stay or Should I Go" - The Clash.

Am I sitting in an unhappy cage?

Why do I like sitting in an unhappy cage?

What is wrong with sitting in an unhappy cage?

Should I stay, or should I leave an unhappy cage?

What if I do nothing?

What are the risk and challenges?

What are the benefits?

What is the price I have to pay in advance?

What if I do something?

What are the risks and challenges?

What are the benefits?

What is the price I have to pay in advance?

What is my decision?

Do benefits outperform challenges?

Am I ready to pay the price now?

Should I have my last confrontation with my internal and external voices and beliefs?

Personal level:

- It is my democratic right and duty to make myself informed and watch the daily news. Danger can always lurk around the corner.
- I cannot imagine my life without a good and long-lasting American mystery, comedy, or drama television series every night. After my busy day, I need to sit and relax.
- There is so much diversity in our country, and to ensure we coexist in peace, we need a very strong legal system. We cannot simply trust each other because we do not know each other well enough.
- For sure, I trust my doctor on prescription drugs. If he/she says I need pain killers or opioids, I take them, like millions of other Americans. I need to manage my pain to be effective.
- I think I am pretty good with the quality of my relationships, usually meeting many people regularly during my daughter's soccer games and my son's baseball tournaments. On Saturdays, I have a quick chat with my two neighbors when cutting the lawn – without any doubt, we have a good connection. On Sundays, I greet so many people at my community church. In addition, we have two close family gatherings around Thanksgiving and Christmas.
- I am so happy. My business is doing very well.

National Level:

- We are the greatest nation.
- We are the happiest people on Earth because we can dream about and do anything we want. Pursuing happiness is our human right, enshrined by law.
- We are the world's leader, we are helping other nations to succeed, and we help maintain world peace, as we are the strongest power of all.

How do we escape our unhappy cages?

- Remind yourself of the purpose of your life or ask yourself what your purpose is.
- Take full responsibility for chasing that purpose.
- Remind yourself what is wrong in sitting in an unhappy cage.
- Define a realistic goal to escape from your unhappy cage.
- Decide and pay the price upfront, knowing the risks and benefits. You will be able to gain something much more valuable, but you will also lose something in exchange.
- Take small steps today and continue every day.
- Monitor whether you stay on the noble path. If necessary, correct the course.
- Make sure you love what you do! Do something for yourself, and something for your family, community, and country.

Below, I am listing randomly selected examples of possible next steps. Realistic possible next steps can only be defined by you, and effectively executed by you. Do not overwhelm yourself but do what is in your sphere of influence. You can always extend your capabilities and sphere of influence but do it in tiny steps to stay motivated.

My level:

- **Spend quality time with yourself.**
- Have a daily routine.
- Introduce routine, and maintain the basic structure of your day: set up a wake-up time, shower time (one of the most important items on the to-do list of Elon Musk - famous founder, CEO, and chief engineer/designer of SpaceX, early investor, CEO, and product architect of Tesla, Inc., founder of The Boring Company, co-founder of Neuralink and co-founder and initial co-chairman of OpenAI), time to make your bed, breakfast time, time to get through what is on your to-do list, prayer/meditation time, time to help others, time to reflect on your day, and bedtime.
- Get adequate sleep every night (e.g. 8 to 10 hours).

- Seek quiet (go to a quiet place, such as your car, the park, the free public library, the B&N bookstore, your church, or your basement, and lock the door). If you need white noise or background music, go to your favorite coffee shop. But nothing can beat a totally quiet space.
- Proceed with multiple self-check-ins per day (e.g. three times a day: in the morning, afternoon, and evening; ask yourself these questions: 1) where am I? 2) what am I doing and how am I feeling now? 3) why am I doing what I am doing and why am I feeling what I am feeling? 4) What is my purpose? 5) Is there anything I can do differently to be closer to my life purpose and to feel even better?)
- Pray every day.
- Meditate every day for a minimum of 5 minutes (you always have 5 minutes a day – there is no excuse for not taking them).
- Feel your body or scan it to feel it every day.
- Walk alone for minimum 15 minutes every day.
- Proceed with an "examination of conscience" at the end of every day (How was my day? What decisions did I make? What feelings did I have? How did I react to my feelings? What was good about my day? Who became a better person because of me? Am I a better person at the end of the day?)
- Plan your next day (remind yourself of your purpose in life, your life mission, and key personal goals you have. Think about what responsibilities to take on, and what tangible actions to take to stay on track to fulfill your life's purpose. Write them both down. What are you going to do, and more importantly, how are you going to become a better person? Also, plan what you are not going to do. "Becoming a better person tomorrow" means becoming better than you were yesterday, and growing according to your own ideals, day by day, step by step. As per Jordan Peterson, it is smarter to compare yourself to yourself from the past, than to compare yourself to anybody else).
- Plan your future (write it down) but live your life now.
- Reduce your expectations, and consciously limit your and your family's options. You can't eat an entire cake at once, so it's much better if you savor each piece individually, taking intentional breaks between each bite.

- Be grateful, and practice gratitude every day. Before you go to bed, write down in your "gratitude diary" who and what you are grateful for.

- **Spend quality time together.**
- Build and maintain meaningful relationships. Connect with people.
- Eat together every day and sit at the same table as your family or friends.
- Dedicate a minimum of 15 minutes to face-to-face talks at the table, maintaining physical closeness (for instance, try to make your knees touch each other).
- Walk together in the evening.
- Plan and spend long vacations together, far from home.
- Go to church together.
- Go to the gym and join group activities or go and eat some ice cream together.
- Play with your kid, or if you do not have one, play with other people's kids (if their parents or guardians agree).
- Meet regularly (at least once a month) with your friends, neighbors, and family.
- Invite your friends, neighbors, and family to your house, including for overnight visits.
- Play board games (thank you, my amazing neighbors!).
- Engage in deep conversations without smartphones (about the meaning of life, your purpose, dreams, and goals, your next family projects, your hobbies or your spiritual life).
- Read books to one another, tell one another jokes and stories.
- Sing and play instruments together.

- **Manage your information diet effectively.**
- Be intentional; be very selective.
- Decide what you want to consume at your information breakfast, lunch, and dinner.
- Check your smartphone or e-mails a maximum of 3 times a day, for no more than 45 minutes); check social media a maximum of 3 times a day (for about 15 minutes total); inform the world (if you must/have to) about your existence, share your life-stories/life-

events only when the day is over: be fair, and discuss your successes and your failures. Be real in the virtual world.

- Turn off live television for good. It is best not to have a TV at home, but if you must have one, do not keep more than one unit. Allow only on-demand content to reach your attention. Plan your viewing time carefully (e.g. Wednesdays at 8:00pm, or during weekends; watch recorded TV or video on demand, including news, but again only if you must/have to). Do not allow the external flow of information to steer your life. Go on an information diet.
- If you must/have to know what is happening around you, ask others. There are always people around you who are always up-to-date with the news, they will share with you anything you need, with great pleasure.
- Limit exposure to video games to a minimum, e.g. a maximum of 30 minutes twice a week (if you must/have to).
- Put smartphones in a basket when entering shared spaces at home. Never bring your smartphone into a restroom.
- Read books like *12 Rules for Life: An Antidote to Chaos* by Jordan Peterson, or *How to Stop Worrying and Start Living* by Dale Carnegie, or *Atomic Habits: An Easy and Proven Way to Build Good Habits and Break Bad Ones* by James Clear, just to mention a few titles. Pick-up one thing/rule/recommendation that inspires you or resonates with you the most and apply it immediately to your life. Only apply one recommendation at a time. Be prudent, not greedy.

- **Be curious all the time.**
- Spend some time abroad – the longer the better. Visit model countries. Try to immerse yourself in different cultures. Try to understand their thinking patterns, processes, beliefs, behaviors, norms, and the effect they have on the overall quality of life, perceived happiness, and prosperity.
- Learn something new every day. You can read any 365-page book in a year by reading one page a day. Watch a TEDx speech on "The first 20 hours -- how to learn anything" by Josh Kaufman.[cv] In other words, build your new skills.
- Watch or listen to intellectually stimulating podcasts or other media, like the official YouTube channels of Jordan B. Peterson, Bishop Robert Barron (also take a look at WordOnFire.org), 'The

Rubin Report,' the talk show led by Dave Rubin, Sam Harris and his 'The Making Sense' podcast, or the video podcast, 'The Ben Shapiro Show,' available on the official YouTube channel of Ben Shapiro, or 'The Daily Show with Trevor Noah,' led by Trevor Noah, or the Oprah Winfrey Network (OWN).

- Sign-up for "The Science of Well Being"[cvi] course developed by Yale University and taught by Professor Laurie Santos. The purpose of the course is not only to learn what psychological research says about what makes us happy, but also to put those strategies into practice.
- Sign-up for the "Search Inside Yourself[cvii]" program, which teaches practical mindfulness, emotional intelligence, and leadership. It was originally developed by leading experts at Google.

- **Decide on your life's purpose, and take responsibility for your own life.**
- **Do something every day to fulfill your life duties and realize your life's purpose.**
- But before you do anything else, "clean your damn room first," as Jordan Peterson used to say. It means that before changing the whole world or coming up with gigantic ideas, start small, start with your own surroundings, start from your own environment and improve day by day, compare yourself only to yourself from yesterday and not to anybody else. When you master cleaning your room, move beyond it, and clean the world.
- **Be kind to yourself and to others.**
- Serve others. Fill up your time with projects for others - not for yourself. Stop thinking about yourself. Be careful, it is a "suggestion" trap, you cannot stop thinking because the thinking process is automatic and is always happening in your brain. Stop thinking about yourself means be aware of your thoughts, and consciously decide not to follow those that are oriented toward your desires. Instead, be selective, and consider those thoughts that are oriented toward others. If none of your thoughts are directed at others, provoke them. Challenge self-centered thought and without too much internal debate start thinking more about how to help others.

- Enjoy the process. Happiness is a state of mind filled with peace, joy, and love, and not a simple item on a to-do list that can be checked off once and forgotten.

Country level:

- Make informed decisions about the right candidate with the right political program, and vote in mayoral, congressional, or presidential elections.
- Educate yourself about current socio-economic situation

For instance, you may want to check the USAFacts website (usafacts.org)

"USAFacts is a not-for-profit, nonpartisan civic initiative providing the most comprehensive and understandable source of government data available. [...] We do all of this to give Americans the tools to ground public debates in facts. Serious, reasoned, and informed debate on the purpose and functions of government is vital to our democracy... USAFacts is a new data-driven portrait of the American population, our government's finances, and [its] impact on society. We are a nonpartisan, not-for-profit civic initiative and have no political agenda or commercial motive. We provide this information as a free public service and are committed to maintaining and expanding it in the future." USAFacts provides "government data from over 70 sources organized to show how the money flows, the impact, and who "the people" are."[cviii]

USAFacts was founded by former Microsoft CEO Steve Ballmer.

- Stand up to racism and injustice.
- Make a phone call, and send a letter or e-mail to your political representative (e.g. state governor, city mayor, president) and ask him or her questions about his or her goals and strategies for a wiser human-oriented economy and how he or she aims to create a happier and less problematic society.
- Set up a personal meeting with your political representative and ask him or her important questions: "What are you doing to make my family, my neighbors, and me happy?" "What is your plan to

further improve the quality of life of your constituents and bring them joy?"

- Vote in elections.
- Organize local community meetings, invite people to garden parties at your home, and start discussions on the quality of life, living less stressful lives, living happier lives and the "human flourishing index." Ask everyone, "What can we do together to create a better future?"

Global level:

- Think for instance, about how to engage in the realization of the Sustainable Development Goals of the United Nations.
- "The Sustainable Development Goals are a call for action by all countries – poor, rich, and middle-income – to promote prosperity while protecting the planet. They recognize that ending poverty must go hand-in-hand with strategies that build economic growth and address a range of social needs including education, health, social protection, and job opportunities, while tackling climate change and environmental protection."[cix]
- Have a look at the 17 Goals to Transform Our World:
- GOAL 1: No Poverty // GOAL 2: Zero Hunger // GOAL 3: Good Health and Well-being // GOAL 4: Quality Education // GOAL 5: Gender Equality // GOAL 6: Clean Water and Sanitation // GOAL 7: Affordable and Clean Energy // GOAL 8: Decent Work and Economic Growth // GOAL 9: Industry, Innovation, and Infrastructure // GOAL 10: Reduced Inequality // GOAL 11: Sustainable Cities and Communities // GOAL 12: Responsible Consumption and Production // GOAL 13: Climate Action // GOAL 14: Life Below Water // GOAL 15: Life on Land // GOAL 16: Peace and Justice Strong Institutions // GOAL 17: Partnerships to achieve the Goal[cx]
- You can be the change!

CHAPTER 3

Fake Right to Liberty

Abandoned without money and education

"In my own country, I feel robbed of my livelihood and can barely make ends meet."

Have you ever heard that story?

Deborah and James, our middle class representatives, have 2 and a half children, 2 and a half pets, a 2 and a half bedroom house with a mortgage, 2 and a half yards (back, front, and side), 2 and a half cars, 2 and a half TV screens, 2 and a half other screens per person (smartphones, tablets, play stations, etc.). They obviously have 2 and a half loans, at least 2 and a half credit cards per person as well as 2 and a half other commitments per person (monthly paid cable TV, Internet, iTunes, Netflix, Spotify, YouTube, or membership in a sports clubs, city gyms or other organized activities). Because their 2 and a half kids would like to go to paid colleges, our couple will very soon need 2 and a half new loans to send them there. To be able to deal with all this, Deborah and James have 2 and a half jobs per person and spend 2 and a half more time at work than usual. Deborah, James and their children wake up 2 and a half hours before the whole world to catch up well in advance and prepare for the new challenges of the new day and be two and a half times more productive and fully realize their "2.5" potential.

There are certainly more 2 and a half(s) in their reality and in their dreams. We better stop here, because the math is getting too complicated.

Have you ever heard such a story? You may respond, yes, maybe or never. Of course, this depends on where you are on the ladder of socioeconomic classes and how far you have developed in the area of self-awareness, self-control, personal effectiveness or broadly defined personal excellence.

Let's pretend for the moment that we are middle-class citizens, born into this class, forced to be part of this class, or there without knowing why.

I can imagine many immediate reactions to stories like the one about Deborah and James, like:

- Oh yes, that is normal. That is the average lifestyle in "my class." There is nothing special about it.
- Oh yes, although that seems complicated, that is more less what we have and want to have as a family.
- Oh yes, it may seem like too many commitments, but by that we know we are alive.
- It is so cool and practical that every member of the family has his or her own room, bath, car, bike, favorite toy, TV, speaker set, smartphone, tablet, PC, Internet access, electric toothbrush, x shelves of books, y pairs of shoes, x+y trousers, x+y+z skirts, x+y+z+v T-shirts education paths, hobbies, "you-name-its."
- Oh yes, it is sometimes hard to catch up with all technological advancements, new offerings and promotions or in the end labor market requirements, but still we can count on our banking system, our credit cards and so far, good credit scores to finance what's needed. We are so grateful for all those credit cards. You can even get one at the grocery store these days. Awesome.
- It could be overwhelming, I agree.
- We still do not know how to save for our kids' education, but we will figure it out. Most probably we will take more assignments in

the afternoon and take advantage of new credit line offerings. Last time, we saw 0% for the whole year. What a deal.

One could argue,

- Why do they need so much stuff in the first place?
- Why are their family lives so complicated?
- Why can't they live much simpler lives?

We may enter a philosophical debate on what's more important "to be" or "to have," or what's more important "not to be" or "not to have" or maybe ("to be" and "to have") vs. ("to be" and "not to have,") or we may want more "to be" than "not to be," and we may want more "to have" than "not to have." And, that is not a question.

By the way, "to be or not to be" (, that) is a question that will be covered in the next chapters.

Poverty level and common sense adjusted poverty level

So, how much do we really need to survive, how much do we really need to survive and at the same time have some fun (not too much, but at least some), or how much do we really need to survive, have more fun and really enjoy our lives?

"So, if we look at the dimension called life satisfaction, we can see that money does matter for well-being and happiness. I mean, on average, richer countries are happier. On average, richer people are happier. The mechanism here is, being without money is a cause of unhappiness." - Meik Wiking[cxi]

"People who pursue only money and say, I'll be happier the richer I am, turn out to be less happy. […] Balance is the formula for happiness. Aristotle had it right when he launched the study of happiness 2,300 years ago." - Jeffrey Sachs[cxii]

"According to Aristotle's Golden Mean, good behavior lies between two vices, excess and deficiency."[cxiii]

Let's take as our starting points the following facts:

- **The top wealthiest 1% possess close to 50% of the nation's wealth.**
- **Almost all wealth is in the hands of less than 20% of the US population.**
- **We, the American People (80% of us,) own only 7% of the country's wealth.**

- It is getting worse and worse. Did you know that productivity in our country improved far more than 70 percent in the last 40 years, but worker's compensation rose only 9 percent in the last 40 years? Money was transferred to the richest and corporations, only.

- **Americans have been robbed.**

- The poverty line[cxiv] in the US for a family of 1 is defined at $12,000 per year.
- **There are more than 40 million Americans living below the poverty level.**

  - the poverty level for a **family of 1** is about **$12,000 per year**
  - the poverty level for a **family of 2** is about **$16,000 per year**
  - the poverty level for a **family of 3** is about **$20,000 per year**
  - the poverty level for a **family of 4** is about **$25,000 per year**
  - the poverty level for a **family of 5** is about **$30,000 per year**

Details can be found in "Poverty Guidelines"[cxv] published by The United States Department of Health & Human Services (HHS), also known as the Health Department.

Allow me to repeat that there are about 40 million Americans living below the poverty line, and this is just the beginning of our analysis. As you will see very soon, based on a "common sense" analysis of our expenditures, it would be better to start thinking about a totally different, more realistic, "common sense adjusted poverty line" or threshold than the above-mentioned official poverty level.

According to the "common sense spending" analysis below, we should honestly talk about $50,000 for family of 1 or $120,000 for family of 4 as "common sense adjusted poverty levels." At the same time we know that about 80% of American households made less than $100,000 per year – which is below the "common sense adjusted poverty level" for a family of 4 (a quick remark: a household consists of all the people who occupy one house or apartment, like families, but also roommates sharing an apartment or people living on their own).

About 80% of American families are living below the "common sense adjusted poverty level."

What is the "common sense adjusted poverty level?" Let's have a look at a simulation made for a family of 4 where obvious cost elements were taken into consideration, like shelter, utilities, food, home supplies, transport, car insurance, Internet, phones, healthcare, clothing, pre-school tuition, entertainment, restaurants, and one-time purchases.

To not run into immediate depression, **the following costs were not included** in the attached simulation: **College** tuition, **Vacation** expenses, Live **theatre/concerts/sports games**, Spotify, Netflix, etc., **Unexpected expenses, Savings**.

Cost Category	$/month	Additional comments
Shelter	$1,700.00	Lease or mortgage on 2-bedroom, 1-bath with kitchen. Of course, rates for renting apartments or houses vary from state to state, and from city to city. Let's take something in between Kansas and New York.
Shelter utilities	$800.00	Clean and waste water, heating/cooling, electricity, gas, trash, real estate/community management...
Shelter maintenance	$100.00	Small house repairs, backyard...
Food	$1,200.00	Breakfast, lunch, dinner, supper at home (groceries $300/week)
Home supplies	$150.00	Toilet paper, dishwasher detergent tablets, laundry detergent packs, soap, shampoo, toothpaste...
Transport (gas, tickets)	$160.00	To school, to work, to store, to clinic, "to church"...
Car lease or loan	$500.00	Lease or debt on 2 cars
Car Insurance	$200.00	Annual insurance plan for 2 cars div. by 12
Internet/TV	$80.00	Broadband internet service
Mobile phone, data plan	$200.00	2 mobile phone plans
Pre-school tuition	$800.00	Tuition for 1 child
Healthcare	$1,300.00	Monthly contribution to the plan plus co-payments plus pharmacy visits, clinic visits plus annual deductible divided by 12
Clothing	$75.00	Once a quarter 1-2 things (shirt, shoes, hat...)
Entertainment	$160.00	Once a month, movie theatre, inexpensive sports game (e.g. baseball game, football game - last row at the stadium...)
Restaurant	$120.00	Once a month family breakfast, lunch or dinner at a modestly-priced restaurant
One Time Purchases (per month)	$180.00	Home equipment purchases in a 5-year cycle. Selected items: TV, DVD, Speakers, Mattress, Phone, PC, Table, Chairs, Dishes, Iron, Kettle, Washing Machine, Dryer, Fridge... Total value ca. $10,000 divided by $5y$ and $12m$
Total costs & expenses with one-time purchases per month	$7,725.00	TOTAL monthly
Annual cash Needed	$92,700.00	Money needed to cover mentioned costs and expenses
Annual income Needed	$118,846.15	Income required based on cash needed plus tax (22% for salaries greater than $38K; only federal tax brackets considered)

Table 2: Monthly household expenses (simulation) for a family of 4.

It looks like that "common sense cost of living" for the family of 4 (2 adults and 2 children with only one kid paying pre-school tuition) is on the level of **$93,000** which translates into **$120,000** of annual income.

Hence, our more realistic, "common sense adjusted poverty level" is $120,000 per year per family without College tuition, Vacation expenses, Live theatre/concerts/sports games, Spotify, Netflix, etc., Unexpected expenses, Savings.

You can say healthcare and cars are luxuries, and that it is better to homeschool kids, or that spending on entertainment, restaurants, or clothing is insane. When I was young, I had one pair of shoes, one T-shirt, and one pair of pants – and it was enough – everyone was happy." O.K., fair enough. Now let's create a less wasteful simulation.

Cost Category	$/month	Additional comments
Car lease or loan	$500.00	Let's take a car lease or debt off (you have just inherited 2 stylish cars)
Healthcare	$1,300.00	Let's take healthcare off (you have incredibly good genes)
Clothing	$75.00	Let's take clothing off (your grandmother is an excellent dressmaker)
Pre-school tuition	$800.00	Let's take tuition off (it's time for high quality home schooling)
Entertainment	$160.00	Let's take entertainment off (sitting on the porch is fun enough)
Restaurant	$120.00	Let's take restaurants off (you never know if they wash their hands there)
One-time purchases per month	$180.00	Let's take one time purchases off (you found a mattress, table, chairs, and a fridge across the street—a garage sale is one of the wonders of the world)
Total monthly costs & expenses to be subtracted	**$3,135.00**	TOTAL w/o tax per month
Total annual costs & expenses to be subtracted	**$37,620.00**	TOTAL w/o tax per year (about **$48,000** to be comparable with income)

Table 3 "Not needed" monthly household expenses (simulation) for family of 4 that have to be eliminated from the total expenses to achieve more optimized monthly household expenses.

Subtracting certain categories (worth about $48,000) we come up with **$70,000** per year for the family of 4. It looks like we ended up with the range of $70,000 to $120,000 for the "common sense adjusted poverty line."

Should we normalize further our calculations and include all "common sense" needs and cost categories into one equation? To reflect the most realistic view, let's keep **healthcare, cars, entertainment, restaurant,**

clothing and **one time purchases** in and add state **college** for 2 resident kids, **vacation** costs for 4 family members, extended **entertainment** (1 time theatre, 1 time concert, 2 sports games) for all, **unexpected expenses,** and finally **savings** (as 10% of income; it should be more but let's not stretch our model too much).

You could ask, how much of my income should I save every month? According to common wisdom or popular advice: "At least 20% of your income should go towards savings. Meanwhile, another 50% (maximum) should go towards necessities, while 30% goes towards discretionary items. This is called the 50/30/20 rule of thumb, and it's popular quick-and-easy advice."[cxvi]

Cost Category	$/year	Additional comments
State college (2 kids, residents)	$20,000.00	Cost for state college for resident 1 child ca. $10,000/year; In case someone would love to attend private university then the calculation is totally different, it would be about $50,000/year per 1 child
Vacation (only 7 days a year, and should be 14+)	$2,700.00	4 people, 7 nights; domestic flight ($150/person), accommodation ($250/night); rented car ($50/day)
Extended Entertainment	$1,040.00	4 people: live theatre (once a year; $40/ticket), concert (once a year; $80/ticket), sports game (once a year; $80/ticket); food ($20/person); Of course, tickets could go far beyond $100 per person
Unexpected expenses	$500.00	e.g. broken shower, broken window, air-conditioning repair, phone damage…
Savings	$10,000.00	Let's take 10% of income (should be 20% according to common wisdom)
Total costs & expenses w/o tax per YEAR	**$34,240.00**	Total expenditures (about **$44,000** to be comparable with income)

Table 4: "Most wanted" additional monthly household expenses (simulation) for family of 4 that should be included in the total to achieve a "realistic view" on total monthly household expenses.

Final income target for family of 4 including all mentioned categories turned to be on the level of **$160,000** (Table 2: $70,000 most basic income + Table 3: $48,000 for healthcare, pre-school… + Table 4: $44,000 for college, vacation, savings…**)** or about $130,000 in cash.

To summarize, the so-called poverty level, line, or threshold defined by government bodies as **$25,000** for a family of 4 ($12,000 for family of

1) is unbelievably and unrealistically low versus a more realistic, common sense poverty level or common sense income level which equals **$70,000** for the family of 4 in the most aggressive scenario and can reach up to **$160,000** if we include healthcare, higher education, vacation, and savings, just to list the most important ones.

It all means the following:

- It is hard to believe that in the most powerful and most prosperous country on Earth there are at least **40 million people living below $12,000 per year.**
- It is hard to believe that the official poverty level is defined at such a low level of $12,000, when the real, common sense one for a family of 1 should be at least on the level of $30,000 and for a family of 4 on the minimum level of $70,000.
- 40% of American households (where the average household size was 2.6 in 2019) earn less than $50,000 per year (as per 2018 stats[cxvii]).
- **It means that about 133 million Americans live below the "common sense poverty line"** ($70,000 for a family of 4; and respectively about $50,000 for a family of 2.6). (There were 128.58 million households and 328.24 million residents in 2019 in the United States).
- 80% of Americans are living below the "happiness level that money can buy".

Your second "you" within you may start whispering that those calculations must have some errors or logical fallacy. There is too huge a disproportion. That can't be true. There is a very easy test that can be performed to test the model – just calculate it yourself, honestly, with full transparency on cost categories, those monthly ones, those yearly ones, and those one-time purchases that span over multiple years. Make sure you annualize them to have a full year's spending picture. Make sure you also include those categories that never show up on your list because you simply cannot afford them, or those categories that represent money you borrowed – not your own money, but your growing credit lines. Be fair, when calculating your costs, for instance, when the credit installments counted in years exceed your projected life expectancy in years then you know you need to live forever to pay it back and be considered a good, credible, trustworthy man.

Your third "you" within you may not be able to withstand such high pressure and start screaming, "that is all crap!" How on Earth can people in some countries (the poorest of the poor) live on less than $1.90 per person per day, which means less than $800 per year, and "you, dear author" are simulating a minimum of $70,000 for U.S. citizens. And by the way, more than 700 million people on Earth are living now with less than $800 per year. Something is not right.

Dear you, we are looking here at the United States of America, at its current economic condition measured in GDP (gross domestic product) which is close to 20 trillion USD per year, 20 and 12 zeros, **$20,000,000,000,000.**

For the sake of this analysis, I would not recommend comparing ourselves to those at the bottom of the list (this is another enormous problem we should resolve) but to those countries at the top – according to our American ambition. The U.S.A. has lots of money, so much that even U.S. citizens themselves cannot see it all, as the pot of money is so big. It is like standing at the entrance to a gigantic skyscraper, or in front of a big elephant, trying to grasp the whole object at once. Simply speaking, U.S. wealth is so great that we have obvious difficulty seeing it. Unfortunately, there are no wealthy elephants in any of 80% of American families' rooms. Elephants can only be seen in those 1+% households because their houses are big enough to house them. Most of us have trouble seeing big elephants in big houses because those creatures are hidden behind security guards, tall walls, huge safes or banking systems. Excuse me for a little bit of sarcasm here.

Let's make a quick, cheap, and not fully accurate calculation, and take U.S. GDP, 20 trillion dollars and divide it by all U.S. households, around 128 million. Now, if GDP was equally distributed, then every household would possess about **$160,000.** This seems unbelievable. I was amazed, too. And by the way, equal distribution is only used here to make this case simple, and of course not realistic. I am a fan of wise or fair wealth distribution, rather than equal distribution, which I am going to explain later.

Does this number remind you of something? Although it is pure coincidence, that is exactly the same value that was calculated as "common sense household income" on the upper end, earlier in this chapter.

In terms of GDP (gross domestic product), one of the primary indicators used to gauge the health of a country's economy – we are unbeatable, simply the best. But, when you look at the individual and family level, we are in "deep mud," to put it nicely.

What about traveling, live theatre, concerts, or sports games, which we love so much?

Now you know why we Americans (80% of us, almost all of us) are not really traveling to different states, not to mention traveling to different countries, and why we don't go to live theatre, concerts, or high-quality sports events. Now you know why we Americans eat "junk" food. We are unable to go to good restaurants serving fresh and heathy food, or to afford fresh, healthy, and high-quality food ourselves.

Let's take a quick look at a family trip to the theatre. Let's take a randomly selected event, e.g. a "Paw Patrol" performance for kids at Kansas City Music Hall. The ticket price per person in the last possible row (to minimize costs) is $55. Multiplying that by 5 people means about $300 for a 2-hour show. The quality of the place is average. Following the strong culture of "popcorning" everywhere you go (even if you are not hungry, you better have one because everyone is eating around you and it is so loud that you cannot hear your own thoughts. I am saying, for your personal comfort, you had better munch, crunch or chomp) we buy 5 bags of popcorn with lemonade which means about $150 in total ($15 per small bag and $15 per small cup of lemonade). So we end up spending about $500 if we include transportation, but not gifts or toys.

That was an extremely light example. For a basketball game, tickets exceed $200-$300 each. For the most recent Elton John concert, decent seats were priced at $2,000. O.K., let's go back to our favorite $100 last row and keep on pretending we are middle class representatives. I love this math game.

How on earth can we Americans attend anything like that? More than 50% of Americans do not have $500 for unexpected situations, like car accidents, plumbing and heating issues, or other home repairs. How on earth can you go to the theatre with your loved ones when your ceiling is leaking?

At least there is a light at the end of the tunnel. I bet most of us can go and watch movies at the movie theatre – what a relief. Movies are effectively used as the powerful steering wheel of capitalism, as they give us the illusion of paradise. They are a great invention and innovation. Thank God we have our movies.

Now, do you want to live in the most prosperous country ever invented, or do you want to live in the most prosperous country ever invented as a prosperous and happy individual? Those two are not the same. Can you see the tragic disconnect here? We are not prosperous, and we are not happy living in the most prosperous country ever invented. Wealth is not wisely distributed. And again, I am not saying equally distributed to not wake up anti-socialist and anti-communist paranoids, subconscious personas in me, in you or in others.

Minimum wage and living wage

Let's proceed with the last consistency check reviewing minimum wage and living wage.

What if we bring to our discussion so-called **minimum wage**, a favorite topic of many politicians? According to Wikipedia: "minimum wage is the lowest remuneration that employers can legally pay their workers - the price floor below which workers may not sell their labor." [cxviii]

- **Federal minimum wage** is **$7.25 per hour.**
- Minimum wage per state varies from $7.25 to $11.50. In the District of Columbia it was $12.50 in 2017 and it was raised each year thereafter until it reached **$15.00 per hour** in July 2020.

So, let's calculate annual income based on minimum wage, taking the amount somewhere between $7.25 and $15.00 - for instance $10 as the average minimum wage.

- Annual income based on average minimum wage = $10 per hour **x** 40 hours per week **x** 52 weeks a year = **$20,800** (assuming one works all year long).

Now, let's cross-check calculated annual income based on minimum wage with so-called living wage. **Living wage** is the income a family needs in order to attain a modest yet adequate standard of living in particular cities in the U.S., following a reliable source, the Economic Policy Institute. Living wages can be calculated using e.g. the *Family Budget Calculator* available on the Economic Policy Institute website[cxix].

Take a look at a sample of living wages per annum for 1 adult, starting with the cheapest cities:

- Kalamazoo, MI, **$32,530**
- Kansas City metro area, KS/MI, **$33,334**
- Orange County, NC, **$40,639**

And ending with most expensive cities:

- New York, NY, **$57,257**
- Oakland, CA, **$57,383**
- San Francisco, CA, **$69,072**

How on Earth can one live on the minimum wage of $20,800 even in the cheapest places in America? That would mean a gap of $10,000 to $50,000 dollars.

To be able to survive - people are living under pressure, and with huge debts.

To compare living wages per area for different sized families, like 1 adult and 1 kid or 2 adults and 2 kids, please visit the Economic Policy Institute website and run one of their simulations.

What is the "happiness level that money can buy"?

"Money makes people happy [...] but it isn't a simple relationship between money and happiness – it's what we call a curvilinear relationship [*A Curvilinear Relationship is a type of relationship between two variables where as one variable increases, so does the other variable, but only up to a certain point, after which, as one variable continues to increase, the other decreases.*] [...] the first dollar you earn is a source of great joy and every other dollar or euro [...] afterwards brings you just a little less happiness. **Moving people out of poverty into the middle class dramatically changes their lives.** Moving them from the middle class to the upper class, well, it does increase their happiness, but not that much. And moving them into the stratospherically wealthy does almost nothing at all. Now, where on this curve is the line, [...] the inflection point, the point where there's really not much more benefit to having more money?

In U.S. dollars you get 95% [ninety-five percent] of all the happiness that money can buy if you earn $75,000 [seventy-five thousand dollars] per year. I should note that 80% [eighty percent] of Americans don't earn this amount, but this is nowhere near being rich.

Why does this line curve? Some people believe it's a law of nature. Money is like pancakes [...] you eat one and it's fabulous, the second is pretty good, the third is starting to feel like too much and after that you're feeling sick."[cxx] - Dan Gilbert, an American social psychologist and writer, Professor of Psychology at Harvard University, and the author of the international bestseller *Stumbling on Happiness*

Effectively, **we are almost all quite "poor citizens" in the richest country** in the universe.

The Richest

Why don't we come back to Earth, and instead of talking about 80% of Americans who are not able to live according to The Declaration, focus for a minute on the Americans who fulfill their American Dreams. Let's have a look at our role models, sports stars, music stars, show business stars, and giant entrepreneurs, both chief executives and owners.

Before we start, to be very clear, it is not my role to judge anybody. What you will see in the next paragraphs is the product of our perfect capitalism, or the pleasant side effects of it – or exceptions to the rule. People are getting awfully rich because the system allows them to become rich. Nobody is perfect. We need not analyze every single titan because who knows what truth we would find there. To be fair, we should look into our own lives before we even consider judging others. It can be, like with anybody else who belongs to any socio-economic group, that we will find people with big hearts, compassion, kindness, gratitude, and willingness to share with others and make the world a better place. We could also find people who are far from role models, and who are trapped in their own weaknesses, greed, and pride, unable to see their good fortune. They usually keep their distance from others, and are not interested in communal wealth and prosperity. Good and bad people can be found in any social groups, at any social levels, so it would be very unfair to judge people's lives based only on their level of wealth.

Let's take some examples from Internet search results:

- The NFL's highest-paid players 2018[cxxi]: Aaron Rodgers: **$76 million**, Matt Ryan: **$57.5 million**, Jimmy Garoppolo: **$43.1 million**, Khalil Mack: **$41.8 million**, Aaron Donald: **$41.1 million**, and so on. These were earnings in one year. Let's assume they play

5 successful seasons, so they should be able to collect approximately **$200-300 million each**.

- The highest-paid actors[cxxii]: 7. Tom Cruise: **$43 million**, 6. Robert Downey, Jr.: **$48 million**, 5. Jackie Chan: **$49 million**, 4. Adam Sandler: **$50.5 million**, 3. Vin Diesel: **$54.5 million**, 2. Dwayne Johnson: **$65 million**, 1. Mark Wahlberg: **$68 million**.

- The highest-paid actress[cxxiii]: 10. Amy Adams: **$11.5 million**, 8. Julia Roberts: **$12 million**, 8. Cate Blanchett: **$12 million**, 6. Charlize Theron: **$14 million**, 6. Emma Watson: **$14 million**, 5. Mila Kunis: **$15.5 million**, 4. Melissa McCarthy: **$18 million**, 3. Jennifer Lawrence: **$24 million**, 2. Jennifer Aniston: **$25.5 million**, 1. Emma Stone: **$26 million**.

- The highest-paid CEOs[cxxiv] (Chief Executive Officers) or owners with company profits: Warren E. Buffett: Berkshire Hathaway company revenue $223.6 billion and **profit $24.1** billion, Larry Page: Alphabet [including Google] company revenue $90.3 billion and **profit $19.5 billion**, Jeffrey P. Bezos: Amazon.com company revenue $136.0 billion and **profit $2.4 billion**, Gail K. Boudreaux: Anthem company: Anthem, Inc. is an American health insurance company with revenue: $84.9 billion and **profit $2.5 billion**, and so on, and let's not forget about Mark Zuckerberg: Facebook company revenue: $27.6 billion and **profit $10.2 billion**, Brian Duperreault working for AIG with total **compensation: $43.1 million**, Dirk Van de Put working for Mondelez International with total **compensation: $42.4 million**, Mark V. Hurd working for Oracle with total **compensation: $40.8 million**, Robert A. Iger working for Disney with total **compensation: $36.3 million**, Jeffrey L. Bewkes working for Time Warner with total **compensation: $32.6 million**, and the last example from a very long list, Indra K. Nooyi working for PepsiCo with **total compensation: $31.1 million**, or Stephen J. Hemsley who works for UnitedHealth Group Inc. and receives total **compensation** on the level of **$17.8 million** (UnitedHealth Group Inc. is an American company that offers health care products and insurance services, is based in Minnetonka, Minnesota, and was ranked #5 in 2018 in the Fortune 500 rankings of the largest United States corporations. For the fiscal year 2018, UnitedHealth Group reported **earnings of $11.98 billion**, with an annual revenue of US $226.2 billion).

- Quick note: assuming the basic monthly payment for healthcare coverage without a deductible per person is approximate $440 ($5,280 per year), then for the aforementioned $17.8 million compensation of UnitedHealth Group Inc.'s CEO, **we could cover 3,300 people** or **1.3 million people** when we take the whole company's earnings.

The above-mentioned figures are only annual incomes. Imagine what the total wealth of our sports, entertainment and business stars is. On top of salaries, bonuses, and stock options, many of them have collected private jets, yachts, summer houses, winter houses, horses, farms, pools, giant cars, and investments.

Why, in the first place, do we need those celebrities, those angels floating above our heads? What kind of law is working here? Is there any natural law in charge here? Business stars in the most optimal case are to create new jobs or sustain them. That is key for our economy. But what about other clearly non-essential privileged ones? Were we enchanted by Disney's magic dust and turned into unconscious content payers, fiction's receivers? Maybe we need them because we are in fact extremely unhappy people living our grey and painful lives. We must continuously switch between the real world and the illusory one. We blindly follow celebrities' stories. We cheat our "mirror neurons" and immerse ourselves in dreams of luxury and happiness to feel part of a wonderful fairy tale. We do it every day, for at least 1 to 3 hours a day. Can't we see this mechanism? Do you think in other wealthy and at the same time happy countries, people are as addicted to celebrity culture as we are? Do they give them such mountains of money to help them live their lives on behalf of those who sponsor them? Not really. That is not the model in Germany, Italy, France, Japan, Sweden, or other countries. Of course, we could always find exceptions. Is there something wrong with our model? Should we reflect on our assumptions, market processes, value flows and value distribution, incentive mechanisms or general understanding of common wealth ideas and wealth creation? Does our system support society's flourishing or its dysfunction? Does our system create equality and happiness for all? In light of those simple examples of those enormous incomes of the rich, the experiences of ordinary people seem depressing.

What is the overall value of a housewife's work, househusband's work or teacher's work? What does the value of the first responder's work look like? Who are our real heroes - important for our lives?

Let me pay tribute to those who have just devoted themselves and sacrificed their lives for us, our real heroes.

"If there is a silver lining to the corona crisis then it's the fact that the world finally CELEBRATES the REAL HEROES! And it's not, with all due respect, football players," [cxxv]'any-sports' players, singers, actresses and actors, casino owners, or the overpaid CEOs of irrelevant or harmful enterprises.

"These are the heroes of the coronavirus pandemic.

Every crisis has its heroes, every disaster its displays of selflessness and sacrifice. Firefighters race into burning buildings. Police officers place themselves in the line of fire. Soldiers march into war.

And now, amid the coronavirus pandemic,

our health-care workers, doctors, nurses, EMTs, and support staff who risk becoming infected themselves — who risk infecting their own families — are making extraordinary sacrifices to care for the rest of us. They do so, most infuriatingly, even as they have been put at greater risk than necessary by the avoidable shortages of masks, face shields, and other personal protective equipment."[cxxvi]

- Ruth Marcus, The Washington Post, March 27, 2020

Do we still have doubts about how to design our system to properly distribute money to those who care about us?

For some of us, net worth is calculated in billions.

Let's take a closer look at the so-called Wealthiest Americans[cxxvii]. At the very top of the rankings we can usually see the following successful individuals (I present just a sample put in alphabetical order): Bill Gates, Charles Koch, Elon Musk, Eric Schmidt, Jacqueline Mars, Jeff Bezos, Jim Walton, Larry Ellison, Larry Page, Mark Zuckerberg, Michael Bloomberg, Michael Dell, Rupert Murdoch, Sergey Brin, Stephen Schwarzman, Steve Ballmer, Steve Cohen, and Warren Buffett). Depending on criteria (net worth, annual salaries, other incentives, stocks' value, properties' value, etc.) we can create unlimited rankings of the top 10, top 100, top 400, above $100 billion net worth, above $50 billion, above $10 billion, above $2 billion... When we analyze, for instance, the top 400, we can see the following:

- Accumulated net worth ranges from $2.1 billion to more than **$100 billion per person.**
- Accumulated net worth by this group of the top 400 Americans is on the level of $3 trillion = $3,000 billion = $3,000,000 million = **$3,000,000,000,000.**
- Assuming the **median net worth** of the average **U.S. household was $97,300** in 2018, the accumulated net worth of those top 400 is equal to **25% of all the American households' net worth taken together, which is 30.8 million households or approximately 80 million Americans.**

Breathtaking, or "just the way it is."

Now,

- As per the United States Census Bureau's data, there were **38 million Americans below the poverty line in 2018.**[cxxviii]
- **So, even if our top 400 magnates would keep only 2.1 billion of their net worth for themselves, still 22.2 million households or 57.2 million Americans could be secured by the remaining worth – eliminating poverty in America entirely** (without going into any details of the sophisticated nature of markets)
- This is either the beauty of aggregations and math, or it is "just the way it is."

The Rich and Waste

While some of the wealthiest spend at least a fraction of their fortunes to create a greater common good, investing in solutions to the biggest world problems like disease, danger, food and water insecurity, the lack of economic opportunity, poverty, income inequality, discrimination, wars, climate change, insufficient government accountability and transparency and more, others waste their fortunes on socially and morally harmful projects, causing society's regression and destruction.

One doesn't have to be a genius to notice:

- The cumulative net worth of only **10 individuals** shaping the **information search and exchange industry** is on the level of **$363 billion,** which translates to almost **10 million Americans**[cxxix] who could have their basic net worth ensured. $363 billion taken from citizens in exchange for more effective buying processes, for more effective information searching, for connecting people together - via virtual platforms imitating human-to-human conversations, and finally in exchange for users' personal data enriched by their behavioral profiles with a thorough understanding of their past-present-future needs. There are of course, huge pros and "some" cons of using new digital and social technologies but the key question is, if that capital is accumulated by ten people, is that the best example of value and wealth distribution? The distribution of value to consumers can be questionable.

- The cumulative net worth of only **25 individuals** shaping **gambling in investment and stock exchange industry via hedge funds** practices using high risk methods, such as investing with borrowed money is on the level of **$168 billion,** which translates to almost **4.5 million Americans** who could have their basic net worth ensured. **$168 billion is being wasted.** Waste is a very polite word; "people are being robbed in white gloves".

- The cumulative net worth of only **9 individuals** shaping our **money management industry** via borrowed money is on the level of **$45.5 billion,** which translates to almost **1.2 million Americans** who could have their basic net worth ensured.

- The cumulative net worth of only **4 individuals** shaping **gambling in the casino industry** is on the level of **$43 billion,** which translates to almost **1.2 million Americans** who could have their basic net worth ensured.

- The cumulative net worth of only **7 individuals** shaping the **media industry** is on the level of **$39 billion,** which translates to almost **1 million Americans** who could have their basic net worth ensured.

- The cumulative net worth of only **5 individuals** shaping **addiction in the alcohol and tobacco industry** is on the level of **$16 billion,** which translates to almost **half a million Americans** who could have their basic net worth ensured. Some of that waste can translate directly into destroyed human lives.

- The cumulative net worth of only **3 individuals** shaping **addiction in shooter-survival games or the gambling machine industry** is on the level of **$10 billion,** which translates to almost **300 thousand Americans** who could have their basic net worth ensured. To clarify, players of cooperative shooter-survival games usually use firearms or some other long-range weapons in combination with other tools such as grenades, armor for additional defense, or other accessories. Most commonly, the purpose of a shooter game is to shoot opponents and proceed through missions without being killed. The focus is almost entirely on the defeat of the enemies using available weapons.

I hope you are getting my point. The above-mentioned group of people and areas of interest are just examples, the tip of the iceberg. I assume you already know that almost all wealth is in the hands of 10% of the population, and more than 40% is in the hands of 400+ people. Decisions made by that small group influence so many aspects of our lives. They can, of course, have a very positive impact on society. However, it is unfortunate when the richest spend their money on the following:

- Drug dealership; drugs purchased for personal or other use (cocaine, amphetamine, LSD, opiates, cannabis products, non-medical marijuana),
- Alcohol purchased above one's physical and emotional needs, overused by oneself or offered to others for abuse
- Sponsoring or attending expensive drug and/or alcohol parties
- Sponsoring, promoting, or benefiting from prostitution
- Sponsoring, promoting, or contributing to non-ethical movies, games, or art production (e.g. showing violence, porn, or racism; violent computer and console games for kids and teens full of death, blood and hate)
- Overspending on property (5th vacation home, 5th boat - some never used)
- Other activities and behaviors harmful to society

Excessive money in the hands of those who do not care about others can create (and already does) parallel, artificial, destructive, unwanted and unnecessary markets.

80% of Americans live below the "common sense income level" and some princes and princesses of our time are playing around using our country's money – demoralizing and destroying themselves and at the same time demoralizing and destroying our communities and nation. It is a lose–lose situation, and as such should be stopped and punished.

We could continue digging even deeper and discover even more nasty initiatives financed by American money magically distributed to magically gifted privileged ones. The purpose of this simple exercise is not to blame anyone, not to spread jealousy or hate, not to try to change it by force or dare to take this wealth by force and redistribute it using another magical formula. The purpose of this analysis is to have honest, individual as well as group reflections and discussions, to inspire critical but constructive thinking, to motivate change for the better, and to advance more modern, more adequate, human-centered capitalism—in other words, "happy" capitalism.

There are so many diseases yet to be cured: cancer, allergies, asthma, Alzheimer's disease, arthritis, AIDS, diabetes, epilepsy, hearing loss, multiple sclerosis, Parkinson's disease, pulmonary hypertension, addiction, obesity, and other genetic diseases. And we waste our intellects, lives, and resources, including money, on so many outrageous false promises. Other uncured diseases include anxiety, depression, loneliness, lack of meaning, and unhappiness. As a country, we also need to be more unified.

A very important assumption has to be made here: that in most cases, we do not really know those at the top because we have never met, spent time with, or lived with them. As such, we cannot say anything about their intensions, true lifestyles, or value in society (taking into consideration the total balance of "good" and "bad," "profits" and "losses" like we would do for everyone else), or what their individual happiness index is.

Although we could see some of the outcomes "most probably" caused by their decisions, interventions, influences, invested capital, invested time and attention, we will never be sure what their real motivations are, what their deepest values and beliefs are, what their moral choices are, what internal battles and internal conflicts they confront on a daily basis. Let's avoid any false accusations or quick judgments. Before accusing anybody in public, we need to study their entire life—both their good and bad behaviors, good and bad "fruits" they have produced and the good and bad external situations that have fundamentally shaped them.

What if some of these people became rich by accident? Of course, to ensure such an opportunity, one had better be in the right place at the right time (be in the right intellectual, emotional and financial state.). We may also believe that in the vast majority of cases those successful

American dreamers were working hard, and that they were extraordinarily focused, devoted, and persevering; that is why they've achieved what they've achieved. Even if someone inherits everything, all possible financial resources, education, or behavioral patterns rooted in personal values, discipline, passion for excellence, and the highest standards of perfection, he or she still has to put time and effort into orchestrating all of it successfully. I can hardly imagine anyone prospering without any attention.

Giving

Fortunately, we have generous givers at home!

- "Americans gave **$410.02 billion** to charity in 2017."[cxxx]
- "America's 50 most generous philanthropists gave out **$14.1 billion** in 2018."[cxxxi]
- The top 5 givers by name: Warren Buffett, Bill and Melinda Gates, Michael Bloomberg, the Walton family,   and George Soros.
- The top 25 givers in alphabetical order: Bernard and Billi Marcus, Bill and Melinda Gates,   Charles Koch, Chuck Feeney, Dustin Moskovitz and Cari Tuna, Eli and Edythe Broad, George Soros, Gordon and Betty Moore, Hansjoerg Wyss, Irwin and Joan Jacobs, Jeff Bezos, Jim and Marilyn Simons, John and Laura Arnold, Ken Griffin, Lynn and Stacy Schusterman, Mark Zuckerberg and Priscilla Chan, Michael and Susan Dell, Michael Bloomberg, Pierre Omidyar, Sean Parker, Steve and Connie Ballmer, T. Denny Sanford, W. Barron Hilton, the Walton family, Warren Buffett.

What is worth noticing here is that the "act of giving" is not a "one time" act. Rather, there is a very high chance that these donors will continue giving in the future. For instance, in 2010, Bill Gates and Warren Buffett announced **The Giving Pledge**, a campaign and charitable organization with the goal of inspiring the wealthy to give at least half of their net worth to philanthropy, either during their lifetime or upon their death. The pledge claims to be a moral commitment to give, not a legal contract. On The Giving Pledge's website, each individual or couple writes a letter explaining why they chose to give.[cxxxii]

Have a look at some motivational letters from the rich who have joined The Giving Pledge:

Dear Warren,

> *Karen and I are delighted to join you in the Giving Pledge, and commit at least half—I expect that we will commit substantially more than half—of what we have to charity. It is much easier to be generous if you have more than you need, so this is not a difficult thing for us to do. That said, I don't think being charitable is innate. In my experience, it is learned from the examples of others. My earliest memories include my father's exhortations about how important it is to give back. These early teachings were ingrained in me, and a portion of the first dollars I earned, I gave away. Over the years, the emotional and psychological returns I have earned from charitable giving have been enormous. The more I do for others, the happier I am. The happiness and optimism I have obtained from helping others are a big part of what keeps me sane. My life and business have not been without some decent size bumps along the way, and my psychological health and well being have made managing these inevitable challenges much easier. While my motivations for giving are not driven by profit, I am quite sure that I have earned financial returns from giving money away. Not directly by any means, but rather as a result of the people I have met, the ideas I have been exposed to, and the experiences I have had as a result of giving money away. A number of my closest friends, partners, and advisors I met through charitable giving. Their advice, judgment, and partnership have been invaluable in my business and in my life. Life becomes richer the more one gives away. In college, I had the opportunity to read John Rawls, and learn his methodology for determining how to organize the world. It made sense to me then, and still does. Rawls advised that you should imagine yourself in what he called "the Original Position." Pretend that you have not yet been born, and don't know to what family or in what country or circumstance you will find yourself. He argued that the world should be organized from such a vantage point. In other words, I believe the fairest distribution would require something along the lines of the Giving Pledge. Rawls proves that charitable giving is the right thing to do from an objectively fair vantage point. I am not a particularly religious*

person, and believe that my limited time on earth is all that I am going to get. And I have lived with that understanding, doing my best to extract as much out of life as I can. I get tremendous pleasure from helping others. It's what makes my life worth living. We are incredibly grateful and honored to join you in the Giving Pledge.

Sincerely, [cxxxiii]

"The more I do for others, the happier I am." [cxxxiv]

To The Giving Pledge,

It is with gratitude that we find ourselves with this capacity to give. We are committed to our philanthropic endeavors and devote our time and energy to this work.

We spend our days at organizations pursing different missions, but with a shared belief in an individual's right to dignity, agency, justice, and self-determination. In the practice of our philanthropy, we are committed to the values of being in service to the public trust, upholding transparency in our work, providing general operating support, continuing to learn and adapt, and trusting grantees and the communities they serve.

This is an ongoing journey and we are excited to learn and grow from our community and fellow pledges. [cxxxv]

Where does the money go? Let's have a look at some examples:

- Warren Buffett: donates to various foundations fighting poverty, promoting women's rights, and backing social justice initiatives.
- Bill and Melinda Gates: fund global health, agriculture development, international development and U.S. education. They support the eradication of polio, vaccine delivery, and the treatment and prevention of HIV and malaria.
- Michael Bloomberg: major gifts go to funding climate change initiatives, to combatting opioid addition, and to supporting public

health and education domains - including funds for student financial aid.

- The Walton family: donates to support K-12 education, to build or renovate school facilities, and to protect rivers and oceans.
- George Soros: gives to early childhood education, anti-discrimination initiatives, social development, and resources and tools for libraries.
- Mark Zuckerberg and Priscilla Chan: support eradication of diseases including Alzheimer's and Parkinson's; support improvement of education and the criminal justice system.
- Pierre Omidyar: gives his money to health improvement technologies, to ending human trafficking, to addressing civic engagement, to media freedom and to digital rights issues.
- Brian and Tegan Acton: started family foundation dedicated to supporting the basic services of low-income families with young children ages 0–5. They also provide support for safe spaces and organizations that ensure food security, housing stability, and healthcare access.
- And so on and so forth. Wonderful. Voluntary self-taxation, if you will. Isn't it amazing?

"People are happier when they are generous and when they feel that the society that they're in is a generous society." –Jeffrey Sachs[cxxxvi]

So, what can we reasonably conclude here? As with most things in life, we can use them to create greater good, create "Heaven on Earth," or use them to destroy what's already good, or create evil. It starts with individual choices, which sooner or later radiate onto families, neighborhoods, larger communities, the nation, and the whole world. But which came first individual choices or the environmental conditioning that shaped the thinking and reasoning of that individual that led to his or her individual choices?" Putting aside the undeniable impact of our genetically programmed bodies, which strive for many deterministic choices, the impact of an environment on an individual life is overwhelming and undeniable. Environmental impact is seen by many as being the highest single factor affecting our worldviews and decision-making. Of course, at the end of a day, when trying to evaluate one's contribution to the world, what matters most are our individual choices. Keeping ourselves accountable for decisions we make seems to be critical to a long-lasting, morally stable social system.

Anyway, we should be proud of our givers, winners, influencers, history-makers, Santa's helpers or Santa Clauses themselves. There is also no doubt that being such an unlimited giver generates an unlimited stream of positive emotions, and we should only hope that those givers experience many moments of joy. You decide when, you decide how much, you decide for whom – which makes "doing good" pleasant.

How can the rest of us Americans make similar experiences part of our lives? We have proof that it is possible to live like that, so maybe everyone can do so. We also have plenty of studies about self-made millionaires. We know how to be inspired and uplifted simply by listening to all those success stories about going from rags to riches. But is this concept of "self-making" real? What if it is not? What if there are some hidden but mandatory ingredients that have to be used?

The common denominator of all those success stories' holders, without any exception is, they were given something by someone.

Usually, they were given unconditional love, care, attention, wisdom, a good education, initial capital, access to a professional network, access to industry knowledge and practices, personal mentoring, and/or a well-functioning brain to process information. They may also have been in good health, and had food, shelter, and safety. Even when they faced poverty or abuse, they always received something that helped them build their bright futures.

To achieve "success" in any possible broad meaning of that word, you had better be given something by someone. What about being truly gifted, with intelligence (both IQ = intelligence quotient, EQ = emotional intelligence, or emotional quotient) going far beyond that of the average person? Would we be able to succeed only with our talent without other people's support, without opportunities, without doors being opened for us? Would our talent alone guarantee success? Maybe yes, maybe no. Most probably not. After an honest analysis of successful lives or even our own lives, we can always see someone, somewhere, somehow pushing us forward like an invisible wind. We can always think of someone who offered a helping hand, either directly or indirectly – changing the world around us and allowing us to choose a different path and make progress.

What if we jointly design our magic formula for our "new economy," a "prosperity and happiness- focused economy?" Will we be able to ensure that that magic formula is applied to all of us citizens? Knowing that we will not be able to ensure that everyone contributes the same, due to natural differences between people, knowing also that we will not be able to satisfy everyone's needs and desires in the same way, is there a fair and practical way to ensure individual and social prosperity and happiness in our country? Maybe it is all about open minds and hearts as well as a good enough definition of what we're trying to solve and a good enough recommendation on how to solve it. It seems that amazing GDP growth, an historically low unemployment rate, and a few billionaires do not bring satisfactory results for individual Americans who dream about individual prosperity and happiness. These are not sufficient conditions, although they are necessary ones. What if instead of "equal" wealth and "equal" happiness distribution we focus on ensuring "equal" human dignity for all – going far beyond the fulfillment of basic needs (such as food, shelter, clothing and basic care)? Maybe we should base our definition of human dignity on our contemporary understanding of human nature and its potential after thousands of years of survival and evolution. Human dignity should be the baseline for all further considerations and improvements. Looking at the "positive" side of humans: we think, imagine, remember, learn, communicate, collaborate, solve problems, improve our life conditions, create structure out of chaos, improve health, and live longer. We express ourselves through art and spiritual and transcendent practices, and enjoy doing it. Those who view or experience others' work, art, or spiritual practices also enjoy them. Humans are able to recognize and name different physical, psychological, or emotional states. Ultimately, humans love being in a state of joy and are also able to devote their own lives to others - that's when they "love", as they used to say.

Will we be able to ensure "dignity for all?" Will we be able to ensure equal access to prosperity (not equal prosperity), happiness, and opportunities, regardless of people's different starting points?

That is a fundamental, very broad and deep question. Will we be able to share accumulated capital and happiness with others, reinvesting that capital in a socially responsible manner?

What if we

- Ensure **human dignity** via **decent living conditions** (food, shelter, clothing) for all
- Ensure **human dignity** via **early care and education** (starting with pre-school) for all
- Ensure **human dignity** via **safety and basic healthcare** (reducing the ubiquitous fear of death) for all

After all, we will all get the chance to become generous "Santa Clauses" for one another, to become someone's hero, or to become our own heroes. Why should only some of us play those exciting roles?

"People don't want you to be their hero... We can equip and inspire others to be their own heroes in their stories"

> -   *Liz Bohannon: Beginner's Pluck, talking to the leaders.*

It is so joyful to receive gifts, but it is even more joyful to be the one who gives them.

I wonder how the following quote from *Winston Churchill* resonates with you:

"We make a living by what we get, but we make a life by what we give."

Socialism vs. Capitalism

I wonder what your reaction is when you hear, "let's ensure something for all," where something could be anything: healthcare for all, education for all, universal basic income for all, work for all, transportation for all, and so on and so forth. Do you like it, or are you ready to explode with anger, shouting: "stay away from evil socialism?"

I wonder what your reaction is when you hear, "to become successful and get rich, all you need is hard work," "all your gains, rewards, and incentives have to be the result of merits – the best measure of contribution (merits could be understood as performance, credentials, scores, education levels, tangible accomplishments, achieved SMART goals [cxxxvii])." Do you agree, or do you react angrily, shouting: "I'm not a robot, I only hear about mindless productivity, and where is the place for a deliberate, mindful, and reflective life, with interpersonal relationships, and time to rest?"

Finally, I wonder what your reaction is when you hear, "money is everything," "accumulated capital is the ultimate measure of success, prosperity, wellness, and contributions," "Money makes money. And the money that makes money makes more money," as Benjamin Franklin used to say, or "money attracts more money," or "reinvesting capital is the most important and relevant activity, not work or merits." Do you agree, or shout: "bloodthirsty, soulless, immoral, and inhuman capitalism?"

I can image many of us would easily overreact here, becoming very passionate about the topic, in defense of our points of view and beliefs.

To calm ourselves down a bit, let's be a bit sarcastic:

What about this one? "Men are like bank accounts. Without a lot of money they don't generate a lot of interest." This is the law of attraction in its essence. If I knew who said this, I would give him or her credit.

Staying in the money context, we could also hear from some idealists that "Money is not the most important thing in the world. Love is." Beautiful. One could respond by saying: "Fortunately, I love money." Brutal, but funny.

Frustration or nonviolent forms of aggression can be seen as natural, civilized reactions to disagreement and effective energy moving the discussion forward. But when it takes the form of meanness, insanity, or violence, it is not civilized anymore; it immediately ends dialogue, burns bridges, cuts off bonds, stops progress, destroys value, and kills hope. Why do we overreact so easily? Because we care about our lives, about our country, because the absurdity is so unbearable, or we are treated by politicians and powerful groups like uneducated adults who can be manipulated. It is so simple to steer the masses by calling them socialists, capitalists, or meritocrats. "You are here to keep your power and don't care about people," or "You are in foreign intelligence service," an infuriated citizen would say.

"Don't call me names," a child would say. Are we not respected, or are we being cheated? Maybe it is about us sitting in our mental cages or on a whole spectrum of shades of blue or red.

What is the America we would like to live in? Is it one where everyone is equal, and the most important social services are available to all, or one where not everyone is equal, so it is up to individuals to arrange their own access to the most important social services? In addition, individual outcomes should determine quality of life as well as social services offered on the open market." I believe that those who already have a lot would say: "It's my business how to live my life and make a living, and I do not need the state to provide me any social services (maybe except military/defense), or force me to donate to any central funds of goods and services for further central redistribution to others. People should take responsibility for their own lives and work hard to achieve what they want." By contrast, those who have next to nothing in their budgets would say "I was not so fortunate. I had a difficult start, and I would like my country to help me organize my life and ensure fair treatment in exchange for my hard work and patriotism." Of course, we can imagine a variety of other different responses or arguments, and these are only hypothetical examples. Going through this exercise, we may get the impression that it is quite a complex problem to solve on such a big scale, trying to satisfy everyone in such a big country.

Let's go little bit deeper and elaborate on critical questions:

Can everyone be equal? Does free healthcare and free education mean socialism? What is socialism? What is capitalism? What is the most optimal "-ism" that could move the needle and push us forward to a more happy and joyful America?

We may hear at least three possible answers: "Yes, people are equal," "No, they are not," "It depends." Some of those who think "people are equal" explain it using the broader context of life and death. In fact, they would argue, "no one asks to be born, no one chooses the exact time, location and social environment, including family they were born into, not to mention sex." By the same token, we all are going to die sooner or later, and having the universe's age as a reference, it will be sooner rather than later. It is an equality resulting from the same "lack of influence", "lack of choice of initial circumstances, including body and mind characteristics". Religious people would say, "we are equal under God," "we were created equal by God, equal for God and equal in God," "our equality should be measured by a measure from God." Naturalists would say, "we are all equal under nature – all humans versus 'others', animals." We do not need to search too long to see the concept of equality embedded in our socio-political system. What about our Declaration? Doesn't it mention equality?

Now, why do many people believe that <u>everyone is not equal</u>? Let's for instance analyze our productivity. To the newly born, pure, immaculate, unblemished man we add additional properties that can be measured and compared with himself and others in time. We enrich our bodies with artificially created requirements and the expectations of the world. If people are equal, they will produce the same outcomes or at least very similar outcomes, one might speculate. But looking around, we can see that that is not true. In fact, outcomes can differ. One person can write an amazing book in two weeks, while another person can write a mediocre one in two years. Now, when we assume everyone has to contribute to society, producing outcomes, and based on these outcomes, will be rewarded, then immediately, we learn that outcomes and rewards will differ. As a result, if we start comparing people based on this artificial concept, we quickly come to the conclusion that people cannot be equal. There is evidence that people are not equal. Is that a valid simplification? Again, yes and no. For some of us, this reasoning is a simplification or even a dangerous confabulation, but for others it is just normal and easy. The direction of reasoning and its effect will always depend on the first assumptions we make, how in our minds the world is constructed or conditioned, what the world is like, what our purpose and our goal are, and who we really are.

So far we have said that people are equal because have similar needs and advanced brains (in comparison to animals), and they have the same lack of initial choice (animals too) and the same most valuable asset on Earth, which is their life - available to them throughout their biological life (animals too) and conscious life (not available to animals). At the same time, we have said, people are not equal because they produce different quantities and qualities of outcomes. Outcomes are not equal, therefore, their achievers should not be equal. I bet you have noticed that there is a subtle but life-changing difference between these worldviews: people are people vs. people are "people AND their outcomes" (performance is a mandatory and integral component of human value). Until we agree on the most fundamental definition of a human being and his or her value, no matter how hard we try, how pure our intentions are, what reasoning we employ, we will not be able to reach a consensus about whether we are equal.

Some might ask, how did we come to such an extended definition of "people" as "people AND their outcomes" in the first place? What about the following alternative definition of "people:" "people" are "people AND their equal inability to survive without external help, especially in the very early stages of life or during serious illnesses, and they have to make an ongoing effort to stay alive." What a complicated definition, but it seems to be true. Don't you think?

The consequence of such a worldview may be that people's major motivation and goal is to support themselves and others (especially babies and seriously ill or elderly people) to stay alive. Another logical consequence is that those who have already achieved a certain level of maturity and independence (at least they think they have) decide to give back to those who have helped them, or in a broader sense, give back to society. Also, we can easily imagine those mature individuals becoming aware of their own aging, and as a result, deciding to pay it forward. Don't you think this would change us from being purely individualistic, disconnected human entities to being more social and interconnected? "Does such reciprocity help us in ensuring equality? How are we going to measure it at the individual or societal level? Should we normalize it? Regardless of the exact metrics we use, the assumption here is that everyone wants to give back, and everyone wants to take to survive. The overall goal could be to ensure equilibrium.

So, why don't we create social, healthcare, education, and work systems that are available to all? There is nothing strange about such an approach. What if, for example, 5% of the population suffers from a serious illness which requires expensive treatment? What if 3% of the population memorizes, calculates, reasons, and thinks better than the rest, and therefore consumes education services more effectively and in greater quantity? What if some people contribute more than others because they have more energy, more physical, mental, or emotional predispositions, etc.? It seems we have to accept that some of us will need more (care, help, attention, and resources) than others depending on chemistry and biology, our personal situations at any given time, our place in a given environment—none of which are equal. In the end, to fulfill the assumption that we are all equal, we have to come up with a pretty complex formula for reciprocity. Maybe such a formula is achievable, but it may require super or at least quantum computers.

Allow me to proceed with the last crazy simulation. What if we reverse our reasoning and say: "If everyone is equal, let's ensure the outcomes are equal, too. Let's design the system that controls production and by design equalizes it across all the people. Those who can produce more need to slow down, and those who produce less need to speed up. Or even better, everyone slows down to the level of the slowest person in society. Everyone is equal, everyone produces the same outcomes." We can sense here that this approach is not healthy. Forcing people to create less goes against their natural curiosity, drive, talents, predispositions, or personal needs, and without a doubt impacts their personal freedom. Now, we have a trade-off between being equal and being free. Forcing people will not only reduce personal freedom, and may eventually will lead to violence and tyranny.

Isn't this debate similar to the everlasting debates on socialism and capitalism? Despite the fact that most of us want the best for everyone, differences in definitions cause polarization. As the majority of Americans are less and less satisfied with living in a "people AND capital AND outcomes" system, no wonder younger generations now call for "socialism." No wonder more socialist ideas can be heard on political stages these days. Of course, we have to be very careful of accusing anyone of being a socialist, not knowing if their understanding of the definition of socialism is correct and appropriately used. Making something more social versus making it socialist is not the same thing. A simple lack of historical knowledge can cause huge problems. Let's look at some examples.

What is socialism?

We can also ask about specific variations of socialism like Marxism, Communism, Leninism, Stalinism, and Maoism. Not to go into too much detail or to go too far back in world history, let's start with "twin brothers" Marx and Engels, who authored "The Communist Manifesto" and envisioned a perfect society. Marx observed that as countries transitioned from centralized monarchies to quasi-democratic-capitalist economies, workers were being exploited by those who owned factories and farms - "the means of production." Marx argued that whoever owns the factory or farm is benefiting more than workers in those factories and on those farms. That creates an inherent inequality. To fix that problem, Marx recommended that society shift power from owners (the bourgeoisie) to workers - allowing workers (the proletariat) collective control of the means of production. Marx concluded that "socialism," which aims to limit worker exploitation, eliminates the influence of economic classes in society, eliminates inequality, and is a precursor to "communism." It is the next logical step after "capitalism."

In "socialism:"

- There should be no classes.
- There should be no inequality.
- The state controls the means of production.
- There should be no competition.
- All people contribute to the greater good and share equally in it, ensuring all are happy, healthy, and free.

Communism could be considered the next step: in addition to the state controlling the means of production, the state aims for total "collective" ownership of all aspects of society and economy.

In "communism:"

- Society should be classless.
- There should be no inequality.
- The state controls "everything," including the means of production.
- There is no private property at all. No private companies hold ownership.
- There should be no competition because there is only one owner, the state, and prices are determined centrally.
- Ideally, society should be moneyless, and even stateless.
- All contribute to the greater good, and share equally in it, ensuring all are happy, healthy, and free.

In short, everybody gives what they can and takes only what they really need in return. Everyone is equally responsible for contributing to the greater good. In turn, everyone can take from that social good when in need.

Is "non-market" socialism or communism a good or bad thing? Analyzing existed or currently existing implementations we tend to say, "it is bad because successful implementations are not known." Some may say, "although it is a noble idea or set of noble ideas, we were never able to make it work properly." Instead of freedom, happiness, and prosperity for all who participate in the system, we see freedom, happiness and prosperity only for those who control the system. Total control leads to or requires total power. Total power leads to or requires corruption, forcing those who have power to surround themselves only with those who are completely loyal and supportive of this source of power. Total control becomes very destructive—it makes countries totalitarian, eliminates personal freedom, and ultimately leads to poverty for everyone, except those in control, who are members of the Communist party, who are corrupted and wealthy. They monitoring and influencing every single step taken by others. This is like being watched by Big Brother.

If one is not obedient, one must immediately be expelled from society, killed, or worse (for the system) sent to forced labor camps for years or till the end of one's life. Disloyal citizens have to be punished, and in many cases, do not get a second chance. Instead of being free, they are enslaved. Instead of being happy, they are fearful. Instead of prospering, they are poor. At best, they cannot envision something better. They are hopeless, and cannot make progress.

The world should never forget the histories of (or in some cases current realities of) the former USSR, China, North Korea, Vietnam, Venezuela and similar socialist and communist regimes.

What else do we hear about socialism?

- "This is the story of an evil that inevitably and inexorably leads to poverty, starvation, and ultimately violence.
- This is the story of the continued false allure and sophistry of an evil that has killed millions of people and even today threatens a new generation of the naive.
- This is the story of an evil well documented and yet still somehow enticing, even in America.
- This is the story of socialism in all its drab and dreary machinelike destruction of individual thought, creativity, and ambition.
- This is the story of socialism in all of its violence, bloodshed, and tyranny. It is a cautionary tale of how America has so far eluded the siren call of something for nothing, of an equality determined and

enforced by the government—but also of how close we still are to succumbing to socialism."[cxxxviii] This is from the introduction to the book "A Case Against Socialism" by U.S. Senator Rand Paul.

- All is "taxed" as all inputs and outputs belong to the state. Outcomes are only centrally distributed.
- There is no free market, capital market, or possibility of owning businesses or investing in them.
- Goods and services are not superior because there is no competition, comparison mechanisms, or motivation to fight for customers' attention. The value of goods and services is not dictated by real market demand or real need, but rather by an artificially created supply and demand formula with artificially set prices steered by the all-knowing body.
- There are no incentives to innovate or to solve major problems.
- There is no freedom of choice when it comes to educational paths or professional development paths.
- All is centrally decided, sourced, governed, and measured.
- There is no free speech. All media are fully controlled by the Party.
- To keep the system running, the ruling body has to tightly monitor each and every citizen to ensure that no one goes against the formula; that no one thinks on his/her own, or under any circumstances talks and spreads his/her own ideas for achieving social justice. To ensure that everyone is in line and behaves appropriately, secret agents eavesdrop on every private or professional conversation to assess its compliance with communist policies and rules. Spies can be found on every corner, placed in almost every workplace, every school, every community, even within families. If one family member doesn't want to collaborate, the whole family can be harmed.
- There is no religious freedom. In fact, no religion is allowed, unless it is used to steer the masses.
- There is no trust at all among the people.

Are there any good ideas worth considering that could be found in those philosophical, social, political, and economic ideologies? Analyzing existing implementations we could say, "yes, there are some elements worth considering." For instance, some elements of public schooling, universal healthcare, social security for all, voting rights for all, social services like police departments, fire departments, military services or common infrastructure are already embedded in most capitalistic economies. So, again, we have to be very precise when talking about individual examples to not throw all the eggs into one socialistic basket (what if there is a one golden egg among the broken ones) and prevent ourselves from learning and improving our own society. Of course, the same applies to those who tend to blindly follow simplifications and could expose us all to enormous social disaster, if certain ideas inherited from "The Communist Manifesto" are realized. All participants in mature, fair, and responsible discussions have to put an extra effort into explaining clearly, precisely, and honestly what they really want to explain. If not, any misunderstanding can lead either to practical exposure to real risks (a consequence of not respecting historical analysis) or to lost opportunities and possible improvements (a consequence of not listening and being fixated on the status-quo). Name-calling (calling someone a socialist) is destructive, and doesn't unite us as one strong society around critical issues. Even "healthcare for all" is not a truly fair and inclusive statement. "Healthcare for all" means all and nothing. It is like calling names. To show that we really care and want to solve problems we should communicate with surgical precision. If not, it may mean we don't want dialogue or cooperation. All we want is to push on what we have already decided in our heads. If we don't consider other points of view, we will be quickly called fundamentalists and ideologists. That is a dead end. What if we say, "healthcare for all; here is why and how… and what do you think?" We are a nation that solves problems, we are nation of inventors and innovators – somehow predestined for continuous evolution, including the evolution of its own socio-economic system. We should never doubt that.

What is capitalism?

On the other hand, what could be the simplified definition of capitalism?

- "Capitalism is an economic system based on the private ownership of the means of production and their operation for profit."[cxxxix]
- It allows and supports private property.
- It allows for and motivates voluntary exchange.
- It allows for and motivates capital accumulation.
- It allows for and motivates the creation of competitive markets.
- "Prices and the distribution of goods and services are mainly determined by competition in goods and services markets."[cxl] Prices are not artificially and centrally set up in the majority of cases.
- "Decision-making and investments are determined by every owner of wealth, property or production ability in financial and capital markets."[cxli]
- "Different forms of capitalism feature varying degrees of free markets, public ownership, obstacles to free competition and state-sanctioned social policies. The degree of competition in markets, the role of intervention and regulation, and the scope of state ownership vary across different models of capitalism."[cxlii]

Is "capitalism" (in the broad sense) then a good or bad thing? The question of whether capitalism is good or bad is already a bad question. Let's treat that question as an introduction to something more. The question of whether socialism is good or bad is also my mental shortcut. Analyzing existing implementations, we tend to say in general, "capitalism is good because successful or adequate implementations are known (to mention a few in alphabetical order: Austria, Australia, Belgium, Canada, Denmark, Germany, Ireland, Netherlands, Norway, Sweden, Switzerland, and of course the U.S.A.)." We tend to say, "yes, it is good, because 'over time, capitalist countries have experienced consistent economic growth and an increase in the standard of living.'"[cxliii] "Supporters argue that it provides better products and innovation through competition, disperses wealth to all productive people, promotes pluralism and decentralization of power, creates strong economic growth and yields productivity and prosperity that greatly benefit society." [cxliv]

Is "capitalism" the Holy Grail for modern civilizations? What do we hear from critics of capitalism?

- It is an engine of inequality. There is no promise of wealth equality. Income (social) classes can be determined based on an income brackets definition.
- Capital is held in the hands of the capitalist class, which owns the means of production, and classes of workers must work for wages.
- Real power is kept "in the hands of a minority capitalist class that exists through the exploitation of the majority working class and their labor." [cxlv]
- It is an engine of economic instability.
- "It prioritizes profit over social good, natural resources, and the environment." [cxlvi]
- Capitalist societies are built on money-based social relations.
- Once one has extensive capital, one doesn't need to work anymore because capital works for him/her.
- It is an engine of corruption. Capital holders can and do influence political decisions steering government and the whole country's trajectory.

Let's take a look, for instance, at how a majority member of the United States House Committee on Oversight and Reform, Rep. Alexandria Ocasio-Cortez (AOC) directly called out (February 2019) the fault in our political system, describing damaging behaviors and how easily our democracy can be manipulated. [cxlvii]

- *(AOC): "If I want to run a campaign that is entirely funded by corporate political action committees, is there anything that legally prevents me from doing that?"*
- *HF: "No" (response given by Mrs. Hobert Flynn - democracy reform activist and Common Cause President[cxlviii])*
- *AOC: "So there is nothing stopping me from being entirely funded by corporate pacts, say from the fossil fuel industry, the healthcare industry,*

big pharma, [...]. Let's say I am a really, really bad guy. Let's say I have some skeletons in my closet that I need to cover up, so that I get elected."

- *AOC: [...]* **"Green light for hash money. I can do all sorts of terrible things. It's totally legal right now for me to pay people off. And that is considered speech. That money is considered speech."**

- *AOC: "So, I use my special interest, dark money funded campaign to pay off what I need to pay off and get elected. So now I am elected, now I am in. I've got a power to draft, lobby, and shape the laws that govern the United States of America. Fabulous. Is there any hard limit that I have in terms of what legislation I am allowed to touch?* **Are there any limits on the laws that I can write or influence, especially based on the special interest funds that I accepted to finance my campaign and get me elected?"**

- *HF:* **"There are no limits"** *(response given by Mrs. Hobert Flynn - democracy reform activist and Common Cause President[cxlix])*

- *AOC: "So, I can be totally funded by oil and gas. I can be totally funded by big pharma [...] there are no limits to that whatsoever."*

- *HF: "That's right."*

- *AOC: "Awesome. Now, the* **last thing I want to do is get rich with as little work possible. Is there anything preventing me from holding stocks in an oil or gas company and then writing laws to deregulate that industry and cause stock values to soar and accrue a lot of money in that time?**

- *RM:* **"You could do that."** *(response given by Rudy Mehrbani[cl], Senior counsel, Brennan Center for Justice)*

- *AOC: "So, I could do that now with the way our current laws are set up?"*

- *RM: "Yes."*

- *AOC:* **"Is it possible that any elements of this story apply to our current government and our current servants right now?**

- *RM:* **"Yes."**

- *HF:* **"Yes."**

- *AOC:* **"So, we have a system that is fundamentally broken.** *We have these influences existing in this body, which means that these influences are here in this committee shaping the questions that are being asked of you all right now. Would you say that's correct?"*

- *RM:* **"Yes."**

Does this really mean that American capitalism is fundamentally broken? Something in us cannot accept this possibility. We have heard so many good things and success stories about our system for decades that such a slandering statement seems to be inconceivable, and this thought seems like a big lie. Don't you think it's quite hard to formulate a fair and final judgement by looking at most philosophical, social, political, and economic systems, ideologies, movements or implementations, without a thorough analysis? Saying that something so complicated and multidimensional is good or bad is cheap manipulation. That is why we should be very vigilant. In any case, it seems that systems like communism or capitalism collapse or malfunction largely due to people in power, who, instead of using that power to help society to prosper, abuse it. Do we have to take human nature into consideration when designing any ideal social, political, or economic system?

Is it a coincidence that in both systems we see powerful and rich magnates who decide the fate of the world and organize the lives of those beneath them according to their rules and their cravings? In communism, power is usually taken by force (like revolution, civil war, killing or imprisoning key political and economic rivals), or by taking advantage of the weakness of the current system (an economy that is going through a recession or rising after the destruction of war) and making promises that are very attractive to the masses. In capitalism, power is usually taken by those with the most accumulated capital because they create jobs, pay wages, and shape legislation. In "democratic capitalism," people believe that power stays with people who are well represented by elected Representatives, honorable, trustworthy people. But as we just learned from the quoted dialogue, real power can and usually does remain in the invisible hands of the richest, and we are not talking here about the famous "invisible hand" of the free market introduced by Adam Smith in his famous book "The Wealth of Nations," published in 1776. That "invisible hand" was of course a metaphor describing the unobservable market force that helps the demand and supply of goods in a free market to reach equilibrium.

If both systems are corrupt, is there any hope for us? As we have already noticed, there is no evidence for good implementations of communism or socialism but there are examples of adequate realizations of capitalisms. And again, there is evidence that "good capitalism" can improve over time. Capitalist countries have experienced consistent economic growth and an increase in the standard of living over time. Also, "democratic capitalism" offers to its followers greater freedom, or at least the greater perception of freedom. After all, it will always be a fraction of the total freedom or a fraction of the perception of total freedom because all systems can create cages.

If we find enough curiosity and courage within ourselves and decide to rattle our cages, then I personally believe that there is a hope for advancement based on "democratic, human-centered capitalism." Do we need a new economy? I think we really do. We definitely don't want socialism or communism {period}. We want a better version of capitalism {period}. But also, we have to make a promise to ourselves that we will never turn that better version of capitalism into any "extremism" – because the pursuit of extremes never ends well.

What about capitalism with elements of a social welfare state? Here's what former President Barack Obama and Bill Maher said to one another during an interview:[cli]

Bill Maher:

*"I'm just wondering **why someone who was accused of being a socialist before** {Barack Obama is laughing} what do you think about the idea that in America, yes we are capitalists, but some things just should not be for the profit motive: health care, prisons, the military, elections, and I would add, newsgathering. People say, get the money out of politics. I think you've got to get out of the news business first or we're never going to learn anything."*

Barack Obama:

*"Well, a couple of things I'd say. First of all, if you look at the United States, Canada, Europe, and all the advanced democracies, then clearly **you've got to have a market-based system** because it's really **productive** and it spurs on **innovation** and **freedom** and **entrepreneurship** and **you've got to have a social welfare state** and in some ways the **label socialism doesn't make that much sense in a context where there is no economy that doesn't have some***

socialist elements. Meaning that there are some common goods that we all agree everybody should have. That's what Social Security is, that's what Medicare is to some extent, that's what public schools are. We all chip in to make sure that everybody, no matter of circumstances of your birth, has these baseline goods."

In the meantime, take a look at Nick Hanauer,[clii] a serial entrepreneur and wealthy man who gave a presentation entitled "The dirty secret of capitalism — and a new way forward" at the TEDSummit in 2019. He talked about bad economic theory resulting in inequality and growing political instability in our country.

"I am a capitalist, and after a 30-year career in capitalism spanning three dozen companies, generating tens of billions of dollars in market value, I'm not just in the top one percent, I'm in the top .01 percent of all earners. Today, I have come to share the secrets of our success, because rich capitalists like me have never been richer. So, the question is, how do we do it? How do we manage to grab an ever-increasing share of the economic pie every year? Is it that rich people are smarter than we were 30 years ago? Is it that we're working harder than we once did? Are we taller, better looking?

Sadly, no. It all comes down to just one thing: economics. Because, here's the dirty secret. **There was a time in which the economics profession worked in the public interest, but in the neoliberal era, today, they work only for big corporations and billionaires, and that is creating a little bit of a problem.** *We could choose to enact economic policies that raise taxes on the rich, regulate powerful corporations, or raise wages for workers. We have done it before. But neoliberal economists would warn that all of these policies would be a terrible mistake, because raising taxes always kills economic growth, any form of government regulation is inefficient, and raising wages always kills jobs. Well, as a consequence of that thinking, over the last 30 years, in the U.S.A. alone, the top one percent has grown 21 trillion dollars richer, while the bottom 50 percent has grown 900 billion dollars poorer, a pattern of widening inequality that has largely repeated itself across the world. And yet, as middle-class families struggle to get by on wages that have not budged in about 40 years, neoliberal economists continue to warn that the only reasonable response to* *the painful dislocations of austerity and globalization is even more austerity and globalization.*

So, what is a society to do? Well, it's super clear to me what we need to do.

We need a new economics."

Role model economies

So, what could be the way forward for our country? What should be our next step? Is there a shortcut to a better future? Is there any reference point, proof of concept, or place where people can live under democratic, free-market -ism and have happy lives? And everybody says, what about Scandinavian countries? For some of us, Switzerland, with the highest per capita GDP in the world, and amazingly high life satisfaction, comes to mind. Every self-respecting politician nowadays must know at least a few basic facts behind the extremely successful societies and economies of Scandinavian countries or Switzerland. Or at least Sweden, to make it simple. Some people say that it is a role model. Others say that it is a socialist economy, while still others say it practices capitalism, but offers generous social services. Because the above-mentioned economies are so special, definitions of their systems tend to escape straightforward categorizations.

What can we see, on a relatively high and generalized level, looking at **Scandinavian** countries?

- **They are the happiest societies in the universe** (#1. Finland, #2. Denmark, #3. Norway, #7. Sweden).
  - Let me remind you of the top 10 countries in the Ranking of Happiness 2016-2018: 1. Finland, 2. Denmark, 3. Norway, 4. Iceland, 5. Netherlands, 6. Switzerland, 7. Sweden, 8. New Zealand, 9. Canada, 10. Austria. The powerful U.S. is not in the top twentyish.

- **They are one of the richest societies in the universe** (#2. Norway, #6 Denmark, #8 Sweden, #12 Finland in GDP per capita) ranging from $80,000 to $55,000 per person. The U.S. is also doing well with $64,000 per person.
  - Let me name the top 10 countries in the World Population Review[cliii], GDP per capita, 2019: #1. Switzerland, #2. Norway, #3. Ireland, #4. United States, #5. Singapore, #6. Denmark, #7. Australia, #8. Sweden, #9. Netherlands, #10. Hong Kong, #11. Austria, #12. Finland. The <u>powerful U.S. is in the top 4.</u> What a relief.
  - It is worth noticing that Norway has unbelievable access to natural resources, being a relatively small society of 5 million people, but so does Venezuela. Systems matter!
- **They are the countries with the lowest income inequality in the universe** (#2. Norway, #3. Denmark, #4. Finland, #6. Sweden)
  - Let me name the top 25 countries based on The World Economic Forum's Inclusive Development Index 2018[cliv]: #1. Iceland, #2. Norway, #3. Denmark, #4. Finland, #5. Czech Republic, #6. Sweden, #7. Belgium, #8. Slovenia, #9. Slovak Republic, #10. Ukraine, #11. Netherlands, #12. Luxembourg, #13. Hungary, #14. Kazakhstan, #15. Germany, #16. Switzerland, #17. Croatia, #18. France, #19. Japan, #20. Ireland, #21. Mauritania, #22. Korea, Rep., #23. Canada, #24. Burundi, #25. Sierra Leone. The <u>powerful U.S. is roughly 56th.</u> We are behind so many other countries.
  - I named the top 25 countries to show the dangerous trap of oversimplification. If the lowest possible inequality (as low as possible according to the Net Income Gini Index) is our ideal then obviously we can see on the ranking list such countries as Burundi and Sierra Leone, which seem to be light years ahead of the U.S. when it comes to inequality. However, the inequality index without the GDP per capita can be extremely misleading. Would you prefer to live in Sierra Leone with around $455 GDP per capita or in your homeland with close to $60,000 GDP per capita? Again, we have to be very careful what we are comparing and how we draw our conclusions. That is why it would be very wise to filter the dataset of countries by GDP per capita, for

example, greater than $10,000, and then study the inequality index. Still from the list of about 40 countries, the U.S.A. is #35.

What else we can say about Scandinavian economies, or to be more specific about Sweden, based on various sources?

What about the economic system?

- Sweden's economy is **based on the free market.**
- Sweden **has a stock market.**
- **Sweden is a capitalist country.**
- **The Personal Income Tax Rate** in Sweden remains one of **the highest** in the world and is about **57.19 percent** (2019). In the Netherlands it is 51.75 percent, in Germany 45 percent, in Switzerland 40 percent, in the **United States 37 percent**, and in Canada 33 percent (per KPMG).^{clv} For clarification: in the U.S., Tax Rate varies depending on taxpayer income levels, from 10% to 37% (called short-term, ordinary income tax brackets).
- **The Capital Gains Tax Rate** in Sweden remains one of **the highest** in the world and is a flat **30 percent**, whereas in the **United States tax** is progressive, starting from **0 percent** (for incomes up to about $40,000), **15 percent** (for incomes up to $435,000), and **20 percent** (for incomes above $435,000).
- **The Corporate Income Tax Rate** is one of **the lowest**. The corporate tax rate is **21.4 percent** (2019), whereas in Germany it is 30 percent, in the **United States 27 percent**, in Canada 26.50 percent, in the Netherlands 25 percent, and in Switzerland 18 percent (per KPMG).^{clvi}
- **Sweden has Value-Added Tax (VAT)** on the level of **25 percent** (there are also reduced rates: 6% and 12% for specific goods and services, like books, copyrights, foodstuffs, restaurants, and catering services), whereas "**The United States does not impose a national-level sales or value-added tax.** Instead, sales taxes and complimentary use taxes are imposed and administered at the state (subnational) and local (sub-state) levels. Currently, 45 of the 50 U.S. states, the District of Columbia, and Puerto Rico impose some form of sales and use tax. Only Alaska, Delaware, Montana, New Hampshire and Oregon do not impose such taxes. [...] Sales and

use tax rates vary among the states. For each state that imposes a sales and use tax, one uniform rate is imposed at the state level. However, several states impose a lower rate on certain items, such as food, clothing, selected services and medicine, instead of exempting such items outright, and also impose higher rates on items such as alcohol. Excluding additional local sales and use taxes, state-level sales and use tax rates range from **2.9% (Colorado) to 7.25% (California)**." (per EY[clvii])

- "Total tax revenue as a percentage of GDP for Sweden was between 50% and 43%, whereas in the U.S. it was around 25%, over the past several decades." [clviii] Let me repeat, about **45% of GDP is owned by government** while maintaining a very strong free-market economy with a very high competitiveness index.

- **"27% of taxpayer money in Sweden goes towards education and healthcare, whereas 5% goes to the police and military, and 42% to social security."**[clix]

- It has favorable economic growth, low inflation, and a healthy banking system.

- Sweden has traditionally been an export-orientated nation and typically maintains a trade surplus, i.e. the value of goods and services it exports is greater than the value of imports.

- In addition to maintaining competitiveness in goods and manufacturing, growth in contemporary service sectors such as information and communications technology (ICT) has been strong in Sweden.

- It's easy to do business there. It is one of the easiest countries in the world to do business with, according to the World Bank.

- Stable economic policies combined with competitiveness, innovation, and an open approach to trade to make Sweden a model for economic success.

- They regularly monitor the fulfillment of their own policies. Dedicated committees (e.g. Swedish Fiscal Policy Council) of experts audit the government's policy decisions regarding public finances to **ensure that they remain consistent with the goals of growth, employment, and long-term financial sustainability**.[clx]

- They continuously reinvent economic governance with a series of **innovative regulations**. A ceiling for public spending was introduced, and measures were put in place to prevent the accumulation of debt. This ensures that the national debt is kept in check.

- Sweden has a diverse, highly competitive, and successful economy.
- **The Global Competitiveness Index of Sweden is among the highest** (#6 out of 138 per The World Economic Forum[clxi])
- It's **highly innovative**.
- It has good **gender equality**.

What about family care, healthcare, and education?

- "It has the **best reputation**. Sweden tops the ranking this year (78.3 points), of the RepTrak reputation ranking.
- It's a great place for families – it has **16 months of parental leave** [...The United States is one of the only countries in the world and the only OECD member that has not passed laws requiring businesses and corporations to offer paid maternity leave to their employees.[clxii]]
- **[It has] free day care services.**"[clxiii]
- "**It offers free education from age 6 to 19.** The Independent School Reform of 1992 made it possible for families to send their children to any school – state-run or independent – without having to pay fees. The law states that children have equal right to education regardless of their gender, ethnic, or political background, or the economic status of their families. Several checks are in place to ensure equal conditions for private and public schools throughout the country. [...] Independent schools in Sweden can open as long as they meet the nationwide educational requirements. Once accepted by the Swedish National Agency for Education, the schools receive government funding and must in return not charge any student fees; they are, however, allowed to accept private donations."[clxiv]
- "**Healthcare in Sweden is largely tax-funded, a system that ensures everyone has equal access to healthcare services. [...]** Swedish healthcare is decentralized – responsibility lies with the county councils and, in some cases, local councils or municipal governments. This is regulated by the Health and Medical Service Act. The role of the central government is to establish principles and

guidelines, and to set the political agenda for health and medical care. [...] All patients should be in contact with a local health center the same day they seek help and have a doctor's appointment within seven days. After an initial examination, no patient should have to wait more than 90 days to see a specialist, and no more than 90 days for an operation or treatment, once it has been determined what care is needed (regulated by a healthcare guarantee from 2005). If the waiting time is exceeded, patients are offered care elsewhere and the cost, including any travel costs, is paid by their county council. Statistics from 2017 indicate that about 79.1 per cent of the patients see a specialist within 90 days and receive treatment or are operated on within a further 90 days."[clxv]. As they claim themselves on their official country website: "Challenges include funding, quality, and efficiency."

- "Sweden **ranks third** overall in the Global AgeWatch Index 2015, which measures **the quality of life for older people**. Sweden's strengths lie in the capability of its older generation – they have above average employment rates (73.6%) and levels of educational attainment (68.7%) [...]
- It invests in green living."[clxvi]

What about safety?

- **The intentional homicide rate in Sweden is about 4 times less than that of the United States** (Sweden's is 1.1 whereas the United States' is: 5.3 based on the U.N. Office on Drugs and Crime's International Homicide Statistics database.)[clxvii]
- **"It is illegal for a civilian in Sweden to carry a firearm**, unless it is for a specific, legal purpose such as hunting or attending shooting ranges. Gun laws are quite stringent in Sweden. To be a gun owner requires a license, and this is tightly controlled by regulations. A potential gun owner needs to meet requirements to be granted a license. To apply and obtain a gun license, the prospective gun owner approaches the local police. The applicant must be in good standing and at least 18 years old. The applicant must be a member of an approved shooting club for at least six months or have passed a hunting examination."[clxviii]

What about the culture?

- They have very a strong and broad **egalitarian ethic**, believing in the principle that all people are equal and deserve equal rights and opportunities.
- They have **low levels of corruption**.[clxix]
- They have **transparency in the media**.
- They have very **high social trust**.
- They have very **strong social cohesiveness**. Bonds among citizens are tight and strong and that is why the Swedish are more inclined to participate readily and to stay with the group. Social cohesion can be further broken down into components, like social relations, task relations, perceived unity, and emotions.

Does diversity affect happiness? According to Jeffrey Sachs, a professor at Columbia and the co-editor of the World Happiness Report:

"A lot of countries with relatively homogeneous populations, similarities among people ethnically or in terms of religion and so on, are not very happy. So it's no guarantee. And on the other hand, it's possible to have a lot of diversity and more happiness. Our northern neighbor in the United States, Canada, ranks higher." So there is hope for us, too.

- **Population size may also be a helpful factor** (common sense assumption) in shaping unity of values, beliefs, thoughts and social cohesiveness. Sweden's population is estimated to be 10.04 million in 2019, whereas the United States' population as of August 2019 is estimated to be 329.45 million (almost 33 times larger than Sweden's).
- "**Religion in Sweden has, over the years, become increasingly diverse**. Christianity was the religion of virtually all of the Swedish population from the 12th to the early 20th century, but it has rapidly declined throughout the late 20th and early 21st century. In 2018, legally registered Christians comprised 57.7% of the total

population. Sweden had so called The Lutheran Church of Sweden — which was the state religion until 2000."[clxx] That could also have an impact on "unity" at the level of moral values. Discrimination on religious grounds is illegal, including discrimination in the workplace and in the provision of public and private services.

- **"Pressure is low**. Whatever you do, at work, you can be yourself, you have time, you will never be solely responsible, and you know you can theoretically fail without fearing dire consequences. Sweden understands like no other that five happy specialists with average pay are more resourceful than one specialist at astronomical pay who is panicking.

- **There are plenty of good examples**. Sweden is full of things that went well. When you can easily grab a thing for reference from where you sit, and learn from it, your job is already a bit easier. We used to call that "standing on the shoulders of giants" when I was still involved in research. Use a top example and go from there. Creative people are usually those who grew up around creative things. It's simply their world. Creativity and entrepreneurship tend to cluster.

- **There is a democratically-determined vision with long-term views, and everyone's input counts**. Some may call that "design by committee," but in actual fact, if you gather some brains around a table to formulate solutions to problems, you can set yourself up for success from the start. The Swedes are masters in the art of reflecting on the problem and its root causes until they really know what needs to be tackled to make a profound difference, being open to surprises, and changing course for the project if need be."[clxxi]

O.K. Let's take a deep breath. I think this is enough information to have at least a high-level overview of a "role model" economy. Now, is there anything we can learn from it? What ideas would be worth considering and applying in our situation? I am with you; it can be painful to admit that we really have a problem. But let's assume proudly that as a thoughtful and group of highly competitive individuals who learn quickly, we are not afraid or ashamed to admit that. Now, let's fix it.

What are the obvious differences between our economies, and how might we fix them? Again, these are possible areas to start with and investigate further. Let's not get fired up immediately or jump to quick conclusions based on emotions, saying that something is obviously a good idea, and another thing is definitely catastrophic. Excuse me for repeating it over and over again, but I think to achieve spectacular or even positive results, we have to discipline ourselves in active listening and saying "yes, and," or searching for benefits before challenges, appreciating other points of view, and enriching our collective thinking process. A social, economic and political system that includes (or is extended by) cultural aspects, acceptable and expected values, beliefs and norm, morality of a society, lifestyles, worldviews, approaches to upbringing new generations, education methods, healthcare, legal framework, taking care of nature... and ultimately acceptable and expected equilibrium between safety (defense), prosperity and happiness – is very complicated. I have a feeling that the exponential growth of data capturing, data analysis, and data transparency (enabled by exponential growth in computational power and information storage capacity) is going to help societies make truly informed and better decisions about their future, gradually improving quality of life on our planet.

What are some obvious differences between our economies, and what are some practical ideas for improving ours?

- "They" (Scandinavian countries and Sweden) are some of the happiest societies in the universe.
- "They" are the richest societies in the universe and so are we.
- "They" have the lowest income inequalities in the universe; we don't.
- "They" are capitalist countries, and so are we.
- "They" have huge taxes: Personal Income, Capital Gains as well as a "tax on everything" called VAT, which we "practically" don't have.
- "Their" Corporate Income Tax is lower than ours.
- "Their" government owns 45% of GDP from tax revenue; the U.S. one owns around 25%.

- "Their" Global Competitiveness Index is among the highest and so is ours.
- "They" have 16 months of paid parental leave; we don't (as the only country in OECD).
- "They" have free daycare services; we don't.
- "They" have free education, free colleges and universities; we don't (of course more analysis is required here because the cost of living is higher in Sweden and students may incur debt to cover their daily expenses. But interest rates there are usually below 1%, and here are closer to 5%-6%.
- "They" have a tax-funded healthcare system that ensures that everyone has equal access to healthcare services; we don't.
- "They" forbid civilians to carry a firearm (it is illegal); we do not .
- "Their" intentional homicide rate is four times lower than ours.
- "They" have great social trust, but we don't (per the Happiness Report).
- "They" have very strong social cohesiveness and a strong culture; we don't. We are a diverse society.
- "They" believe and live according to the principle that all people are equal and deserve equal rights and opportunities. We also believe that people are equal in accordance with the Declaration, but in practice, that equality manifests itself differently. Do we believe in equal opportunities for all? Not yet.

So, what do those "happiest" Scandinavian countries have?

"They have a high level of prosperity, to be sure, but they're not the richest countries in the world by any means.

[They lead balanced lives.]

You don't have to get super rich to be happy, they believe.

In fact, if someone's super rich, they [wonder,] what's wrong with that person? So, they're not [societies where people are aiming to become] gazillionaires.

They're looking for a good balance of life and the results are extremely positive." [clxxii] - *Jeffrey Sachs.*

What shall we do now? Why don't we leave the recalculation of those sophisticated taxation models to the biggest brains of economics and data science in our country, expecting that they will find ways to improve them sooner or later? Those geniuses have a proven record of personal integrity and trustworthiness, and must come up with solutions that serve us in the best possible way. Of course, we have to ensure that digitized data sets used for any calculations follow the highest standards as well, ensuring data authenticity, security, integrity, consistency over time, reliability, validity, and accessibility. For instance, after reading the article "The Rich Really Do Pay Lower Taxes Than You" published by *The New York Times* in October 2019 (quoted below), some would say, "how can this be?" "How do the richest pay less than 99.9% of Americans?" Raising taxes for the wealthiest would make sense, wouldn't it? Unfortunately, this strategy is ineffective, as the wealthiest entrepreneurs can leave the country, searching for more favorable "tax paradises." I am not saying we should not tax them or that we should tax them more, but that we should be aware of the bigger picture. This particular area of our taxes can quickly show us that common sense is not too common. Some of us used to say, the most moral approach to taxation is when everyone is paying the same tax percentage, whereas others also used to say that a more progressive model is fairer, where the more you earn, the higher your tax bracket. If I were asked to use common sense, I would immediately increase taxes on corporations that do not create new jobs, innovate, create real value for society, make our economy more vibrant and effectively sustainable, or reinvest for growth. I would immediately increase taxes on corporations that harm society, stimulate addictions, and induce participation. I would closely look at the overstated real estate market and banking system – which create an illusion of vibrant industry by persuading and urging clients to take on debt. It is so easy to create the illusion of a vibrant market, even under a free market economy, by using enough capital and regulatory impact, increasing real estate prices, increasing education prices, and then luring people into debt. We should not point fingers at one another, but rather acknowledge that we have an imperfect system. Do we want to fix it? If yes, then how?

"The 400 wealthiest Americans last year paid a lower total tax rate —
spanning federal, state and local taxes — than any other income
group. [...] The overall tax rate on the richest 400 households last year
was only 23 percent, meaning that their combined tax payments
equaled less than one quarter of their total income. This overall rate
was 70 percent in 1950 and 47 percent in 1980. For middle-class and
poor families, the picture is different. Federal income taxes have also
declined modestly for these families, but they haven't benefited much
if at all from the decline in the corporate tax or estate tax. And they
now pay more in payroll taxes (which finance Medicare and Social
Security) than in the past."[clxxiii] --*The New York Times*

Inequality matters

Unequal distribution of wealth causes social and economic instability,
according to some respected economists. Thomas Piketty, author of
Capital in the Twenty-First Century is one of them[clxxiv]. When reading **The
World Inequality Report 2018**[clxxv] we are clearly warned about the
"catastrophic consequences" of excessive inequality: "Economic
inequality is widespread and to some extent inevitable. It is our belief,
however, that if rising inequality is not properly monitored and
addressed, it can lead to various sorts of political, economic, and social
catastrophes." Also we can see the important clarification made by The
World Inequality Report's authors: "Our objective is not to bring
everyone into agreement regarding inequality - this will never happen,
for the simple reason that no single scientific truth exists about the ideal
level of inequality, let alone the most socially desirable mix of policies
and institutions to achieve this level. Ultimately, it is up to public
deliberation, and political institutions and their processes to make these
difficult decisions. But this deliberative process requires more rigorous
and transparent information on income and wealth."

What are our key takeaways about the United States from The World Inequality Report 2018[clxxvi]?

- **"Income inequality in the United States is among the highest of all rich countries.**
- The approximately 117 million adults that make up the bottom 50% in the United States earned $16,600 on average per year, representing just one-fourth of the average U.S. income.
- The income share for the top 10% was 47%, with average pre-tax earnings of $311,000. **This average annual income of the top 10% is almost five times the national average, and nineteen times larger than the average for the bottom 50%.** Furthermore, the 1:19 ratio between the incomes of the bottom 50% and the top 10% indicates that pre-tax income inequality between the "lower class" and the "upper class" is more than twice the (1:8 ratio) difference between the average national incomes in the United States and China, using market exchange rates.
- Average pre-tax [clxxvii] real national income per adult has increased 60% since 1980, but it has stagnated for the bottom 50% at around $16,500.

[Rephrasing it:] "National income grew by 61% from 1980 to 2014 but the bottom 50% was shut off from it."

- While **post-tax cash incomes of the bottom 50% have also stagnated**, a large part of the modest post-tax income **growth of this group has been eaten up by increased health spending.**
- **Income has boomed at the top.** While the upsurge of top incomes was first a labor-income phenomenon in 1980s and 1990s, it has mostly been a capital-income phenomenon since 2000.

[Rephrasing it:] "The rise of the top 1% mirrors the fall of the bottom 50%."

- The combination of an increasingly less progressive tax regime and a transfer system that favors the middle class implies that, even after taxes and all transfers, the **bottom 50%'s income growth has lagged behind average income growth since 1980.**

[Rephrasing it:] "Among the bottom 50%, the pre-tax income of working-age adults is falling."

- Pre-tax **income inequality has risen notably** since the 1980s, slightly more than post-tax income inequality.
- Taxes have become less progressive over the last decades.
- Transfers essentially **target the middle class**, leaving the bottom 50% with little support in managing the collapse in their pre-tax incomes.
- Increased female participation in the labor market has been a counterforce to rising inequality, but the glass ceiling remains firmly in place. Men make up 85% of the top 1% of the labor income distribution."

[Rephrasing it:] The reduction in the gender wage gap has been an important counterforce to rising U.S. inequality.

What is really alarming here is the resemblance to the years of the great crashes. Take a look at former U.S. Labor Secretary Robert Reich's commentary in the movie "Inequality For All,"[clxxviii] where he makes a compelling case about the serious crisis the U.S. faces due to the widening economic gap:

"[...] Two researchers, Emmanuel Saez and Thomas Piketty [...] looked at IRS tax data, not just over the last few years but all the way back to 1913, when the income tax was instituted. It showed that there were two peak years. 1928 and 2007 become the peak years [when] the top 1% [took] on more than 23% of total income. [...] This graph becomes very central for explaining what has happened to the U.S. economy and, indeed, what's happening and has happened to our society. It looks like a suspension bridge. What happened the year after 1928? The Great Crash. And what happened just after 2007? Another crash. The parallels are breathtaking if you look at them carefully. Leading up to those two peak years, as income got more and more concentrated in fewer and fewer hands, the wealthy turned to the financial sector, and in both periods, the financial sector ballooned. They focused on a limited number of assets: housing, gold, speculative instruments, debt instruments. And that creates a speculative bubble in both times. We also know that the middle class, in both periods, their incomes were stagnating, and they went deeper and deeper into debt to maintain their living standards. And that creates a debt bubble. That's why you see, in both these periods, economic instability."[clxxix]

Let's hope that we will be wise enough to prevent the next crash.

But again, we have to be very careful with any quick judgments and conclusions. What if we accept the reasoning of Dr. Jordan B Peterson, a professor of psychology at the University of Toronto, who believes that **"inequality is the fundamental rule of existence"**?

"Marx was concerned about inequality and there are reasons to be concerned about inequality. But the problem with Marxism is that it lays the cause of equality at the feet of the fundamental institutions of the West: the free-market democracy, capitalism, patriarchy the hated word. Inequality is not caused by the institutions of the West. That's wrong. **Inequality is the fundamental rule of existence** *[...]. The thing about the Western systems, every system we know produces inequality when it's run as an operative process. All of the systems produce inequality.* **What we've developed in the West is the only system that produces wealth along with the inequality.** *And you might say well the wealth isn't equally distributed [...] that's true, hence the inequality. But at least there's some wealth. [...] The number of people in absolute poverty in the world [decreased from ca. 30% to ca. 15%[clxxx]] between 2000 and 2012 - three years faster than the U.N. was hoping for in its most wildly optimistic projections. People are getting comparatively richer at an absolute level with unbelievable speed. It's never been seen in the entire history of the planet. [...] First it happened in the West obviously [...] And even in the last 75 years there's been an unbelievable increase in the standard of living, and now it's starting to happen everywhere else. The fastest-growing economies in the world are in sub-Saharan Africa. That's a hell of a good deal. There's no starvation in China. There's no starvation in India. And in the places in the world where*

there still is starvation it's because of political reasons. It's not because there isn't enough food; it's because one group of people sets out to starve another group of people to death. [...]

Inequality is a problem. [...]*'clxxxi*

It seems that many of us strive to ensure equality in a naturally unequal world. Isn't that counterproductive? Shouldn't we stop fighting Mother Nature? Is this a fair duel? But what if our next "evolutionary" step is to counter established impulses, conditioned reflexes, and determined social behaviors, or at least to rise above these patterns? Can we flourish more? Will the reduction of the inequality gap result in an increase in social trust and ultimately an increase in the happiness levels of individuals?

Have a look at how political commentator Bill Maher describes the American way of life to an international audience, and mentions income inequality[clxxxii]:

Participant of The Oxford Union's debate*: "If you could import a certain cultural way of life which country or area [you would choose from]?*

Bill Maher: *"Well, I guess the best of all worlds would be to eclectically take from each society what works best. I certainly know Europeans in America who came to America because they felt that where they lived was not affording them the economic opportunity that they wanted. In Canada they say they cut down the tall trees. I've heard that from other people, too. I know French people; I know British people in America... [...]*

I like the economic freedom that America affords me. Of course, the downside for us is that it's sort of a winner-take-all system we have, especially now. Our income inequality is horrible and getting worse. We don't really take care of everybody. It's an every-man-for-himself system. We elevate greed to a level I don't think any other country does. So, we are coming along on the social issues. We are becoming a little more like an enlightened western European democracy [...]. So, I think in a lot of ways America is becoming a more enlightened, kinder, gentler nation, but we have a long way to go. And I think the root of it all is greed. We just worship the almighty dollar way, way too much. And until we get over that we're never going to truly become a society that they envisioned 239 years ago."

Life in capitalism and particularly life in a meritocracy is hard.

"Life in capitalism and particularly life in a meritocracy is hard. It's a constant struggle in competition with others. No institution or person gives you the basic things that you need to flourish without your fighting to get them. And that means that success under those circumstances requires enormous amounts of support early in life and deep into adulthood, and that support is incredibly expensive. It's expensive in time. It's expensive in money. It's expensive in expertise. And that means that grown-ups who are struggling themselves are not in a good position to provide the advantages for their children that the children will need to compete in the next generation. Whereas grown-ups who have abundance themselves are in a much better position to do it. And that explains how inequality that in some sense looks like it's narrowly economic based on income or wealth can become comprehensive, can reach into family structure, childbearing, it reaches into religious practices, it reaches into consumption practices, it reaches into exercise..." [clxxxiii] - Daniel Markovits, Guido Calabresi Professor of Law, Yale Law School

We have a long way to go. Let's take from each society what works best. Let's keep an eye on income inequality trying to find the best balance between both "sufficient" wealth creation coming from economic freedom AND "sufficient" happiness creation coming from well-perceived social justice. Individual "sufficient" creations may still result in a well-integrated system.

Problems and Solutions

What shall we do? I believe we can do a lot, and are only limited by our imagination.

Let's take a look at our gut feelings. What if we try to resolve the following problem?

We can try to ensure the best possible balance between human and animal well-being AND social well-being AND our country's economic power AND our country's security as represented by a new socio-economic model for our country that reflects current and possible future situations. This model should define respective Key Performance Indicators, Measures, or Indexes that can be tracked and improved over time (such as a Human Flourishing Index).

To do that, we can draw on the work of the strongest intellectuals in the country, and benefit from the best science labs, colleges, universities (Harvard University, California Institute of Technology, University of California, Berkeley, University of Chicago, Princeton University, Cornell University, Yale University, Columbia University, MIT, Stanford, University of Minnesota, to name just a few).

We can increase the poorest Americans' minimum base of dignified life.

Why don't we focus first on those 40 million Americans who are living below the poverty line? There is a very high chance that their life is miserable, and their development restricted. They are crying out for help. While analyzing individual cases, one quickly realizes that they are trapped in the vicious cycle of poverty.

Low income results in low savings, which results in low investments, which results in low economic growth and low levels of education and healthcare, which results in low productivity, which results in unemployment, which results in low income.

There could be variations on this cycle, for instance, adding a **high birth rate** or **low access to technology**), but the essence is always the same. It is a vicious cycle of poverty which is very hard to break.

Let's assume we want to lift disadvantaged people up. There is already a thriving school with an extraordinary, business-focused principal who is able to attract funds from various charities, voluntary initiatives, and governmental programs. Despite the unbelievable and unique potential that schools may have, many children are literally living on the streets, sleeping with their parents in cars, garages, and shelters, and unable to attend class or focus. Poor and uneducated parents want to work and be paid but in some districts there are no job opportunities at all. Finding a job would require traveling across town to work in selected factories. To travel, they would need affordable transport, but with no cars, no gas, no money they feel trapped. I can imagine people saying that external support should be brought directly to this area. This is easy to say, but harder to execute. To be really successful and achieve a long-lasting effect an intervention has to be thought through and managed diligently. There are millions of dollars flowing to "forgotten" and "scary" places all over the world, and although they address and solve urgent problems, they usually fail to solve problems in a sustainable way. It would be exceptional if the external flow of money was permanent. Handing out money to random people without proper market-creating mechanisms, and the proper knowledge and transfer of skills to the new market participants and stakeholders will result in failure. The powerful influence of political systems on overall rescue missions and the long-term potential of selected regions should not be forgotten.

Car sharing makes it easier for adults to travel for work. We assume that such populations have no savings and cannot cover any travel expenses in advance. What if a shared ride service like Uber or Zipcar enters the market with a three-party agreement between the company, the factory, and the worker and offers dedicated group (public) transportation from our miserable district to selected factories? The business model may be as simple as that: the worker pays the shared ride service for transportation using a pre-paid traveling card issued by the factory. The shared car can only drive certain pre-defined routes to eliminate abuse of the system. Of course, shared ride companies do charge fees as a percentage (%) of each transaction. Workers cannot use pre-paid cards for anything else. Factories deducts all accumulated transportation costs from each individual employee's paycheck. Also, factories, using transportation software, are able to detect any inconsistencies or irresponsible uses of pre-paid cards, and question such transactions.

We can think of something even less sophisticated like the introduction of dedicated factory buses that drive through workers' communities and collect people one by one or at the agreed bus stations (like a school bus for factories). Of course, transportation is paid by the factory after it deducts that money from its workers' wages.

Adult education centers make it easier for adults to access education. Making it simpler for people to access their jobs is one thing, but again, to break the cycle of poverty we need education as a key ingredient. Adult education centers could be created with clear and mandatory rules: those who have attended classes there are to give back by teaching others; every course has to offer practical knowledge that can be immediately applied in the local ecosystems of factories, businesses, and community activities; everyone has to go through personal finance basics, effectiveness basics, communication basics and "my purpose and my hobby development" basics. Classes could be held virtually, and if adults do not have Internet service at home, then adult education centers' classrooms may be used). These efforts could be supported by churches, human-centered foundations, companies with social responsibility ambitions, associations, rescue teams, emergency units, you name it. However, this situation is far from ideal. Such a local system has to become a self-sustaining one as soon as possible This is the beginning of a market of its own, which creates new personal and social needs of a higher level. It should continue to provide ideas on how to meet those newly manifested needs, should also pull in more and more participants into this new marketplace and reality and inspire the community's growth.

We can significantly decrease the income inequality gap and reduce injustice in the following ways:

- Improve our taxation system, calculate, adjust, implement, measure, repeat – experiment.
- Increase taxation on capital and corporations that harm society.
- Increase taxation on capital and corporations that don't create value for society and markets but only enhance the welfare of one individual or his/her family.
- Increase economic opportunities for all Americans and increase social capital.
- Calculate the sweet spot of the new socio-economic model, securing sufficient free-market competitiveness and securing the "common sense dignity income level" for everyone.

It is a giant problem, but with new technologies, we are closer than ever. Starting with computer simulations doesn't hurt at all.

We should ensure the fair market valuation of existing jobs and work models which nowadays are not valued at all (not appreciated by the market or system, which don't give them reasonable or fair value) or are much undervalued. What is the value of a **housewife's** or **househusband's** work? What is the value of a **homeschooling parent's** work? What is the value of a **pre-K teacher's** or an **assistant's** work? What is the value of **construction workers'**, **hospital nurses'**, **painters', musicians' or poets'** work?

Have a look at early care and early education. Can you see the unbelievable contradictions there? When you ask most people what the most important aspects of their lives are, or what they are proud of at the end of their lives , usually you hear, "my children" (from people who have been blessed with their own or adopted children) or "my family" or "my friends" or "my business" (especially ones that helped other people). If children are so valuable, why are childcare services undervalued? If we were conscious enough, we (as a society) would put much more attention, energy and money into this area. Have we given up on the best possible daycare, pre-K, pre-school or school care and education? From contemporary science on human development and growth, including education patters, behavior and need patterns, we know that to ensure that adults flourish, they have to have childhoods filled with love, compassion, respect, active listening, attention, quality time, unlimited acceptance and inclusion, and education. Human beings have to be taught to love, manage their emotions, cooperate, compete with others, fail with dignity, win fairly, and take responsibility. Human beings have to be taught from a very early stage what their values are so that they can define their purpose in life, pursue goals and meaningful relationships, and find joy and happiness.

And now, look what we have: we give away our money (the result of our hard work) to the "clowns in the circus arena" (excuse my language), and having nothing left in our wallets to reward those who care for our children. We build fortunes for "show business avatars," forgetting to invest in our own children. It is insane! It is sick! It is crazy!

Of course, we have far more similar occupations which are undervalued where people with some or no interest in moneymaking are not appreciated by our system. People whose passions include nature, humans, beauty, peace, music, art, health, support, voluntarism, or spirituality are excluded from current capitalistic machinery. What about those who do hard physical labor on our infrastructure, mines, forests, and coasts? Can they lead dignified and enjoyable lives?

To flourish as a whole, we have to take care of everyone, not in a socialistic sense, but in a modern, scientifically proven, best of all, well-defined sense. And that is a powerful, purposeful goal worth pursuing.

We can define the maximum available income or income ceiling.
When anyone exceeds this high bar, he or she has to give back to the

system and contribute to highly important initiatives. In other words, what is beyond this threshold has to be reinvested in social causes like education, health, insurance, security, violence, addictions, and suicides. Of course, the devil is in the detail and in the proper design. At the same time, we have to acknowledge that we do not like to give back to the system because it has bad connotations for us. That is why we need smartest of the smartest to figure it out. How might we calculate an income ceiling?" I believe we can find a reasonable approach. It should be quite easy to list all critical versus luxury items. Knowing our "common sense income level," $100,000 or $160,000, which includes 2 kids' education, some savings and vacation time, we could just double, triple or quadruple it to come up with a satisfactory "common sense luxurious happiness income level." My intuition tells me that $500,000 per year for a family of 4 should be sufficient (minimum) for those at the top of the hierarchy, but it is just my intuition, and everyone has a right to a different one. Now, to calculate lifetime total "cash" wealth for the richest, we could base our calculation on reasonable, lifetime financial freedom requirements. Let's assume we need 40 years of financial freedom, which means in dollars 40 years x $500,000 = $20,000,000. $20 million of a wealth in cash plus some assets. Please be aware, I am calculating it on a napkin, spending not more than 5 minutes on it. I bet we can come up with a much more reasonable and realistic dream income (ensuring that the unknown needs of the richest are also taken into consideration) that is not based on intuition, but on science. Our goal is to stimulate and provoke different thinking and different approaches to centuries-old assumptions, and to bring us closer to being an ideal state.

"On average, richer countries are happier. On average, richer people are happier. But, once we get to a certain level of income, an additional $100 a month is not going to impact how people feel about their lives. So, with money, like with everything else, we see diminishing marginal return." - *Meik Wiking*[clxxxiv]

We can create dedicated pro-human innovation funds from money recovered from the ceiling income policy, from harmful business taxation, or from other creative sources. Innovation funds would allocate resources based on ranking coming from publicly transparent investment "beauty contests" which prioritize all competing ideas. Under a new financial ecosystem, these dedicated funds would also be treated as available financial incentives for all these entrepreneurs and enterprises willing to make advancements in important areas like education and income equality, healthcare access equality, loss of work due to automation and digitization, and remedying climate change. The recovered money should be devoted to projects which are innovative, socially responsible, create markets and jobs, generate long term growth, and solve our major problems.

By the way, the richest, who would be asked to subsidize innovation funds, would still be able to own those new socially accepted innovative enterprises and stimulate markets, grow salaries, increase the quality of education, and most importantly improve the lives of 80% of us. They may say, "that is so socialistic; we are going against our American values. If you start regulating our economy, it will fail fast." The good news is that our economy is already regulated. Every implementation of capitalism is also regulated in its unique way. Our aim should be to move not into pure socialism, but to a better version of capitalism, which we might call "happitalism," ensuring all men are equal, free, able to live and able to pursue happiness.

We can introduce market-creating innovations as proposed by the team led by Clayton M. Christensen, Harvard Business School professor, the architect of and the world's foremost authority on disruptive innovation, author of *The Innovator's Dilemma* and co-author of *Prosperity Paradox.*[clxxxv] They believe that smart entrepreneurs could create totally new and successful markets within the poorest areas, countries, and economies in the world. Those explorers have to recognize critical unmet and unknown needs of local societies and then try to come up with tailor-made low-cost offerings (specially designed products, services and experiences for very specific customer groups) that have to be produced and consumed by them. In turn, these new affordable products and services should meet their never-before-fulfilled needs as well as newly formed ones and naturally stimulate their appetites for more. Initially poor, helpless and non-entrepreneurial citizens become hungrier for newer, better, healthier, happier lives. When desire and knowledge are finally there among locals, another stimulus, incentives and most importantly adequate market and business models with solid business processes can be brought in by the original investors to create jobs and awaken market forces. In a perfect situation, new markets should be self-created and self-maintained by locals themselves - by a new generation of entrepreneurs and by qualified managers and workers. The key success factors are: to establish solid innovation processes with clear governance to make them sustainable, and to achieve alignments with local political powers, ensuring key stakeholders see their benefits and support the change in a long term.

What about Digitalization and Artificial Intelligence?

Per some futurists' predictions, in a few years, millions of current jobs will be replaced by robots and artificial intelligence algorithms. We should address that important change which is definitely coming. It is not hard to imagine self-driving tractors, cars or trucks, software that calculates taxes, prepares financial statements and legal agreements, and automated call centers, etc. It seems that we will be faced very soon (if not now) with new challenges like how to ensure more jobs in a world of fewer ones, how to ensure human resources reeducation, retraining, and recertification synchronized with very fast-moving market changes, how to ensure fair wealth distribution in digitally dominated markets or how to contribute to a human flourishing index for all Americans. Those who will make it work should be adequately rewarded and honestly "glorified" by society.

What if in couple of decades we can create a work-free world? Will we be able to function properly in such a world? For now, psychologists, sociologists and economists are in the early stages of considering such pessimistic scenarios. I believe there will be always a space for healthcare innovations, sports innovations, or leisure innovations. In a work-free world our attention may focus on resilience and healing, improvements to our health, and changes to our psychological, emotional, and spiritual lives (e.g. perfect body building, perfect diets, perfect mineral-ization and "vitamin-ization", perfect bacterial balance, sleep and regeneration, "any part of the body" transplants, "any part of the body" prosthesis, micro-chips implantations, broadening the senses, memory expansion, access and search of information using thoughts, including thoughts controlled devices - advanced brain-computer interfaces, interpersonal and inter-general-artificial-intelligence-avatars communication steered by thoughts, advanced and targeted gene therapies; perfect peace, perfect meditations, perfect thoughts control, perfect needs control, perfect children upbringing and education methods, perfect consciousness and infinitely many other things). We can also focus on community development through new types of social events, social games and social interactions. We will also continue our experiments with immortality by transferring memory from the brain to the computer. Let me open my eyes again and come back to now.

We can increase access to preschool education for all.

Per research that focuses on very young children up to 5 years old, the return on investment in their education is much higher than the return on investment in other age groups. Those first years of life are critical to building the foundation for later school and life successes. Positive change in early childhood education leads to better outcomes for the entire society and the economy. Shall we consider granting access to it to everyone, for free? If so, how do we satisfy both sides: our strong belief in an economy where the government plays a limited role and our belief in a human-oriented economy at the same time? This is a nonpartisan or bipartisan issue, because the prize is our life and prosperity, and taking sides may prevent us from having an open and productive discussion. What a puzzle to solve. I am sure thousands of debates have already taken place on similar topics in our country, especially during election season. Some of the obvious concerns are still there: "Who is going to pay for it and why?," "How do we ensure the high quality of such free public education?" "Free public education and high-quality education are mutually exclusive." "What if I can afford anything I want, and I do believe in the enormous power of high-quality education - will I be able to participate in a tailor-made education system?" We can see that equality in access to education, although a very noble idea, is a very challenging one and it is a high risk promise that one could make. There will always be a level beyond which not everyone will be given access and offered "equal" treatment. How can we treat everyone equally, knowing that not everyone is equal even when it comes to their own expectations? Although everyone is equal under God, or when facing life and death situations, there will always be a level where someone is not satisfied. In a free economy, that seems to be the reality. But you never know. What if we are making a fundamental mistake in defining equality, assuming that everyone requires the same high-quality education? So, what's the problem? Let's brainstorm:

We can steal with pride from the best in the class. First of all, are there any high-quality education systems out there in the world? The answer is, yes. There are successful education systems in Finland, Denmark, Norway, Singapore, Japan, South Korea, Netherlands, and Canada just to mention a few. The United States of America's pre-college education is far behind that of other developed countries, usually not making the top 20 (based on reading, math, and science tests, which high "schoolers" take prior to applying to colleges and universities). Secondly, are there any high quality AND education systems available to everyone out there in the world? The answer again is, yes. You can find free education for instance in Finland and also realize that it is one of the best education systems on Earth, you can find it in Germany, Denmark, Norway, Austria, France, Sweden, Poland and in many more places. It seems it is doable. The **United States of America's preschool education is not mandated by law and generally not even considered part of primary education, and as a consequence, preschools are costly or not realistically available for the majority of Americans.** The irony is that the most important phase of human brain development which is happening between 0 and 5 years of age (as already mentioned) is not supported by a systematic governmentally-endorsed approach in our homeland. And of course, let's remember, nothing in the world is really free, hence, to understand any free, high-quality education system we would need to analyze the entire ecosystem of a particular country and find out how the money really circulates there and who gains and who loses because of such a design.

We can shift currently utilized subsidies to early education. Wait a minute, don't we have some form of free-public education in our country already? Even if we have, it seems we prefer to sponsor, invest or "burn" our money, putting it into the later developmental phases. And again, according to available knowledge, it is ineffective and inefficient because we simply try to catch-up and close early education GAPs. As said before, the highest return on an "investment in a human future potential" is at the earliest stage of its growth. What if intellectual "deficits" cannot be restored anymore? What is the logic of our system? I hope my spontaneous reaction and solution idea do not come as a surprise. Without asking for more funds or proposing more taxes, why don't we shift currently utilized subsidies or property taxes and move financial resources from later education phases to the first, most rewarding phase – early education? This would not harm capitalism: we would use the funds we already have in but allocate them more effectively.

We can apply additional funds to early education. What if we try to be braver and think about something more radical? What if we keep currently used subsidies for public elementary and middle schools and at the same time ask for additional funds for early education pre-schools? Now, I am a real genius? (LOL[clxxxvi]) The rich would say, "I already pay for my kids' private education (where educators serve my kiddos at private preschools, private daycares, private kids clubs, private sports clubs, private cultural centers, private education centers, or at my home), so I have no obligations and no interest to pay on top." The poor would say, "I would love to, but I don't have spare taxable money, I have no money to contribute." Fair enough on both ends. But is it fair completely? Aren't well-educated citizens the same as clean air or clean water for the whole society? Isn't education a kind of common good? "Socialist, Socialist, Socialist," I can hear some of you. "People should work harder, take full responsibility for their own lives, and if they want an education, they had better earn it." Another person may argue, "come on, these are just kids, we are talking here about 0-5-year-old "workers." How on Earth they could contribute and earn money for themselves? It is simply blaming (or cursing) the children for the mistakes of their parents." I can imagine another genius (so many of them here in this book) saying, "let them participate in free education for all but they have to pay it back" (Ladies and Gentlemen let me introduce one and only, "The Baby Loan for Educated Life"). We already have a student loan disaster happening right before our eyes. To fix our unhappiness problem (where education is our big issue and one of the "root causes") we had better change something. Human flourishing does not happen by accident, but rather is the result of bold decisions and determined actions.

Money is important, but it is not everything.

One more important thing I would like to mention here. Like with human happiness and the amount of money that can buy some of it (you may recall $75,000 and the curvilinear relationship presented earlier in this chapter) – there is (most probably) a magic break-even point beyond which any additional money that can be invested in a school system will not make any significant difference in terms of performance or quality. There is proof based on a quite famous and for sure serious experiment from Kansas City that no matter how many additional millions you pump into the system (here the troubled Kansas City, Missouri, School District, KCMSD[clxxxvii]) it will all be in vain if other foundational elements of the puzzle are also not provided. "Mentioned experiment failed on every level. Graduation rates didn't increase. Every major goal they set out to accomplish failed. Except spending money, they very much succeeded in that respect."

That is why we always have to remember that money is a very important ingredient to move our world forward but that it is not sufficient to create exceptional results. To get those we have to have at least very good leaders who show great levels of integrity, competency, passion, and people skills. They have to be visionary, loving people who want to grow and who have a solid understanding and experience of how to design, run, and maintain complex systems and organizations. They have to know how to speak effectively, make stable alignments with various stakeholders' groups, and protect the highest values and policies that shaped the enterprise.

———————

We can introduce an education tax (Edu-Tax). Shall we raise taxes on the wealthy, on corporations, and on other eligible entities? Looking at healthcare as an example, there is theoretically no healthcare tax in our "healthy" country (why should there be?), but there are deductibles and hidden, confusing charging mechanisms which can be easily classified as "mysterious taxation." The so-called "edu-tax" could be collected not from the parents, legal guardians or children's caregivers but from educational content, products and services produced by commercial or non-commercial organizations (e.g. Disney movies, children's museums, toys, etc.) The logic should be built around the objectively assessed importance of available content. For instance, the most important element of early childhood education is a real, living, physically present, competent, empathetic, caring, and demanding teacher. The next item could be a preschool facility, including key educational toys and books, writing and drawing tools; less important content (in the whole broad spectrum of learning possibilities) could be subscriptions to Netflix to watch "Super Why!" episodes (where four fairytale friends go on magical adventures and preschool children follow those Super Readers as they jump into books that come to life). Other less important content could include trips to amusement parks, which are still educational but not as much as schools. What if we introduce taxes based on such a ladder of importance? Then our preschools will be free to all, and less important educational content will be "fairly" taxed. That would be the most complicated taxation model ever created but without a doubt, some beautiful minds will quickly figure out how it should work in the most optimal way.

———————

We can introduce taxes on any socially irresponsible practices, activities, products or services like violent video games, which are stealing valuable childhood time by offering clear harm to the society and wasting our money that should be invested in proper education, which is valuable to the public. Can you imagine that we are imposing a "pro-edu-tax" on the entire gambling industry? There are endless examples where we fail and destroy people's dignity, humanity and hope, and there are endless examples of how can we fix it and create a happier world.

We can close the gap, looking at a practical example by COR.ORG.

Let me give you one more example of the exceptional initiative and engagement of people from a particular church who decided to change the world in a practical way, making it a better place. The Church of the Resurrection[clxxxviii] from the Kansas City Metro are (with several locations: Leawood, Olathe, Kansas City, Blue Springs, and Overland Park) has defined its clear and powerful Vision 2030 – to simply "close the gap between what is and what should be in our lives, our community, and our world." Members as well as guests of that church strongly believe that they are called to CLOSE THE SPIRITUAL GAP, CLOSE THE GENERATIONAL GAP, CLOSE THE JUSTICE and KINDNESS GAP and CLOSE THE OPPORTUNITY GAP. In the "opportunity gap closure" part we can read the following vision statement with specific goals:

"Break the cycle of poverty for children in Kansas City, giving each child the possibility of attaining a future with hope.

1. Ensure every four-year-old who will attend our partner schools has access to pre-K education so that they are prepared to succeed in elementary school.
2. Ensure children in the communities surrounding our partner schools have access to basic health care through mobile medical clinics offering basic health care, vision, dental and hearing screening.
3. Address childhood hunger in the neighborhoods surrounding our partner schools by establishing new food pantries or supporting existing pantries.
4. Increase the number of partner schools from the present eight to ten, including one partnership in each campus's surrounding community."

Knowing this church community and its mind-blowing accomplishments, I am sure they will deliver and will change the world as they promised. What generous, inclusive, loving, action-oriented and faithful people they are. "A piece of Heaven on Earth." Just come and visit.

We can significantly improve the early education of the youngest in the following ways:

- Increase access to daycare and early education for all who want it.
- Improve the goals and quality of daycare and our early education system:
  - Children should receive attention, acceptance, recognition, and inspiration.
  - Children should learn how to be curious.
  - Children should learn how to be responsible for their own lives and be socially responsible.
  - Children should learn what it means to live joyful, peaceful, and happy lives.
  - Children should learn about American culture and what makes us unique and united.
  - Children should learn how to be mindful and intentional.
  - Children should learn critical thinking, constructive criticism, and decision making.
  - Children should learn how to solve problems and generate new opportunities.
  - Children should learn how to create economic value and human value (personal happiness, social happiness, and the protection of nature).
  - Children should learn how to cooperate and how to compete, and the difference between the two.
- Increase the quantity and improve the quality of interactions between children:
  - Significantly increase unsupervised play time (to stimulate the natural development of social skills, cooperation, competition, problem solving... and building trust within a peer group).

- Introduce mandatory, scheduled, and long playground time together.
- Introduce mandatory, scheduled, and well-designed teambuilding sessions together (getting to know each other better, have ability to connect, in action).

"The power of your ability to connect with the people you want to influence is the most powerful of all."

–Ben Sherwood, American writer, journalist, and producer, and the former President of Disney-ABC Television Group and ABC News

- Introduce mandatory, scheduled, and well-moderated conversation sessions (meaningful talks, on a personal level, giving dedicated time and attention to one another, discovering other human beings, building social bonds).
- Increase the availability of parental leave for all who want it.
- Increase the competitiveness of the teaching profession (to make it one of the most prestigious and well-paid occupations, controlled by hybrid government and free-market forces. The best candidates should get the job).

We can significantly improve the education of the whole of society, especially the 9-19 age group in these ways:

- Increase access to higher education for all who want it.
- Improve the goals and quality of the education system (as above).
- Increase the quantity and improve the quality of children and teens' interactions (as above).
- Increase access to practical group projects and initiatives for all who want it:
  - Real problem solving (posted by state, county, city, church, industry),
  - Leadership, entrepreneurship and voluntary education for all who wants it,

- Startup incubators, seed funds and mentors for those who qualify.
- Increase the competitiveness of the education profession (as above).

Are there any role models for this?

What are critical success factors that could lead to exceptional results? Why don't we choose Finland as our benchmark, given that it routinely outperforms the United States in reading, science, and mathematics?

- The formal goal for education is "to support pupils' growth toward humanity and ethically responsible membership in society and to provide them with the knowledge and skills needed in life."
- Equal access to education is a constitutional right (at all levels, pre, K, primary, middle, high and college/university).
- There is a guarantee of multiple educational paths that can be freely chosen.
- An educational path never leads to a dead end.
- Early education is designed around the concepts of "learning through play" and "balanced growth" (the personal and social preferences of each student are taken into consideration). Curiosity and critical thinking are developed through well-designed, proven methods and tools, including story-telling, songs, games, drawing, imaginative play, and improvisation play, with lots of outdoor, "social bond-building" time.
- School days are short (shorter than anywhere else).
- There are no standardized tests at all (the only one standardized test is taken at the end of the school, and scores are used as part of college applications).
- The final ingredient or secret of all the secrets is that there are extremely professional teachers:
  - Teachers are very well respected and trusted by society.
  - The teaching profession has great prestige and benefits.
  - It is quite hard to become a teacher because there is enormous competition.
  - To be qualified, in addition to proving solid knowledge, candidates have to have appealing stories about their higher purpose that explain why they really want to be teachers.

- The expectations at universities are high.
- Teachers are well paid (that is unimaginable in our reality).
- Teachers are in a continuous process of learning and professional development.
- No additional personal financial investments are required to participate in the educational path.

It seems that there are successful free, high-quality education systems. Should we review our approach? Of course, we have our own, specific situation, embedded in our history, in our unique ambitions, values ,and beliefs. Because we always have an appetite for more and better, I have no doubt we will do something about it. It should be a no-brainer that fixing the problem as soon as possible is in our best interest because we know that there is a very strong correlation between an educated mind and the availability of life opportunities. It would be a masterpiece if we could incorporate human happiness into our schools' curriculum, going far beyond obvious human intelligence properties – measured by scores in reading, writing, math, science, or problem solving. What a noble goal we could have.

"To support pupils' growth toward humanity and ethically responsible membership of society and to provide them with the knowledge and skills needed in life."

We can always ask, what are the definitions of "humanity" or "ethically responsible?" What does "needed in life" mean? We may have different opinions. In the Mission Statement we would also like to see, as Americans, additional phrases like "be able to realize our own dreams, create our own destiny," "be able to create and run our own for-profit enterprise or non-profit organization," "be able to pursue happiness," etc.

Can the system be for all who want it?

When I say "free for all," it doesn't mean that the solution should cost nothing; after all, nothing in the world is free - except perhaps an act of pure, unconditional, perfect love. What I am trying to achieve here is the best approximation of the most affordable system for all who want it. Giving something to someone will mean taking away something from someone. It is all about our priorities. At the same time, I believe one day technology will allow us to find those neuronal networks of gives and takes and help transfer social value from one place to another seamlessly. Society is a living organism, and a dynamic system, and at the given point in time there is always someone who has something that I want, and at another given point in time there is always someone else who needs something that I have. Mastery will come the moment we match this "demand and supply." Of course, we have protected our free-market, which should enable overall value flow, competitiveness, and growth – but the governance of the whole system should come from diligently and democratically elected "ethics" that keeps people at the center. This could become one of the many success stories of our new, human-centered capitalism. We should dream big.

> **"More equal access to education is key to addressing the stagnating or sluggish income growth rates of the poorest half of the population."**
>
> –The World Inequality Report 2018[clxxxix]

As you can see, I just shared my initial wish list. It was relatively easy because it was a "massive simplification" and generalization, but I had to start somewhere. I wonder what your ideas are. In case you are more advanced than me and already engaged in practical research or in implementing your ideas, please continue. Why don't you shake the cage? Shake it till you make it! What if I do not want to leave my comfortable cage?

Shall we, at the end of this chapter on money, analyze two randomly selected, hypothetical mental traps and try to motivate them to co-exist and cooperate? Let's take the rich man's world and the poor man's world as our extremes. Will they ever be able to connect, discuss, and partner? Before we analyze them, let's recall our ultimate goal, to bring happiness to our lives via human flourishing.

Imagine a person born rich. What could be the natural motivation and thinking patterns of this person? He or she would want to retain his or her wealth and protect it from others. Let's also assume that our character plans to keep secrets, and so keeps others, including family members and business partners, less informed, and steers them accordingly. Being several steps ahead obviously gives him or her a tremendous "competitive" advantage. Would such a person ever think about the happiness of others, happiness for all, and equality of opportunity, not to mention equitable wealth distribution? Of course, it depends on the person. Let's assume in our case that this particular person does not care about others. Will this person be willing to leave his or her comfort zone? Most probably not. Even if most of us feel and think that bringing happiness to everyone is the noble and right thing to do, it may not be the first priority for this and other hypothetical rich people. That is the rich man's world. That is the rich man's cage. That is the rich man's privilege.

What about a poor man? What could be the natural motivation and thinking patterns of a regular poor man? To work harder, to demand equality and equal treatment, to demand wealth equality, to demand fairer wealth distribution, easier access to education and healthcare, access to capital, access to life opportunities, to give up and do what he/she did before, or to stop doing anything at all. Some people may turn their frustration into anger against the rich or those in power. The poor are in cages, far removed from those of the rich.

What if being rich or poor largely depends on luck? What if you are very wealthy today because you are simply very lucky? Imagine that you were born in an extremely poor, remote village? Your chance of becoming wealthy is close to zero. What if you are well educated today because you are simply very lucky? Imagine that you were born into an extremely toxic family and environment, had no opportunity to attend any school (or to attend a good school). Imagine that you never had a book in your hands, never sat on your own, in your own room, in peace, thinking deeply about reality, about the wonders of life, about the best possible ways to solve everyday problems, about your future. Finally, imagine that you didn't have any encouraging role models around you. Your chance of earning any degree is close to zero.

Knowing that people are not equal when it comes to intelligence, creativity, energy level, motivation, emotional and mental conditions, vulnerability, health, etc., how can we make them more equal, or how can we make them luckier? Knowing that we are all different when it comes to our places of birth, "families of birth," or times of birth – how can we make ourselves more equal, or luckier? Also, capital which was inherited or given to us by others may not be the most accurate measurement of equality. We have no influence on how much wealth is given to us. So maybe, equality measured by self-earned capital is the best possible candidate for a quality index. But to be completely honest, just self-earned capital would need to be calibrated by other initial conditions that contributed to its generation. So, again, brain power, personal potential, health conditions, skills, knowledge, capabilities, wisdom, etc. are all important ingredients of initial conditions. I feel like I'm chasing my own tail. How can we make people more equal and luckier?

Capital is just one of many fuel cells accelerating the work of complicated and complex social machinery. The best machineries are those with the best performance and durability, those that are able to self-renew and self-improve over time. These systems can maintain their independent activities (=independence), maintain the good condition (=prosperity) of all their components (= members of society), keep all moving parts well oiled, well synchronized, well calibrated and well interfaced (=joy, unity, and love) and provide sufficient funds to keep such a giant organism alive. Pure capital has to go hand in hand with human capital, social capital and other capital, and remains an important building block in keeping everything rolling. When wheels are spinning, everything seems to be all right.

Coming back to our two worlds, how do we make them communicate and collaborate with each other?

At a minimum, equality could manifest itself in dignity, respect for rights (life, liberty), compassion, and a willingness to satisfy at least the basic human needs of every individual in a responsible way. Equality could be measured as quality of life we give and take because we are all interconnected and should stay connected in the healthiest way. If we disconnect, we will malfunction, degenerate and suffer on an individual as well as a societal level.

What about creating one united cage to inspire human flourishing and make ourselves happy? "But, why should I agree to anything like that? Why should I share my wealth with everybody? I have worked hard for it, so I deserve it. I hate this idea."

Looking at these different life cages which have their own awareness levels, hidden motivations, comfort zones, and principles, we may realize that this is a really big project. To accomplish so called "human-oriented capitalism" that includes all of society seems to be a gigantic undertaking. How to reconcile the conflicting interests of different mental cages? I think we need to go down to the core. We need to revisit our purpose, our values, our beliefs, and how we prioritize them, and how we walk our talk. We also need a clear and comprehensive understanding of what the right to live, the right to freedom, and the right to pursue happiness really mean. After all those revisions, we have to sit down together and agree on our new collective purpose, highest priority values and beliefs, culture and initiatives. That will start the greatest transformation process ever seen.

Our target human-centered capitalism would require capitalism and democracy embedded in a superior moral system based on **human dignity**, **responsibility**, and **love**, supported by a human- centered legal system that works for the people and not the other way around, regardless of how deep people's pockets may be. The definition of human dignity should acknowledge that humans have their own free will, and ensure that all are provided with decent living conditions, food, shelter, clothing, early care, and education (starting with pre-school), as well as basic health and safety.

My description of the target of human-centered capitalism is of course influenced by my personal worldview. I am aware that others' perspectives may differ.

Human and Country Flourishing Index

What if our goal for the coming years is to define, agree on, and introduce a new "country performance indicator" not represented by GDP (Gross Domestic Product) but rather a "Human and Country Flourishing Index" that measures the overall condition of the economy (GDP-like) AND the overall condition of the economic situation of the majority of citizens (a prosperity index of the people with "common sense dignity level" as its baseline) AND the inequality gap AND happiness level? We could call that a happiness index, a well-being index, or a universal quality of life index. The science of happiness will definitely help us define what needs to be measured and how.

Let's not forget, **"We make a living by what we get, but we make a life by what we give."**

Let me repeat: **In U.S. dollars you get 95% of all the happiness that money can buy if you earn $75,000 per year. 80% of Americans don't earn this amount. Moving people out of poverty into the middle class dramatically changes their lives.**

Self-reflection time

Although it is not self-improvement, and does not increase your wealth, I still encourage you to spend some time reflecting and making your own decisions. Getting out of a financial cage may be long and painful, but in the end, it may be very rewarding. Enjoy the process. If you don't believe in change, stay where you are, but not for too long.

"Should I Stay or Should I Go"[xxc]

Am I sitting in a financial cage?

Why do I like it?

What is wrong with it?

Should I stay or should I go?

What if I do nothing?

What are the risks and challenges?

What are the benefits?

What is the price I have to pay in advance?

What if I do something?

What are the risks and challenges?

What are the benefits?

What is the price I have to pay in advance?

What is my decision?

Do the benefits outperform the challenges?

Am I ready to pay the price now?

Should I confront my internal and external voices and beliefs?

On a personal level:

- I believe I am not intelligent enough to earn well.
- I believe I am already working like crazy and have no chance of improving anything.
- I believe money is not important.
- I don't need to travel.
- I like my house and my porch.
- I can realize my American dream.

On a national level:

- We are the greatest nation on Earth.
- We are the wealthiest country on Earth.
- We are the biggest power on Earth.
- Even if I cannot afford much, I am living in the most prosperous place in the world.

How do I get out of a financial cage?

- Remind yourself of the purpose of your life or ask yourself what your purpose is.
- Take full responsibility for chasing that purpose.
- Remind yourself what is wrong with sitting in a cage.
- Define realistic goals to help yourself escape from the cage.
- Decide on and pay the price upfront, knowing the risks and benefits. You will be able to gain something much more valuable, but you will also lose something in exchange.
- Take small steps today and continue every day.
- Monitor whether you stay on track. If necessary, correct your course.
- Do something for yourself, and something for your family, your community and your country.

Below, I am listing randomly selected examples of possible next steps. Realistic possible next steps can only be defined by you, and effectively executed by you. Do not overwhelm yourself but do what is in your sphere of influence. You can always extend your capabilities and sphere of influence but do it in tiny steps so that you stay motivated.

My level:

- Define your financial survival threshold for you and your family and do your best to guarantee it.
- Think long-term to eliminate stress in the future, e.g. calculate and monitor your financial progress, know your target, and plan to reach that target. Review your progress on a weekly basis. "Financial freedom" is understood here as the number of days you and your family can survive after sudden financial loss due to bankruptcy, job loss, or unexpected tragedy (sickness of a family member, fire, flood, etc.). In other words, how long you can pay for your food, shelter, bills, communication, and important commitments without having access to any new income sources like a new job or business opportunity? (Let's assume your household monthly cost of living is on the level of $5,000. Hence, to survive one month you would need $5,000 in your saving account. To survive two months you would need $10,000, and so on. Define your comfort level in terms of how long you believe you would need to find a new job or income source).
- Start saving $5 per day, which will give you $1,825 of savings per year. After 10 years you will have $18,250.
- Start saving $500 per month and accumulate $25,000 in 4 years. Because of that you may achieve financial freedom for yourself in 6 months. That will give you peace of mind in case of an emergency.
- Calculate and monitor your weekly cash-flow (what's available and what can really be spent and what has to be saved).
- Save money in advance for expected and unexpected expenses (healthcare insurance deductibles, car insurance, property taxes, vacation, birthday parties for your kids, your haircut four times a year, unexpected health issues, car repairs, home repairs, air-conditioning repairs, tax advisors, or new shoes). This can add up to more than $6,000.

- Stop using credit cards. In extreme situations you may use one while booking a car or hotel room, because third parties usually require deposits or insurance. In other cases, there is no need to live on credit, especially short term "credit card" credits. Of course, smart debt-to-equity financial strategies can be learned and applied, and leveraging debt can have business benefits. It requires knowledge, preparation, risk analysis, and discipline to make it right without putting others in real danger.
- Watch personal finance basics videos on YouTube or attend finance management basics classes (find free ones at churches, non-profit education centers, etc.).
- Simply practice not buying anything, except food. It is fun, I promise.
- Instead of consuming, create something (think, design, talk, teach, educate, and discuss).
- Make a list of your expectations and reduce the list to minimum. Per nearly three-thousand-year-old wisdom, we know that to reduce human, existential suffering, one has to eliminate desire. Without it, there is no tension between what is and what could be or what should have been. Eliminate all but one desire, and practice doing so for at least three months.
- Learn something new every day. You can read a 365-page book in one year. My quick recommendations on socialism and capitalism, to gain a broader perspective would be:
  - *The Case Against Socialism* by Rand Paul
  - *Guide to Political Revolution* by Bernie Sanders
  - *Capital in the Twenty-First Century* by Thomas Piketty
  - Make sure you always read reviews of any book you read and then form your own opinions. Adjust your opinions as you learn and experience more.
- Read *The Meritocracy Trap: How America's Foundational Myth Feeds Inequality, Dismantles the Middle Class, and Devours the Elite*, by Daniel Markovits[cxci].
- Build your skills:
  - According to e.g. Malcolm Gladwell, to become an expert it takes 10,000 hours (or approximately 10 years) of deliberate practice, as discussed in his bestseller, *Outliers*. Deliberate practice is a specifically defined term. It involves goal setting, quick feedback,

and countless drills to improve skills with an eye toward mastery. It is not "just showing up," and it's not fun anymore. To climb a 10,000 feet mountain, you always need to take many steps.

- To achieve this expertise, there is an excellent and practical TWO-MINUTE rule (from *Atomic Habits* by James Clear): "*When you start a new habit, it should take less than two minutes to do.*" This is as easy as it sounds. My simple examples are:
  - "Exercise every day for 1 hour" starts with "Put your sportswear on, including shoes."
  - "Read to my children everyday" starts with "Read one page, close the book, and make up your own story."
  - "Shop every week" starts with "Create a simple shopping list."
  - "Prepare snacks for your kids," starts with "Pull out lunch boxes as well as all ingredients the evening before."
  - "Take out the trash every second day" starts with "Take out new trash bags and place them on your trash bins the evening before."
  - "Graduate from university" starts with "Open your book at the chapter you need, and pull out your notepad and pen."
- Prepare your own business idea based on the clear problem of the clear target group. Make sure it is built on your talent, interests, and passions. Go and show it to successful entrepreneurs, and ask for candid feedback.
- If you are a musician, painter, or other artist, prepare your own product or service for selected group of people, show it to your future customers, and get their feedback.
- Turn off real-time television for good. It's better not to have a TV at home at all. Allow only on-demand content to reach your attention. Plan it very cautiously. Consume selected content mainly during the weekends. Don't allow external information to steer your life. Go on an information diet.
- Become a monk – what about that?

Country level:

- Send a letter or e-mail to your political representative (e.g. state governor, city mayor) and ask him or her questions about his or her goals and strategy for wiser wealth distribution.

- Request a personal meeting with your political representative and ask him or her important questions, "What are you doing to attract more businesses to our area?" "What are you doing to ensure our wages are at least at the 'common sense dignity level'?" "What is your detailed plan for improving the well-being of your citizens?"
- Vote in elections.
- Organize local community meetings, invite people to garden parties, and start discussions on the "cost of living," the "quality of life" and "the human flourishing index." Ask everyone, "What can we do together to create a better future?"

CHAPTER 4

Fake Right to Life

Intimidated by guns

"In my own country I feel scared and terrorized with all the guns pointing at me."

"The rate of murder by firearm in the U.S. is the highest in the developed world."

"We are killing ourselves at the highest rates in decades."

Have you ever heard that story?

Let's return to the story of Deborah and James, our middle-class representatives. They possess two and a half guns. Deborah inherited hers from her father, who has many more in his private arsenal, and James got his on his 30th birthday from his loving wife. It also became a family tradition that James gets his gun license renewed on every 3rd birthday to ensure there is at least one state-of-the-art gun at home, just in case. Deborah keeps her weapon in her safe in the basement following her family tradition, and to keep it out of the children's reach. James carries his gun every time and literally everywhere, while sleeping, walking, driving, even when he does nothing during the day and at night. He is safe because he is armed. He could be even better armed, but he doesn't want to exaggerate. Also, his kids have no access to his gun simply because it is never left unattended.

Deborah and James's neighborhood also seems to be well-armed because most of their neighbors have their own arsenals at home. There are some strangers or outcasts in their community, as Deborah and James used to say, who claim they have no weapons at all because they are against them, in general. But those are suspicious individuals. "Maybe they are not Americans, or they have just moved here, and do not yet understand our culture and our rich heritage. They definitely need more time to adjust," they used to say to themselves.

Deborah, James, and their kids go to a local church every Sunday. That is their family's weekly ritual. It makes them feel united, as well as a meaningful part of local society. Although they put all their trust in God, they feel much safer and comfortable seeing armed security guards on duty, welcoming them with a wide smile as they enter the chapel.

Because they cannot bring guns to church, having trusted bodyguards around is what James really needs to peacefully participate in the morning mass. His shooting equipment is waiting for him in the car – well concealed. It is more and more annoying for Deborah and James when they see "No Guns" signs at the doors of more and more places. "Why can't we carry guns to our favorite restaurant, our favorite theatre, or our kids' schools?," they complain from time to time.

Deborah and James also watch the news during the day, in real time. Their TV is off only if there is nobody at home. The first person who gets home turns it on to listen to the latest local and national news. Because Deborah and James hate to waste their time, when they get into their cars, they immediately turn on their radios to hear what is happening. No music is allowed. To further optimize their time, Deborah and James are now considering transforming their old-fashioned house into a more intelligent house, so they can control their media devices remotely from their smartphones. "Always being informed is our democratic right and duty. It gives us time to prepare and react to major events or threats."

"There is so much crime" – they used to say, and everyday there is something new – "another kid committed suicide, another mass shooting happened at a school in a neighboring state, another mass shooting at the church, another gun fired accidently during a teenage party, another conflict at a crossroads where angry people ended up shooting, another life-threatening situation in a local sports bar between supporters of opposing teams." "Therefore, we must always carry our guns with us and renew our licenses regularly. That is also why we need to be very well-informed every day, every hour, and every minute, to know how to protect one another, especially our children."

"By the way, have you heard about the friend of our neighbor's child who stayed with them overnight and when all the adults went to work, the next morning he pulled out a big machine gun and started firing from the first floor bedroom window at any car passing by the property, and immediately after the police arrived, he killed himself with a shotgun? He was that kid's best friend. What a tragedy! Our neighbors spent their evening at the police station and in front of the TV screens. "That is why I am keeping my gun in the safe," says Deborah. "And it is good that you, James, always carry yours," she adds.

Have you ever heard such a story? How you respond depends on many factors, like family traditions, a traumatic or non-traumatic childhood or adulthood, the past and present community in which you live, and so on.

Civil War

Do you know what has recently shocked me to the very core? When my good friends from abroad, who visited America for the first time, asked me the following question: "Are you guys in any kind of civil war or something?" In most cases they whispered in my ears as politely as possible, trying not to insult me in any way or cause any tension. They were simply wondering what is really going on here, in such a "civilized" country as ours. Coming from a "parallel universe of different norms" they were reacting to seeing guns everywhere with embarrassment and worry and also with childish curiosity. Of course, they were confused and afraid. "Who is against whom? Who is the most dangerous here? Are we safe at your house? Does gun violence only occur in poor areas? Why is everyone so careful when arguing? Why is everyone so careful when approaching someone's property (even when they just want to borrow sugar or baking powder to make their birthday cake)? Why is everyone so careful when stopping at the gas station in a small country town? Why, why, why?"

"Why, almost two hundred and fifty years after declaring independence, do American citizens still feel the need to protect themselves against themselves?"

"Those foreigners have no clue about our history, or if they do, they don't take it seriously because this is not their country," we can quickly respond. "It is obvious that without guns in people's hands we would never have gained and maintained our independence. Hence, we should never forget what led us to our freedom and never relinquish that most basic and important right to keep and bear arms as guaranteed by the 2nd Amendment[cxcii] to the United States Constitution which indeed protects the right of the people to bear arms and was adopted on December 15, 1791.

Is this story we learn at school, from mainstream media, government officials, or our parents true or false? Let's take a look at some high-level statistics:

- **There are more than 390 million civilian-owned firearms in the United States.**
- **The United States owns close to 50% of the entire global stock of civilian firearms,** and firearms owned by law enforcement agencies or militaries are not included in this percentage.
- **We are the civilian gun capital of the world.**
- Is this good or bad? Should we be proud of such leadership or does it show us something else, another hidden truth?
- **In 2017 only 40% of American households (out of almost 120 million households) reported gun ownership.**
- **Knowing only 40% own guns implies that those who do have on average 8 guns per household.**

So we allow Americans to carry guns, but the majority of us are not taking advantage of that right. Are we putting ourselves in danger, or is there no real threat? Why do some of us still take the 2nd Amendment seriously, cultivate tradition, and collect more weapons than "common sense" would suggest, breaking another world record? There is a certain imbalance and inconsistency here.

Do we need those guns or not?

The problem is that even if someone decides not to keep a gun (because he is disgusted with killing, he is paralyzed in case of killing, he is an advocate of the civilization of love and trust, he believes in friendship, unity and care for each other) there always will be someone who exercises his or her right, creating an imbalance of power and generating natural conflict and tension between members of society. Such a society is clearly far from optimal.

Paradoxically, the majority of Americans are not well-protected against the minority of armed ones. Of course, there would not be any paradox if everyone would fulfill their constitutional right. But it seems the right is somehow fictitious nowadays. Usually, where there are more exceptions to the rule, the rule needs to be reconsidered, adjusted, and enacted to reflect what is acceptable at this very moment. The healthiest situation would be to ensure either all Americans keep guns or none do.

This is a never-ending debate. The question is, why?

Is there anything happening behind the scenes? It seems in addition to deeply rooted traditions and historical circumstances ("I need a gun to defend my family against past and future 'loyalists', including my own government, I need a gun to defend against a whole list of enemies such as psychopaths, thieves or avengers, I need a gun to defend against wildlife or simply to maintain my sniper skills in case I am called into the army") there must be something more fundamental and more powerful behind the whole gun thing.

What if we examine the capital employed, the money that stimulates the gun industry and ensures its protection and sustainability? What if there are far more subtle, powerful, and dangerous forces keeping the bullets flowing? What about going back to the reactions of my foreign friends? "Why are you so afraid, why are you so scared in your everyday life, you Americans?" Of course, our mentality always (or in most cases) navigates between one cage or another. The question is, which cage approximates the reality that we would like to have.

What if there is a battle happening for our souls, minds, and decisions? What about the concept of keeping society fearful so that the masses can be controlled? This is a very old idea, but an effective one. Before going into any conspiracy theories, let's look at the obvious signs, causes, and effects that shape our opinions.

Why do we need guns in the first place? Why were they made? Why are they still being manufactured? Common sense dictates that **guns were made to kill others more effectively!**

According to the dictionary definition, to kill means to cause the death of a person, animal, or other living thing. You can say there were reasons why man got better at killing and greatly improved his tools, obviously, to survive. Survival is one of the most important impulses, instincts, and desires of most living creatures. Before humans discovered other possible options directing us toward eternal being, survival was and is still the most important "thing" in life for the vast majority of the population. To survive means to protect and to fight for biological life.

Who is really threatening us today?

- **Distant countries**, especially autocracies (those with a vague system of social values, ruled by dictators),
- **Neighboring countries**: Canada, Mexico? I don't think so.
- **Majorities**,
- **Minorities**,
- **Poorer neighborhoods**
- **Our own neighborhoods (**mainly those neighbors I don't really know, or those I know too well),
- **Random passersby**

- **Thie**ves
- **People seeking revenge** for the past or present, consciously or unconsciously
- **Drunk, semi-conscious or maybe mentally unstable or ill people**
- **Animal hunters** who missed their target.
- **Family members**
- **Myself,**
- **My dog,**
- **Pistols that accidently fire themselves**

Of course, this list is not complete, but it already gives us an overview of enemies we face.

The shocking fact is that we are killing each other at extremely high rates.

Violence statistics and findings

According to an article by Kieran Healy[cxciii], professor of sociology at Duke University:

- "**America is a violent country.**"
- "**The United States is a society where an unusual number of people die violently, at least in comparison to other rich, capitalist democracies.**"
- "**But there is little doubt that the tendency for assault to be lethal in the United States has a great deal to do with the easy availability of guns.**"
- "**...Horrific, high-visibility mass shooting[s] appear to have become more common in the United States in recent years.** It is by now well institutionalized as a mode of violence. When one happens, everybody knows what to do. The past decade has seen innovations in terrorist violence elsewhere in the OECD, too, such as random knife and acid attacks, or driving vehicles into crowds."

But, **"Using a truck as a weapon is just less efficient than using a weapon as a weapon."**

- **The United States is outperforming OECD countries in Assault Death rates.** (OECD, The Organisation for Economic Co-operation and Development, is an intergovernmental economic organization with 36 member countries, founded in 1961 to stimulate economic progress and world trade).

According to the Pew Research Center[cxciv]:

- **About 75%** of gun owners say owning a gun is **essential to their freedom**; only **35%** of non-gun owners say the same.
- **About 67%** of gun owners say that **protection** is their major reason for owning a gun.
- **About 40%** of gun owners say **there is a gun that is both loaded and easily accessible** to them when they are home.
- **About 44%** of Americans say they **know someone who has been shot.**

According to the BBC's article[cxcv] "America's gun culture in 10 charts" from October 2018:

- **"...the rate of murder or manslaughter by firearm in the U.S. is the highest in the developed world."**
- **In the U.S.** in 2016 there were almost **15 times more** gun-related killings as a percentage of homicides **than in England and Wales** and close to 6 times more than in Australia.

According to the investigative magazine *Mother Jones*:

- Of the **33,594 people who died** in 2016, there were **22,938 suicides**, **14,415 homicides** of which 71 died in mass shootings, plus 1,305 others, including accidental deaths and war casualties.
- There have been **more than 90 mass shootings** in the U.S. between 1982 and 2016.

According to Gallup[cxcvi]:

- Do you think there should be a law that would ban the possession of handguns, except by the police and other authorized persons?

- Asked in October 2018: **71% said no**
- Asked in July 1959: **60% said yes**

U.S. public opinion has changed dramatically over the last 60 years.

The gun industry in the U.S.

According to an MSN.com article[cxcvii] based on data sourced from the NSSF's 2017 Firearms and Ammunition Industry Economic Impact Report:

- **"Guns are a big business in America.** In 2016 alone, the gun industry was responsible for roughly **$51.3 billion** in both direct and indirect economic activity across the country."
- "The firearms industry is responsible for more than **300,000 jobs** and more than **$15 billion in wages**, when you count direct, supplier and induced jobs and wages, according to the NSSF report. For 20 states, the total economic impact of the gun industry measures in the billions."

Who is lobbying against gun control?

- **"The National Rifle Association (NRA)** campaigns against all forms of gun control in the U.S. and argues that **more guns make the country safer.**"
- "It is among the most powerful special interest lobby groups in the U.S., with a substantial budget to influence members of Congress on gun policy."
- The NRA officially spends millions of dollars per year to influence gun policy, and in the last 17 years it increased that spending about 3 times.

No more statistics are needed at the moment. The general picture should be clear enough. Let's take a deep breath and reflect on what is really happening in our gun cage.

Programmed to Kill or Manipulated to Kill

Is it better for society to teach kids violence or love and compassion? The answer could be, "it depends." First, we may want to ask, "but what do you want to achieve?"

Let's assume you are part of the group of terrorists that has one major goal, to eliminate those who are different (and the whole list of differences can be elaborated here, starting from religious differences). How would you like your society to function? What mindsets, behaviors, and culture would you want? You would definitely vote for Hate Civilization. What do you think the Taliban army does? It takes 3-year-old kids and turns them into killing machines.

Why do they do this? Why they don't take the strongest teens or adults, train them professionally, and send them on a mission? The answer is that the rulers would like to own the souls, thoughts, and desires of their soldiers. They don't just want physical fitness or smart fighters, they want fanatic predators, killers, and murderers.

And this can be effectively achieved only by programming very young brains in accordance with well-known research and theories of early childhood moral development.

Morality is our ability to learn the difference between right and wrong and understand how to make the right choices, and that learning process takes place within a strictly defined timeframe. Already between the ages of 2 and 5, many children begin to show moral behaviors and beliefs, hence, that is the best moment to shape their thinking processes, their values, their world maps, foundational compasses that will influence every future decision, both conscious and unconscious. On top of that, children between the ages of 5 and 10 think that authority figures such as parents and teachers have rules that young people must follow. The understanding of it is so powerful. It can be used to create angels or devils, and depends on the content "served" to fresh and growing brains, which are like sponges.

It is not too difficult to come up with another extreme example of a group of people, society or nation motivated to create a flourishing, peaceful, joyful, united, compassionate, economically stable, and happy society. The recipe is there and is known – especially when to start the process (the later ones does, the harder and more complicated it is). Children have to have loving, caring, compassionate, supportive, encouraging, mindful, individually as well as socially oriented parents, caregivers, teachers, neighbors, community members, government representatives, etc. who are investing their time and attention in teaching them how to love themselves and others, how to take responsibility for their own decisions and actions, and how to be generous and give back to the world, and as a result achieve fulfillment in their lives. To be able to experience the wonderful effect of this "happiness generation cycle," which brings deep joy to us humans, adults have to intentionally program new minds. As already mentioned, the basic knowledge is already there. Adults should start their kids' education immediately after their arrival. Most of the brain paths responsible for language abilities are more or less shaped before the baby reaches its 9th month of life. Talking, smiling, stimulating, playing with those tiny ones is recommended, and should be obligatory.

Where do you think we are as a nation? Do we invest in a society that focuses on the flourishing of people, giving everyone freedom, the right to live, the right to equal treatment, the right to be part of one family and one nation, and the right to become and be happy?

New evolution

Do we invest in a society to strengthen its Darwinian world order based on natural selection as described in the theory of evolution and treat it as the primary or only right? Natural selection seems to be one of the strongest natural forces that has been shaping the character of life on Earth and most probably will be shaping it in the future. In such a society, the smarter you are, the more powerful you are, the wealthier you are, the more powerful you are, the healthier you are, the more powerful you are, the more armed you are, the more powerful you are.

If this power is not used for the common good it will very quickly generate significant inequalities which in turn will trigger frustrations, tensions, and conflicts between groups of people. Many commentators with the highest degrees in economics, sociology, philosophy would say, but that is normal, that is natural, that is according to the famous 80/20 rule (known as the Pareto rule): there is no equality in nature, there will always be a hierarchy, 80% of wealth will be in the hands of 20% of the people, 80% of work will be done by 20% of people, etc.

I agree, if we decide as humans to keep the status quo and act according to the laws of nature, all this is true. The stronger wins - the winner takes it all. The Pareto rule is valid and nothing more needs to be said, except that we are still the most intelligent and eloquent species in this world and could think it through and decide on the best possible way forward.

What if we decide that with help of our enormously developed brains and unquestionable advantage we have gained over animals, we will start a new evolutionary path - the true evolutionary path of man? We could design our own human mind-based world. Of course, as intelligent and wise creatures, we have to respect the laws of nature to simply survive, but maybe not all of the laws of nature must be obeyed – especially killing and eating one another.

My point is, **we do not need to kill one another while living under the same roof**. It is the 21st century. Don't you think we are able to fix this problem? Paradoxically, if we continue killing one another, it should not be called "living under the same roof," but "dying under the same roof." Unfortunately, it looks like we are doing our best to sustain the status quo.

Media

Our children, teenagers, and adults are bombarded by violent content from media and directly from our streets. Try to turn on the news and you will hear crime story after crime story – all day long, 24/7. You may say, we are such a big country, more than 330 million people, so of course, something, somewhere is happening, and by use of instant media the whole nation is informed immediately. That is true. But watching your local stations you find exactly the same pattern with similar frequency and the law of big numbers has no application whatsoever. Let's be clear and transparent, crime stories are the best possible stories humankind invented. It is so close to our survival instincts that in the blink of an eye we are alert and ready. In microseconds we assess the overall danger level. We listen, we are focused, our attention is grabbed by the tricky and calculated manipulation of media designers.

After the tragedy, the media evoke excessive excitement and exaggerate to the limit. "They" amplify the crime to make it even more terrifying. Commentators become so passionate as if they were competing for an Oscar for the best supporting actor or actress. The thriller is born in real time, and must remain on air for as long as possible. Success is measured in terms of how many viewers tune in to a particular station. The overall effect is that everyone within a certain radius is terrified and has already lost touch with reality. You can be sure that every living witness and his/her relatives and friends will be asked for an interview, every animal that passed by that particular crossroad will be examined, the weather conditions will be carefully checked, violence statistics for that specific area will be pulled out and thoroughly analyzed. Every single new fact will be studied for hours. On top of that, throughout the day we will be hearing additional information about the shooter, and facts will be provided one at a time to ensure the audience is kept on the edge of their seats. At the end of the first day, we will have a fairly good understanding of the shooter's personal profile. His or her motives and specific life situation will be discussed by a group of passionate panelists. People will be also dialing in to add multidimensional and fresh perspectives. The show must go on. For the people outside of our American cage, this looks like a reality show. This is an all-day reality show. It is invasive, brainwashing and it serves a certain hidden purpose.

Video games

Our children, teenagers and adults are bombarded by violent video games, in which crime is the underling narrative of the game. You sit in front of your video station "relaxing by shooting." At least this time you are the victor, not a victim (following the phrase of one of our famous TV pastors). You are there voluntarily, you wanted it, you are a commander, you are a shooter, not a target. Although, ironically, in most cases, the shooter is at the same time the target for hundreds of other hunters. Your main goal is to eliminate as many enemies as possible to survive and to excel with your skills. You kill not only algorithm-steered avatars but also avatars steered by other people hooked up to the same apocalyptic network. There is blood all around you, there are human body parts all around you, you are breathing in gunpowder, you are listening to a symphony of shots, moans, and despair. There are hundreds of bullets flying in your direction. You are sending hundreds of those per hour as well. Some advanced players can send hundreds per minute.

There are different opinions about the real impact of video game violence on human thinking, emotions, and behaviors. Some anti-violent video game lobbyists claim that there is a tremendous impact, especially on young children. Other lobbyists dealing with video game violence claim that there is very minimal impact. Here are comments supporting both sides, taken from ProCon.org:

- "Violent video games have been blamed for school shootings, increases in bullying, and violence towards women. Critics argue that these games desensitize players to violence, reward players for simulating violence, and teach children that violence is an acceptable way to resolve conflicts."[cxcviii]
- "The controversy over violent video games resurfaced following the massacre of 13 people at Columbine High School in Jefferson County, CO on Apr. 20, 1999. The two teenage shooters were revealed to be avid players of weapon-based combat games Wolfenstein 3D and Doom. Following the shooting, 176 newspaper articles across the country focused on the allegation that video games were the cause of the tragedy."[cxcix]

or going to another extreme:

- "Video game advocates contend that a majority of the research on the topic is deeply flawed and that no causal relationship has been found between video games and social violence. They argue that violent video games may provide a safe outlet for aggressive and angry feelings and may reduce crime."[cc]
- "Defenders of violent video games argue that the research has failed to show a causal link between video games and real-world violence. They argue that correlations between video games and violent behavior can be explained by youth predisposed to violence being attracted to violent entertainment"[cci]

What really amazed me in the last quote was that it is not the fault of widely available and accessible violent games, but a problem of the presence or existence of young people who are predisposed to violence and therefore naturally attracted by violent entertainment. Unbelievable reasoning. Of course, there are individual preferences, predispositions, and psychopathic types, but if there was no violent content around us no one would be attracted to it (of course, there will always be exceptions). That doesn't mean we would totally eliminate aggression and violence, but that the "dark side" of human nature would not be so often triggered or activated due to ubiquitous stimulants.

What is also worth mentioning here is that most of those barbaric stories teach our kids, in a very smart way, effective killing methods by creating well-designed scenarios, well-analyzed and tested reward mechanisms, and by manipulating users' subconscious minds to keep them engaged and addicted.

The higher the level you reach, the better the equipment you gain, and the more virtual deaths you can cause. This is excellence in killing.

Gaming experience is more and more subtle and impactful. The use of virtual reality and augmented reality features, the use of improved sound engineering, the use of 3D, 4D, XD dimensions to mimic natural physical interactions including shaking chairs, steering wheels, rotating cabins, artificial wind, rain and smell effects is a great step forward. It will not take us too much time to introduce human-brain interfaces (as already used in healthcare), implanted chips or hormone regulators. The list of new functionalities will grow, and I bet, will never stop. And don't get me wrong, this is a powerful educational platform, and as with any invention, it can be used to create good or evil.

Although a debate continues about whether or not our children should be exposed to violent video games, I think we don't need to be sophisticated scientists or clinicians to be able to come up with an initial hypothesis on their negative impact on the youngest brains. It goes without saying that innocent minds are extremely receptive to any new content, including violent content. The degree to which that content will determine their thinking patterns and understanding of the world - especially in the area of building healthy, rewarding relationships, being able to properly manage their emotional lives and making internally coherent and socially acceptable decisions – will depend on multiple factors and cannot be easily predicted or measured. But our belief and available science suggests we better shape it consciously, intentionally and mindfully towards foundational values, virtues or rights, like love, respect, kindness, responsibility and the right to individual and group happiness. Telling violent bedtime stories to our new generations will not move us in the right direction and will not make us a successful society.

Some would say that the video game industry, threatened by a federal regulatory commission, already created a game rating system in 1994, and kids should be well protected if exposed to proper categories: "Early Childhood", "Everyone", "Everyone 10+", "Teen", "Mature", "Adults Only" or "Rating Pending".

Imagine a teenager (who is obviously less receptive to bloody screenplay than a 5-year-old player), who enjoys his or her leisure time by murdering aliens, is accompanied by his or her younger siblings who proudly cheer and scream for more victims. Let's not forget about an innocent child who plays in a warlike atmosphere in the middle of a home battlefield. Depending on the individual's level of maturity, it may be very difficult to distinguish what is real and what is not. Overdosing on daily "screen" shooting may have serious consequences in real life. Whose fault is it? It is parents' fault – no doubt about that. But do we make it easier or more difficult for them to raise their children properly? The parenting environment is becoming more and more complex and challenging. Parents, other family members, educators, and caregivers are forced to build barriers against the overwhelming toxicity of products of a modern, progressive society.

Let us now take a look at some key figures:

- **U.S. gaming revenue** is close to **$25 billion**, making it the second largest market behind that of China.
- **More than 95% of U.S. kids age 12-17 play video games.**
- **More than 50% of the 50 top-selling video games contain violence.**

Movie Theaters

Do you really want me to move into the film industry and uncover the violence in most widespread productions? Please consider it, and form your own opinion. There is blood leaking from the screen, I assure you.

We do not need to kill one another while living under the same roof called America, but we are still doing it.

How do we escape this cage?

Can we imagine life outside of it? We were born and raised in this particular cage and we have inherited behavioral and thinking patterns, social norms, and formulas for success that are valid and appreciated here. That is not, I hope, any breakthrough discovery. It can be easily observed on a smaller scale looking for instance at different family models. In a family where kids regularly see acts of kindness, they will most probably behave similarly in the future. In families where parents resolve most of their problems by screaming at each other and blaming one another, most probably their kids will use similar problem-solving methods in their adult life. In families where members glorify and value their own race as superior to that of others, their children may be narrow-minded, requiring everybody to adjust to their vision of life. In a family where instead of competing for resources, which generates a lot of stress, members share resources, usually experiencing brotherhood and deeper joy coming from such practices, members may later value cooperation over blind competition. In a family where their members are forced to follow army-like discipline and to show the highest performance, those members will likely be well-organized citizens and future soldiers or managers – I hope. There is a high probability that we will be able to guess the behavioral patterns of future generations by simply looking at their childhood experiences.

It is not hard to guess what the thinking process and argumentation line around gun policy would be for someone raised in a family of gun lovers and users. Of course, those kinds of predictions coming from generalizations may be seen as unfair, but statistically that is the more likely scenario.

From a psychological point of view, it is very hard to break all internal schemas that evolved in us and be born again into a new life. Clinical psychologists, psychotherapists, sociologists, and philosophers know how tough the problem of changing human perception is. The vast majority of them (as they continue to practice their profession) believe it is shapeable, but it takes years to achieve visible effects.

"Carved in stone" perceptions are sometimes called paradigm. A paradigm is the way we perceive, understand and accordingly interpret and judge things. This is the lens through which we see the world - it is simply our point of view. We think we see the world as it is. In fact, we see the world as we were conditioned to see it. That is our invisible mental map. We are in a mental cage thinking that we are living the only possible version of our lives. So how do we ensure paradigm shifts? How do we know that we wear right or wrong lenses? How do we know that we are sitting in a right or wrong Cage?

- Is the Earth still flat?
- Is lightning still a sign of the revenge and anger of the gods?
- Are bacterial infections witch's curses?

- Is schizophrenic behavior a result of demon possession?
- Can boys and girls attend the same school, and even the same class?
- Can people with different skin colors ride the same bus at the same time?
- Can women and men work in the same company and receive comparable salaries?

These questions are super easy. But as we all know, they were super difficult in the past. Try to talk to Millennials or Gen Z about those topics, and they will look at you as if you came from another planet. Their reaction would be the first indication of powerful paradigms working at both the personal and collective level.

When we analyze history, we know that changing or shifting those paradigms wasn't an easy process. It required scientific breakthroughs, in many cases accidental breakthroughs coming from planned or spontaneous observations and trials. It required enormous tragedies caused by nature or triggered by people, enormous suffering and pain - including wars and torture.

It also required patience, focus, mindfulness, reflection, openness, humility, acknowledgement, courage, risk acceptance, repetition, taking responsibility for new discoveries, taking full responsibility for consequences, people boldly spreading news and risking their own reputations, lives, and family members' lives.

Changing the paradigm can be very risky. But it can also be enlightening, and can lead to greater beauty and diversity. The reward can be enormous and fulfilling. The reward can be a flourishing life.

How do you respond to the following questions?

- Should we allow same sex marriages?
- Should we allow same-sex couples to raise children?
- Are there more than two human sexes? (It would be good to start with the definition of gender.)
- Can the economy be oriented to human flourishing?

- Can we distribute our wealth fairly to all? (It would be good to define fairness first.)
- Can we live in a work-free world?
- Can we live in a gun-free country?
- Can we ever live in a gun-free world?
- Can we ever be united and flourish as a nation?

You can engage in a lengthy discussion, and other millions or billions of people can do the same. Now, how can we run these discussions in a "civilized" way? To move things forward in a productive and durable way will require realignment and redefining common goals. The beauty of such big questions is that whatever answer you bring to the table there will be so many interdependencies and possible side effects caused by your proposal. Various participants will see things differently, as very positive or very negative and all happening at the same time. To reach social consensus, many people will have to push past their own paradigms to be able to discover a "new normal."

How can we get closer to the truth?

There are hundreds of examples of how we were able to shift our paradigms over the course of history. Are we captured by the gun paradigm? It is difficult to know; we need to visualize new possibilities and benefits before we even make changes.

The good news is, we have some useful tools to begin with. They are not perfect because we are still learning the subject. We have root-cause analysis, we have problem solving methodologies, we have sophisticated scientific methods, we have psychoanalysis, we have experience, we have a huge amount of data and clinical cases, and we have knowledge and intuition. We have intuitions that go beyond materialism, we have spiritual intuitions, encoded in philosophies and religions. So, we are not beginners.

How do we stimulate our brains to start seeing things in a new way? I bet there are multiple approaches. Shall we use a very analysis to see where it will lead us? Let's use these questions to define our framework.

- Why do we live?
- What is the most important thing in our life?
- What is our purpose in life?
- What is human nature like?
- Why was the gun constructed?
- What are the purposes of carrying guns?
- What are key observations associated with guns?
- What should be considered during gun policy discussions?
- What are possible conclusions?
- What are the inconsistencies and contradictions?

Let's try to come up with some answers.

Why do we live?

- There are many concepts.
- We were created by our Creator (e.g. The Declaration's view). We are here because of the Creator. We live for the Creator.
- We are here by accident, by chance.
- Our life is the result of evolution, which started with the Big Bang. Matter and antimatter have organized and continue to organize in almost endless configurations, and it has happened that living organisms have emerged and evolved from the most primitive to us - the most sophisticated and intelligent. There is a high probability that there are endless universes as well as endless incarnations of ourselves in those universes.
- We've always been here. We are a God. We will live forever. There is nothing more than "we" and we don't need to be more than "we" because we are all and everything. We are even more than everything because everything happens in us, within us, around us and by us. We are "we" and we are "I." We or I are endless incarnations of The One God on Earth. We never die, we never get bored. I can live infinite lives and not even be aware of it. When I

wake up, I realize that I was embodied in a limited micro-life living in a limited environment that limited me – but this limitation was designed by me to enjoy the process. Unlimited possibilities, configurations, creativities, and excitements – that's what life is all about.

- In fact, we don't live – our life is an illusion which was projected on the endless canvas of consciousness. We are consciousness embodied in physical form, but only because later we become a completely different form of the same consciousness. There is no me or you, there is only consciousness.
- And many, many more possibilities, just use your imagination.
- To put it short, let's summarize selected options:
  - We were created as persons who will die for sure, but have received a promise that we will live forever.
  - We happened to emerge as persons who will die for sure.
  - We are God – omnipresent, almighty, and purpose-driven person.
  - We are Consciousness – omnipresent, not a person, without a purpose.
  - And many, many more.

What is most important in our life?

- Our life now, our life in the future. Depending on our paradigms, some of us want to live here and now, some of us want to live here, now, there and in the future. Some of us would like to live eternally. Some of us would like to reincarnate (even in a slightly different form, such as stone, tree, butterfly, dog, elephant, whale, eagle...) and continue to live. There is also a very small group of people who would like to disappear because the burden of suffering in their lives is unbearable.
- In general, we want to survive with the least amount of suffering and pain possible.
- In the best case, we would like to experience joy or happiness.

What is our purpose in life?

It would be optimal if we lived meaningful lives and we knew beforehand what meaningful life really is. To live meaningful lives, we must have purpose. Of course, having purpose or not having it may depend on answers to the previous questions. What could be our purpose?

- To survive.
- To be happy.
- To have a good life.
- To have a family, to have kids, to have loving partners.
- To be good. To change the world for the better.
- To love. To help one another.
- To earn eternal life by doing good according to given religious or ideological commandments.
- To be reincarnated in higher forms.
- To not suffer.
- To have as much fun and pleasure as possible.
- To possess as much as possible.
- To control and rule.
- To live a normal life.
- To build a house. To build a rocket. To start a business...

What is human nature like?

- It is the most powerful among species and vulnerable– we can hurt each other with one look, one word, or one touch.
- There is a place in our hearts for love and hate.
- There is the light and the dark side of us, we have the potential to do good as well as evil.
- We can be programmed to create good or to destroy it.
- We are able to procreate and care for life and kill at the same time.
- Mostly, we aim for peace, collaboration, support and unity because it creates less existential suffering and helps us live less stressful and longer lives.
- We are conditioned by past experiences (pleasant or painful and traumatic) and by the design of our biological bodies (genes, senses, brain, emotional reactions to stimulants, etc.) and for those who accept spiritual dimensions – we are conditioned by our spirits and their maturity.

- Some "consciousness driven" scientists and para-scientists are risking the hypothesis that humans don't have their own free will, and all that they do is deterministic.

Why was the gun constructed?

- To better defend and to eliminate the opponent or enemy. It is an improvement on tools like knives, slingshots, and swords.
- To kill effectively

What are the purposes of having guns?

- "Facilitating a natural right of self-defense,
- enabling the people to organize a militia system,
- participating in law enforcement,
- safeguarding against tyrannical government,
- repelling invasion,
- suppressing insurrection, allegedly including slave revolts"
- The people have the right to bear arms for the defense of themselves and the state.
- For fun
- For sport
- To hunt
- To feel strong, powerful, and independent
- As a hobby; to collect weapons as historical objects

What are the key observations associated with guns?

- We are killing ourselves even more than decades ago, in America.
- We own most of world's firearms.
- We program our brains with violence (media, social media, video games, movies).
- We put an enormous amount of money into the gun industry.
- We put enormous amounts of resources into the promotion and availability of weapons.
- We have the 2nd Amendment, allowing us to keep guns.
- 40% of us have a gun or guns, whereas 60% don't.

What else should be considered during gun policy discussions?

- We can observe greater polarization (various causes: use of modern technologies that allow people to "freely" communicate and exchange ideas; the microaggression of anonymous members of digital social platforms, hate propagation and amplification by dedicated social platform algorithms, pre-filtered, personalized content served to individual consumers to shape opinions, yet big questions of identity politics, policing reform, systemic racism, injustice, pandemic, unemployment, immigration policy are not fully solved).
- Mass loneliness, addiction, lack of education, and depression are sky-rocketing, as are suicide rates.

How can we further develop our discussion and try to escape the gun cage based on these very basic assumptions or observations?

Let's look for obvious conflicts, conflicts of interest and goals, conflicts of needs that want to be fulfilled or conflicts of assumptions and beliefs. The obvious area of conflict comes immediately from our being conscious, living organisms: unconscious participation in a natural growth process (similarly to bacteria, plants or animals) and more conscious desire to live long and comfortable lives. To live, meaning to survive, we had better ensure physical safety. To live meaningfully, we had better ensure fulfillment of higher-level needs, like belonging or love. Of course, the higher we climb on the pyramid of needs, the more complex it gets because more resources are needed to meet all accumulated needs of all lower levels. Now, depending on someone's location on the globe, time in history, individual and social characteristics, it may be either easier or harder to find enough resources to fulfill those needs.

Suddenly, the natural force shows up and pushes individuals to acquire, collect, and surround themselves with resources that will guarantee fulfillment of their needs, because if not, something unpleasant is going to happen. What if there are no resources available, or worse, what if resources are almost within reach, but unfortunately, they are unavailable because someone else already possesses them? Resources that are taken, owned or in the process of being consumed by others are "unavailable resources".

What if people get what they want, but others, who are more desperate, try to take those things away by force? What if somebody caused by great hunger appears with an attitude close to madness and tries to take away what does not belong to him? Questions like this make violence seem natural.

The fundamental question arises, how can we live together and ensure all our individual needs are satisfied? Some would say that in a world of unlimited resources, this is achievable, while others would be doubtful that we will ever be able to meet everyone's needs.

It is clear that in these circumstances, I will try to safeguard my resources from others. If someone tries to take them away from me, I will hide them or defend them. I will fight.

Similarly, when I am in need, I will ask for what I need, or take it by force. I will fight.

How do we resolve that conflict? Two good people will fight each other. To save their own lives, they will put their lives in danger.

It may be that the winning societies of today and the future are those that offer the broadest and most seamless access to resources to all their citizens. This is particularly true of fundamental resources like food, shelter, safety, belonging, love, and opportunities for growth.

Winning societies are those which are able to offer access to education to all of their citizens, especially access to fundamental programs like early childhood education, wellness programs (where human nature with all its beauty and complexity is truly explained), mentoring programs for parents and caregivers, and programs that focus on community growth. The more knowledge and wisdom are spread, the more credible, reliable, self-regulated, trustworthy, and unified society becomes.

We can also do nothing, as a result of which society will remain unequal and become more polarized. Frustration and anger will increase. To ensure our safety, we would, of course, need to provide ourselves with more guns - hoping for a miraculous self-regulation process - to naturally solve our problem. Is this a good alternative? Maybe there are other alternatives. I encourage you to take your time and think seriously about them.

By the way, by supplying more arms to people, we give them a very clear signal – "we don't trust you, we don't trust one another. And it is unsafe here!" The effect is predictable. People are fearful, smiling on the surface but ready to explode and react with aggression. Give them strong enough stimulants and you will see revolutions, protests, rallies, fights, acts of vandalism, and violence. "Civil war" is a reality here.

By the way, by supplying more arms to the people we encourage ourselves to think about further improvements in weapons of mass destruction because we simply become fanatical in thinking that everyone is our enemy. We must be prepared in the best possible (and most advanced) way. Everything is interconnected and nothing will be forgotten - the results depend on the path we decide to take - as always.

Do we have the same goal?

The highest purpose of life for almost all people is to survive. Other purposes also exist and can differ from person to person, from group to group, from nation to nation. If two or more representatives or groups of representatives have different purposes, especially conflicting ones, it is hard for them to reach a resolution.

Let's assume, my purpose in life apart from survival is to have fun, to have anything I want and to control others, and your purpose in life apart from survival is to have family and friends, to love and to serve others with your talents.

Who is mentally closer to the desire to have and use his or her gun?

I am more willing to possess a gun, per my underlying ideology. I have only one life, and I would like to maximize pleasure, even if that means taking advantage of "weaker" people. I need a gun to defend my status and keep "thieves" out of my home.

The person full of love and compassion may want to have the right and means to defend himself and his family, too, although he would never initiate violence, but rather would react to it. But overall, in the given scenario, I clearly recognize the imbalance between these two purposes and how they can lead to the desire to have a gun. To prove such a hypothesis, we would need more data and more useful statistics. There could be additional difficulty in collecting true "personal" data because what people usually declare may differ significantly from how they would respond to real life-threatening situations. But at least we could try to collect preferences per precisely defined target groups.

Now, to be even more provocative, let's say that the loving person believes in an afterlife. Let's go even further and assume he is a Christian who believes in "unconditional love" and "loving one's enemies," and is willing to sacrifice his own life for others.

Who is mentally closer to the desire to have and use his or her gun?

The person who loves his or her enemies doesn't need weapons.

So, the discussion - if to have a gun or not - on the lower than the top level of hierarchy of purposes is useless, and it will not lead to long lasting agreement, because everyone will always bring their own personal reasons that together cannot be easily reconciled. The only criteria that can be used here is to refer to the highest level of hierarchy of purposes. Do people prefer to live or not, to survive or not to survive?

Because we want to live and guns are for killing, the only logical step forward would be to reduce the number of guns and ultimately eliminate them entirely from a civilian space to effectively protect our lives.

Our brainwashed, programmed minds may not accept this reasoning. That is not because we are not intellectually capable, but rather because it is simply uncomfortable for us to accept. To proceed with similar reasoning seems so irrational, unbelievable, or ridiculous. Why waste energy on such reasoning?

Even someone who has been living in isolation and has not been indoctrinated by the infallibility of The Constitution (in that particular aspect of life), and in addition has been raised in a loving family valuing life and treating it as a gift and a miracle may have a problem resolving this gun problem. Why? Apart from the problem itself, there is an unsolvable implementation problem. Guns are everywhere, so there is no practical way to take them away from people.

I hope you get what I am trying to say. Even if we finally agree on the importance of life and on gun elimination as mature, responsible, knowledgeable, aware human beings, we are still unable to move forward.

Why is such a mature, advanced, intelligent, innovative, motivated society not able to solve the gun problem? There seems to be something more fundamental than the dilemma of "having or not having a gun", something that prevents us from starting the problem solving procedure. The most common belief is that because we have had guns for some time and in huge quantities - there is no way to take them away from society.

Again, as one of my favorite commentators, with a pretty amazing bio, a scientific background in philosophy, neurology, sociology and other fields acknowledged that the problem is not solvable:

"Although, I am not a 2nd Amendment person...

If you ask, why shouldn't we just ban guns? [You are probably not aware of how] impossible that project is, politically and practically in the United States. We have 300 million guns on the ground, we have at least million people or probably more... for whom gun ownership is the most important variable in their lives. ...People who are telling us, they will fight a civil war to defend their right to own all the guns they want and guns they already have.

You cannot take those guns back from those people!"

After repeating his assumption that we are not able to take guns away, he recommended better gun control, monitoring, background check mechanisms, training systems, and more modern mindsets appropriate for the post-September 11th era. After this well prepared 30-minute speech with some elements of reasoning and some elements of storytelling this was all he could offer. Maybe that is a good starting point. I am not angry at him or at others who try to engage honestly in really difficult debates. I am astonished that even talented, exceptional and rare brains are not able to break the pattern and uncover an ongoing conspiracy. What is the truth? I am also amazed at how powerful and subtle the underlying paradigm is - the basic perception, the mind map imprinted on us.

Implementation problem

So, our problem is one of implementation. In many people's minds there is the following "true" hypothesis: if we would start America from scratch, and rediscover it again (maybe in the near future by colonizing the planet Mars), knowing what we know now, we probably would not introduce guns. As most people know they bring more harm than benefits or pleasure, and clearly are against the most fundamental right to live."

We don't know how to collect all those 390 million civilian-owned firearms from our citizens. There are some of us who are determined to start another civil war just to retain the right to bear arms, and some who think that repossessing guns will create more of an imbalance in society as those who return their weapons first will immediately feel more vulnerable and defenseless. And looking at the volume and scale, it is impossible to collect 390 million assets in a single step, for instance during mandatory Guns Collection Day.

"You cannot take those guns back from those people!"

Despite abandoning the solution to the main problem, my admired intellectualist did not entirely give up and at least started suggesting some possible improvements – broadening and deepening the topic of a new social mindset and the new model behavior of new citizens. In summary, he recommended:

- Managing the problem of gun violence in our society. Each individual should increase his or her self-defense skills. He himself loves martial arts, especially Brazilian Jiu-Jitsu.
- Also, to manage the problem of mass shooting, everybody should be trained on how to quickly attack the shooter and not hide from him or her.
- The advice was: if you see a mass shooter and you are in the crowd, you should immediately run and jump at this person. You must act like a hero. For sure, some people will die or will be seriously wounded. But this is normal, and this is how it should be.
- Also, he himself loves to go to the shooting range regularly. This is so much fun.

To be very fair, this particular thinker also made a clear opening statement: his proposals are only valid in the current situation. If society did not have any guns, he would be against the Second Amendment.

I would like to underline one additional aspect here. Have you noticed that while giving his recommendations, he was also exposing his own personal preferences? You could hear: "I am not a Second Amendment person but I love my shooting practice." It is so difficult to attack the problem when there are conflicting needs. In one situation you want to satisfy one need and in another situation, one minute later, you want to satisfy the other – but both cannot be satisfied, especially if they are in conflict. This reminds me of a standard psychotherapeutic situation.

A good psychotherapist is able to recognize in his or her client big inconsistencies, internal conflicts, conflicting motivations, conflicting assumptions about reality - regardless of the analyzed reality. In many clinical cases, one person has to deal with many concurrent realities: a reality directly experienced and interpreted by consciousness, a reality pushed into the unconscious and not easily accessible, or other realities determined by our different emotional states, contexts and situations. We are dealing with many personalities that do not simplify the whole process of discovering the most real reality and bringing us closer to the new world outside a toxic cage. In many cases, in order to get out of the cage, we need external intervention like another person - an honest and enlightened friend or a highly qualified professional who knows what to do. Another way to get out of the cage is to survive the trauma. No one would wish this for an even worse enemy. Finally, in order to get out of the cage, it is so important that we talk, continue the conversation, learn from each other how to participate in an effective and value-creating debate.

It looks like the more we deviate from the main problem, the more caricatured the ideas we bring to the table, like "Let's sell even more guns and train even more people." What an unfortunate paradox. We don't need to search too long and too deep to find other public figures offering similar proposals. What if we follow the though process of the prime-time national news host who believes that America's problem isn't too many guns, but it's not enough guns?

"I have been calling for a long time for every school to secure its perimeter. Equip them with retired police and military. [...] I want guys to donate 15 hours. I think we could cover every school, every hour, every day, add a metal detector, and I think we're going to have safer schools. Have one armed guard on every floor of every school, all over every mall, the perimeter and inside every hall of every mall. Now, that gives us an instant response opportunity that we wouldn't normally have."[ccii]

If we follow these recommendations we will need security guards at every gas station, every church, every movie theater, every cafe, every bar, every restaurant, every concert hall, every farmers' market, every pumpkin patch, every sunflower patch, every apple orchard during the apple harvest season... at every train station and inside every train, every bus, every office and government building, every elevator and escalator.... To serve all these places, almost everyone would have to be called up as an armed guard. Is this the right thinking? A "reliable and trustworthy" source of information says yes. Is that really a reasonable approach? Something inside of us is telling us that it cannot be. Many of us feel that something is wrong. When we consider such an alternative, it immediately causes internal disagreement, anxiety, or anger. Do we want to live in a country that resembles a military base (military zone, occupied area, refugee camp or ghetto with barbed wire, perimeter fences, metal and gunpowder detectors with CCTV cameras on every corner, on every vehicle, built into every baseball hat, installed in every bag, in every school bag and of course placed on every teacher's desk with facial recognition feature and instant access to full personal profiles)? Absurd or possible reality? I bet it's absurd, in a free country, but the reality in countries enslaved, ruled by dictators. Everyone is ready to attack, holding a loaded guns in their hands. Of course, everyone is ready to "react" in defense (we are not talking about "attacking" here). Isn't that synonymous with civil war? Is this the scenario we are looking for? A society that lives in prison, a society that lives in a cage, a gun cage.

The good news is that in our country we can endlessly generate and articulate ideas and hear all sorts of individual preferences. Anybody is allowed to express his or her opinions, points of view, wishes, requests for changes, complains even without explaining the reasons, because it is a luxury of our democracy and the power of free speech.

What about "guns for all, because some of us like to hunt", "machine guns in every house, because some of us returned from military service" ("those who have not yet had the opportunity to serve should get used to machine guns at home before they are recruited into the armed forces").

We quickly realize that it is not so easy to craft a one-size-fits-all solution to keep everyone happy. Although many requests can make sense in specific, isolated cases, they cannot be populated on a mass scale without rising social tensions and calling for injustice.

Are there any role models?

There are countries that allow their citizens to keep their guns, like Switzerland, and the project seems to be successful. Switzerland is one of the most heavily armed nations in the world and has almost zero gun violence.

There is mandatory military service in Switzerland, meaning almost every man goes into the army. As a result, "every man" should have a very good understanding of what guns are for, is well-trained, and has hands-on experience. In case of any foreign invasion, every citizen turns into a qualified soldier. In addition to the mandatory military service, respect for guns and for life, there are mandatory background checks requiring that owners not have any existing convictions. There is a well-defined gun approval process with exact waiting times, there are mandatory safety courses that have to be completed, and instructions that have to be followed. Also, ammunition has to be carried separately from weapons. All of this creates unique gun culture there.

There were no mass shootings in Switzerland (except one in parliament almost 20 years ago, whereas in the U.S. there were almost 2000 mass shootings since 2012), it means no school shootings, no mall shootings, no street shootings, no concert shootings... "There can be miracles when you believe."[cciii] I don't think we need a miracle, we need to think more clearly. Although, I would still encourage everyone to believe in the miracle of life, and truly protect it.

To proceed with a Swiss-like approach, we would have to change our gun culture. And while waiting for our savior – a courageous, brave, bold, mentally fit and morally healthy statesman—our lawmakers should start working on the following long list of good practices, as quickly as possible:

- Universal background checks, both criminal and mental
- A written request to authorities and a waiting period
- A requirement to have clear record
- Gun education and proper training (e.g. unloading a gun when not in use)
- An assault weapons ban

- A high capacity magazine ban
- Justification for and traceability of arms ownership
- Respect for guns and human life

But do we want to make every citizen a soldier?

At a minimum, let's eliminate the pathology we have today: we require that hunters be educated, certified and have clear papers before they kill animals, but we do not require anything from the rest of us who are able to kill people. You cannot call it a little oversight, or that we "forgot", "never thought about this aspect", "we need to control the animal population and to do so, we need to educate hunters", "weapons for all serve mainly defensive purposes, so why should we learn to hunt people"?

We have to face the truth, that it is not right, and that it is against any basic logic. It brings us down below animals' levels, when it comes to the right to life. "The right to life is a moral principle based on the belief that a human being has the right to live and, in particular, should not be killed by another entity including government."[cciv] Some could also accuse us of being stupid. We are smart people. We could even risk the statement that we have been able to attract the world's biggest talents, becoming the smartest of the smartest - but something shady is definitely going on here. Of course, interests and the forces of industry could be one thing, but being trapped in a cage mentality could be another. You may be the wisest of the wisest, but if you are trapped in a fundamentally wrong world, a wrong way of thinking based on a fundamentally wrong understanding of how the right world should work, all your mind can come up with is a "better bad world", which really means, a more bad world. Of course, without an external reference point, all the progress and improvements made in the wrong world are seen from within as positive developments and achievements. But you don't have to be a genius to detect that in fact the most intelligent solutions introduced by the wisest minds in this wrong world are causing this wrong world to develop backwards in the eyes of the outside, the right worlds - making this wrong world even worse. Isn't this the same as looking at aggressively growing cancer cells in a healthy body? The world of cancer appears in the form of a Trojan horse in a still well-functioning larger world, and by using its intelligent mechanisms of rapid multiplication it tries to defeat its host, this larger world. If it is not stopped by external force, external intervention - will win the battle, spreading its own "wrong life" over the "proper life" and destroying it. However, the endgame is doubly tragic, because when our "proper life" ends (death of the host), the "wrong life" ends too. Although the short-term strategy of cancer and its execution seemed brilliant, it really led to self-destruction and annihilation - without even knowing it. What if our gun cage is our "wrong world," our "wrong thinking," our "wrong approach to life"? Wrong thinking will always result in wrongdoing.

While sitting in our cage, we may see, from time to time, rays of hope breaking through the bleeding sky of our fearful lives, letting us know that there are better alternatives, social orders, and lifestyles. We involuntarily react with laughter or with contempt or in disbelief hearing those crazy but normal ideas, and we usually don't pay enough attention or don't give them enough credit, and without honest reflection we reject them. What about giving new ideas a try?

When you hear such a comment, made by the former governor of Arkansas: "The common denominator in all of this is not the particular weapon. It's the hate inside the heart. It's the loss of morality. It's that disconnecting from a God who values all people," [ccv] what is your reaction?

Can we really defend ourselves?

Imagine the following situations:

You walk alone on a dark street and suddenly you are surrounded by 3 people with big guns - will you be able to defend yourself, will you be able to act like a hero?

You walk together with your 3 well-armed colleagues on a dark street and suddenly you are surrounded 20 gangsters - will you be able to defend yourself, will you be able to act like a hero?

I think that one gun in one hand is not sufficient anymore. Even multiple guns in multiple hands may not be sufficient today.

It is lie that you personally can defend yourself with your personal arsenal of weapons from today's organized enemies. Effectively, you cannot.

It is a lie that you personally can defend yourself from bad government with your personal arsenal of weapons. Effectively, you cannot.

In less than a second, the U.S. military forces (Army, Navy, Air Force...) can blow up your whole property. You will not have anyone to fight with – you will be gone. Even if you get more than a few seconds, you'll have to face an army of micro drones invading your property, just like a mosquito's infestation. You will not have anyone to fight with – you will be gone.

The U.S. Armed Forces

Although we cannot individually defend ourselves from heavily equipped, highly skilled and I hope high-tech U.S. military, we should not forget about our bigger home and fortress - called America – which has to be protected as the most precious treasure. We have to be able to defend ourselves and I hope we can defend ourselves from any external enemies. Without a free, independent, self-regulating country – we would not be able to talk about "any" social happiness, including in most cases any individual happiness at all. Defending our American borders should be our highest priority and giving our full respect to those who serve our country should be our citizens' duty, more than regular acts of kindness or courtesy. Paradoxically, every country thinks the same, hence keeping world peace is a very complicated and complex project, which requires continuous and focused effort, intelligence in shaping relationships and foreign policies, defining a balanced flow of information, goods and people across borders, aligning on joint approaches to global problems (and you can be for or against a given idea, and it all depends on your values and beliefs, age, scientific evidence, political party membership or membership of an industry group...). Let's not conflate the topic of bearing arms with the possession of an arsenal of weapons by our armed forces. And to make it clear, The United States Department of Defense (DoD) is in charge of supervising and coordinating all agencies and functions of the government directly related to national security and the United States Armed Forces. The DoD is the largest employer in the world with more than 1.3 million active-duty service members (soldiers, marines, sailors, and airmen). Do you really want to go against this power, yourself? Or, do you really believe we need to grow our army to 300ish million members – making all of us quasi-active soldiers, marines, sailors, and airmen? As the DoD is an executive department of the federal government, one way to influence its quality and loyalty to us is through active engagement in our social and political life, strengthening our democracy, and active engagement in our family and community's lives by explaining, teaching, sharing our core values with young generations and showing one another what it means to be patriotic as well as responsible and loving U.S. citizens. Without a doubt, we want a strong and loyal military with amazingly effective military equipment.

Some would say, "but to have such a strong military, we have to have strong, competent and brave individual soldiers who know at least how to use personal guns effectively, and ideally how to operate other military weapons as well. And because they have to be in the "always-ready" mode, they have to be allowed to keep their guns anywhere and anytime and practice their shooting skills regularly and frequently." We can go even beyond simple gun possession by all. What if we start shaping people's beliefs, attitudes and thinking patterns by transferring deep and broad military knowledge and expertise to each and every individual? In so doing, we can be sure that gun and military culture will be successfully created, implemented, and followed. If the sovereignty of the country is paramount, all aspects of life should be subordinated to this highest priority.

So maybe gun possession is not only appropriate for our militia (that long ago emerged from armed civilians in the face of a sudden and demanding historical situation; we proudly recall its heroic attitude and victory), a way to fulfill the gun industry's financial needs and desires, or about hunting, entertainment, and self-defense. Maybe it is designed to help us with our highest priority – our national security.

What could we gain from an army-like education for all? Clearly, a lot:

- A love of our homeland and its people – patriotism,
- Becoming part of something bigger then yourself,
- Discipline,
- Taking responsibility,
- Perseverance,
- Obedience and respect for hierarchy,
- Loyalty, trust, and honesty,
- Physical strength,
- Survival skills,
- Self-defense skills, with or without weapons,
- Skills for defending others with or without weapons,
- Knowledge of how to help during natural disasters,
- Knowledge and skills in various fields, such as logistics, telecommunication, computer science, strategy and management, cooking, etc.
- Employment (there are already 1.3 million active-duty service members),
- Basic needs such as food, shelter, and clothing being met
- Support in education and personal development via coaching and subsidies,
- Volunteering

What can we learn about military life by listening to James Norman Mattis, an American veteran, retired United States Marine Corps general and former government official who served as the 26th United States Secretary of Defense?

- Excellence!

- You need a specific set of skills, a mentality of excellence, and a mentality that does not give up, that does not complain that something cannot be done, cannot happen. Being a soldier - for a general of the Marine Corps - means a willingness to be a part of something bigger then yourself. Instead of shrinking yourself into specific tasks or behaviors, you can experience self-expansion and greater meaning.
- "On the battlefield there is no trophy for second place, so you have to win."
- Affection!
- "What holds soldiers together is an affection for each other that no matter what happens they will keep fighting [...] and the affection is the opposite in its own way of popularity. Popularity brings favoritism [...]"
- Trust and Respect!
- "When you going around making people get up and move when they don't want to, when you are telling people [...] to jump into a mud puddle because you do not want them to be reluctant to hit the deck in the mud when they get shot at, you are not doing things that make you popular, but you find, too, that if you've been honest with your troops, if they trust you, then they will stick with you."
- "It is affection that builds on trust and respect but it's not popularity"
- Overcoming Fear!
- "There is nothing strange about the fear, it's going to be there [coupled with a fatigue that goes beyond words], it's part of every fight. [...] But you are well enough trained, but what really drives you forward [...], what keeps you going really is that affection, that love for one another, that I don't care what happens, I am not going to leave him or her uncovered."
- Discipline! Learning from Mistakes!
- "For all of you, because you are all going to be leaders of something [society, on the job, families], if you want to be, that's your choice, make sure you know the difference between a mistake and a lack of discipline. If [we] can help people get through mistakes and use them as learning opportunities it doesn't in any way accept lack of discipline that's not in moral turpitude."
- Coaching!

- "In the Marines we don't call it command and control. [...] Marines believe in command and feedback."
- Problem Solving!
- "Einstein, when confronted with the problem of how to save the earth [having only one hour], allegedly said, I would spend 55 minutes defining the problem and save the world in 5 minutes"

Of course, to be totally honest with ourselves, we should also speculate on possible side effects that may or may not occur after serious involvement in the military world:

- Post-Traumatic Stress Disorder (PTSD): a disorder in which a person has difficulty recovering after experiencing or witnessing a terrifying event. The condition may last months or years, with triggers that can bring back memories of the trauma accompanied by intense emotional and physical reactions. Symptoms may include nightmares or unwanted memories of the trauma, avoidance of situations that bring back memories of the trauma, heightened reactions, anxiety, or depressed mood.[ccvi]
- Exposure to excessive violence may in some cases trigger violent behavior.
- Exposure to excessive death may in some cases cause callousness, or repression of emotions.
- Exposure to hermetic obedience-based training may cause reduced ability to think independently and critically, including reduced self-esteem and reduced sense of agency at being outside of a hierarchy.
- Exposure to a hermetic work environment based on rules, policies, and procedures may result in reduced ability to shape and maintain emotional relationships with other people, including proper functioning in civil society.
- Being taken care of by the Employer (as long as you follow the orders) and detached from challenges, one's own decision-making, and the norms of normal social life.
- Coming back to civilian reality may be very tough, full of misunderstandings, disappointments, frustrations (what was normal and rewarded in the military is simply not normal, not rewarded, not understood, or even acceptable).

- "You cannot go into something like that and not be changed [...]"
- "The only way you can return young men to civilian society as better citizens is to make certain you don't allow the grim aspects to basically define them. They've got to be able to do very bad things without becoming bad or evil in the process. That is a tough line and it takes constant nurturing of the young men who oftentimes are so young. You are really acting as their parent."[ccvii]

Would you like to bring military life into your "normal" family life? Could you imagine that in your case the advantages outweigh the disadvantages? Is this the right project to stand up for, sacrifice your life? What if we do need to maintain a certain level of discipline, obedience, and even aggression in society to be alert, ready to react, ready to defend, and ready to fight? Maybe living comfortable lives is already weakening us and preventing us from being soldiers.

What is the right balance, between me being a soldier and me being a civilian citizen, between me carrying a gun all the time and me not carrying a gun at all, between our aspiration for national security and our aspiration for happiness? What is the highest priority? What matters more, individual or national security? Can we consider one without the other? Isn't this a phenomenal question? To build an army, we need people who are alive. To have people who are alive we need certain conditions and protection to keep them alive, we need an army on duty, day and night. What if both worlds, military and civilian, are out of sync? What if they have conflicting visions, desires, goals, agendas, and motivations? What if military leaders disagree with political leaders, or even disagree with the president?

- "At times military leaders have to bring wars [grim realities] into the discussion with politicians who are trying to go for peace and prosperity and healthcare and education--all the things we care about. Again, we defend the country so it could have those things and somehow we have to bring that thinking into the decisions made in war which is completely alien to what we are trying to do in this beautiful democracy and bring the harmony of our team together in this country (at least I hope we are) [...]
- If you believe in the Constitution, if you are going to uphold the Constitution then you keep faith with it, and you carry out the

orders of the civilians unless you think they are immoral." [In my case] I thought [that political decision] was strategically unsound [but] under me we did pull these troops out because that was his [the president's] right as the elected commander-in-chief and you do not suddenly think that you start telling the civilians when we are going to war or when we are not going to war. [...]
- I don't believe people with military backgrounds should come out and make political assessments of civilian leaders [unless when running officially for office]"[ccviii] – as the general explained.

Very interesting. Isn't it? There are indeed two parallel realities, separated but tightly interconnected and interdependent: A) being powerful, striving for excellence, "winning as the only option," following orders, intimidating others, unity with and affection toward comrades in combat - military versus B) remaining peaceful and prosperous, "ensuring democracy as the only option," following the will of the people, and pursuing happiness. Life and love are common denominators. Most competencies and capabilities cannot be effectively used in another, or at least they cannot be transferred one-to-one without major adjustments or modifications.

Shouldn't this be our ultimate ambition and goal--to have safe borders with loyal, strong and highly effective U.S. Armed Forces able to defeat any enemies and neutralize or kill external aggressors and at the same time to have peace at home with responsible, loving and happy people able to defeat their enemies and internal problems without hurting or killing one another? In the best possible scenario, these realities coexist. The wisdom is to do it in the most optimal way and aim for perfection. When people freely give their lives for others, we experience that perfection. We used to call that "loving thy neighbor" – the noblest act of care, kindness and service – happiness in its essence and purity. Although happiness is born in pain, we are united, we are in love. What a paradox.

When asked, "what is the greatest national security threat facing the United States today?" our former U.S. Secretary of Defense responded that besides terrorism, it is us being not united:

"**We are separating into these little warring tribes** [similar observation and warning formulated by Lincoln already time ago], we won't talk with each other. We are contemptuous of others. We don't think that the person we disagree with might actually be right once in a while and as we go into this more contemptuous role we are almost perpetually in elections [...] That isn't the right model to stay in governing where you try to divide and get yourself elected. Once the election is over you have to go into governance and governance is about unity, not dividing. We've got to come together, spend those 55 minutes, roll our sleeves up to find the problems and let's take time to do that and then solve it [in the remaining 5 minutes]."[ccix]

Which room do you want to stay in, *Soft* or *Sharp*?

Let's proceed with the final consistency check. Let's assume you are a parent of Emma, a 4-year-old girl. You just decided that she will enroll in a pre-school and go there every second day starting from the early morning till 3p.m. You have been given a choice, you can either send Emma to the "Soft mascots" class or the "Sharp sharks" class. They are held in two different rooms:

A. "**Soft mascots**" **Room**
    - Where there is an abundance of colorful toys, games, and children's favorite books.
    - There is a variety of play stations, Lego tables, tables with wooden, softly rounded blocks, tables with railways, trains and bridges, arts and crafts tables, and many more.
    - There are no sharp objects (scissors, knives, forks, metal and plastic swords, sharp tips...), toy pistols, slings, metal balls, laser pointers, matches, lighters.
    - Instead, there are lots of fluffy pillows and mascots.
    - In accordance with the rules, you are not allowed to bring anything like that.
B. "**Sharp sharks**" **Room**
    - There is an abundance of colorful toys, games, and children's favorite books.

- There is a variety of play stations, Lego tables, tables with wooden, not softly rounded blocks, tables with railways, trains and bridges, arts and crafts tables, etc.
- There are many sharp objects, as well as various types of toy guns, slings with stones, metal balls, laser indicators, matches, lighters.
- There are few fluffy pillows and mascots.
- You can always bring in any toy you want.

This particular pre-school believes in children's wisdom and in the importance of emotional and social intelligence. That is why pre-school staff focus on the development of students' social skills, enriched by creativity and critical thinking. To realize its vision, the education program assumes as much as possible unsupervised time for pupils, plus many micro group projects, where in addition to tangible results, kids are motivated to show key behaviors, like "taking responsibility" and "collaborating." Also, based on a very clear rule, no screens are allowed.

Which room will you send your Emma to?

Would you prefer a room full of dangerous objects or a more secure environment?

Nobody in his/her right mind will leave his/her child alone with "dangerous objects." That should be one of the basic principles of parenting.

Now, coming back to the adult's world, can you guarantee that every adult behaves according to commonly accepted social norms and laws, sitting in a "Sharp shark" American room? We will never be able to ensure that everyone uses their "gun toys" appropriately – simply because we are all conditioned otherwise (having our own personalities, our own life situations, our own problems, our own ways of dealing with these problems). Someone will overreact in response to someone else's behavior or his/her own behavior, or will not respond at all, becoming an open target for the reactions of others.

Let me leave you alone with this mental exercise. It is about your own reflection here.

The ultimate question is, "Do you agree with the National Rifle Association (NRA), which claims that more guns make the country safer, or do you have a different opinion?"

Don't you think this is a good time to leave the "Gun Lovers" or "Gun Addicts" room and open up to other options? We can at least try to open the doors of other available rooms and look inside with curiosity. One of them may be the "Life Lovers" Room or the "Human Lovers" Room.

I really wonder what conclusions can be drawn from all this? Have you managed to find any inconsistencies, well camouflaged contradictions, any signs of a different, parallel reality in your life, in your family and community? If not yet, you can just start listening to your body. What does your body tell you? What is your state of mind? What is the state of your emotional life? Do you experience peace and joy, or frustration and overwhelming anxiety? You look for motivations that are in conflict with each other and by naming them, confronting them, you give yourself a chance to discover the real problem, the root cause. Perhaps you will find new cognitively acceptable avenues, new possible scenarios, and finally you come up with new considerations and new world models - worth exploring. Even if you only awaken your initial curiosity, it can already change your life. What if you assume that the new truth is really true? What if you try to live according to this new truth? In the worst case, you will learn something new. At best, you will gain a new life - you will get freedom.

Problems and Solutions

How can we really solve our problem, knowing that even the Presidents of The United States were not able to solve it before?

If you want to become president, unfortunately there is a very minimal chance that you will do so by promoting a "no guns" policy. No president and no government will ever be elected by going against 300,000 people who work for the gun industry. No clearsighted politician will go against their own voters. No one would dare to manipulate a $56 billion industry. These are also reasons why the problem cannot be solved.

What shall we do now? I believe we can do a lot and are only limited by our imagination.

Take a look at the following ideas:

Significantly decrease assault deaths in America to the level of OECD countries' average - as a first step. As a next step, to outperform those developed countries and go below the average assault death rate. Let me recall here, "...the rate of murder or manslaughter by firearm [in the US] is the highest in the developed world."

And to achieve that (again) we use our strongest intellects we already have in the country and benefit from the best science labs, colleges, and universities.

Significantly increase safety by decreasing gun violence.

No guns on the streets. Guns should only be allowed on the gun owner's property. I bet no change to the 2nd Amendment would be required. Of course, let's not confuse "guns on the streets" with armed forces and national defense, our highest priority. Compliance would be ensured by real-time police tracking of each gun. In addition, specific guns would only be activated by their owners. And all this thanks to current and future technologies, like GPS, Internet of Things, and biometric gun safes...

No guns on the streets and on private properties, except for dangerous wilderness areas. I bet no change to 2nd Amendment would be required. The idea is to move guns into Citizen-Owned Armed Spaces, so that they would only be stored at certified Gun Storage Locations – Shooting Ranges – Recreation & Competitive Shooting Ranges - Hunting Areas. Guns would be stored in known locations. Specific guns could only be activated by their owners thanks to the new technologies. "Keeping and bearing arms" would be ensured in dedicated locations. Immediately after implementation, respective monitoring and gun violence measurement would be activated. Policies would be regularly reviewed and adjusted based on detailed statistics.

Implementation Problems

Of course, we are playing with fire here, trying to solve the unsolvable. But then again, we never thought we would travel in gigantic aircraft, we never thought we would land on the moon, and even recently – we've just sent people on the SpaceX autonomous mission fully controlled by computers, we never thought artificial intelligence algorithms would search for new molecules on behalf of humans to cure diseases, we never thought we would edit our genes, we never thought we wouldn't be working on weekends as well, etc. It seems it is a matter of time, focused effort and money before we see achievements.

Let's acknowledge that this problem is political, and more socially sensitive than "just" scientific, hence more holistic and tailor-made problem-solving methods should be used. How do we know that this problem is solvable? Because there is clear evidence that there are well-functioning countries, economies and social systems, even better functioning than ours, where there are no guns at all. Do we want to be the best? Do we still want to be the first? If so, we will become even greater only by solving even greater problems.

Now, to overcome the implementation problem ("how to collect all the guns from the civilian space") maybe dedicated incentive programs for and businesses should be required to stimulate the creation of new industries. Also, new educational systems and training programs on how to bear arms in a socially responsible way need to be created. In case the implementation problem cannot be resolved in one step, multiyear transformation process needs to be designed. Maybe an entire generation must pass to successfully conclude this project. That's why it will be so important for the new educational program to reach younger audiences.

Transform a $60 billion industry into a new industry or set of industries and ensure jobs security.

Where are you - economic geniuses, where are you – world changing businessmen and businesswomen, where are you "hungry for growth" investors? What would successful entrepreneurs do? What they usually do when they see their industry is shrinking due to changes   in customers' behavior, needs, preferences, or due to disruptive innovation that enters their market, or crisis that is caused by other adjacent industries' condition (oil prices go up, banking systems do not perform, the stock market crashes), or due to crises that are caused by natural forces such as floods and earthquake. Of course, there is no one-size-fits-all formula, but there should be a set of steps to effectively reposition and recover. For instance, we could study the following areas:

- **Mega trends in the economy:** clean energy, digital farming, computational life-science, gene-editing, and gene therapies, remote healthcare, self-healthcare with real-life evidence, organic food, self-driving cars, self-flying parcels, just to name a few.
- **Current gun owners' needs**: safety, the identity of being American, the feeling of being independent, the pleasure of hunting, the pleasure of collecting historical or new models, to name a few.
- **Current gun industry stakeholders need**: including the richest, and celebrities who think they need personal protection, politicians, gun manufacturers, factory workers, company owners, distribution network owners and workers, investors, all other indirect gun

industry beneficiaries who "benefit" from gun violence, like hospitals, lawyers, funeral homes, etc. Their possible needs should be considered and somehow met.

- **Competition to guns industry, alternative products and services, possible disruptions:**

Alternative products: tasers{a weapon firing barbs attached by wires to batteries, causing temporary paralysis}, smartphone tasers, tranquillizer guns[ccx] that shoot darts with a hypodermic needle tip, filled with a dose of tranquilizer solution that is either a sedative or a paralytic, and which once injected will temporarily impair the target's physical function to a level that allows it to be approached and handled in an unresisting and thus safe manner, or other varieties of traps and non-lethal devices.

What about the newer generation taser (NGT) or stun gun that temporarily numbs your body with X volts of energy or Y dose of proven chemicals, which whenever used, sends real-time information to "911" receiver stations informing the police and other rapid response units about: "gun" usage, its geo location and the person who used it (based on ownership data, voice recognition, fingerprints or heartbeat rates). Immediately after enemies fall, their vital signs are also captured and transferred real-time to "911" receiver stations. Accordingly, a dedicated rescue mission is immediately initiated by properly trained and proven algorithms, and both certified personnel and specialized robots are sent to the place of tragedy. Our new product and service (NGT) would not be designed to kill but to prevent. Imagine, that minutes or seconds before any tragedy, authorized units would already know that something may happen by getting and interpreting real-time data on the level of anger and if the gun is now being held in the hands of a possible suspect. I don't think it's just a dream or an unrealistic vision. We are almost there.

Disruptions: intelligent drones, intruder detection systems based on heat, movement, electromagnetic field, image and chemicals recognition, 24/7 monitoring systems, nanorobots, lasers, real-life evidence and wearables, innovative EMI and RFI shielding solutions (electromagnetic interference and radio-frequency interference) used against devastating electromagnetic pulse attacks, cybercrime and cyber defense and believe me, many more options that are in testing phases or already out there being used by our special forces. There are so many things to invest in.

Guns as a service - **gun rental and storage industry** similar to car and ski rentals, with requirements and restrictions? We would still allow the right to own the gun, but storage would only take place in predefined, government-certified, very well-protected locations. The solution would entirely eliminate guns kept in homes, but at the same time would broaden access to guns in a very controlled way. Obviously, to rent or store own gun one would need valid paperwork, including a background check. You could rent the best or the newest pistol or rifle model – never used by anyone before. You would have access to hundreds of rental places all around the U.S. We would respect our rights and control "the environment" at the same time.

Far substitutes: martial-arts courses, equipment and gadgets, "self-defense in the world without guns" courses, equipment and gadgets, archery-like activities, paintball-like or laser-shooting-like activities with surrounding toolsets and gadgets (Will anyone finally design and bring to the market our dream lightsaber – a Jedi colorful and buzzing weapon?), virtual reality adventure games, virtual and real reality games (Pokémon Go-like augmented reality games), all kinds of sports or new sports that may arise, and many more interesting alternatives.

Without a doubt, there are lots of questions that need to be answered, like how to satisfy the needs of future customers, how to create a new need in the current or new market, how to design profitable business models with all possible revenue streams and efficient cost elements, how best to finance new enterprises, what the key stakeholders are, what policies and regulations are needed, and what a "corporate" social responsibility strategy is, which will ensure that we create something much better for humanity than what we have now.

Isn't it fun to brainstorm new ideas to known problems? So why instead of stuns, tasers, self-defense courses, or other destructive tools and methods, won't we turn to life-promoting themes? I think we have to be revolutionary here and cut ourselves off from the past. We should create something new. This is a fantastic moment for us Americans to start chasing the new American Dream and activate what's best in us: innovation, curiosity, competition, collaboration, entrepreneurship, persistence, and belief. A mind seeking happiness and freedom wants to create something new.

Become a proud American without the support of the 2nd Amendment, and feel safe and powerful without the 2nd Amendment being a shield.

Introduce relevant, factual, compulsory educational content for all Americans: about our heritage, about our American culture (as described in the chapter Fake Happiness) and about the new normal – the era of no guns. We should ask ourselves several honest questions, like: what our heritage really is, how we benefited from our heritage in the past – why we needed it, how we can benefit from it now, what part of heritage should be left behind the museum's windows because it doesn't fit our contemporary society, our adjusted understanding of the world, our new mindset, and technological advancements. And although some heritage pieces have been placed on the shelf, we should never forget about them. We also would need to train ourselves on resolving disputes and defending ourselves without guns, as well as on how to build solid and long-lasting social trust, how to build a happy, prosperous, united society based on contribution to the greater good. There is so much we could do. Just think about it.

Self-reflection time

Am I sitting in a gun cage?

Why do I like it? What is wrong with it? Should I stay or should I go? What if I do nothing? What if I do something? What is my decision?

Should I confront my internal and external voices and beliefs?

On a personal level:

- I cannot imagine life without guns.
- I live on a farm and I have to protect myself and my family from coyotes.
- I love my gun, it's my family treasure.
- My community is very safe.

On a national level:

- We gained independence because we had access to weapons.
- We are the biggest power on Earth, because everyone can have a gun.
- I live in the safest place in the world.
- We are the greatest nation, and guns are part of our identity.

How do I get out of a gun cage?

- Remind yourself of the purpose of your life or ask yourself what your purpose is.
- Take full responsibility for chasing that purpose.
- Remind yourself what is wrong with sitting in a cage.
- Define realistic goals to help yourself escape from the cage.
- Decide on and pay the price upfront, knowing the risks and benefits. You will be able to gain something much more valuable, but you will also lose something in exchange.
- Take small steps today and continue every day.

- Monitor whether you stay on track. If necessary, correct your course.
- Do something for yourself, and something for your family, your community and your country.

Below, I am listing randomly selected examples of possible next steps. Realistic possible next steps can only be defined by you, and effectively executed by you. Do not overwhelm yourself but do what is in your sphere of influence. You can always extend your capabilities and sphere of influence but do it in tiny steps – to stay motivated.

My level:

- Simply practice not buying any guns.
- Simply practice not carrying a gun. In fact, it can be much easier than not carrying your smartphone.
- Define what it means for you to feel safe and then advocate for it within your community and when talking to your governmental officials. Feeling safe is a foundational right and starting point for other aspects of one's personal and social life. Feeling safe is the single most critical prerequisite of a happy life.
- To build social trust, make sure you educate yourself and your family. Base your knowledge wisely on different (sometimes antagonistic/in conflict) information sources and come up with your own opinion about at least key topics: health care, crime and guns, inequality & employment, education, immigration, racism, identity politics, abortion, drug addiction, legal and financial system or climate change.
- While communicating, listen actively first, before giving any advice or expressing your quick judgments.
- Take enough time to get to know the subject matter as well as the people you are talking to, including their individual motivations, aspirations, knowledge, experience, thinking patterns or communication styles and culture.
- Learn how to discuss showing respect and protecting other people's dignity.
- Learn something new, every day.

- Reading one book about the military, for instance: *Call Sign Chaos: Learning to Lead* by Jim Mattis and Bing West.
- Turn off real-time television for good. Allow only on-demand content to reach your attention. Go on an information diet.

Country level:

- Send a letter or e-mail to your political representative (e.g. state governor, city mayor) and ask him or her question about his or her goals and strategy for domestic peace.
- Request a personal meeting with your political representative and ask him or her important questions, "What are you doing to keep me, my family and my neighbors safe?" "What is your detailed plan to improve the safety of your citizens on the streets, in schools or in their homes?"
- Vote in elections.
- Organize local community meetings, invite people to garden parties, and start discussions on the "how to live a safer life," the "quality of life" and "the human flourishing index." Ask everyone, "What can we do together to create a better future?"

CHAPTER 5

My Happiness

Mindful, responsible, socially connected

and giving to others

How do I know I am happy?

- I am satisfied with my life most of the time.
- I am satisfied with the way my life is going, regardless of whether I laughed or smiled yesterday.
- But to be honest, I tend to laugh and smile almost every day.
- I perceive my life as meaningful and worthwhile.
- I feel that my life is good. It could always be better, but it's not bad.
- I am experiencing much more joy and positive well-being than sadness or dissatisfaction.
- I am experiencing more (not many more) "positive" emotions than "negative" ones. All of them are important for me and critical for self-assessment, self-control, and self-calibration. Of course, "positive" ones trigger pleasant feelings, and I prefer them to unpleasant ones.
- In fact, I am usually in the so-called "normal" state, without exaggerated emotions.
- I have a sense of fulfillment.
- I feel gratitude.
- I have and maintain social connections based on trust and kindness.

Unfortunately, my brain and body have formed some inappropriate habits which generate short-term pleasure, but at the same time cause adverse long-term consequences. I am not addicted to any substances or to gambling, but that doesn't mean my physical body "rests in peace" and has no wants or temptations. My current state is the result of luck, morality, and free will. I govern my own needs and desires rather than becoming their servant or slave. When you play with the same toy long enough, the toy may start playing with you, or playing you, steering you, and manipulating you. The addictive nature of human beings is not foreign to me and forces certain levels of alertness. I sense it more like stinging stress than burning anxiety. It is a dynamic process that requires an effort to balance it all. Without going into the details some of my weaknesses, like cravings for chocolate or eating before bed, are repetitive in nature. These already have a negative impact on my overall well-being, and may become more damaging if they are not tamed.

Despite these addictions, I think I am living a good life, that is, one with a sense of meaning, deep contentment, and solid connectedness to the world.

What makes me happy?

Small things:

- The tender words of my wife, her smile, and when she hugs me and gentle strokes my head. No more details are necessary.
- When I come back home after a business trip and look at the happy faces of my wife and my children.
- When my children cuddle up to me, especially when we are lying in bed, before they fall asleep.
- When I take a morning shower in a hot water, and I have amazing ideas and visions.
- When I play the piano and interpret songs in my own way.
- When I listen to beautifully harmonized jazz music, and the piano is the leading instrument.

- When I play semi-competitive soccer for "dinosaurs"- it has to be "painful" and tough.
- When I immerse in the mysterious world of theater or musicals. I love reading poetry as well.
- When I eat (European) chocolate mousse or (natural) whipped cream cake with raspberries.
- When I drink hot green tea or black tea with lemon or organic iced green tea.
- When I listen to audiobooks or podcasts while driving.
- When I watch documentary movies or psychological thrillers.
- When I have even short conversations with my friends (in person or over video).
- When I buy anything I want, whenever I want, as long as it does not cost more than $100. That is a positive side effect of limited desires for material things. What financial freedom.
- When I eat my favorite breakfast or lunch at my favorite places, as long as it does not cost more than $25. What a luxury.
- When I finally go to bed. I love going back to my bed at the end of the day. It's a blissful feeling.
- When I go to bed in the middle of the day (rarely on Saturdays). This is the greatest luxury I can experience without any major investments.
- When I go for massages. This is the greatest luxury I can experience with some investments.

Bigger things:

- When I have a "deep" conversation with my children, and I am amazed by their natural wisdom.
- When I have "deep" conversations with people.
- When I am on stage interacting with large audiences and having heated discussions.
- When I work with people. When I orchestrate. When I lead.
- When I brainstorm ideas, create prototypes, and shape business models. When I solve problems.
- When I work on ambitious projects, and when I see progress and tangible results.
- When I engage with the Youth Ministry leadership at the Church.

- When I design my life-coaching workshops.
- When my family goes for 3-week vacations to unknown, foreign places.
- When my family organizes special family events (birthdays, Christmas Eve(s)…).

Larger things:

- When I write a book for 12 months or more.
- When I relocate with my family to different countries for 3 or more years.
- When I engage in life-saving interventions for others (providing water, heat, clothing, shelter, housing, assistance in recovering from addictions or anxiety, and inspire, motivate, and bring hope to others).

What is the root cause of my being happy?

The shortest possible answers are:

I was loved, I am loved, I hope to be loved by others.

I loved, I love, and I want to love others.

I got, I get, I hope to get from others.

I gave, I give, I want to give to others.

"We make a living by what we get, but we make a life by what we give". [ccxi]

Who gave me what I got?

Who and what have influenced my happy life?

* * *

My wife: *Love, affection, tenderness, sacrifice, life, time and attention, acceptance, faith...*
My mother: *unconditional love, care, time and attention, acceptance, courage, curiosity, support, perseverance, playing the piano, faith (spirit)...*
My father: *presence, love, responsibility, knowledge, perseverance, joy from music, humor, English, faith (mind)...*
My brother: *perseverance, strength, focus, how to raise small children, minimalism, faith...*
My grandmother: *time and attention, perseverance, patriotism, nature, painting skills, faith...*
My grandfather: *responsibility, perseverance, entrepreneurship, respect for people, work, money, car, faith...*
My mother-in-law: *time and attention, acceptance, trust, sacrifice, faith...*
My father-in-law: *time and attention, acceptance, trust, responsibility, faith...*
My brothers and sisters-in-law & families: *acceptance, trust, fun, joy...*
My sister-in-law: *self-development, critical thinking, courage...*
My cousins: *acceptance, fun, joy...*
My aunts and uncles: *time and attention, acceptance...*
My American aunt and uncle, Sharon, Bill, and my cousin Stefan: *time and attention, encouragement, Love, joy, a healthy distance from the world, wisdom, and all those gifts, presents and greeting cards you have sent to me...*

* * *

My early education primary school teacher: *inclusion, care, tenderness...*
My middle and high school physics teachers: *inspiration, curiosity, my first science and physics concepts...*
My high school English teacher: *inspiration, joy, critical thinking...*
My music teacher: *trust, appreciation, joy, love for music...*
My piano teacher: *acceptance, joy, love for music, playing the piano, improvisation...*
My high school PE teacher: *acceptance, joy, love for sport...*

* * *

My friends:
Krzysiek & family: *time and attention, acceptance, support, fun, joy...*
Marcin & family: *time and attention, acceptance, support, fun, joy...*
Artur & family: *time and attention, acceptance, support, fun, joy...*
Maciek & Gosia: *time and attention, acceptance, support, fun, joy, lifetime friendship, god-fatherhood to my child...*
Tomek & Mirka: *time and attention, acceptance, support, fun, joy, lifetime friendship, god-fatherhood to my child...*
Father Wojciech & Father Tomasz: *time and attention, acceptance, support, fun, joy...*
Grzesiu & family: *time and attention, acceptance, support, fun, joy...*
Maciej & Monika: *time and attention, acceptance, support, fun, joy...*
Michał & Agata: *time and attention, acceptance, support, fun, joy...*
Adam & Anka: *time and attention, acceptance, support, fun, joy...*
Gosia & family: *time and attention, acceptance, support, fun, joy...*
Grzesiu & family: *time and attention, acceptance, support, fun, joy...*
Marek & family: *time and attention, acceptance, support, fun, joy...*

Seba & Joanna: *time and attention, acceptance, support, fun, joy...*
Sławek & Beata: *time and attention, acceptance, support, fun, joy...*
Gośka & Tomek: *time and attention, acceptance, support, fun, joy, god-motherhood to my child...*
Stefan & Evelyn: *long-life friendship, support, international experience, fun, joy...*
Marta & Harry: *time and attention, acceptance, support, fun, joy...*
Agnieszka & Arek: *time and attention, acceptance, support, fun, joy...*
Kristin & Franzi: *openness, balance, diversity, real-life discussions, fun, joy...*
Iza & Sam: *time and attention, acceptance, support, fun, joy...*
Leah & Steve: *time and attention, love, inclusion, acceptance, support, U.S. culture, fun, joy...*
Jessica & Valentin: *time and attention, acceptance, support, fun, joy, board-games time, grill, blower...*
Kelly & Tim: *time and attention, acceptance, support, fun, joy, lawn support, scooter...*
Uzma & Tariq: *time and attention, acceptance, support, fun, joy, fresh vegetables and mint...*
Bethani and Adam: *time and attention, acceptance, inclusion, U.S. culture, fun, joy...*
Jennifer & Rolf: *time and attention, acceptance, inclusion, support, love in action, friendship, U.S. culture, fantastic humor, fun, joy...*
Ann & Bill ("American father & mother"): *love, time and attention, acceptance, lifelong friendship, wisdom, joy...*

* * *

My business leaders:
Dariusz: *inclusion, trust, appreciation, discipline, sense of humor...*
Rafał: *inclusion, attention, trust, curiosity, goals setting, situational leadership...*
Yves: *trust, group dynamics, informed decisions, education, co-financing MBA...*
Edwin: *discipline, warmth, trust, international exposure & development...*
Steve: *managing politics, wisdom, trust, international exposure & development...*
Thomas: *trust, inclusion, appreciation...*
Rolf: *time, roles and responsibilities, processes, attention to detail, discipline...*
Regina: *time, passion, joy, smile...*
Noel: *trust, talent development, growth, sense of humor, efficiency...*
Matthias: *trust, talent development, growth, efficiency...*
Helmut: *inclusion, time and attention, support, composure, leadership...*
Bill: *strategic thinking, leadership, emotional-intelligence, sense of humor, growth...*
Ana Maria: *trust, courage, dedication, transparency, friendship, warmth...*
Drazen: *trust, experience, complexity management, high-level pictures, strategic thinking...*
Bryce & Chad: *ownership, speed and inclusion...*
Dirk: *time and attention, active listening, mentoring, executives' perspectives, leadership...*
Joyce: *focus, discipline, customer orientation, faith, executives' mindset, leadership...*

* * *

My employees and co-workers:
Andre, Beth, Bob, Bobbie, Casey, Chandar, Dale, Danny, Dave, David, Deb, Debbie, Deborah, Dennis, Gordon, Julie, Kathleen, Kumar, Kyle, Madhukar, Mike, Nan, Phil, Ray, Roxy, Ron, Snell, Stan, Steve, Teresa, Vijay, Bill, Zach; Marek, Jarek, Jarek P., Wlodek, Sławek S., Robert, Sławek, Michał, Dariusz, Robert N., Zsolt P., Zsolt T., Krzysztof, Vladimir, Radomil, Zbynek, Agnieszka, Jolanta, Sylwia, Norbert, Beata, Michał G., Marek C., Mietek, Magdalena, Agnieszka S., Halina, Beata, Dariusz D., Dorian, Mateusz, Zoltan, Roman, Michal M., Maciej, Gaweł, Tomasz, Marcin, Peter, Peter D.; Shafie, Ehsan and other excellent colleagues: *hard work, reliability and credibility, teamwork, professionalism, partnership, trust, tolerance (you tolerated me), joy...*

* * *

My functional peers and partners:
Markus, Harald, Martin, Stefano, Marc, Malcolm, Dave, Francisco, Irmgard, Lars, Philip, Christian, Uwe, Orit, Atanas, Selwyn, Duncan, Marin, Duncan, Sandrine; Isaac, Nazim, Franjo, Rene, Holger, Sharon, Torsten; Brian, Ravi, Brian L, Kathleen, Alex, Carmen, Chris, George, Mark C., Robert H., Brian K., Marc, Bill P., Lisa F., Richard, Thomas, David A., Jorge, Shawn H., John K., Allison, Joan, Jim M, George N., Kim, Susan S., Carl T., Philip V., Pat, Sharon B., Farah, David S, Stefan R., Cyndi, Johannah, Vincent, Katie, Mike, Terrie, Traci, Tom, Daria, David H., Terri, Tony, Greg, Sangeeta, Hobart, Tierdyn, Peter, Christopher, Lisa, Jay, Zsuzsanna, Jesus, Priscilla, Henning, Mark, Sai, Kathy, Dave, Meg, Melissa, Risa, Dirk, Julia, Diana; Alan, Clay, Daniel, Sandra, Michael, Stephanie, Christian, Kevin, Eric, Brad, Thomas, Chris, Ivonne, Elizabeth, Victoria and other excellent colleagues: *teamwork, professionalism, partnership, leadership, tolerance (you tolerated me), joy...*

* * *

My business peers and partners:
Andy, David M., David, Greg, Jessica, Kent, Lauren, Monique, Nancy, Robert, Sebastian, Stefan, Tim; Joshua, Beatrix, Jaan, Ann, Brian, Douglas, Josh, Jim, Bob G., Scott, Susan, Jim, Zachary, Scott, John, Dion, Elizabeth, Lynn, Jeriel, Barb, Lance, Praveen, Ihsan, Mark, John, Larry, Mason, Brian, Alex, Asela, Kristine; Kevin, Rhett, Laura, Mary; Peter, Ted, Marek, Frumi, Lisa, Kayla, John FK, Ethan, Jacob; Marek K, Paweł; Tomasz K., Tomasz N., Marcin, Marta, Krystyna, Maria, Krzysztof, Marcin P., Adam S., James, Anna, Justyna, Monika, Remigiusz, Paweł F., Paweł Ł., Beata, Krzysztof S., Michał W., Marek, Hanna, Daria, Marta, Edyta, Dariusz, Tobias, Jost, Christophe, Charles, Markus, Liska, Matthew and other excellent colleagues: *teamwork, professionalism, partnership, leadership, tolerance (you tolerated me), joy...*

* * *

My spiritual leaders:
Pope John Paul II: *faith, who God is, being a role model, courage, strength, Holy Mary...*
Father Robert Skrzypczak, Father Piotr Pawlukiewicz, Father Janusz Chwast, Father Adam Szustak, Bishop Robert Barron: *faith, knowledge, who God is, what love is, what spiritual life is...*
Pastor Adam Hamilton: *faith, knowledge, critical thinking, who God is, what love is, what practical love is, what life is, what family is, what diversity and inclusion are...*

* * *

My thought leaders:
Eckhart Tolle, Jordan Peterson, Oprah Winfrey, Sam Harris, Trevor Noah, David Rubin: *although we have never met in person, I am thankful for your inspiration, stimulation of my critical thinking, your fight for a better world and that you seek the truth...*

* * *

My Rezlife[ccxii] Student Ministry leaders and co-leaders:
Rev. Ashley, Taylor, Chris, Evan, Alex, Dan, Bill and other leaders: *mentoring, youth ministry orchestration, leadership, life examples, testimonies of faith...*
My sophomore guys from Rezlife[ccxiii] Student Life Group:
Adin, Aiden, Andrew, Ashton, Baxter, Ben, Benjamin, Cole, Drew, Gabe, Garrett, Hunter, Jackson, Jake, JD, Jonathan, Kaleb, Lance, Mack, Ryan, Rylan, Seth, Thomas, Ty, Tyler, Sam and Cooper: *honesty, frankness, energy, faith, fun...*

* * *

My soccer team buddies:
Kalesony's teammates, Rock 'n' Ball's teammates, Imports' teammates, OP Ballers' teammates, FC KC's teammates, Bayer's teammates, Schering's teammates: *brotherhood, persistence, prowess, joy...*

* * *

Santa Claus: *Lego box, formula1 toy, tape player with radio, Atari computer, and at least 43+ more presents...*
Eater Bunny: *10s of Kinder Eggs, 10s of Chocolate Bunnies, and at least 43+ more small presents...*
Tooth Fairy: *in fact never gave me anything – maybe she didn't know where Europe was. I forgave her years ago.*

* * *

My own children:
Paulina: *unconditional Love, happiness and joy, fatherhood, walk-the-talk, creativity and not giving up...*
Szymon: *unconditional Love, happiness and joy, fatherhood, walk-the-talk, passion and patience...*
Kornelia: *unconditional Love, happiness and joy, fatherhood, walk-the-talk, sense of humor and helping others...*

* * *

My godchildren:
Julia: *love, joy, "unclehood," independence, carpe diem, filmmaking...*
Jagoda: *love, joy, "unclehood," perfection, hardworking, ambition...*
Piotrek: *love, joy, "unclehood," passion, perfection, overcoming adversity, playing chess, soccer...*
Marcel: *love, joy, "unclehood," passion, courage, playing video games...*

My family's children:
Jacek, Kalinka, Magda, Iwo, Oluś, Piotruś, Alan...: *love, fun, joy...*

My family friends' children:
Jaś, Staś, Kapi, Nina, Marta, Julia, Karolina, Natalia, Mateusz, Matylda, Misia, Jaś, Staś, Ola, Krzyś, Piotr, Maciek...: *fun, joy...*

* * *

I can go on and on. It is overwhelming to look at what I have been given. I am speechless. I am grateful.

I am not exaggerating here at all. Those meaningful relationships have formed me. Those meaningful gifts have equipped me and prepared me well for tough adventures in life. Those meaningful friendships have made me fearless. This is not rocket science, this is simply the power of meaningful connectedness. I got my life wisdom taking from those trusted wisdoms. I know that in difficult times I have people that I can lean on, people whom I can trust, people who will support me and help me, no matter what, anytime, anyplace. One "look" away, one "word" away, one "phone ring" away, one "e-mail" away, one "short text message" away. I never talk to them through social networks. I should say, I never pretend that I talk to them through social networks. We talk using spoken words. We talk and hear each other at the same time. We even talk, hear, and can see each other at the same time. We interact. We feel each other's presence, we feel and anticipate each other's emotional states. We listen to hear, we talk to be heard. These are real, existing, tangible, ready-to-respond, ready-to-stand-up for me human beings. And, I am for them anytime, anyplace, too. We act, we react, we prevent, we solve, we participate, we collaborate. We trust! We connect!

In times of serious suffering, although surrounded by those who truly love me and wish me well, I am alone. There are moments in our lives in which we are always alone, no matter how great the empathy or compassion of those who surround us is. There is no way we can pass all of our suffering or pain on to anybody, even if a person who immeasurably loves us is voluntary asking for it. Regardless of one's mastery in mindfulness, meditation, and contemplation, there is always a pain that turns back our illusion of "selflessness" back into an illusion of the "self" who begs for mercy. In moments when pain is not bearable any more, what makes us want to survive is staying with those we love, or fulfilling our life purpose and then giving meaning to this extreme suffering.

My biology: *formed me into my life, gave me my body, energy, health, thoughts, "illusion of self," talents and more.*

It was not my plan to be born the way I was born. It was not due to my effort. It was not my personal achievement or my merit. It was pure luck. A small dose of self-awareness and knowledge helped me to keep what I got and stay alive.

My God: *life, hope, fearlessness, love, compassion, mercifulness, meaning, purpose.*

Finally, I decided to believe in God's existence and God's "I AM-ness" in response to God's grace - to consciously accept God's gifts for me. I have no doubt that this decision has opened me up and has given me access to the ultimate source of the deepest and broadest love, peace, joy, happiness, and life in an abundance. Although, I am very far from the "prosperity gospel's" reasoning, I experience abundance in my spiritual life and "just enough abundance" in my so-called material life. Trusting in God results in fearlessness. Fearlessness is the foundation of happiness, freedom, courage and creativity. Once you have no fear, you don't need to meditate eight hours per day in seclusion or become an impersonal consciousness. Once you have no fear, you don't need to be afraid of your own thoughts, of yesterday, today, and tomorrow. Once you have no fear, you don't need to be afraid of other people's opinions. Once you have no fear, you can trust. Once you have no fear, you are hopeful. With this decision, I have opened myself up to fearless life in an existential and non-existential sense. Fearlessness and love (which includes responsibility) paired with "just enough life conditions" make us well-evolved, flourishing, happy humans.

"Let your faith be bigger than your fear"

That one sentence can have tremendous power to change people's lives.

I have no doubt that I know that I believe in God. Scientifically advanced atheists would immediately challenge that statement, saying, "There is no God because there is no evidence of God's existence," "You didn't decide anything yourself, you were taught (or brainwashed) early enough to believe, and because it became your worldview (your truth about the world) you had no choice not to believe," "But what are we talking about? There is no "you," there is no "I" in the first place. Your brain generates thoughts by itself, creating the illusion of your existence as well as any God's existence," "You need God, because you are in existential fear," "You need God, because you believe in your existence, and by that you separate yourself from everything that is," "You are alone in fear and you need help," "You haven't yet exposed yourself or practiced enough deep mindfulness to be able to see a different, alternative reality. You haven't been confronted with the indescribable experience of being enlightened." "You haven't discovered oneness with everything, and with that, a lack of personal identification and personal suffering." "Or maybe you are poorly educated and believe in stories told by the gifted storytellers." Later in this book, I describe why God exists for me, and that there is no rational or scientific way to challenge such a statement.

I decided to believe in God's existence, to consciously accept God's gifts for me, these are: my life itself, other people's lives, the possibility of peaceful unity of all that is, the reality of love – to will the good of others[ccxiv] (including acts of kindness between beings) that leads to unity, no fear, the hope that everything that happens makes sense, that everything that happens has a meaning, a purpose, and a happy end. With no evidence of an afterlife, would you prefer for there to be an afterlife or not? You may say, it depends. What if the afterlife is worse than the present? Then the perspective of the afterlife is obviously not attractive. But what if there is an equally probable option and there is a wonderful afterlife? Since no one can prove that any scenario is correct, or invalid, it seems it is a matter of individual decision – what reality or "after-reality" I hope to see. I have already made my decision. What about you? What do you prefer? What is your decision, at least for now?

In addition to all that I received, listed above,

I was given freedom from the past and current generation of heroes.

I was treated with respect and dignity.

I was provided with decent living conditions (food, shelter, clothing), care, education and safety.

I got access to life opportunities.

I am overwhelmed at what I got. I am shocked. I have no words. I am lucky, or using my language, I am blessed. I am happy. I am so grateful.

Here is my private message to those beautiful people I mentioned above and many others I didn't mention (only due to limited space in this book): "You made me! I am a product of your availability, readiness, willingness, effort, interventions, actions, goodness, care and love!" If

God is hearing me now: "I indeed was born again, because of You. You gave me my purpose".

"What an unrealistic view," some would say. I admit, after I wrote these things down, I was suspicious and confused as well. "It cannot be that I am so lucky." "But in fact, I am." All of those meaningful relationships have been formed, all of those other gifts have been given and received. Of course, this is my brain that creates my perception of reality and helps make it more positive than negative. That is obvious. But what caused this in the first place? I bet it was caused by the things that my brain was exposed to (especially in the very early stages of life). Its own characteristics and predispositions play a huge role as well. So, again, it was an enormous amount of luck, and a bit of free will (which operated on the basis of the accepted ultimate goal and moral system). Some scientifically advanced atheists and non-atheists could argue that there is no such a thing as free will, and that everything is deterministic. Thoughts come and go by themselves. There is no need for me to influence them. Later in this chapter, I refer to the reality of free will, that on the human level, it does exist, and it reveals itself in a conscious decision-making process. The negation of "free will" may come from a misunderstanding of how the properties of complex systems, such as the mind, arise, or may come from a misunderstanding of the definition of "free will" and the expectations we have for it, or it is the result of intentional manipulation to achieve hidden benefits or other goals.

What I would wish my children to be given to live a happy life?

I would respond:

1. Give them **acceptance**, **care**, and **love**. Teach them to love.
2. Introduce them to the **unconditional love** of God as well as to the concept of **eternal life**.
3. Give them **hope, fearlessness,** and **purpose**.
4. Give them **food, shelter, clothing**, a **clean environment**, **education**, and **healthcare**.
5. Teach them **responsibility** and **self-control**. Equip them with a **moral compass**.
6. Teach them how to create **meaningful relationships**.
7. Teach them **critical thinking** and that every **decision** they make shapes their destiny.
8. Teach them how to be **mindful** and how to **listen** and **talk to God**.
9. Give them **freedom**.
10. Show them how to **give** and **give thanks**.

What if someone is less lucky and not equipped to become happy?

Unfortunately, there are millions of people in our country who were not adequately prepared and equipped to experience happy lives. Fortunately, there are millions of others who were. So, how do we move forward? Isn't it an obvious call for all of us to become more sensitive, mindful and intentional, and thus notice each other more, see each other's presence, life situations and offer encouragement and support? Isn't it an obvious call for all of us to start giving, sharing, supporting, helping, designing better ("more-lucky") social systems, teaching people how to contribute to better social systems, teaching generosity, and sharing? Giving and teaching others to give back sounds like a good formula.

"We make a living by what we get, but we make a life by what we give".[ccxv]

What if someone is less lucky and not equipped to become happy? What if we help him/her? As with everything in life, we may want to keep a healthy balance and not overload the recipient so that he/she remains curious and motivated to grow. We need to provide strong foundations and then let him/her go on his/her own. Let's give them acceptance, care, love, food, shelter, clothing, a clean environment, education, and healthcare. Let's teach them love, teach them to walk, teach them to fish, teach them to think, teach them to solve, teach them to search, teach them to cooperate, teach them to give back. Because there will always be a deficit of love, we need to introduce them to unconditional love.

Will it be possible to heal all the wounds we have collected throughout our lives, including those of physical abuse, emotional abuse, abandonment, rejection, betrayals, poverty, etc.? Probably not. To heal them partially - in a way that they no longer block us from experiencing happiness in our lives, I think the answer is, yes. We have developed many useful psychotherapeutic and healing methods that help us get back to our desired state. Some of us may require medical intervention to experience happiness, in which case specialist-led treatment improves our quality of life in a sustainable way. What is also worth mentioning is that our human hearts are so deep that to satisfy them, in full, is impossible. Those desires make our lives exciting, but at the same time cause suffering - the tension between what is and what we want it to be. We also have countermeasures to address those tensions, from ancient practices, to modern spiritual and religious practices, to extremes, like the psychedelic practices that produce hallucinations and apparently expand consciousness, providing at least short-term relief from accumulated daily life stresses. Because continuous and frequent exposure to psychedelic dreaming causes disastrous consequences like depression, addiction, or death, we cannot rely on that path at all. We can engage in meditation and mindfulness practices following, for instance, Buddha's teaching and walking His paths – and by losing our "selves," and the associated desires, ultimately reduce our suffering. But the moment we gain the illusion of "no self," the illusion of "self" wants to be noticed – it wants to come back. The "self" also has a natural need to cling to other selves and interact with them. This "being together" thing is a mysterious property of the self. It seems there will always be something in us wanting something else. Maybe these dynamics, this movement, this balancing, this unstoppable trading-off is called life. Don't you think? Such a life happens on a continuum between these two extremes: either you make yourself "selfless," or you blow your illusory self ("ego") out to extreme and in so doing separate yourself from the world, become lonely and fearful. The more you move away, the more alien and scary the world becomes, the more frightened you become. Is living a good life a process of finding a good balance between such extremes? Being yourself instead of being a "impersonal existence". Being alone vs. being together. Being safe vs. being excited about risk. Being spontaneous or being structured. Maintaining status-quo or changing. Staying or leaving. Believing versus knowing. Loving yourself vs. loving others. Our 'self' wants to have both conflicting attitudes at the same time - this causes frustration and anxiety. Let's assume we decide to live a "normal" human life, spend some time alone, spend some time with others, engage with the world by solving important problems, raise kids, help elderly people, have fun and rest. Experiencing little bit of the "self," we immediately experience a little bit of separateness and fear, as well was a lack of unity and love. In fact, from the moment we separated from our mothers, we have been fearful, and will be till the end of our days. Unconditional love and unity are gone. We miss it. So, now we need to balance fear with love. How can we do that? We need another person to "generate" and experience love. We cannot learn and then practice love alone. Love emerges in a relationship. Does this mean, we need each other? Hell yes!

What if I am less lucky and not equipped to become happy? I had better search for help. I had better seek acceptance, care, and love. I had better ask compassionate people for food, shelter, and clothing, a clean environment, an education and healthcare. I had better act. There are responsibilities on both sides, for lucky people as well as unlucky ones. Unlucky ones are those who have never been given enough to begin their journey to true humanity. The lucky ones are those who have been given enough to flourish. But, as Louis Pasteur[ccxvi] famously said, "Luck favors the prepared mind." Meaning I have to work quite hard to get luckier. It is also worth remembering that lucky ones can at any time, usually unexpectedly, become an unlucky person. "I fell to the ground, woke up in the emergency room and didn't remember anything from my previous life as a lucky man". Such a fragile luck is. Does this mean, we need each other? Let us never forget that.

At the end of the day, as human beings, we are not able to become perfectly lucky or perfectly happy. Our desire for love, to be loved, will never be satisfied. No one and nothing can satisfy our need for love because our human, imperfect love cannot satisfy perfectly. The only hope may come from believing in a perfect love that may exists in a perfect reality practiced by a perfect being.

How do we become ourselves?

Being aware of the fact that I am a product of the evolutionary process as well as a product of all the information that has been registered and accumulated by my body or exchanged with or within my body (including the influence of chemical compounds, e.g. hormones, microorganisms, electromagnetic fields and the like, on one end, and the influence of other people's opinions, on the other) - my "experience of self" and/or my "experience of the illusory self" suddenly asks fundamental questions: Who am I? Where am I from? Why am I here? What 'caused' or created me? What made everything around me happen? Who caused it, instead of, what caused it? 'Am I' a real existence? Assuming 'I am' a real existence, will my existence end one day when my body turns to dust? Already today, as I sleep, I experience the disappearance of the "experience of self" or "illusory experience of self". Does this mean that under certain conditions I can wake up, but under different conditions I will be gone forever? Or will I wake up in another reality of existence and the "experience of self" or the "illusory self"? What is the best possible life I can live now?

What do you think about such a simplified chain of events?

A human baby is conceived in the mother's womb, experiences an enclosed environment, can hear sounds, and can react to stimuli. When she is born, her whole world collapses. Darkness is replaced by light, warmth is replaced by cold, the muffled sounds of the aquatic universe are replaced by the squeak of the airspace, and the baby is separated and is under extreme stress. The baby lies on her mother's chest, hears her heartbeat, hears her voice, calms down, and reunites with her, albeit in a different way.

The baby is growing. As long as she is attached to her mother, there is a big chance she stays calm. Quiet moments end with sudden attacks of crying and screaming if the baby is hungry or has colic - fluctuating pain in the abdomen caused by intestinal gas. No matter how much tenderness is offered, or care is given to the child, when she is hungry or feels pain, she will let everyone know, and will not voluntary stop. Our tiny baby learns to experience the world, which is mainly her mother. When mom goes away the world collapses again, she panics, she is disoriented, and she doesn't like it. Fortunately, mom always comes back. It's a "nice" world.

As the child is growing, slowly but surely, she separates from her mother. It is a period full of suffering, most probably lots of fear and stress. She would prefer to stay together. Instinctively, she prefers it. In addition, whatever she touches, this thing becomes part of her. This is a natural extension of "self". The baby and each of her toys are now one body. When someone tries to take a toy away from her, she screams and shows serious frustration. That is far from "happiness," isn't it? The child and her hunger are also one. A child becomes "a hunger" when she is hungry.

As she grows, thanks to her brain development and external stimuli she becomes more aware of her body. She receives a lot of feedbacks from the world and is exposed to repeated rituals performed by her parents (if anybody smiles, she smiles back, if anybody talks to her, she talks back, if anybody touches her, she touches back, if anybody shows her something, she copies that). She realizes that she has control over her body parts. She starts to move from one place to another. She can see herself in a mirror. Her eyes can see themselves in the eyes of other people (the headless being discovers her head. Later in life she will also discover that this head will carry its central processing unit, the brain - the whole world enclosed in a "narrow mind"). She starts calling herself by name, and finally by "I." This always evolving "I" is like painting a picture incessantly, layer by layer, shape by shape, color by color. This "I" is like an enormous sponge absorbing water, but instead of water it absorbs huge amounts of sensual experiences, encodes them into information and stores them. Whatever the "I" hears, it treats it as a "new self" or "enriched self". Each new experience becomes part of an "adjusted self". One day the "I" is Spiderman, another is Superman. When the "self" hears from its loved ones: "You are so beautiful," "You are so smart," "You are so brave," "You are so good," "You are so talented and so hard working" - the "I" immediately believes in it and becomes what it believes in. Yesterday the "I" was the winner of the Super Bowl, today the "I" is the commander of the spacecraft, etc.

"I" never stops its expansion, never stops learning, never rests. It mainly develops by repetition, by imitating others. "I" never stops thinking, and as of now, it thinks that it really thinks. There comes the day when our grown-up child's big "I" meets another "I," bigger or smaller then it, which does not glorify it, does not even accept its presence, way of being, style, behaviors, reactions, thoughts or decisions. Big "I" is totally confused, it feels under attack, becomes frustrated, sarcastic, angry and ready to fire back. Instead of "love" it feels something else, similar to the feeling of being hungry, being separated, being robbed of part of itself. It feels a little bit smaller, but still strong enough to react and defend itself. "How dare you treat me like this?" "How dare you tell me I'm not a genius scientist, a brilliant painter, or a great businessman and leader?" Alien "I" tries to influence and change our big "I," but it faces opposition. Big "I" suddenly stops learning as it used to learn before. There comes the day when our grown-up child's big "I" does not receive what it has always been receiving. "How is it possible that there are no more free rooms?" "Why am I not allowed to park here?" "What does it mean that I don't work here anymore?" "Are you telling me I don't have any money?" "What cancer are you talking about? There must be a mistake." "Are you leaving me or is this a joke?" "Is he alive?" "Oh, no."

There are times, when "I" is afraid of being "I." There are times when "I" does not want to be "I" anymore. But, fortunately, the "I" we are talking about got solid foundations at the very beginning. In those horrible moments, moments of trial, its brain starts its core program (like a computer 'BIOS' - booting program) and comes to the rescue. A brain wired with hope starts seeing meaning in this suffering. The process of leaving the dark has just begun. Who knows, if "I" will fully recover, but with strong "fearless" roots, surrounded by other friendly "I(s)," and a strong work ethic, the chances are pretty high.

What about a child who wasn't hugged right after her birth or afterward, who wasn't served when she was hungry, who wasn't comforted when she was in pain, who wasn't surrounded by people to take care of her. What if her mother had to work three shifts to make a living and had no time to offer an unconditional love to that innocent child? What if her violent father left her family before her thirteenth birthday. But before he abandoned her, he hurt her deeply and damaged her for the rest of her life. Such a picture of false fatherly love will determine all his future relationships and ways of solving problems. "You're a loser." "I'm ashamed of you." "How can you be so stupid." "You don't try hard enough." "You never win." "It's your fault." "I can't help you anymore." "No, you can't do it." "Don't do it." "I forbid you." "You broke it again." "I don't want to see you again." Her "I" has just found out what it is and what it is not and never will be. Her "self", though larger than the child's initial self, is a product of threats, hatred, betrayal, failure and guilt.

Her "I" does not dream about anything special. It wants peace and silence. Her "I" does not dream about creating anything good, but rather plans revenge and feeds its anger. She is convinced that she is useless, and the world reflects that back to her. It is a self-fulfilling prophecy. How can she become a happy person or at least a little bit happier? Her brain was programmed for self-destruction, her life experiences gave her enough reasons to believe that there would not be any way out. We are not yet even talking about education, or access to healthcare. We are at the very bottom of the pyramid of needs, where dreaming of something incredible, contributing to the greater good, enjoying the beauty of art, admiring the beauty of nature, immersing in spirituality, calling God our father and Love of the world etc. is totally out of reach. First things first. "I" must be loved first, so that it can love in return. Is this a hopeless situation?

Each of us was hurt by someone in our lives, to a greater or lesser extent. The most severe hurts are usually caused by the people we love the most and those who should love us. There was no way that all your needs were always met, there was no way that your fears were always mitigated. Each of us has been hurt and, as a result, transfers this trauma back into relationships with others - in most cases, doing so unconsciously. I believe there is a way out, especially for those "I(s)" without serious psychosomatic conditions. What about the following logic? This is an enormous simplification, of course:

- I was born into a dysfunctional family, though not of my own will.
- My life situation is the result of good or bad luck.
- Despite my level of luck, there is never enough love that could satisfy me, hence I experience fear.
- I got hurt by someone I loved, or who was supposed to love me. I carry a lot of emotional wounds.
- My adult "self" has been shaped for many years by the forces of nature, other people, and my brain's activity.
- My adult mind is thinking its thoughts without my intervention. I have the illusion that I think.
- My destiny is built of every decision "I" made (on behalf of me).
- Because decisions are made in a "self-thinking" brain, they are not really my decisions. This is not my destiny.
- My behaviors and my actions are mainly triggered by the decisions that "I" made (on behalf of me).
- My brain observes the results of my behaviors and actions and confirms to itself that "that's the way the world is" (Or as Forky from "Toy Story 4" would say: "That's just the way the cookie crumbles![ccxvii]"). I stay in my mental prison and grow into it more and more.

How do I break this cycle? How do I condition my brain to think my own, better thoughts? We may try to come back to our virgin "I," the most core "I," without any layers, levels, labels, imprinted thinking patterns, worldviews, regrets, or desires. Arriving at a state of pure being would be the most optimal one.

There are some promising practices that can be used, like mindfulness, meditation, prayer, contemplative prayer, various psychology and psychotherapy schools or other mind-oriented trainings. Although I am not suggesting any very lengthy therapy, as it is not about the past, but about the present and the future.

"We actually have the chance to reframe things in our life in [...] powerful ways [...] It means we can use these framing techniques to change around our experience. We don't actually have to change our physiology to change whether or not some experience makes us happy or sad." ccxviii – Laurie Santos, Associate Professor at Yale University

"We actually don't even have to change the past or have avoided certain negative experiences in the past if we can reframe them in the future. [...]

You are always free to tell yourself a new story about the past. [...]

You can actually just change your relationship to something that used to be a source of suffering for you and in that sense reach into the past and put it to some order." ccxix – Sam Harris, an American author, philosopher, neuroscientist, and podcast host.

I propose to enrich these statements with one additional mandatory condition: "We actually have the chance to reframe things in our life in powerful ways" and become much happier as long as we set the immaculate ideal as our new reference point.

- Reaching pure presence or at least a kind of "beginner's mind" (having an attitude of openness, eagerness, and a lack of preconceptions or judgements, just as every beginner has) may require lots of effort and self-discipline. Such an intentional and non-judgmental attitude of the observer of his own thoughts should lead to the acceptance of the world, forgiveness for those who have hurt us so much and freedom from guilt for the life that was led on our behalf by one of the unconscious versions of the illusory "I".

- Now, to be able to come back to reality and enjoy human interactions, especially with loved ones, we have to build our proper reasoning based on the best possible recipe. The whole process can be compared to the restoration of an old house.
- First, we dismantle our house. We do it layer by layer, starting with removing the roof. Then we disassemble the attic, and eliminate the stairs. Then we demolish the walls and garage. We continue until we encounter the hard core of the basement and foundations (like peeling onions).
- Second, we build a totally new house, but on solid foundations.
- To experience "free will" and be in charge of the shape of our future house – our life, we have to stay as close as possible to our consciousness - being in our "meta-thinking" that observes the thoughts of our mind. We need to be ready to define our ultimate life purpose, goals, and the best possible way to achieve them – our path of truth we want to walk, our role model we want to follow, our moral framework. We may want this moral framework to be ideal, and also practical. This is the most critical element of our renewal. We need a true mentor for our souls.
- It would be miraculous if someone loved me unconditionally before I started my new life. It would be wonderful if I also fell in love with this first and pure love – my first meaningful relationship. It would be beautiful if someone could show me how to do it best, accompany me support me, and wait for me at the end of the road with open arms and a smile.
- Once we have realized our "fake self" and we are ready to re-build it, once we have defined our life purpose, something bigger than ourselves, once we have an idea of how can we contribute to "the greater good" of the world, we can decide what path we want to follow and who we are going to walk with. It would be very good to have at least one kind and wise human being next to us and one ideal being beyond our comprehension. The ideal represents someone who never gives up, betrays, or leaves us, and who never stops supporting and loving us.
- We are now ready to be born again. Our life is in our hands. Our decisions, which are validated based on the moral framework of our chosen ideal, give us firsthand experience of our "free will" – the most critical property that evolves only in us, in the whole universe

– the quality that makes us true human beings. Our decisions, which originate from an agreed purpose and goals, make us the main constructor of our own destiny as well as a key influencer in the world around us.

Now, the key question is, what is the best reality of the highest ideal to which our "free will" would like to refer and would like to follow. On the way back to our more real "self" and happier life, we may not yet want to aim for purpose in the afterlife, or wrestle with perfect moral systems. But the danger is that whatever human-type-idol we select as our role model and travel partner, he/she can always fail badly, disappoint us and hurt us badly. The decision is up to you. I decided to follow my ideal, my highest truth, my God. And to be more practical, I decided to follow Jesus of Nazareth, the son of God, and God himself – my unquestionable role model (I explain it in the chapter, My Creator). And to be honest, I don't know if that was my autonomous decision to follow Him, or if I was chosen and asked to follow Him (this is what I decided to believe). I know at least that I have been continuously trying to respond to His Grace and cooperate with It as much as I can to stay on track. And if you ask me, "what am I really risking here?" The answer is, nothing. Simply nothing. I just decided to believe in the best possible scenario. The highest possible risk of being wrong is that I gain nothing. The highest possible benefit, in case I am right, is I gain everything, including ultimate happiness and an everlasting life.

And of course, let's not confuse happiness with pleasure. There is a huge difference between having pleasure and being happy. There could be situations where one is in pain, but still happy and internally joyful.

"So, when it comes to what we're doing here, we don't just follow what other people say, we learn how to find out for ourselves. So, we start off in life, enjoying our life, you know finding fulfilment in pleasure. There's lots of things to find pleasure in, in this life. You know in movies, in Harry Potter, in Superman, you know and obviously just in travel and all the things which you spend a lot of your money on, seeking pleasures in life, sex, relationships. But we always find out that search for meaning in physical pleasure, even if

it's going to see this amazing scenery. [...] But you know, you go and see beautiful landscapes... I remember going on a pilgrimage once, going to the Taj Mahal. It's supposed to be one of the places to tick off on your, what they call these days, bucket lists, to see these great monuments which people say are the wonders of the world. You just go there, and you sit there, and you ask – Why is this beautiful? Why do so many people come here? Is there something inherently beautiful in the structure or is it just because I'm a sheep, and other people have said it's beautiful, therefore it must be beautiful, therefore I'll go there and get my photograph taken there, tick that one off. You know, always as a monk, as a human being, you're always questioning. Is that really it? You know to see all these places. And of course, there's no end to the places you can visit these days, on these tours. And is that the meaning of life, to actually to go and see [...]

Then I started reading books by Robert Burns and he had a passage there which totally abolished the illusion of finding happiness and pleasure. It was that "Pleasures are like poppies spread, you pluck the flower and the bloom is shed," – the particular type of flower, as soon as you pick it, the petals fall off, or "like the snowfall in the river, white for a moment and then gone forever". [...] But that was the essence of this poem. Pleasures are like poppies spread – we search for meaning in pleasure and we have a lot of pleasure in life.'[xcxx] – Ajahn Brahm, Buddhist monk

That is the process of becoming happier that I know, and that is what I consider part of my worldview. In this case, knowledge is not enough, faith is also required. Again, you challenge motives and truthfulness by observing thoughts, emotions, decisions, results and the overall happiness in your life. After a while you realize that something is not right, that there are so much untamed internal conflicts, contradictions, and inconsistencies. The further away from the "inherited false self," you are, the easier it is to get rid of judgements, toxic relationships, and damages. You move away from "yourself" until you vanish or meet your intellectually and emotionally **naked "I."** You look into the mirror and through the eyes of your "soul" (the purest and most virgin version of your existence, which wants only life and love) and you see everything but your old self. To participate in the world and be a loving valuable human being, you decide to leave the stillness of consciousness and start moving and interact. Being in a deep state of awareness of your purity, you decide to return on your own terms and conditions, in the best possible way. **You decide to follow the most perfect and practical model of a happy life**. You decide to follow the best possible scenario of the best possible life. Although it is hard to understand it, it may be easier to believe it. To take the last step, you need a practical example, a reason to believe that a happy life is possible. You need a life coach, mentor, or authority to listen to, talk to, and follow. You had better pick the best possible master.

You must touch the bottom to be able to really bounce back. That is a life changing process that I know, and I believe in.

Is this a long process? I would say it depends. Its duration depends on one's individual situation, and it can last one short moment or one's entire life. Every process is different for every person. It is usually a painful process. It is a process of dying and being born again. The realization that I am not who I thought I was is very disappointing, sad and painful. Dealing with shame afterwards is painful. Dealing with pride, which immediately rejects a new, uncomfortable truth, is painful. Dealing with pride is crucial, but also very difficult. The "Great Ego" is terrified by the vision of its annihilation. The process of acceptance may be lengthy. After we finally "rest in peace" (with a dead self, but with a living body and "soul") we start the process of rebirth. The world as we knew it, the world as it knew us, does not accept our "new self," or our new "truth-based ego" so easily. Our new life requires the renewal of all relationships, commitments, habits, behaviors, actions, and decisions. It all comes from completely different motivations, goals, and purposes. Renewal means change, cancellation, or establishing something brand new. Is this an easy or difficult process? It can theoretically be a very easy process, but in practice, it is a complex one. The greater the enlightenment you experience, the easier the process will be. The more you trust the Ideal of ideals (your new God) – the easier the process will be. Ultimately, it is worth doing, because it is a highly rewarding transformation.

Don't hesitate to work with professionals like psychotherapists, mindfulness teachers, spiritual leaders, and of course yourself. Your destiny is shaped by each and every decision you make every single day.

It is an action of accepting responsibility, which in turn repays with a sense of meaning. "Do you prefer to watch another episode of the questionable value of a TV series, or do you prefer to create a new episode of your own, happier life?" Here's the question. Make up your mind. And remember, when you say "yes" to something, you always have to say "no" to something else.

Is there such thing as free will?

Mr. Sam Harris says, "There's no such thing as free will".

> *"I've argued that there's no such thing as free will. So, what is there? Well, there's luck, both good and bad, as well as what we make of it. Actually, that's not quite true. What you make of your luck is also just more luck. Once again, you didn't pick your parents. You didn't pick the society into which you were born. There's not a cell in your body or brain that you created nor is there a single influence coming from the outside world that you brought into being and yet everything you think and do arises from this ocean of prior causes. So, what you do with your luck and the tools with which you do it even down to the level of the effort and discipline you manage to summon in each moment is more in the way of luck."*[ccxxi] – *Sam Harris*, an American author, neuroscientist, and podcast host.[ccxxii]

Although I can agree with many hypotheses and proposals coming from Mr. Harris, in some cases he seems to fall into specific mental traps. "There is no free will." Really? Maybe yes, maybe no. "There is no 'I'/'self'." Really? Maybe yes, maybe no. "There is consciousness." Really? Maybe yes, maybe no. In many cases, to start any discussions on these and similar matters, first, we need to agree on clear definitions.

Can "I" sit on a chair?

Imagine entering a room and staring at the chair and the table next to the window. In the center of this table is also a nice vase with spring flowers. One might say, "Although you think you can see the chair at the table and beautiful flowers, in fact, there is no chair, table or flowers. Those are just illusions. To prove it, please come closer, for instance one inch away from the chair. What can you see? You might think, it is at least a piece of flattened wood with a smooth surface, light brown in color – this is what I can see. But, in fact, there is nothing in front of you. It is another cunning trick, another illusion. To prove it, please come even closer to this wooden board. What if you wear glasses, bring a microscope with you, or better, a transmission electron microscope? What can you see? I can tell you right now, you can see some strange objects, let's call them particles, somehow interconnected or interrelated through invisible but real forces or fields and finally organized in 'three-dimensional' larger structures. Gazing at them, can you really see the original chair, table, or flowers? No way. I bet you already forgot about that light brown color, or that you could sit on this thing you called a chair. There is no chair, table or flowers. There are particles." As you may guess we can continue such a journey endlessly, either scaling it down or scaling it up. It is so easy to imagine flying away from that particular chair, room, house, or even the Earth and say, there is no chair, room, or house... Our worldviews, though, depend on one's point of view, point of reference, location, proximity and other variables. Our worldviews are determined by the situation or circumstances we are in. They are relative. It seems like there isn't one true worldview. It is so fascinating that depending "where you are sitting" physically or mentally, the properties of observed or experienced "objects" change, the behaviors of interacting objects or systems of objects change, and our perception of what we observe changes. In one particular position the object you are looking at has one color, whereas in another position it suddenly has different color, or no color at all. In one particular position an observable object looks like a regular room in a regular house, in a regular community, in a regular American suburb, whereas in another position it suddenly emerges as just a cabin on a cruise ship or a dummy room in a film studio's hangar. In one particular position, let's assume from the position of curious aliens that are watching us thorough their long-range telescopes, human beings appear to them as unsophisticated, if they (aliens) didn't know that those humans could think and talk, they would quickly classify them as just "animals." Now, being in another position, let's say, directly sitting inside of the human brain and seeing all of those millions of signals going back and forth, you would immediately glorify human superiority over the animal kingdom. Assumptions one can make have tremendous consequences. If humans are animals, you do not need to discuss and align with them, you just decide yourself and push for execution. If humans are humans, you discuss and align with them – and it's a totally different process, much sophisticated, and much longer. Also, the approach to interactions, cooperation, how we talk about our purpose and goals, how we plan actions, and how we decide on execution methods, will vary greatly, depending on what position you take.

Do "I" exist?

What if in one particular position you say, "There is only the brain which is simply processing information (or exchanging electric impulses between its neurons) – on its own. There is no 'me', no 'you', and no human personality. You do not need "you" to exchange those impulses, as there is no role you can play. You do not start, you do not stop, and you do not maintain this process. You are not important. Who are "you" in the first place? There is no "you," but there is a molecular, chemical, biological form that does something in a phenomenal, repeatable way, and it is very hard to point at one and only one conductor orchestrating all internal operations of this form. It's not you, for sure. You have nothing to say. You are the side effect of this complex processing. This processing has to reach a certain complexity level for you to arise as a fake you, and you take it for granted that you exist – but in fact you don't. Without this involuntary flow of stuff within the brain, there is no "imaginary" us that can think of it right here, right now. Without this brain there is nothing.

So, what could be another position in which we could have a slightly different opinion? Let's simply forget that there is a functioning brain, like we usually forget that there is a functioning engine in the car we drive without which fast and long-range movement would not be possible. There is the flow of gas, oil, electricity, and air in that same car, but we do not pay attention to it anymore (as long as it is functioning well). How do we forget that there is a processing brain? Doesn't this happen when we get deeply involved in the activity we love, or when we face huge danger, or when we experience unbearable pain? Physical suffering is probably one of the most powerful reasons why we immediately return to "ourselves," feeling that we exist here and now and trying to survive. There is also existential suffering that immediately reorganizes our priorities and understanding of "ourselves."

What if we never met anyone like us, or never had the opportunity to look into the "mirror," or never saw our own body parts including shadows on the ground or on the walls? Would we be able to recognize our own unique physical presence? If no one ever was looking at us, looking at our face, looking into our eyes, how could we really know that we have a face, or that we are observable objects in the Universe? Maybe then we would never develop self-awareness or separate from the world. A world that looks at itself with its own eye. Being "headless" (or "no headed") is certainly a possible theoretical scenario, perhaps also practically possible to some extent in a laboratory environment or in a computer simulation. The film "Avatar" could be a good analogy and reference point.

But can this be true that my "I" does not exist? My gorgeous 4-year-old daughter woke me up today by jumping on my belly like on her outdoor trampoline. When "I" opened my eyes, "I" realized that I am real. Her beautiful, large, smiling eyes were staring at me. I was sure they were. When I was trying to close my eyes and return to my dreamland, she was not happy, immediately stopped singing and started screaming, "Dad, wake up. It is morning. Time to play!" After I opened my eyes again, she promptly changed into a flying angel, staring back at me with indescribable joy. It seemed like two brains using their pairs of eyes recognized themselves in a very mysterious way and started communicating, acknowledging their own existence, playing an action-reaction game, influencing one another, forming an invisible group of "I(s)" – beings. That is one of the most spectacular phenomena, when two brains a minute before were living in their own, separate worlds of signal processing, and now are pairing up, dancing together, re-calibrating, synchronizing, and going beyond their physical premises. They formed dependency, unity, new quality, new property of the "system", new level, and new relationship.

If we do not pay close attention to those different positions or levels (aggregation levels) – we can easily misinterpret behavior. On an atomic level, there is no "us" as we used to think of ourselves as "us." So, it's true, there is no "I," "me," "you," "he," "him," "she," "her," "we," "us," "they," or "them." Even if we assume we could exist on different levels, still, without that atomic level, there is no chance we could exist on any other higher levels. There is a really intriguing interdependency between levels, bottom-up as well as top-down. What about our existence on the level of thoughts? Let us assume that we agree that there is a unique ability of the human brain to remember life's events, to access these events at any time and, of course, to produce thoughts, usually interrelated ones which are in a logical cause and effect relationship. The question is, am I my thoughts? If they are not mine, then whose are they? It should be obvious that those thoughts belong to brain, and as blood is circulating in my bloodstream without my intervention, or my cells are multiplying without my motivation, thoughts are arising in my brain as well without me helping them. Do we really know what our next thoughts will be? Many of us have some doubts. If we do not create our own thoughts purposefully and intentionally, we should not even say, "I am thinking," but rather, thoughts are "thinking of me," or thoughts are "making me up" assuming "I" am at least "my" body in which thinking is happening unintentionally.

Can "I" decide?

Some of us can go even further and broaden the scope to adjacent levels and say that human beings' thinking, and behavior is fully deterministic. It is determined by the "natural" design of their brains and interconnected sensors embedded in multiple organs – the very unique product of awfully long evolution. All participating elements of the "physical" world were fine-tuning themselves and organizing themselves in a way - to ultimately manifest their unique features and functionalities. Thinking became one of the breaking-through features. But what does that mean in practical terms? Mr. Sam Harris says, as I already mentioned, "There's no such thing as free will." Just one of the consequences of such a determinism.

Is this the only truth that I do not freely decide myself about my life, especially what thoughts to think of? Are there any other truths? In the morning of The Super Bowl day, where my home town team, The Kansas City Chiefs, was expected to win (and they won!) the World Championship trophy after 50 years of trying, my teenage daughter approached me with a kind and honest question: "Dad can you help me with my math? Tomorrow, I have a major test, and I still don't understand some of the concepts. Please." "Please, just not today" – my brain started thinking, but mouth was not saying anything yet. "It was all Saturday, yesterday" - my brain generated another thought and this time it decided to make it public. My daughter's eyes immediately turned into much larger than normal – they expressed her helplessness and repentance. "I don't believe it." "This is the most important game I've waited for so long." "Everybody confirmed they will come." "I can't just disappear when all my friends are here" - my brain was at its best, conducting its energizing brainstorming session. It created thoughts after thoughts and created many catastrophic scenarios as well. "For the first time this school year she came to me asking for help." "I had always asked her to do so, kindly offering my support." "Here she is". "But, why today?" My vocal chords remained still - I was quiet. The brain acted like an unstoppable factory - thought after thought - producing not my thoughts, but somehow illusory mine.

Although I wanted to watch the whole game, my brain decided to help my daughter's brain and spend the 2nd and 3rd quarter on solving math problems and the 1st and 4th watching the game. "I" wonder now, why in the first place, my brain "likes" to watch the game so much (it never played it itself - it never played any outdoor game or even went out of its head for a short walk).

I can agree with Mr. Sam Harris that my thoughts arise before I can really think them. Isn't it fascinating? I have the impression that when we "try to think" them, we can see them emerging one at a time, and one by one, continuously, uninterruptedly, like watching an extremely large family photo album with thousands of pictures in an automated slideshow mode – where picture after picture is showing up on the screen of your computer. There are pictures we wanted to store, but the vast majority of them have been stored without our being asked or even knowing about it – they have been stored on behalf of "us" by our brains. In addition to billions of pictures, metadata about how they are interlinked is also stored. Watching frame after frame creates this "illusion of thinking" or "illusion of being in control" - it is the illusion of free will, which is capable of making its own decisions. If we pay enough attention, we can become quiet observers of our brain's thoughts, seeing them come and go, arrive and depart, arise and subside. That is the magical moment when we start experiencing "I."

In fact, one of the definitions of meditation is the state of becoming quiet, not judging one's own thoughts, and at the same time staying still, experiencing the here and now, experiencing all that really is (not all that was or can be) within one's own body (breathing, sensing blood circulation, energy flow including temperature changes, the interaction of the senses with "outer" world stimuli) and experiencing all that really is outside of our body. In the end, there is no separate body. The body and the world are one. Energy flows and its levels may be different, but in the end, it is all the same.

We experience some form of "I" being such an observer. But is this really already that "I" that we want to be? We can be an actor who follows a script and has no influence on it whatsoever. We could become, with some effort, a spectator in the movie theatre that shows our life story. At least we can react with cheering, booing and in extreme cases we can leave the theater. Can we be something more? Can we become the screenwriter, director, or the producer of our own saga? Sam Harris, if I understood him correctly, would say, "No, you can't." There is no you. Your thoughts are predetermined by the biology and history of your personal body and were born before you came up with them. Your thoughts have already been created before you realize their existence. You do not think. It is your brain that has already thought about it.

Let's come back to my example with the Super Bowl and the math dilemma, to watch my favorite local football team's game and throw a party, or skip it and support my daughter in her preparation for the math test. After being asked by her personally for help, knowing how independent she wanted to be, what were the possible scenarios? After considering whether to help, my brain decided to do math with my daughter. She is more important than a game. Again, can this decision be made by the brain without asking me for permission? Let's assume that it can. It is a "simple" decision-making process based on inputs (a finite number of criteria and a finite number of incoming data points), relations between these input data, their weights and time. "I" do not need "myself" to make such a mechanical decision. There is no free will.

What were the possible scenarios and were these scenarios really available to me as decision options? Let's assume that the following thoughts appeared on my brain canvas: "No way, I can't miss this game," "All my best friends will be here," "She should be more responsible," "I've told her so many times, don't procrastinate, prepare for the tests well in advance," "It will be a very good, but of course, painful life lesson she has to learn today." The brain has decided: I will watch the match, no matter what. Then, I would say: "I can't help you, darling, I'm sorry. I have my own commitments for tonight." Can this decision be made by the brain without asking my permission? Suppose so. It took "all" of the available facts and the interconnectivities of those facts and the associated weights of the importance, and through a "simple" decision-making process (a criteria-based algorithm) – it made that decision.

What if the following chain of thoughts emerges in my brain: "No way, I can't miss this game," "All my best friends will be here," "She should be more responsible," "I've told her so many times, don't procrastinate, prepare for the tests well in advance," "It will be a very good, but of course, painful life lesson she has to learn today." (The following new thoughts appeared) "*It seems that this test will determine her final score at the end of the year before she goes to college*", "*We have already invested so much in her education*", "*All those hours of math tutoring on weekends, all those Internet courses (especially Khan Academy website* [cxxiii]*)*", "*In fact, everything is already prepared: food, drinks, and Ola will be there to talk to my guests*", "*I can go in and out from time to time, maybe nobody will even notice that I'm not watching with them*"...

That is how my brain decided to do the math with my daughter.

Now, if we have more time, we can come up with many scenarios, like: "don't watch, do the math" vs. "watch the 1st quarter and do some math" vs... "watch the whole thing and do not do the math at all." But again, one of many options will be chosen. Who decides? And how are decisions made? When does the brain know that this is the right moment to make a decision? From this simple simulation we see that apart from "all" the resources available at this moment (memories -

facts that are categorized, formed in relationships and weighted), it is the time (which the brain gives itself to process information) that is very critical for determining the final result. Some important thoughts have not yet flashed on the "conscious canvas" of the brain, but the decision has already been made. What if the brain waits a little longer? The decision may be completely different.

"I don't have time to visit John in hospital today, I will try to come tomorrow" versus "I don't have time to visit John in hospital today, I will try to come tomorrow. But wait a minute, isn't he in a life-threatening situation after this terrible accident an hour ago? I am cancelling all my appointments today, and I am going to the hospital, now."

One even tiny new fact changes "our" decisions. Can we say "we" (an "imaginary we") have something to say? Could "we", for example, move into a more "conscious" state, the state of the thought observer and at least take control of the clock. The observer is most likely another thought, a meta-thought, a parallel thought that drives very slowly on the right lane of the brain highway and sees all the thoughts of the left lane that pass it at much higher speed. It would be so close to the feeling of being the true self that steers this process. The "I" returns to control (I am in control). But it is still a meta-thought, not "me"? We can play this game endlessly, going up or down the hierarchy of thoughts or climbing the stairs of our abstract house of consciousness.

Do we make a mistake in reasoning?

I think, it's a "Leveling Problem" (what I call it). We are trying to explain the properties of one system, which has its own specific complexity level, with a totally different system that has a different complexity level - superior or inferior, higher or lower than the observed one. Without a doubt, we can find people who have very limited access to their more sophisticated meta-thoughts. This is because, they are probably children and their brains are not yet sophisticated enough to form an experience of meta-thought or they have damaged or not fully developed brains (for various reasons) or have never been told or never discovered themselves that they can be the time keepers and referees in their own game of life. It could also be a problem of reference points, where a more sophisticated brain looks at less sophisticated brain and concludes that the host of the less sophisticated brain is not aware of what is really going around it. Such a reflection may have an important impact on the "stronger" brain which could be tempted to take advantage of this situation, and for instance, try to control the "weaker" one from outside. We can also imagine a scenario in which a more advanced brain decides to help the other one, or it doesn't care. Even a sophisticated person living in his/her highly sophisticated society could be classified as "not capable of grasping the essence of life," by another more sophisticated brain. I bet, many of us experience different levels of "personalized or impersonalized consciousness," especially when compared to different people. "Impersonalized consciousness" is considered by some of us as enlightenment. We could say that there is no boundary between the world and us. The "personalized I" does not exist and is fully aware of this. The "I" is everything and nothing at once, the "I" is consciousness. We can move from total unconsciousness to consciousness, knowing that our personalized existence may exist at certain levels of complexity, or may not exist at all. Which state should define us as 21st century human beings? Another question is, should the state define human beings, or should human beings define the state? Which state would be the most optimal and lead to the happiness of human beings? Some of these states may be theoretically noble and ideal, but hard to put into practice. Instead of personalized names, we can always use our impersonalized Social Security Numbers.

So, is Sam Harris right or wrong by saying that there is no "I," or that there is no such thing as free will?

With the memories I have "on hand" (in my brain) and limited time for analysis, my brain tells me that he is both right and wrong. He is right when he looks from the perspective of pure brain biology, current knowledge and our best guesses as to how our brains work. The brain as the physical and neurological organ, made out of particles, formed into higher level chemical structures and even higher-level biologic structures, acquires and processes signals (or "information") as its main function. It does it through our lifetimes, behaving like an enormous sponge thrown into the water. Electrical blinks "are" our thoughts (of course, at a higher abstract level), and there is no higher level "I" that is required to make them blink. "I" can only emerge from complex enough blinking patterns, their amount, speed, regularity and so on and so forth. So, "I" cannot think those blinks in advance. They blink, and then "I" can start thinking that it thinks. Now, is it really the brain that makes those electrical blinks within it, or are there electrons that bounce around from one atom to another pushed by some forces and energy levels? As you may sense now, it is a logical dead-end, a fallacy in reasoning. Isn't it? So, in my opinion, Sam Harris is wrong applying or extrapolating the properties of one lower level system to a higher-level system. This applies to any levels in nature, where one thing is made up from others.

I agree, there is no such thing as free will – in the brain's world.

But there is such a thing as free will – in the conscious human beings' world.

There is no such thing as Starbucks coffee that you can drink in a world of nanoparticles.

But there is such a thing as Starbucks coffee which you can drink on the 43rd and Broadway in Manhattan, New York.

Another insufficiently good argument that Sam Harris used to defend his thesis of "no free will" is that our brains, although they can store enormous amounts of memories, can only access a few of them at a time. Then, our brains process them according to algorithms to produce final outcomes - our decisions. Let's forget for a moment about "subconscious processing." "Conscious processing" is even more limited. In his flagship experiment, he asks the audience to pick their favorite celebrity in the predefined experiment time. As a summary of the experiment, he would conclude that you are always limited in your selection of this particular list of celebrities that has just shown up in your brain during that particular experiment. If for some unknown reason Keanu Reeves wasn't on your short-term (memory) list of celebrities – you would not have had the opportunity to consider him your favorite. He cannot be your favorite actor, even though you admire him the most. Your options had already been narrowed down and pre-determined before you could make your final choice. What kind of free will is that? You had nothing to say. I can easily agree that options were already determined in the given experiment timeframe. It reminds me of the restaurant situation and the specific **menu in that restaurant**, where the only dishes you can order are those listed on that menu and the restaurant owner is not willing to adjust them even a tiny bit so that the restaurant can maintain its reputation.

Isn't this a "leveling problem" or a "time keeper problem", again? But what if I repeat the experiment? I can generate different outcomes and then choose from them. I can write them down on a piece of paper and then try to decide, by using my next best meta-thought, my more conscious mind. I can also master and fine-tune along the years my own external (to my brain) decision-making algorithm with pre-defined questions, criteria, and timing. And all of it, to mimic my own specific biology, higher level needs, higher level values, beliefs, and history, including the history of past interactions with other human beings. Of course, this menu, in this particular restaurant, at this particular time, is fixed and determined, but I can always decide to leave the restaurant and go across the street. I can keep changing restaurants until I am satisfied that this is what I want to eat for tonight's dinner, and of course, for the price I am willing to pay. My choice is indeed limited by the time my brain has, before it changes from already being hungry to starving.

"Leveling" is like making a **fishing net**: you start with one rope, and it is useless (you can play with it like your jumping rope or swing on it in the yard). Then you lay another rope over it, and it is still useless (it has already lost its functionality as a jumping rope but has become a more sophisticated swing). You lay more and more ropes horizontally and vertically, you create nodes at the intersection of those ropes (interlinked memories) and depending on the expected size of the fish you want to catch, you add or subtract ropes to or from your net. Now, if you go too far and add too many ropes to your finishing net, then the mesh size becomes invisible – preventing water from penetrating your net. A fishing net that is impermeable to water becomes useless (but you can still have a pretty nice flag, hammock, umbrella and many other useful things). It is useless at the beginning of the process and useless at the very end. Only with a well-designed grid made of ropes can we expect our finishing net to function according to its purpose. What a paradox. To navigate between levels, including levels in our consciousness, requires a certain knowledge about the nature of complex systems and their properties and the behaviors we are about to observe. It also requires a very systematic approach, prudence, care, patience, and humility.

So why does Sam Harris formulate such a thesis? By saying there is no such thing as free will, his brain and his highest-level meta-thought most probably decided to raise the lower level bar of the less complex system and bring it over to the already existing higher level, a more complex system of aggregated thoughts. Overlap between these levels immediately creates confusion. At the very beginning, it can create the illusion of discovering something new or revolutionary. It is very important to note that some manipulations at lower levels can lead to amazing and very positive results observed at higher levels. Influencing the thinking patterns of young children can shape them into good adults. Also the development of well-functioning and proven gene therapies (lower-level manipulation) can save millions of lives, and strengthening the foundations and walls of a house can prevent it from falling apart during a major storm. Unfortunately, the opposite can be true, too, in that what happens at lower levels can negatively affect what happens at higher levels. Take as an example modifications of molecular structures that have known side effects (such as PFAS, highly toxic "forever chemicals" produced by humans, which are used to produce hundreds of everyday products). In addition, dangerous ideologies that brainwash young, flexible minds with fascism, communism, or indoctrination by the doctrines of sects, cults or religions that are dangerous to humanity. Using one level to explain another may be a very good intellectual trick and method for achieving visible improvements or important breakthroughs for the people and the world.

I agree, there is no such thing as free will – in the brain's world.

But there is such a thing as free will – in the conscious human beings' world.

We should not forget about some clinical cases where our brains have real difficulty in staying conscious.

Now, if the main problem was a limited and finite list of options (which the brain has to process), we may want to determine how many options we need to say the system is non-deterministic. This may mean that all we need is the right number of required brainstorming cycles. Some of us would say that having only two options already makes their system non-deterministic because they can choose either one or the other. On the contrary, someone would say that "before I make my own non-deterministic decision, I need to review an almost infinite number of options and choose the best possible one". For different problems we can use different magic number of cycles to generate "the best" possible options.

> To buy a drink at a gas station, we might need five minutes, and I guess, about ten brain cycles to generate good decision candidates. "I want a Coke." "I already had one soda today and I promised myself I wouldn't exceed one a day." "So, maybe Gatorade?" "Orange, pink, yellow...?" "They are so sweet" "What about hot tea? It's so cold in here. Black or green?" "They only have fruit tea." "Let's take the blue Gatorade" "What about my kids? They will beg for Gatorade right after I get in the car." "Too much stress". "Water, please." This is an interesting game of juggling thoughts. At least at some higher level of illusion I was able to force it to play for longer than usual and thus experience its true self - my true self. To buy a house, we might need one month of brainstorming and maybe hundreds of scenarios to study. However, in order to buy a new pair of shoes, I hope to do so during one visit to the mall.

At higher levels, a mind is able to form thinking (processing) patterns or criteria as meta-thoughts which determine the flow and sequence of lower level thoughts. At a pure biological level this could be seen as permanent, stronger electrical connectivity between specific sets of neurons. Hence, patterns or criteria could be seen as meta-thoughts, gateways, or weights put on selected memories or chains of thoughts that pop up more often than others when triggered by particular events. Those judging meta-thoughts can be called values, beliefs, or preferences. At a certain aggregation level, and after enough interactions with external world through continuous feedback loops (both receiving, reacting, and interpreting stimuli through the senses and also through other neighboring thoughts) the "construct" consisting of these aggregated meta-thoughts starts calling itself "I." Those "constructs" which deviate too much from universally accepted core values can be called Ego(s). Those meta-thoughts which are able to stay still and remain indifferent to external conditions or types of thoughts or registered and experienced sensations are usually called peaceful, mindful, enlightened thoughts. We need those higher-level meta-thoughts to experience the seamless flow of lower-level thoughts as one thinking experience. We need those higher-level meta-thoughts to be able to retrieve and recognize other different lower-level thoughts, and in so doing, become observers who experiences physical and emotional feelings or individualized perceptions.

The point is, Sam Harris is right as long as he stays at the biological level of the brain or sticks to the basic function of the mind. He is wrong, in my opinion, when trying to apply or impose properties and behaviors of lower level complexity to higher level complexity systems. What an illusion for one level may already be a reality for another level.

Do we know our own motivations and intentions?

Why does Sam Harris's mind formulate this thesis? Don't get me wrong, good discussions, good conversations, and good arguments are the foundation of human progress. So it is a luxury that we are able to challenge one another in a civilized way to move things forward. What is usually missing in such debates is clarity in terms of intentions, goals, and worldviews – which are an enormous waste of time, and cause misunderstandings and frustrations. Dancing around real problems prevents us from achieving more. Of course, many debate partners themselves are very strongly attached to their own ideas, so to achieve anything valuable at the group level or anything that has additional social value is practically impossible. The paradox is that many of them are not fully clear about their own personal intentions, problems, goals and worldviews, so conducting any constructive and promising conversation is nearly impossible. Not knowing the core motivations of contributors, we can pay a huge price and cause negative consequences for humanity – introducing, for instance, harmful ideologies like, "people are pre-programmed robots with no capacity for self-reflection (as there is no self), decision-making capabilities, or free will". Not knowing one's own or someone else's motivation makes it extremely difficult (close to impossible) to reach any mutual agreement.

What if someone is under the strong influence of a peer group and becomes dependent on an intellectual, financial or power level - or even his survival depends on that group? What if someone is trapped in the mental prison of his own pride – being an academic guru, and change of his views is not an option? It may be the end of his career, his sources of income, his followers who follow him day and night. Without followers, indeed, he may cease to exist. What if somebody lives in a cage labelled "I'm famous", chooses the most controversial topics and uses the power of social media to spread a false but very attractive theory? And what if someone sits in his cage because of the clear benefits of this cage, although he knows it is immoral and disgraceful. He is not willing to change anything, because he is so safe. It is better not to reveal any of his intentions, but "to build even higher walls and put additional guards."

Am I locked in a similar cage? Do I know my motivations? Do you know my motivations? Why am I writing this book now? I remember that in the first semester of the school for psychotherapists, I was asked why I wanted to help people. I answered, naturally, because I love them, and I feel I have a life mission and a sufficient set of talents to comfort them, to inspire them, and to help them. In response, I was asked many follow-up questions, and at the end of such a lengthy process to identify the real reasons for my own motives, I almost forgot my own name, and of course, I started to doubt that my love for others was real.

"But why do you need to love others?" "Could you spend a little more time with yourself and find out what the real reason is?" "You said you had a lot of love in your childhood, two loving parents and four loving grandparents, and now you have a loving wife and unconditionally loving children. And you said you wanted to give back" "Is there any compulsion in you to love another person?" "Do you think you must or must love back, or do you want to?" "What do you think of your self-confidence, your self-esteem?" "Could you describe your relationship with your father?" "What about your mother?" "Were you appreciated enough at home? Please, describe how you were or were not appreciated by your mother, father or peers." "How do you feel now?"

What if it's not about other people, but it is more about me – my need for appreciation, my need to be noticed and recognized, my need to be praised, glorified, listened to, and to be in the center. I was close to believing that what I was "really" feeling, experiencing, and considering my life mission was fake. That was the moment of truth. I was discovering my deepest motivations. I came out of this experiment more aware, more mindful, more intentional, more careful, stronger, and more confident. My mission is indeed to love and help, but to love and help in a wise and responsible way, making sure that it's all about others and myself at the same time. "Love your neighbor as yourself," only if you know how to love yourself properly.

So, what is my true cage? What is the best cage in which to live a happy life? Even if we define one, or find one, how do we transition from our current cage to that one? To come to any future settlement will require a lot of patience, good will, transparency, and a shared vision.

How do we escape from our cages and shift our mindset?

- By desiring the **truth**
- By desiring **love**
- By desiring **understanding**
- With an **unconditioned, conscious** and **clear mind**
- With **curiosity** and **open-mindedness**
- With **respect**
- With **compassion**
- By honestly looking at "unconscious conditioning" (the cycle of thoughts-decisions-behaviors-actions-results-thoughts). Is it a negative spiral that pulls me down? Am I **mindful** and **self-aware** enough to see my conditioning or inherited and well-grounded schemas that work in me and steer my destiny? Am I mindful and self-aware enough to clearly see my emotions, where they come from, and how they influence my decisions, behaviors and actions? Am I mindful, self-aware, and **patient** enough to make my own independent decisions?
- By finding **inconsistencies** in my own motivations, conflicting needs, desires, behaviors and actions
- By finding contexts in which opposite and maybe conflicting ideas can be true
- By assuming that the person I am listening to might know something I don't
- By asking control **questions**, like: What is truth?, What if the other truth is true?, Who am I?, Who do I want to be?, Why am I here?, Where do I want to be?, What is my purpose?, Why am I thinking like that?, Why am I feeling like that?, What am I doing right now?, Is what I am doing right now consistent with my personal purpose, mission, and values?, What decision should I make?, What are my alternatives?, Am I ready to pay the price for my choices?, What makes me happy?, Why-Why-Why-Why-Why?, Do I love?
- "Knowing what is true is essential for making good decisions and shaping our destiny."
- "Searching for and defending the truth is a relay race, not a sprint."

CHAPTER 6

My Creator

Fearless, hopeful, loved, and living a good life

"All men are created equal, and endowed by their Creator…"

– The United States Declaration of Independence

You can spend your whole life proving that God does not exist, and you will be right in your own reasoning.

You can spend your whole life proving that God does exist, and you will be right in your own reasoning.

You can spend your whole life proving that you don't care if God exists or not, and you will be right, too.

But before you start proving anything, try to wrestle with the following basic questions:

What is my God like - regardless of God's existence or non-existence?

What is the best possible God like - regardless of God's existence or non-existence?

Why don't I want to believe in such a God?

Why do I want to believe in such a God?

Why is caring better than not caring, or vice versa?

Ultimately, it's about the decision: whether to believe in God or to believe in "not God."

You can't not believe in anything.

I based this chapter mainly on the Christian vision of the Creator, so, if you believe in another God or gods, or no God at all, kindly treat it as an example. I encourage you to join me in this mental exercise, and use your worldview as a basis for your analogies and conclusions. I respect your freedom and independence.

"Look, I am coming soon! My reward is with me, and I will give to each person according to what they have done. I am the Alpha and the Omega, the First and the Last, the Beginning and the End.

Blessed are those who wash their robes, that they may have the right to the tree of life and may go through the gates into the city. Outside are the dogs, those who practice magic arts, the sexually immoral, the murderers, the idolaters, and everyone who loves and practices falsehood."

"I, Jesus, have sent my angel to give you this testimony for the churches. I am the Root and the Offspring of David, and the bright Morning Star." [...]

Let the one who is thirsty come; and let the one who wishes take the free gift of the water of life. [ccxxiv]

(Revelation 22)

What would be the best possible world?

The world exists but doesn't have to exist.
"Authentic religion often begins in this extraordinary experience - an experience of the contingency of the world [no need for a world to exist]. What does that mean? It means this deep sense, intuition: 'the world exists but doesn't have to exist,' 'things are, but they don't have to be,' they don't carry within themselves the reason for their own existence."[ccxxv] – Bishop Robert Barron

What if I am a scientist? I cannot just say I believe in God, whose existence I cannot prove. I will immediately lose my credibility in front of my peers. I will lose my status and authority. Sooner or later, I will be excluded from influential scientific circles. But there is also no evidence that God does not exist, so I should be fine. There is also no evidence of what causes the Big Bang, and what was before it. Science itself can only measure what can be measured and what is measurable. How far can we go below the quark (a type of elementary particle and a fundamental constituent of matter; quarks have not been directly observed, but theoretical predictions based on their existence have been confirmed experimentally)? Even if we successfully go one or two levels "below" our quarks and gluons (those which "bind" them together), still there could be further infinite numbers of sub-levels of sub-matters and sub-antimatters. Once we realize that we do not have sufficiently precise tools, we have to start assuming or anticipating or "hypothesizing" – or using less scientific language – we have to start believing. There are obvious limits to science. Already much of our contemporary science is based on initial assumptions, axioms and "beliefs." The case becomes obvious and the decision can be made between believe in God and/or science (or in neither God nor science.

I encourage you to answer the following groundbreaking questions:

Do I prefer to live in the best possible world with GOD in it?

or

Do I prefer to live in the best possible world without GOD in it?

You may say, "I don't know, depends on the definition of GOD." Unfortunately, the definition of GOD cannot be really formulated, if GOD exists. If we tried to formulate a concept of GOD, then it would mean either we are GOD ourselves or we have a limited view of GOD's perfection and absoluteness. For the sake of this exercise, let's just assume we are talking here about the best possible GOD we can imagine.

At the end of the day, answers to those two questions will lead us to two totally different realities that will have huge existential consequences. The major difference between those two is that "the best possible world with GOD" offers HOPE for a HAPPY END and AFTERLIFE, whereas "the best possible world without GOD" offers DISAPPEARANCE forever, or in the best possible version of "the best possible world without GOD" dissolution in the ocean of energy and matter, or in the impersonal consciousness (which we still do not understand).

So, are you choosing **HOPE** and the **AFTERLIFE** or **NONEXISTENCE**? It's up to you. You can decide. Not making a decision is also a decision. Only if you have never heard these questions, you can remain in unconscious indifference, remain in ignorance. I am telling you, it is worth wrestling with this decision. All your life choices will depend on this groundbreaking selection. The funny thing is, both realities are equally probable and possible. So there is no risk of "not being" well informed.

Is there a God?

This is what I believe I believe in. To be honest, I am continually in the process of letting go of some things that I was taught to believe. At the same time, I am adopting new beliefs. I do not know for sure, which is why I believe. At least, I think I know that I believe.

Usually we can hear the following: there is no scientific evidence that God exists, and there is no scientific evidence that God does not exist. With great devotion, I have been opening my eyes and ears for twenty plus years (of my adult life) to search and find the truth. I have tried to utilize, as much as I possibly could, the computing power of my brain, and its general intelligence. I have tried to pay attention and keep myself honest when challenging biases inherited from my parents, highly influential people, culture, and situations that shaped my "initial worldview." I have been studying historical and contemporary books and publications, listening to debates, conversations, lectures, preachers at church, interviews, observing atheistic movements etc. So far no one has been able to present solid arguments in support of any of these concepts. That is, we cannot know for sure that God exists or does not exist.

As we do not know whether God exists, we can either forget about the topic or choose to believe. "Giving our faith" is as powerful as knowing, although it uses a different set of assumptions and has different consequences. Mankind has been "believing" for at least tens of thousands of years, while knowing for a much shorter time. Some say that we have been doing real science for at most 300 years (e.g. taking Sir Isaac Newton's activities as a good starting point; Newton was an English mathematician, physicist, astronomer, theologian, and author who is widely recognized as one of the most influential scientists of all time).

Believing can be seen as a competitive approach to knowing, but if we think about it deeper, it does not need to be. Believing was, and I hope still is, a complementary and mandatory element of human reasoning oriented around progress. Knowing, that results from scientific evidence, gives us clues about how something works, sometimes with full certainty or sometimes with well-defined probabilities of certainty. Believing, on the other hand, gives us imaginary access to unknowns with mandatory promises of to-be-discovered-certainties in the future. The illusory knowns are possible realizations of knowns in the unknown future. Believing is risking, believing is trying something new, believing is tapping into areas that were never visited - believing is innovating. Believing is hoping. It may be quite hard to simulate what our world would look like without a human strategy of believing. Maybe we would not make any progress at all as species, or maybe we would, but very, very slowly. Not allowing ourselves to assume any unknowns, but following rigorous scientific processes to move ahead step by step could be time-consuming and less motivating. Creating scenarios and hypotheses has to be triggered by believing. Agreeing on assumptions or forming and proposing axioms belongs to the space of believing, more than to knowing. We assume, but we do not know. Funny, isn't it?

That is why I assume that **we are all believers**. We do not know if God exists, and we do not know that God does not exist. So if we want to continue this discussion, we have to believe in God's existence, or we have to believe in God's nonexistence. In both cases, we are all believers. We believe in God or we believe in the nonexistence of God. There is nothing science can help us with.

My point of view is that every person who faces the subject of God and "No-God" must decide for him/herself what to believe in. There is no option to not believe at all, unless someone is unconscious, or not yet confronted with such an existential question, or has been confronted and is able to stay ignorant or has enough inner power to refuse thinking about his/her own, honest answer and positioning. Or has so many other important things on his/her plate that finding time to reflect on what to believe appears to be a luxury, and beyond his/her reach at that very moment.

Of course, this kind of rule of "believing in everything" should apply to any imaginary objects, concepts or hybrids. What could be our answer to the following question (recently asked by my 6-year-old son): "Is Star Wars real?" "Is Yoda a real Jedi?" (assuming that the Jedi is a real concept). In other words, it is a dilemma if we know for sure that Yoda exists, or if we know that Yoda does not exist, or if we are not sure if Yoda exists or does not exist. If we don't know what's real for sure, then we have to believe either in Yoda's existence or nonexistence. I know that Yoda does not exist. But someone can ask: "How do you know that Yoda does not exist? I just saw him a couple of times on the screen, and he is as real as the other characters in Star Wars. "It seems to be a definition problem. I know there is no Yoda in the form of an intelligent being that is able to communicate with others, that can be seen in our physical, matter-created world." Still someone can challenge it and say: "What about Christopher Columbus? Most people know about his existence, but we can't see him anymore. Does this mean that we cannot know and must believe?" In order not to fall into endless loops and make a choice between knowledge and belief, we need to provide as clear and concrete a definition as possible of what we want to know or believe. To sum up, I don't believe in Yoda because I have sufficient evidence that a physical, person-like Yoda didn't live in the past and doesn't live now, and I can trace how, when and by whom "He" was created as a drawing, then a doll, then a computer representation and put to "life" only in film reality. But just in case, although I know, I am not one hundred percent sure.

Some would still ask, "are we closer to believing or not believing in God's existence?" Looking at, for instance, the thirteenth-century discussion of Thomas Aquinas[ccxxvi] with scholars we could be amazed by reasoning that is still very hard to challenge.

"Thomas believed that the **existence of God can be demonstrated**. [...] he considered in great detail five [logical] arguments for the existence of God, widely known as the [...] Five Ways" [ccxxvii] (sometimes called "five proofs.")

"Aquinas did not think the finite human mind could know what God is directly, therefore God's existence is not self-evident to us. [...] So instead the proposition God exists must be "demonstrated" from God's effects, which are more known to us."[ccxxviii]

As Thomas Aquinas himself said: "Therefore I say that this proposition, 'God exists', of itself is self-evident, for the predicate is the same as the subject ... Now because we do not know the essence of God, the proposition is not self-evident to us; but needs to be demonstrated by things that are more known to us, though less known in their nature—namely, by effects. [...]"[ccxxix]

The five logical arguments for the existence of God are: "[...]

1. **Motion**: Some things undoubtedly move, though cannot cause their own motion. Since, as Thomas believed, there can be no infinite chain of causes of motion, there must be a First Mover not moved by anything else, and this is what everyone understands by God.

2. **Causation**: As in the case of motion, nothing can cause itself, and an infinite chain of causation is impossible, so there must be a First Cause, called God.

3. **Existence of the necessary and the unnecessary**: Our experience includes things certainly existing but apparently unnecessary. Not everything can be unnecessary, for then once there was nothing and there would still be nothing. Therefore, we are compelled to suppose something that exists necessarily, having this necessity only from itself; in fact itself the cause for other things to exist.

4.   **Gradation**: If we can notice a gradation in things in the sense that some things are more hot, good, etc., there must be a superlative that is the truest and noblest thing, and so most fully existing. This then, we call God.

5.   **Ordered tendencies of nature**: A direction of actions to an end is noticed in all bodies following natural laws. Anything without awareness tends to a goal under the guidance of one who is aware. This we call God."
ccxxx

I must admit that this is very simple but very powerful reasoning. What do you think? Would you be able to challenge that? Try it. Good luck.

What other reasoning can be marshaled to demonstrate the existence of God? Let me try using my simple, home-grown philosopher mind.

- Would you agree that our thinking happens in our brains, and at a certain level of granularity, it is a transmission, and the storage of electrical impulses (we can call it, information processing) that happen in a certain organized way (the full details of which are still to be determined)?
- Would you agree that we, hosts of such sophisticated brains, experience in a "magical way" our own existence, the illusion of being separated from other objects, other beings?
- Would you agree that we cannot prove that similar "information" processing does not happen at a different level, or in a different environment, in other objects or space in our universe?
- Is it possible that similar information processing (the movement of a physical particle in space or set of particles from point A to point B) happens at a sub-quark and sub-gluon level (a quark is a fundamental constituent of matter) – the level we don't have access to yet because instruments that could measure it have yet to be constructed?
- Is it possible that there is a sub-quark information processing unit similar to our brain? Let's call it a sub-quark-reality brain?
- Is it possible that the illusion of (super) self, which comes from the sub-quark reality, similar to our illusion of self and thinking process, exists? I think that it is possible, but not to be proved by people.
- Now, having clear evidence that our brains can "create," assemble new types of forms, objects or even living organisms (e.g. new

viruses, genetically modified crops, insects, animals, robots, machine learning and artificial intelligence algorithms and "living" software) that never existed before, by building them from available building blocks of matter and antimatter or information (as one particular representation of matter), can we imagine similar phenomena taking place in the sub-quark reality, where the (sub-quark-reality) brain "creates" or assembles new kinds of forms, objects, and even living organisms (including people, as well as the illusory "I"/"You"). Moreover, the whole system of production of new creatures is highly repetitive and durable - thanks to the assembly line programmed by DNA structures.

- What if a similar, but fundamentally different, highly intelligent, and capable being created us from building blocks that we are not able to comprehend?

"Why is there something rather than nothing?"

"[When] the atheists who often claim 'we're the most rational, [and] you religious people believe in your magical thinking and you're caught in these old superstitions and we're the real rationalist around here', I always tease them and say 'you drop the question just when it gets really interesting'. Yes, scientific questions are fascinating, I agree with you, follow them all the way. But the really interesting question is 'Why is there something rather than nothing?' 'Why does the world exist at all?' 'Why is there the realm of nature?', 'Why is there the nexus of contingent things?' That's nursing question. And what do I get from the atheist, time and again: 'I don't know', 'It just is' or my favorite: 'It popped out of nothing'. And I'm getting accused of magical thinking..."[ccxxxi] - Bishop Robert Barron

Is believing in God anti-intellectual? Can we add humility to our skepticism?

"Is God, or belief in God, to be equated with anti-intellectualism, violence, and bigotry? Or would these very human impulses exist regardless of belief in God? After all, the officially atheist regimes [...] burned books, imprisoned and slaughtered millions, and fostered their own forms of bigotry. God or no God, human beings will find reasons to oppress and kill one another. [...] Just as Christians or theists might hold their convictions with a bit of humility, recognizing that the facts leading them to their convictions might have other explanations, I believe atheists would do well to maintain a similar humility [about[the question of God."[ccxxxii] - Adam Hamilton,[ccxxxiii] senior pastor

Could someone who has been blind from birth imagine the light?
From a scientific point of view, we are almost sure that there is a cause and effect for everything in our world of matter and energy, starting from the formation of our universe. We are almost sure that something or someone has made the universe happen. Is that thing or entity more sophisticated (or intelligent) than us? Because we are not able to know everything, due to our lack of sophistication and limited cognitive properties that prevent us from exploring the surrounding world to its fullest, we have to believe in one of two scenarios: to believe that there is no intelligent cause and creator or to believe that there is an intelligent cause and creator behind all of it.

Because we can imagine other beings to be far more intelligent than us (including the one, more intelligent than others), and because we experience internal desire to live now and forever, (we may be willing to give more chances to the scenario that there is intelligence out there, and that there is the possibility of eternal life. Which scenario to choose is up to everyone.

Could someone who has been blind since birth imagine the light Try to honestly wrestle with this question. I doubt you could imagine light in a world of total darkness. Because we have our concrete desires, because we have our specific intuitions, it really gives more credibility to the scenario where God exists. By choosing the version of the world without God and the afterlife, one immediately eliminates hope and the possibility of reuniting with our loved ones. That is a very pessimistic alternative. Why would an emotionally stable person ever choose a pessimistic scenario over an optimistic one, when both of them are theoretically equally probable?

"Faith and reason complement rather than contradict each other, each giving different views of the same truth." [ccxxxiv]

Who is God?

God is not a thing or an individual. We can say legitimately that the modern sciences have indeed eliminated the gods. The sciences in principle cannot eliminate God, because God is not an item within the natural world.

"Here's the thing, the new atheists [among them Christopher Hitchens and Richard Dawkins] believe that God is some reality in the world or alongside the world or above the world, God is the supreme instance, if you want, of the category being (all kinds of beings around). Well that's exactly what God is not. [Thomas says] that God is not in any genus even that most generic of genera namely being. Well, isn't God at least a type of being, and Thomas's answer is 'no,' he's not. God's not a thing or an individual. [...] God is [...] 'the subsistent act of to be itself'. God is not an item within the world. [It can become] a Yeti theory of God. Some people say 'there is a Yeti Bigfoot, some say there isn't. Let's go find out.' Some believe it, some don't. God is not some item within nature within the world. Rather God is that great ocean of existence from which the world in its entirety comes. Not something in the world, but the condition for the possibility of the world, that's God. One way to get at this, too, is to distinguish between God [with a] capital G and the gods. Go back to the old Greek and Roman myths or myths of any culture. [...] The gods are supreme instances of let's say the human type [...] they're like superhumans who are immortal, may have super minds and super skills and powers, but they are finally beings in the world living up on Mount Olympus or down in the sea or up in the sky. There are supreme instances of the human or the natural. They're not strictly speaking supernatural. They exist as denizens within nature. This is why we can say legitimately that the modern sciences have indeed eliminated the gods. With our scientific equipment and our great scientific spirit, we've explored the heavens and the mountaintops and the depths of the ocean, and indeed, we haven't found supreme beings around. More to it, the modern physical sciences have managed to explain most physical phenomena. We don't have to appeal to [...] supernatural divine causes. That's true if by divine you mean the gods. The sciences have indeed eliminated the gods. But here's [...] a point I want to underscore. The sciences in principle cannot eliminate God, because God is not an item within the natural world. God is not some event or phenomena that can be examined by the physical sciences. He's not the subject or object of an experiment. Even in principle the sciences can't eliminate God, they can't address the question of God." ccxxxv - Bishop Robert Barron

Does the existence of bad religions prove the non-existence of God?
I can understand the huge frustration of the "New Atheists" of our times who based on evidence truly hate organized religion. I can find examples in which I agree with them. I do not agree with the reasoning that if there are bad religions, religious systems, or religious institutions (institutionalized religion) there cannot be a God. This is an obvious logical fallacy. Bad religions, or bad religious practices of a "good" religion do not prove that God does not exist. I think discussions should focus on "what God is like" and not "if God exists" because it is very hard to challenge in the first place.

If God exists, what is my and others definition of God?

Based on what I know about the world, my God:

- **Is the Creator of "everything that is,"** "things" that are alive and not alive, visible and not visible to me, known or not yet known to me, and that were and will be. He is the originator of the world in which we live.
  - Everything that was created has a purpose, only known to the Creator.
  - Some of "everything that is" can be very primitive and unlike God, whereas some may resemble God, according to the endless variations of the endless creativity of God. Everything is possible.
  - Some of those less primitive creatures think that they exist and are independent beings. At their level, they know they exist. At God's level it is an illusion of existence, because only God is the real Existence. In many cases they try to mimic God's behaviors or invent their own. As they are always less sophisticated than their Creator, they are not able to fully understand God's

intentions or desires or anticipate God's actions. God appears to them always as inconsistent or unpredictable, because they are not able to see all of God's picture at once.

▪ Some of God's creatures may try to go against God's plan because they feel like God and want to try to be on their own, establish their own world's design, have their own creations. God allows that to happen. Everything is allowed and possible within the limits imposed by the version of the "nature" given to creatures by their Creator.

• **Knows how "everything that is" works** (because it is created by God) and is able to influence everything that is, including changing the course of any events occurring in the world.

• **Is the most perfect Being**, Existence, Entity, not made of matter or anti-matter as we think we know it; is not made of something, and just "is."

• **Has perfect properties.**

• **Is the most intelligent and most perfect person** (if I am a person, then God can be a person too).

• **Is not limited** to anything or by anything (our nature has no influence on God, as God controls created nature).

• **Is almighty**, can do anything, can create something out of nothing.

• **Is eternal**, everlasting, endless, and timeless (is not imprisoned in our illusion of time caused by continuous matter changes and movement).

Shall we also take a look at the definition given by thirteenth century philosopher and theologian, Thomas Aquinas? "Concerning the nature of God, Thomas felt the best approach, commonly called the via negative, is to consider what God is not. This led him to propose five statements about the divine qualities:

1. **God is simple**, without composition of parts, such as body and soul, or matter and form.
2. **God is perfect, lacking nothing**. That is, God is distinguished from other beings on account of God's complete actuality. Thomas defined God as the 'Ipse Actus Essendi subsistens,' subsisting act of being.

3. **God is infinite**. That is, God is not finite in the ways that created beings are physically, intellectually, and emotionally limited. This infinity is to be distinguished from the infinity of size and the infinity of number.
4. **God is immutable**, incapable of change on the levels of God's essence and character.
5. **God is one**, without diversification within God's self. The unity of God is such that God's essence is the same as God's existence. In Thomas's words, "in itself the proposition 'God exists' is necessarily true, for in it subject and predicate are the same."" [ccxxxvi]

If God, the creator of "all that is," exists, it should be impossible to define God from the level of "anything that is," unless it is from the level of God. It is like trying to imagine the most beautiful, exceptional, epic painting which stares back at the painter who has just painted it – and is able (this painting) to recognize and understand the nature of its Master.

> If this example is too exaggerated, what about a small, three-year-old child who is forced to take a disgusting medicine or receive an injection, because if he does not do so, he may die. Does the child understand the meaning of the pain, or the ultimate consequences of not following the procedure, or does the child really understand his parents' "good intentions"? We all know that a three-year-old cannot define reality as an adult, cannot see the danger, cannot predict the consequences, and cannot even imagine what life really is. The child has limited capabilities to understand the world at higher, more complex levels. Someone could say that these examples are just to confirm the assumptions.

What if people create super intelligent computers, like robots, which outperform humans in computational power and intelligence as well? In this case, the creature can understand its creator, at least in some respects. When it comes to the processing of information – thinking, it is highly probable, but when it comes to understanding and feeling what it is like to be human, probably not. Pain and suffering would be one of the key unknowns. To feel like a human, "it" has to become one. "It" has to wear the same body, it has to be able to experience constant attacks by other living organisms, many of which are living inside of humans, and finally be able to grow old and die. To recreate the whole physical body's ecosystem in a computer, with all its functions and limitations, seems to me, as of now, impossible. But even if it is possible (let's use our power of imagination) then it will become another form of human being that is augmented by artificially-created processing power and memory units, asking the same questions, but maybe at a slightly different, more sophisticated level. The question is whether this will be the next evolutionary stage of human beings or the birth of new, human-like species. Now, if this new species is programmed to avoid asking questions about its creators, it will be programmed to not feel physical and existential suffering, and will be programmed with a perfect moral system that allows it to co-exist in perfect symbiosis with others. In that case, the topic of God most probably will not be necessary for them to solve anymore. But, interestingly, Gods "themselves" (people in this particular example) will be very interested in controlling their creatures and placing further limitations on the definition of their existence. Also, knowing us very well, can you imagine happily cooperating humanoids not having to deal with issues caused by computer viruses?

Coming back to the question of God, I assume that it is impossible to get to know God fully, to describe Him fully, or to define, visualize, imagine or even dream about God fully. If I could describe God, I would be God. But I am not the One. At least I know that the existence of God can be demonstrated, and I believe that the nature of God reveals itself in the world.

Admittedly, my image of God has been shaped by the people, events (miracles), intuitions and philosophies, "holy" books, feelings of connectedness with God, and the fruits of His love (my family). I chose to follow one particular story, the Way, the Truth and the Life. The story of Jesus Christ has moved my mind and soul the most, has given me the greatest hope, and has made my life meaningful. That is my God that I decided to believe in, or to be more precise, that is the God who decided to enlighten me first, so that I could believe in him. Some may ask, knowing that one God exists, why do I need the separate incarnation of God, in the person of Jesus Christ? Isn't it too much? Could the story of Jesus be fabricated? Maybe yes. Maybe no. Theoretically yes and theoretically no. Were people able to invent the Bible's stories themselves, without the mysterious influence of "grace"?

"Though one may deduce the existence of God and his Attributes (Unity, Truth, Goodness, Power, Knowledge) through reason, certain specifics may be known only through the special revelation of God through Jesus Christ. The major theological components of Christianity, such as the Trinity, the Incarnation, and charity are revealed in the teachings of the Church and the Scriptures and may not otherwise be deduced." – Thomas Aquinas[ccxxxvii]

Could those holy stories be imagined by people before they were written down? Because we cannot forget what we know (in most cases), we cannot prove that it is possible or impossible to write such stories. There is no doubt that people can come up with unrealistic, God-like stories themselves. But still, we will not be able to easily prove what was the underlying inspiration those concepts. Limits are defined by our creative minds. And we are undoubtedly very creative.

Take a look at such surrealistic visions developed by Scientology, Jediism, Pastafarianism, or Universe People. "Take the whole Xenu thing for example, you only are let in on the secret of the dictator of the Galactic Confederacy that trapped people in volcanos, and that how their spirit 'Thetans' lives on in humans causing them harm, hence the whole Dianetic [a canonical text of Scientology] thing. The fact that they actively threaten people when they try to leave is spooks enough[ccxxxviii]"

How can we guess more about God's nature and God's plans for the world?

As elaborated earlier, we could try to define the best possible world with the best possible God in it and treat it as our closest to ideal definition. But not yet ideal. The best possible God's definition could probably evolve from observations and conclusions about nature, about human beings' behavior and about social systems' performance, behavior and impact on nature and human beings themselves. Don't we already have the principles of natural law, and the economics of good and evil?[ccxxxix]

Haven't we already formulate a variety of philosophies for living a good life, as well as the ethics of doing so? Haven't we also described the transition to the afterlife, including incarnation, reincarnation, resurrection, ascension, or even transformation into God "himself". Even so, we may wonder, what is the real God like? Shall we pick one "philosophy," combine selected ones, or take all of them into account? What if "holy" books are really "holy" and "authored by God," or written by authors inspired by God? Then understanding what God is like should be easier, and can be derived directly from these books. Unfortunately, we cannot prove the holiness of holy books, so treating them as holy leads us back to the space of faith. What if we never had access to any holy books (like the Vedas, the Tao Te Ching, the Pāli Canon, the Chinese Buddhist Canon, the Kangyur, the Hebrew Bible 'Tanakh', the Bible, the Quran just to mention a few)? Would we be able to create similar philosophies, or religions codified in similar holy texts? Would it be possible to write a new holy book for the man of the 21st century? Would it create a new religion - the best religion in history? It is so hard to guess. Civilizations that already have such texts have been shaped by them. It would be very difficult to do any reliable simulation to answer such a question. It is impossible to clear out our collective minds as well as individual ones and look at the world anew. Of course, we could search for those civilizations that have not yet been able to formulate their ideal, so that we could watch them grow.

"God has revealed something about His own heart that we couldn't have guessed on the basis of reason." "Philosophical reason would not be sufficient for someone seeking real communion with God."
"To accept the Revelation of the Bible might be too much for someone, especially today, who's completely outside the ambit of religion, but the arguments might awaken the mind sufficiently [...] to say yeah, I'll take a look at the Bible. I use the example of getting to know a person. So, I'm meeting you for the first time today. [...] I came to my own conclusions about you, watching you in action and reading about you. [...] Let's say over many years we became friends and I came to know you more and more. At a certain point you would tell me something about yourself [...] that I would never have guessed or known independently of that. At which point I'd have to make an act of faith.

I'd have to say yeah, I believe that. [...] I think that's the analogy for reason in relation to faith. When it comes to God you can discover an awful lot of things through the mind by looking at the world and reasoning about it [...]"[ccxl] - Bishop Robert Barron

God is a person who has created us individually.
"Don't tell me for example that the Bible is one more iteration of the mono myth or the Bible's one more version of the universal religious story. It is not. The Bible knows all about God's transcendence. It knows all about [...] the awful, uncontrollable, inscrutable power of the creator of the universe. [...] But at the same time the Bible says that God is a person who has created us individually, who loves us personally, who guides us and who draws us ultimately into his own life. You will not find that in Plato. [...] You will not find that in Emerson or Schleiermacher or the New Age. The Bible then speaks of this personal God. [...] God becomes one of us."[ccxli] - Bishop Robert Barron

We can find "the Word of God in the words of men."
"There are so many people on these forums who mistake the Catholic sense of the Bible with, say, a Muslim sense of the Koran. Catholics do not think that the Bible was simply dictated by God to automatic human recorders. Rather, the Bible is "the Word of God in the words of men." And that means that we have to play a subtle hermeneutical game in approaching this collection of sacred texts. We don't "pick and choose;" we interpret. So please stop knocking down straw men!" [ccxlii] - Bishop Robert Barron

"The Scriptures are God's revelation, passed on through the apostles and embraced by the Church down through the ages. They provide us with timeless wisdom that can reorient our lives - our minds, our hearts, and our actions - as we engage in our world."[ccxliii]

As God is not a category from this world that we could try to understand, God reveals himself to man in man to allow us to understand His nature.

Why believe in God?

Is there a valid reason why we should believe in God? Are there any benefits that come from believing? Or are there any negative consequences that we will have to suffer if we don't believe? Does God have any plan for the world? Does God have any plan for people, for me? If there is a master plan, would that be a good reason for believing? Are there sufficiently good reasons to believe?

Why did I decide to believe in God (if we assume that it was my autonomous decision)?

- To know how to live the best possible life.
- To know how to become peaceful, joyful, and fulfilled with love.
- To know how to become fearless.
- To be open to hoping for an eternal life with my loved ones.
- To know how to reduce suffering, and to accept it by recognizing its true meaning

How do we live according to God?

If my happiness depends on believing in a God with a master plan, how should I cooperate with God, or at least not go against God's will.? Does He provide us with any guidance for living a happy life? As I already mentioned, my heart and mind have responded to the story of the historical teacher, Jesus of Nazareth – Jesus Christ. I decided to believe that Jesus[ccxliv] was and is the Son of God. I decided to believe that Jesus is God. I decided to believe that He won against death and is risen, that He is still alive and living among us.

How do we live according to Jesus?

In addition to understanding natural laws, we need to recognize that God is love to the point of death.
"If God is love, there's lover, beloved, and shared love within the very nature of God. How do we know that? Well, the first Christians knew it from the cross of Jesus that God so loved the world, he sent His only Son into our dysfunction, drawing the Son back to the Father in the Holy Spirit to save us. I can't guess that. […] That was revealed. […] You'd never guess that God is love to the point of death." [ccxlv] - Bishop Robert Barron

Jesus said to them, "If God were your Father, you would love me, for I have come here from God. I have not come on my own; God sent me." (John 8:42)

Then Jesus, still teaching in the temple courts, cried out, "Yes, you know me, and you know where I am from. I am not here on my own, but he who sent me is true. You do not know him, but I know him because I am from him and he sent me." (John 7:28-29)

Then they asked him, 'Where is your father?' "You do not know me or my Father," Jesus replied. "If you knew me, you would know my Father also" (John 8:19)

"I and the Father are one." (John 10:30)

"I tell you the truth," Jesus answered, "before Abraham was born, I am!" (John 8:58)

"Jesus says have you been with me this long that you still don't know the one who sees me sees the father. […]

That's why Jesus compels a choice in the way that no other founder does. Muhammad to His infinite credit never claimed to be God. Muhammad said, I'm a messenger, I received a message from God.

Moses to His infinite credit never claimed to be divine. Moses had received the law from God and gave it to the people. The Buddha to His infinite credit never claimed to be divine. What he said was 'I found a way.' Then there's Jesus who doesn't say 'I found a way,' he says 'I am the way.' How strange that is. He doesn't say 'I found a truth. Let me tell you about it.' [He says] 'I am the truth.' He didn't say 'hey there's this new mode of life that I've discovered. Let me share it with you.' [He says] 'I am the life.' [...]

Those claims are the unique treasure of Christianity and therefore they compel a choice as Jesus himself said 'either you're with me or you're against me.' If Jesus is who he says he is, I must give my whole life to him. He's God. He's the highest good. If he's not who he says he is, he's a bad man. [...] 'Either he's God or he's a bad man and you get to decide.' 'Either you gather with me or you scatter.' And there is the gospel. The gospel is the good news about this Jesus and it compels on the part of those who hear it a decision, a choice. I think that's the most important thing we know about Jesus."[ccxlvi] - Bishop Robert Barron

I decided to follow Him. I decided to believe that He is the way, the truth, and the life.

"I am the way and the truth and the life. No one comes to the Father except through me." (John 14)

"I am the light of the world. Whoever follows me will not walk in darkness, but will have the light of life." (John 8:12)

"If you hold to my teaching, you are really my disciples. Then you will know the truth, and the truth will set you free." (John 8:31)

Don't get me wrong, it's not about preaching to you, it's about giving you a full picture of all of the building blocks of my happiness. It's about being honest with you. It's about sharing the decisions that I have made and how they have influenced my worldview and formed me. These are my fundamental choices that I make each and every day, so as to intentionally steer my life toward happiness. This is my personal and intimate journey that is meant here to serve as an illustration. This is the way of a Christian. At the same time, I respect your individual choices, philosophies, lifestyles, or religions, as long as you respect the right to life and freedom.

In turn, I experience a real relationship with Jesus Christ, my God, my Supporter, my Healer and my Savior. He walks with me, and at the same time, He lives in me. That is what I believe, what I experience, what I feel, what I understand, and what I know.

"Do not let your hearts be troubled. You believe in God; believe also in me. My Father's house has many rooms; if that were not so, would I have told you that I am going there to prepare a place for you? And if I go and prepare a place for you, I will come back and take you to be with me that you also may be where I am. You know the way to the place where I am going." Thomas said to him, "Lord, we don't know where you are going, so how can we know the way?" Jesus answered, "I am the way and the truth and the life. No one comes to the Father except through me. If you really know me, you will know my Father as well. From now on, you do know him and have seen him." Philip said, "Lord, show us the Father and that will be enough for us." Jesus answered: "Don't you know me, Philip, even after I have been among you such a long time? Anyone who has seen me has seen the Father. How can you say, 'Show us the Father'? Don't you believe that I am in the Father, and that the Father is in me? The words I say to you I do not speak on my own authority. Rather, it is the Father, living in me, who is doing his work. Believe me when I say that I am in the Father and the Father is in me; or at least believe on the evidence of the works themselves. Very truly I tell you, whoever believes in me will do the works I have been doing, and they will do even greater things than these, because I am going to the Father. And I will do whatever you ask in my name, so that the Father may be glorified in the Son. You may ask me for anything in my name, and I will do it." [ccxlvii] (John 14, 1:14)

Jesus did exist, whether we like it or not.[ccxlviii]

"Occasionally a skeptic will try to argue that Jesus could have been a mythical figure, wholly made up by the early church. But the evidence for his existence is overwhelming."[ccxlix] - Adam Hamilton, senior pastor

In Jesus, God experienced our humanity and became one of us in order to reveal himself to us.

"In Jesus, surely God experienced our humanity. But the Incarnation was not simply to have God walk in our shoes; it was to allow God, literally, to meet us on our own ground – to become one of us in order to reveal himself to us in terms that we could understand, showing us what he is like and what his will is for our lives and for the world." [ccl] - Adam Hamilton, senior pastor

Jesus Christ changes how we live our lives and how we face death.

Jesus has been seen by many believers and non-believers as a great moral teacher. But because he was raised from the dead, and many people claimed to have seen him, touched him, and eaten with him – it proved that he was and is divine.

"Faith in the resurrection of Jesus Christ changes how we live our lives and how we face death [...]" "It's an ever-present sign of God's victory and the triumph of good over evil, love over hate, and life over death." [ccli] - Adam Hamilton, senior pastor

Christ is the privileged way to salvation AND an atheist of goodwill can be saved.

"Christ is the privileged route to salvation. [...] However the [Church] clearly teaches that someone outside the explicit Christian faith can be saved. They're saved through the grace of Christ [...] I mean the grace is coming from Christ, but it might be received according to your conscience. So, if you're following your conscience sincerely or [...] you're following the commandments of the law sincerely, you can be saved. [...] an atheist of goodwill can be saved because in following his conscience [...] the conscience is in fact the voice of Christ." [cclii] - Bishop Robert Barron

So how do we live according to Jesus? My answer is, "Just follow Him." "Just listen to Him." "Just imitate Him." "Just act like him." What else? "Just spend time with people." "Just look at people with care." "Just listen to people." "Just don't judge other people." "Just help those who cannot pay you back." "Just go to a 'desert' alone, calm down, meditate, and pray." "Just take up a spiritual fight. Be brave." "Just quench your desires." "Just stop fantasizing about the pleasure that is going to harm you. Do not flirt with temptation." "Just trust in God in every situation." "Just believe." "Just hope." "Just LOVE!"

Jesus showed us how to live a happy life, how to choose good over evil, how to choose love over hate, and how to choose life over death. A happy life is a result of being fearless and not being a slave to one's desires or possessions. A happy life is a result of internal peace, calm, confidence, being in control (but not full control), having meaningful relationships, experiencing self-fulfillment and having hope that the best possible world is really there and will never end, and that the current life is just the beginning. Jesus is giving us that hope and is taking away our fear. Jesus showed us how to live according to God. He showed us how to love God, how to love our neighbor, and how to love our enemies. Jesus demonstrated selfless and sacrificial love. Life is all about love. Life is a school of love. Love is what matters most.

What is Love?

Love is the single most important word in my life and the cornerstone of my worldview. And, indeed, I treat my earthly life as a school of love – the more proficient I become, the deeper joy I feel. Some monks joke that "the worse one's life is, the better one's life is," but that may sound too crazy. Isn't it true that better schools provide better education, more demanding schools create better quality results delivered by their responsible and knowledgeable students, and tougher schools shape stronger characters? So making our lives harder cannot be the goal in itself. The goal is to achieve and maintain a state of joy for as long as possible, regardless of one's circumstances, adversities, or inevitable suffering. I believe we were created to be happy, but not necessarily to experience pleasure all the time. Those two are not the same things. And true love is the way to true joy.

"For the time will come when people will not put up with sound doctrine. Instead, to suit their own desires, they will gather around them a great number of teachers to say what their itching ears want to hear. They will turn their ears away from the truth and turn aside to myths. But you, keep your head in all situations, endure hardship [...]

I have fought the good fight, I have finished the race, I have kept the faith." ccliii (2 Timothy 4, 3:7)

In other words, at the end of my life, I wish to be able to say:

I have attended the right school and participated in challenging courses. I have graduated with honors. I have kept the faith, hope, and love.

So, what is love?

In my case, I was shown love and I was a subject of love in the first place. Then, I was taught and trained to love others. Next, I was introduced to God's love and advised to be grateful and glorify God for God's love and my creation. In the meantime, I was trying to love myself as much as possible and to love in the right way, by balancing selfishness and general goodness. After a series of deep reflections, I realized, I was who I thought I was. I was a representation of a bigger or smaller ego (EGO can also stand for "Edging God Out"), and the size of it depended on the situation. I came as close as I could to my core, and decided to rebuild my personal profile according to the best role model I could find – the way, the truth, and the life. After that, I entered the reality of a never-ending life, loving others as I did myself, and afterwards I accepted greater challenges in loving others – even those who could be my enemies, to finally prepare myself for the ultimate and the greatest form of love, which is giving my life for others. I don't know if I'm there, but I will know when the time comes.

These are my guidelines that I use to be better prepared:

"You must love the Lord your God with all your heart, with all your soul, and with all your mind." [ccliv] (Matthew 15, 37)

"To love is to will the good of the other."[cclv] - Saint Thomas Aquinas

"You must love your neighbor as yourself."[cclvi] (Matthew 15, 39)

But what if you love yourself improperly? Having the wrong kind of self-love as a reference point may be insidious, misleading, and harmful. There is no way out. We need the ideal.

Who is my neighbor?

"A man was once on his way down from Jerusalem to Jericho and fell into the hands of bandits; they stripped him, beat him and then made off, leaving him half dead. Now a priest happened to be travelling down the same road, but when he saw the man, he passed by on the other side. In the same way a Levite who came to the place saw him and passed by on the other side. But a Samaritan traveler who came upon him was moved with compassion when he saw him. He went up to him and bandaged his wounds, pouring oil and wine on them. He then lifted him onto his own mount and took him to an inn and looked after him. The next day, he took out two denarii and handed them to the innkeeper and said, look after him, and on my way back I will make good any extra expense you have. Which of these three do you think proved himself a neighbor to the man who fell into the bandits' hands? **The one who showed pity towards him**."[cclvii] (Luke 10, 30:37)

So true love is to show mercy, goodness, and loving kindness, to offer someone a helping hand. To really love means to really notice another human being – to stop, to listen, to accept the existence of another human being and to recognize the needs of his heart. To really love is to act.

There are two key questions worth asking and worth contemplating, as rightly pointed out by Pastor Adam Hamilton:

What will happen to me if I stop there to help?
or
What will happen to him if I do not stop there?

"A man only has the right to look down at another when he helps him to lift himself up." - Gabriel García Márquez

"[Let] us not love with words or speech but with actions and in truth. This is how we know that we belong to the truth and how we set our hearts at rest in his presence."[cclviii]
(1 John 3, 18:19)

The point is to be good to those that can't return the favor.
"Real love wants the good of the other and so it makes demands. [...] So, it's not sentimental. We hyper sentimentalized a lot of religious language and that caused huge problems. [...] So, when the Lord says to love your enemies - that's the great test of love. Because if it's your enemy this is not someone who is going to pay you back. So, if I'm kind to you that you might be kind to me, well, that's not love. [...] The point is to be good to those that can't return the favor." [cclix] – Bishop Robert Barron

"Love your enemies and pray for those who persecute you."[cclx]
(Matthew 5, 44)

This is totally counterintuitive, but totally understandable and reasonable in the light of the reality of eternal life.

Love of one's enemies is not a rational principle.
"[...] we're capable of [loving our enemies] because of grace operating in us, not justice of our own [...] will to excel. That's the result of a pure gift [...]."[cclxi]- Bishop Robert Barron

"Love one another. As I have loved you, so you must love one another."[cclxii] (John 13, 34)

"If anyone wants to be a follower of mine, let him renounce himself and take up his cross every day and follow me."[cclxiii] (Luke 9, 23)

Love means effort. Love means letting go of one's ego, acting against one's own desires, and responding to the needs of others. Love means looking up at the sky, looking beyond mortality and the fragility of things. Love means following God - personal and everlasting Love.

"No one can have greater love than to lay down his life for his friends." [cclxiv] (John, 15, 13)

In the absence of life-threatening situations in which our greater love could be tested, to lay down our lives for others may also mean: **to give our time and attention** to them, because the duration of our lives, here on earth, can be (and usually is) measured by units of time. Every "good, whole-hearted" minute that is devoted and offered to others shortens our lives for their sake.

It is all love-based.
"We're being drawn into the divine Love. Do we have to accept that love as an act of faith? Of course. God makes this great offer in Christ. Is it accepted in faith? Yeah. [...] Without faith you can't get into the spiritual life. [...] Now having made that great fundamental act, are you now called upon to be fully engaged, mind, will, passion, body, everything in response to that love [...]? Yes. [...] It begins with grace [...] and then cooperation with grace which manifests itself in a life of love."cclxv - Bishop Robert Barron

Love means taking responsibility for ourselves and others.
"Love means willing the good of the other as other. That might take the form [...] of calling somebody out and saying, look, what you're doing is repugnant to God's will. That's willing your good. That's not coming down hard on you, that's willing what's best for you."cclxvi - Bishop Robert Barron

My definition of love

Love is the most fully expressing and self-realizing, autonomous and conscious **act of the will to engage in action for the good of another human being** which is a gift of self-sacrifice (to the point of one's own death) for others and for one's own good that requires a **continuous effort** in getting to know oneself and another human being as well as developing oneself and others in all dimensions of humanity (physical, psychological, emotional and above all spiritual). It is important to maintain an attitude of **acceptance, lack of judgment, and forgiveness** (after Jesus). The goal of love is to **unite** in **joy and peace**, while **remaining our own individuality, overcoming the feeling of loneliness**, and thus **fear** and **shame**, and **minimizing pride and greed**.

At first, love needs to be accepted. Then, our harmful past needs to be forgiven (not forgotten) and finally accepted, and without any hatred, love can open itself up to an attitude of sacrifice. Such love enables me to serve myself, my family, my community, my company, and other people. The effect of living in love, is the feeling and state of happiness and fulfillment, despite the inevitable suffering inscribed in the nature and misunderstanding the meaning of human life on Earth (suffering as a result of the unavoidable effort put into the process of becoming).

Love assumes and confirms the existence of a personal being – a person - with his/her right to life, freedom and happiness. Love is an act of entering into unity with personal entities of the visible and invisible world. Love is in opposition to attractive philosophies which offer a captivating vision of life without suffering, which in a sublime way reduce man to meta-thoughts, leading to the idea of the impersonal substance, energy, or consciousness.

The model of perfect love (that is, the act of will directed towards union) may be described by the relationship between God the Father, God the Son and God the Spirit. A practical example of such perfect love was explained to us by Jesus Christ as love between men in the context of our present life, and it was shown to us when He offered His own life for us. The love of Jesus, others, and yourself creates the relationship of Love as well as Joy (**J**esus, **O**thers, **Y**ou).

Love is an act of the will to engage in action for the good of another human being.
But what is good for me or for others?
Something is good for me when it:
- Helps me to achieve happiness now and forever.
- Increases the meaning of life and the desire to live here and now, and also there and in the non-existent future.
- Increases the sense of freedom, decisiveness, and responsibility for one's own life.
- Increases one's sense of self-awareness, internal peace, and deep joy.
- Increases one's agency (including problem-solving) and passion for creation (If we assume that I can choose autonomously between action and no action, then both states can be good).
- Reduces feelings of loneliness, anxiety, shame, and prolonged frustration or dissatisfaction

- Balances (based on one's passion for creation) the need for (excessive) desire and enslavement (to anything standing in the way of one's freedom).
- Decreases lust and greed.
- Reduces existential tension (to have vs. be, to know vs. not know, to create vs. consume, to act vs. do nothing, enchant vs. fall in love, friendship vs. love, femininity vs. masculinity, matter vs. spirituality, nothing vs. something, meaning vs. meaninglessness, time vs. timelessness, here-and-now vs. there-and-after, creation vs. evolution, God vs. man).
- Helps to secure food, shelter, and basic security.
- Helps to teach responsibility for one's own life.
- Helps and comforts in the face of disease or loss.
- "Offers" me someone's time and undivided attention.
- Reminds us that love is expansive and provides freedom in unity (versus non-love which is drawing in, enslaving and devastating).

The goal of love is to unite us with others.
But what does "to be united" mean?
To be united means that we are one in joy and peace, while maintaining our own individuality. To be united with another human being means to create a close relationship, to provide a sense of security, to instill confidence and tenderness. It means to pay attention to the "good" needs and "good" desires. It is a balance in giving and receiving. "I am You" at the level of our hearts. "I am not You" at the level of matter, talents (forms and tools of giving), experiences, "good" desires, etc. When I look at you, in fact, I look at myself at the core, at the level of our souls. At that level it is very hard to hate anyone, it is very hard to reject anyone, it is very hard not to be united.

If I love, I am peaceful, and I dance.
If I do not love, I am afraid, and I fight.

Biblical definition of love

"If I speak in the tongues of men or of angels, but do not have love, I am only a resounding gong or a clanging cymbal.

If I have the gift of prophecy and can fathom all mysteries and all knowledge, and if I have a faith that can move mountains, but do not have love, I am nothing.

If I give all I possess to the poor and give over my body to hardship that I may boast, but do not have love, I gain nothing.

Love is **patient**, love is **kind**. It **does not envy**, it **does not boast**, it **is not proud**. It **does not dishonor others**, it **is not self-seeking**, it **is not easily angered, it keeps no record of wrongs**. Love **does not delight in evil** but **rejoices with the truth**. It **always protects, always trusts, always hopes, always perseveres**. Love **never fails**.

But where there are prophecies, they will cease; where there are tongues, they will be stilled; where there is knowledge, it will pass away."[cclxvii] (1 Corinthians 13, 1:8)

Lecture on wise love

Here is another accurate definition of love that I heard during a lecture on the subject given by a priest[cclxviii].

- Love is **selfless.** We love for nothing, but we do not trust for nothing. Ideal love loves without any merit.
- We must love **irrevocably**, like parents who love their children, especially small children. Ideal love loves forever.
- We must love up **close.** We ensure closeness by hugging, being together, devoting time and attention. I love everyone but love only a few people intimately – my closest family members and trusted friends. We ensure nearness. Hence, love or friendship via social media does not meet the assumption of proximity. There is no

possibility of achieving fulfillment from love over the Internet, via social media. In order to be able to exchange warmth effectively - people need physical presence and touch. This is a prerequisite for a happy life.

- Love has to be **visible.** Love must be seen via presence, sacrifice, tenderness, and patience.
- We have to love **wisely.** We have to love responsibly. Love does not mean pleasing others, love also means admonition. Exhortation should always be respectful and ensure the dignity of others.

How do we start loving?

- I am open to ideal love. I know I am loved by God.
- I imitate that love. I am actively getting to know love, and trying to love more and more.
- I am connected with those who love, too. I choose wisely the people with whom I share my life. I am loved, I love, and I am most connected with those who love the most.

What if I was not loved, or I am not loved by anyone?

- Not everyone was and is loved by someone.
- There are people who hate to be loved because they were never truly loved, they were removed from love, were abandoned or cut off from love, and it is too foreign to them to accept such an act of kindness. Even if someone offers true, unconditional love, they are not able to trust it.
- Without external, transcendent love, there may be no hope for happiness for them. The paradox is that there is no person on Earth who could fulfill our need for love in its entirety. We will never be satisfied with human love.
- **I suffer because I do not love. I suffer because I am not loved. I suffer because I try to love imperfect people who hurt me**.
- **The greatest tragedy is when people are sure that they will never love again. This tragedy is comparable to death – spiritual death**. The physical body can still function, but the person feels an inner emptiness and lack of hope, meaning in life, and sense in living.

- Even being in a very prosperous environment (family, community, society), sooner or later, existential suffering will kick in, and if there is no love, the human soul will be tortured.

When we love, nobody will take away our joy.

Joy is not an emotional state, but a state of soul and mind.

Happiness is the clear result of a life filled with love.

A Buddhist Monk's Definition of Love

"And of course, later on in life, we get into relationships. You know, where we start to experience love. Now, love for another human being, and the closeness of that love, and the trust and the vulnerability of that love, gives a more powerful meaning to things. Sometimes it lasts, sometimes it fades. And if it does last, it doesn't last forever. And I notice that most people in their search for meaning in life, they often stop there, you know, with this thing we call love, and not really understanding what it is, but getting some sense, some taste that there is some meaning in this thing. It can be incredibly fulfilling, for a while. [...] The love your kids show to you which is incredibly sweet - that selflessness - when you come home from work and your little five-year-old just runs to you, "Welcome home, mummy." There's something in that which has far more meaning than any sort of pleasure. And this is something which you look at. Why? That is most people feel that finding that love and experiencing that love and giving that love is the highest meaning of the world. [...] So much of that love is like the poppy, pluck the flower, the bloom it sheds may not be straight away but after a while. [...] You watch someone else from a distance as they go through their relationships and also when they go through the end of their relationships, especially, you know, when somebody dies and passes away, and all the pleasure of that love you shared together is replaced by this almost intolerable pain called grief. And someone you love so much, a young child, gets taken away. [...] How can the mother and father cope with that? The pain of that. [...] The grief always comes with that love. One of the reasons is that if we want to find meaning in life, that particular love, please don't confine it to a person. Keep it separate from the person but include that person. This is one of the things which as a monk, you know people say – don't you miss as a monk, having a relationship? I said, "What do you mean? I have so many relationships as a monk, with each one of you." And I don't mean sexual, I mean something much bigger, I'd been "opening the door of your heart" and including each of you in my life whenever you are in front of me. And I always think when you don't put love onto a person, but you put it around that person, include it, you don't just confine it, limit it to one being or two beings or three beings or ten beings. Then you find when that being goes, the love is still there. This is one of the things which I learnt from Buddhism. We have this beautiful thing called love, but we attach it to a being. We attach it to a thing and then when it's attached to a thing, when that being goes the love goes with it, replaced by pain. But for many people, you know, teaching, learning through meditation, who come to places like this, somebody dies but the love stays. It doesn't go. It doesn't end up with pain, with crying, with grief and not being able to go to work for weeks and years afterwards. That pain of grief is not there when we learn that love is not in a person, but love is just around them, surrounds them, soaks into them but [is] not confined to one particular being. [...] This what I'm talking about by this thing which we call love, changes the space, it's not with the person, it's totally independent of them. Maybe that person sparks and generates that love just like a wood can start a fire or oil starts a fire. But the oil is not the fire. The person is not the love. Love is something which that person ignites which is separate and exists independently. [...] A person dies, the love is still there and is not replaced by the grief, like something has been stolen from you. The person disappears but not the happiness, not the love, not the beauty, that will always remain. [...] Sometimes when we receive that love, we just attach to it. [...] Why is it so nice to be loved? Why do people search for that love? One of the things is because it gives us a sense of worth, at last, that somebody respects us. I must be okay because somebody loves me. That search for meaning of being worthwhile in this life, if we can't get that from many people, at least we can get that from one person, the person who loves us. That's why a mother's love is just so beautiful." *cclxix* – Ajahn Brahm, Buddhist monk

These are very nice descriptions of love, I must admit.

- This thing called love, changes the space, it's not with the person, it's totally independent of them.
- The person is not the love. Love is something which that person ignites which is separate and exists independently.
- Maybe that person sparks and generates that love just like a wood can start a fire or oil starts a fire. But the oil is not the fire.
- A person dies, the love is still there and is not replaced by the grief, like something has been stolen from you. The person disappears but not the happiness, not the love, not the beauty, that will always remain.

Love is a space, Love is a fire, Love remains, and everything else passes. I like this idea very much. However, not all of these conclusions are part of my belief system. "The fire" or "the sound of rushing wind", to mention a few, I believe are visible signs of God's presence in the world - the ultimate source of love and love itself. I am surrounded by this source, immersed in it, and this source is in me. Unlike Buddhism, or in addition, Love is a personal God. For me, love means acting according to God's will and always in relation to the other person. To love means to act according to the best possible strategy for life that guarantees true happiness. Infatuation, affection, passion are not the forms of love we are talking about here. Although it can be incredibly fulfilling, it will last only for a while. Even if it does last longer than a while, it doesn't last forever.

So, should we love a particular person? Should we get attached to others? Buddhist monks' recommendations are not to do so.

This seems like a trade-off between "close love" and pain.

It is indeed a very reasonable way for us to reduce our own suffering over the loss of loved ones. Keeping away from bonding, keeping away from deep and long-term personal relationships with concrete persons seems to be an attractive strategy that minimizes our discomfort in hard times of separation, or permanent detachment. But what is the point of such an emotionally, mentally and physically distant life? We live together but in reality, we live separately. Maybe it is all about a healthy balance, like most aspects of a good life?

I think we are coming back to fundamental questions: Why are we here? What/Who "caused" us? Who are we? What is our real nature? Do we really exist, or do we merely think we exist? Are we individual persons or just random representations of one universal consciousness? What will happen to us after we die, after we lose our awareness of existence and dissolve in the ocean of matter? Will we see each other again? Will we be able to recognize each other and reconnect?

As long as we anchor our current life in the current world – either we will constantly be afraid of losing loved ones and remain fearful, or we will distance ourselves emotionally, not allowing deep and beautiful relationships to happen, and fall into existential loneliness that is either well camouflaged by the stillness of a well-trained mind, or not well camouflaged.

> And what if we were created to live life to the fullest? What if, instead of sitting passively on the "bike of our life" held and pushed from behind by someone who cares about our safety, we could ride the bike ourselves - steering and pedalling with enough power not to fall down. We may pedal faster to have better balance and a little more fun. Of course, there is a limit to how hard we should push and push the bike forward so as not to endanger our lives. Balance is the key word, as usual.

What's the right balance in our lives? Maybe we had better stay at home because so many dangers lurk outside. Something may fall on our heads, we may stumble and fall, we may be hit by cars, etc.

> What would your swimming experience be like if you kept the lifeguard's pool stick in front of you all the time?

> What would your treasure hunt experience be like if you could see the treasure chest before looking at the map?

What would your mountain hiking experience be like if you could only walk around your house in circles connected to video game controllers and glasses?

Would that be a satisfying depth of life experience? What is your gut feeling? What is your intuition?

What would your life experience be if you could only live for a short moment? And what would your life experience be if you could live forever?

I fell in love with a specific promise, and I really expect this promise to come true. I believe that we are unique beings with our own, individual, unique, different immortal souls, with our own, individual, unique, different mortal bodies, created to experience freedom and to participate with great joy in life's journey - to unite in Love. And God, who created us, is our beginning, our love, our guidance and our destiny.

"God is a person who has created us individually, who loves us personally, who guides us and who draws us ultimately into his own life." [cclxx] - Bishop Robert Barron

I believe that after our physical deaths we all will meet again, most probably in different quality embodiments, and will continue our endless adventure. There should be no place for boredom because in the "higher level" reality there will be no time and most probably something much different, broader and deeper than space presenting endless possibilities to us. Thus, it is now beyond our imagination and beyond our senses.

For me, "to love" means to act for the benefit of another person according to a role model and at the same time, not be afraid to have close relationships with loved ones. When the time comes to bid farewell, I would like to look into the future with hope, believing we will meet very soon. In the meantime, when "you" are gone, I suffer emptiness caused by lack of your physical presence, but as the time passes, I hope I will be able to start loving others again and be loved by them. I have no doubt, there are so many people waiting for my heart to turn to them – there is unlimited space for unsatisfied love out there in the world. The desire for love and the action for love is a never-ending project to which we can devote ourselves fully. I can guarantee that in true love you will never be bored, and before you notice, you will start a new chapter of your book of life – singing, "Heaven, I'm in heaven // And my heart beats so that I can hardly speak // And I seem to find the happiness I seek..."[cclxxi]

- "I'd been "opening the door of your heart" and including each of you in my life whenever you are in front of me," says our monk.
- Love any of your neighbors, says my teacher.
- In case it is very hard for you to love a particular person, the first step would be to start loving his/her pure heart with your pure heart (such a Benedictine practice). Love at the level of hearts, not at the level of schemas, egos, or instincts.

At the "deepest" level of our hearts we should all be equal.

What about romantic love?

I remember that I loved that short dialogue from the movie "Meet Joe Black" where the father (Parrish, performed by Anthony Hopkins) encourages his daughter (Susan, performed by Claire Forlani) to be open to finding real love:

"[Father:] - I want you to get swept away out there. I want you to levitate. I want you to... sing with rapture and dance like a dervish.

[Daughter:] - Oh, that's all.

[Father:] - Yeah. Be deliriously happy, or at least leave yourself open to be.

[Daughter:] - Okay. "Be deliriously happy." I shall, uh-- I shall do my utmost. [Chuckling]

*[Father:] - I know it's a cornball thing. But love is passion, obsession, someone you can't live without. I say, fall head over heels. Find someone you can love like crazy and who will love you the same way back. How do you find him? Well, **you forget your head, and you listen to your heart**. And I'm not hearing any heart. 'Cause the truth is, honey, there's no sense living your life without this. **To make the journey and not fall deeply in love, well, you haven't lived a life at all. But you have to try, 'cause if you haven't tried, you haven't lived.***

[Daughter:] - Bravo!

[Father:] - Oh, you're tough.

[Daughter:] - I'm sorry. Okay. Give it to me again, but the short version this time.

*[Father:] - Okay. Stay open. Who knows? **Lightning could strike**.*

[Daughter:] [Chuckling]

[Father:] - Yeah?

[Daughter:] – Yeah. [cclxxii]

In my case, lightning did strike in my life, immediately after I made a decision to love my wife according to the Way, the Truth and the Life. Lightning strikes when I make decisions to stop and help, to offer my time and attention to others, to respond to the needs of other people's hearts that call to be fulfilled. It can be romantic when it is mutual, but it doesn't have to be. It is for sure spiritual – more peaceful than crazy, more joyful than delirious. Having romantic and spiritual love at the same time sounds like the best possible dream.

How do I know I love?

- Did I give you something to eat when you were hungry?
- Did I give you something to drink when you were thirsty?
- Did I invite you in when you were a stranger?
- Did I clothe you when you needed clothes?

- Did I look after you when you were sick?
- Did I come and visit you when you were in prison?

"Lord, when did we see you hungry and feed you, or thirsty and give you something to drink? When did we see you a stranger and invite you in, or needing clothes and clothe you? When did we see you sick or in prison and go to visit you? [...]

Truly I tell you, whatever you did for one of the least of these brothers and sisters of mine, you did for me."[cclxxiii] (Matthew 25, 37:46)

- **Do I lay down my life for my friends?**
- **Do I devote my undivided time and attention to others?**

What if real love is not from this world?

Imagine that as a parent, for the fifth time in a row, you are trying to explain to your four-year-old son that he must not run after the ball into the street, or that he must not slip on the freshly frozen lake, or that he must not throw stones over the bushy fence – to make sure that nothing tragic will happen. Seeing for the sixth time that the behavior of your loved one hasn't changed yet, you may feel disappointed, frustrated, or even angry. Is lack of obedience a sign of ill will, or the malicious nature of a child? Is this more a lack of true understanding of how things work, a lack of imagination, a lack of experience, no sense of responsibility for one's own life and the lives of others, no sense of the true value of life, or a lack of something else? What if we were told a thousand times that to live a happy life, we needed to follow clear guidelines? Imagine now that there is The One who knows it all and comes to us with Good News. He comes with the recipe and we are not mature enough to listen, or open-minded enough to accept a different alternative, we are not brave enough to try, we are not strategic enough to see beyond the horizon of our current, well-known comfort zones (which are not so comfortable). What if real love is not from this world? It seems it isn't. And what if it turns out, to give our souls what they deeply desire, we have to accept this counterintuitive logic of this "alien Love."? What if we have to open ourselves to the new promise and the new normal, before we start experiencing extraordinary and outstanding outcomes – fruitful and flourishing lives? We are so blind to the different reality of life that if someone new suddenly shows up at our doorstep with really good news, we would be ready to crucify Him/Her again. The historical Jesus, who was put to death by those whom he loved "the most," was extremely disappointed. What a strange response to such an offer of love. Again, maybe it was immaturity, maybe it was short-sighted thinking, maybe it was living in a hurry, maybe it was a simple fear of change, maybe it was jealousy, or maybe it was the desire to stay in power. Maybe there exists a much greater, broader and deeper "reality" than ours, and our "visible reality" is a subset of it. How would one feel coming from that "real reality" (beyond the human world) to this "visible reality" (the human world)? How would we feel hearing and seeing such a good stranger who proclaims, experiences this reality, lives according to the "real reality", dies before our eyes, and then returns to that better reality? Although immersed in deep suffering and condemned to death by those to whom He came, He did it all with the deepest peace and great dignity. He didn't beg for life, but rather preferred to return home,

""**My kingdom is not of this world.** If it were, my servants would fight to prevent my arrest by the Jewish leaders. But now my kingdom is from another place." […"] In fact, the reason I was born and came into the world is to testify to the truth. Everyone on the side of truth listens to me.""[cclxxiv] –Jesus (John 18, 36:37)

Living in the Ocean

Let's assume that logic of "real reality" is to guarantee all living creatures (endowed with free will) to coexist forever and in harmony. How could we achieve that?

Let's assume that "real reality" is an ocean, and every single water molecule represents individual beings (body and soul). One water molecule is somehow connected to another water molecule by invisible forces or fields. That connectivity, interrelationship, and direct influence of one molecule on another is a real and observable thing. When we look at the ocean from a distance, let's say from the sky level, we see it as one moving, pulsating, or waving object that resembles a membrane (or enormous trampoline for kids, a flag or a sheet fluttering in the wind). When we look at it from a microscopic point of view, we see particles and molecules – no membrane (no trampoline, flag or sheet) can be seen or even sensed anymore. Let's assume that when the ocean is flat and has no waves, we call it peaceful. When the ocean is peaceful, we assume water molecules are peaceful, too. Beings are relaxed and painful tensions do not arise between them. They remain in perfect balance and distribute accumulated energy evenly to all. It's like people holding hands loosely – a very pleasant feeling. Beings are united and "happy." The best state seems to be the peaceful ocean state. It is hard to notice any individual molecule or group of molecules standing out from that molecular crowd. They are more like one ocean than themselves individually. But it depends on the point of view.

Let's assume one water molecule wants to differentiate itself to satisfy its particular need. It rises higher and higher, but at the same time, it tightens the bonds that it has with other molecules. It can see more – trying to look for beyond the horizon – but it stretches the network of connections. It feels excitement, but at the same time, it experiences a lot of stress being on top of the wave, afraid of falling. It experiences fear while being lonely out there. Although it decided to go there alone, it has pulled the closest ones behind it as well. That generates frustrations on the part of those who were taken against their will. The higher it goes (or lower it goes) relative to the ocean level, the further away it moves from the peaceful equilibrium, harmonized unity, truth of life, "God's reality." Although not moving itself forward or backward (because "In reality, the water in waves doesn't travel"[cclxxv]) it generates huge waves of anxiety for the whole system. The ocean is no longer peaceful and relaxed. ("Ocean waves transport energy over vast distances, although the water itself does not move, except up and down. This may surprise you, but if you think about it, once you are past the breakers on your raft, you pretty much just bob up and down."[cclxxvi])

It's like when people hold hands, and someone decides to go in a different direction and tries to pull the whole group behind him. It is not pleasant anymore – it is difficult and painful to hold hands and not disconnect. When one soul decides to follow its illusory "I" (ego) and fulfills its own needs and desires, forgetting about the relationships it stays in - it generates tensions between all, it causes suffering for all. One molecule can cause a chain reaction – wave reaction – a storm. The higher it jumps away from the surface of peace and unity, the greater the fear, alienation, and fallout. The more it tries to keep the balance by responding to needs of others, the more it "loves."

Now, if you know that we live in such an ocean of body and souls, molecules of the "water of life," (or we live on an endless membrane, trampoline, flag or sheet of our "real reality") AND you come to the people that live in the so called "just visible reality" (human reality), who have no clue that other superior reality exists, imagine how hard it would be for you to explain the different rules of life to them. (By the way, Membrane theory 'M-theory' is an existing theory in physics that unifies all of the consistent versions of superstring theory; and 'String theory' is a broad and varied subject that attempts to address a number of deep questions of fundamental physics). In the best case, you would be ignored, in the moderate case you would be called insane, and in the worst case you would be imprisoned or killed because your theory of everything would conflict with the worldview of those who currently rule and benefit from the status quo.

The problem is, it is not obvious that we live in the ocean or on a membrane, being one of many tiny particles located on its surface. There is no way to understand this logic in its totality. (It's like explaining to a child why people from the opposite side of the globe don't fall into space. After introducing the concept of gravity, still walking upside down remains a mystery to most of us).

There are some signs, signals, interpretations of natural laws, intuitions, gut feelings, and pangs of conscience that allow us to think there is something more than a localized view of our "visible reality," something more powerful and more intelligent. But interestingly, those who become believers have no problem accepting the truthfulness of the holy-ocean-reality. They have no problem living close to the surface of united souls, by practicing perfect love to ensure balance for themselves and others. Giving to others guarantees no storms or hurricanes. Exchanging perfect love eliminates internal and external tensions and in turn brings greater peace, joy, and happiness.

What if one or multiple water molecules evaporate from the ocean due to too much sun and too much wind? Droplets of water are now floating in the sky – that is their reality of death or life after death. They are now free, they are in Heaven. What a transformation, what a metamorphosis. Believing molecules (believers) are not afraid of death, they are waiting for it to experience something more powerful and more intelligent.

So, what if our spiritual life really happens on a similar, but obviously more sophisticated ocean, or membrane? (And throughout the ages we have had so many similar intuitions and scientific theories around oceans, membranes, strings, parallel universes, consciousness, All is God, souls, spirits, The Holy Spirit, Heaven on Earth, Heaven in us, Heaven in our hearts? As per beautiful song by Anna Maria Jopek "Niebo/Heaven": "If Heaven, eternal Heaven is the sum of our souls, we are almost there, so close to it, so close"[cclxxvii]).

Let's assume that the logic of "real reality" world is to guarantee all living creatures eternal and harmonious coexistence. How could we achieve this? Doesn't my free will give me an opportunity to do anything I want? Doesn't your free will give you the same opportunity to do whatever you want? How do we ensure that all of us coexist? What if I I help you to fulfill all your needs, and you help me to fulfill mine? What if you suddenly would want to satisfy your hunger and I am not ready to share my only meal with you at this very moment? Would you try to influence me, maybe force me to share it or give it away or even steal it from me? Would we allow violence? What if you suddenly wanted to satisfy your sexual needs and I did not want to help you? Would we allow such violence? You satisfy your needs anytime you want, and I satisfy mine anytime I want; that would be an interesting rule of life. I don't think we can solve the problem of meeting such needs so easily, especially in the world of interconnected beings. Imagine that we are talking here not only about two individuals, but billions of us living on our planet at the same time. How could we arrange the world appropriately? Perhaps the intuition of perfect love (love as a relationship, love as the act of doing good to others, love as an attitude and practice of putting others before ourselves) can guarantee the coexistence of all creatures? But what if by practicing perfect love someone sacrifices his own life for someone else, and does not exist or coexist anymore? Will such a perfect love be the solution for all of us? It seems not for everyone, only for those who have survived. Unless we assume that we live forever in this "real reality." Current sacrifices can indeed lead to the peaceful coexistence of all and create the ultimate unity of all creatures – in the long run.

So, what if our spiritual life really happens in a similar, but of course more sophisticated ocean? Do you think our life choices would be different? How would we design our world around such truth? It would be a totally different story. Wouldn't it? I am sure. What if dying is like evaporating and frivolous hovering towards the sun? What if dying is like an accumulation of evaporated drops from the ocean of earthly life into the united clouds of eternal life. All together again, in a slightly different form and closer to the sun. What a nice perspective, what a nice dream. Maybe instead of writing prose, I should switch to poetry. And of course, my example of intuition is far from perfect, there are so many inconsistencies, but that is as far I decided to go, while writing this book. A different book will feature different intuitions.

"The Son is the image of the invisible God, the firstborn over all creation. **For in him all things were created**: things in heaven and on earth, visible and invisible, whether thrones or powers or rulers or authorities; all things have been created through him and for him. He is before all things, and in him all things hold together."[cclxxviii] (Colossians 1, 15:17)

What if we were created in Him, our Ocean, our Perfect Love – allowing us to be united and to live like that forever?

Why there is suffering?

I can understand the huge frustration of the "New Atheists" of our times, proudly represented by the minds of Christopher Hitchens[+], Richard Dawkins, Daniel Dennett, Sam Harris, or Bill Maher, to name only a few, who based on evidence truly hate organized religion. I am really delighted while listening to their arguments and eloquent explanations of how humanity has fallen into the mental trap of believing in an imaginary God and remains blind to all the terrible things that happen in the world, created by that fictitious Creator. Some may say, "How come such a good God created such a bad world? And it's not only about all the forces of nature that prevent us from staying alive, not to mention living happy lives, but it is also about us, violent people capable of domination, slavery, and even murder. Good God versus extreme living conditions. Good God versus aggressive chemical and biological structures, viruses and bacteria on a mission of continuous invasion. Good God versus the image of God – imperfect and disappointing man".

No one has ever guaranteed us that we will live a long, prosperous life free of suffering and pain. Rather we are guaranteed to experience sickness at some point (including life-threatening diseases), we will experience suffering and pain, we will experience different levels of poverty or the real risk of poverty, our loved ones will die, and we will die for sure – the majority of us in our 60s, 70s and 80s, some of us at a very young age, some of us even at conception.

Our suffering usually raises the following questions or doubts:

"If God is loving and just, then God must not be all powerful. Or, if God is all-powerful, God must not be loving and just. […]
Can we reconcile belief in a loving and powerful God with the suffering present in our world? […]
Why is God punishing me?"[cclxxix] - Adam Hamilton, senior pastor

---

Living in an Anthill

If God is omniscient and God knows things, does God influence everything to make it happen? Can you see the future of an ant?
So is God omniscient, or not? Does God know when and what will happen to us? Isn't this like looking at an anthill from a distance and watching hundreds of ants move around in a given moment, simultaneously? We can see them all together and also individually. We know more or less when and where a chosen one started its expedition and more or less when and where it will end it. What we don't know is (unlike God who is omniscient), what their "little choices" will be on their way to their future, their destiny. There are hundreds or thousands of choices to be made when facing a rock, facing a stick, facing a water stream, facing a small tree or a big tree or facing a wall – all classified as roadblocks, obstacles, problems to be solved. We may not know (and in this particular scenario of our imaginary analogy), we may not want to know (leaving some "freedom" to those we watch, to those we "created") if an ant decides to go to the right or to the left, go up or down, or even turn around and march back. This is the "free will" at the local ant level applied to the real life of the ant. have no idea that they are observed from above. Ants have no idea that by walking straight ahead for another five minutes they will be drawn in by the rapid river, they will be trampled by a running child, or squashed by an apple falling from a tree. It is not their fault. It's their world's logic and their world's behavior – it's their life situation. They have zero impact

on most (external) events, but still have some impact on selected ones: go to the right or to the left, go up or go down, turn around a little bit or turn back and march in the opposite direction. Does this remind us of something? Be good or be bad, stop and listen, rush and do not pay attention, stop and help, run and don't care. It can happen that we make a bad turn and miss our mark. We fall from the cliff of happiness to the abyss of misery. In a hypothetical world of local freedom and free will, we let creatures to make these life choices.

Does God allow everything to happen?
I think God allows everything God created to happen, and God allows this created everything to act according to its created nature, according to different degrees of evolved self-awareness, different degrees of evolved self-determination, ultimately different degrees of evolved personal freedom. One important fact about the created world that has to be taken into consideration is that everything is in conjunction and combination with everything else. So, there is no individual being and its individual situation that should only be considered, analyzed and taken care of, but the whole network of interconnected beings needs to be considered, analyzed and taken good care of. In the best possible world, individual and connected others are coexisting (in human words) in perfect harmony, peace, and love. I believe that everything is designed according to God's plan: human beings are free and called to live together. I believe that everything is destined according to God's plan: human beings are to unite and live forever. But not everything that happens at the local human level is planned by God, and that is the beauty of perfect design. To ensure the successful realization of a God's plan, parallel things have to happen in parallel. Beings have to be able to experience life to its totality including the ability to make their own choices of being like God, or not, and whether to continue on their current life path or not. People have to be able to create unity among themselves, if not during their episodic and short earthly lives, then afterwards in their eternal life (maybe with endless and surprising episodes). Unfortunately, looking at the universe's and our Earth's history, we quickly realize how short our human life on the Earth is.

13.799 billion years of the universe versus 300 thousand years of the existence of the human species. In perspective, if the age of the universe was 1 year, Homo sapiens would be there for about 11 minutes. Now, when comparing the life expectancy of an individual person, for example, considering 75 years as an average life expectancy, then the length of individual life would be 170 milliseconds (17% of 1 second) in a 1-year-old universe.

Because our lives are so short, it is hard to imagine we can achieve unity in love for all humanity (7.8 billion of us in 2020) in one step, in one generation. It seems that by design, to be successful in the realization of God's plan, our individual human lives have to go beyond what we know and consider as life. And if that is the case, we live not only here and now, but in the distant future, and the problem of suffering and death is not a problem anymore. Without a promise of eternal life and attainable unity, suffering and death are indeed meaningless and shape an unjust and horrible reality, including an unjust and horrible portrait of God. Having hope for eternal life and united, "loving" beings, we are entering into a totally different story, where suffering and even death take on meaning. Isn't the perspective of an endless life in love the worldview changer? If we were to unite (regardless of the time horizon), aren't all these inconveniences, pains, including the gift of one's own life, the only means of achieving the ultimate goal? Maybe. Also, if we pay enough attention, we may realize that suffering and death are important forces that enable certain qualities in us. When one of us is going through hard times, it can motivate us to do good for him/her. We suddenly become empathetic, we start listening actively, we perform acts of kindness, we arrange personal or group support, including provision of resources and running charities. For sure, suffering and death are powerful forces, indispensable factors in the equation of life that can release enormous amounts of good in us and push us to action.

Does everything happen for a reason?

"If by 'everything happens for a reason' we simply mean that we live in a world of cause and effect, then of course this is true. But if we mean that everything happens according to God's plan, and that God wills everything that happens, this cannot be true. When we say that it is true, then [...] we misrepresent the nature and character of God."[cclxxx] - Adam Hamilton, senior pastor

Is it true that if I believe in God and try to be a good person, God will take care of me and bless me and nothing bad will happen to me?
"The Bible definitely does not teach that those who follow God will have a life of bliss. It describes the dogged faith of those who continue to trust in God despite their suffering, and the comfort, strength, and hope they find in the face of suffering." [cclxxxi] - Adam Hamilton, senior pastor

Is being truly free the greatest good we can get?
"The philosopher Søren Kierkegaard claimed that divine omnipotence cannot be separated from divine goodness. As a truly omnipotent and good being, God could create beings with true freedom over God. Furthermore, God would voluntarily do so because 'the greatest good... which can be done for a being, greater than anything else that one can do for it, is to be truly free'. [...] God can be all-powerful and all-knowing even while people continue to exercise free will, because God transcends time." [cclxxxii]

What about suffering caused by human decisions?
"If we have no choices, and we only always do God's will, we cease to be human and become puppets. We human beings value our freedom above practically everything else. Part of the risk God took in giving us freedom is that we might and probably will misuse that freedom [...]" [cclxxxiii] - Adam Hamilton, senior pastor

Most of the world's pain is because people and societies fail to practice love.
"Who wouldn't agree that most of the world's pain is because people and societies stray from the right path – because they fail to practice love?" [cclxxxiv] - Adam Hamilton, senior pastor

No one does evil but for the sake of a perceived good.
"Ask Yourself Two Questions:
1. Do you believe that all humans have an instinct to benefit themselves?
2. Do you believe that all humans, to the extent that they suffer, instinctually seek to relieve their suffering?

If you answered yes to the above questions, then you can accept the idea that nobody chooses to do wrong when they perceive that the wrongdoing in question will bring harm upon them. To the extent that we simply obey our instinct to benefit ourselves and relieve our suffering, we are not willing to harm ourselves. Socrates believed that persons who seek what they understand to benefit them are not trying to do wrong. They do not act for the sake of the wrong, but for the sake of obtaining the perceived good with which they are trying to improve their lives."[cclxxxv]

I don't do what I want, but I do what I hate.

"We know that the law is spiritual; but I am unspiritual, sold as a slave to sin. I do not understand what I do. For what I want to do I do not do, but what I hate I do. And if I do what I do not want to do, I agree that the law is good. As it is, it is no longer I myself who do it, but it is sin living in me. For I know that good itself does not dwell in me, that is, in my sinful nature. For I have the desire to do what is good, but I cannot carry it out. For I do not do the good I want to do, but the evil I do not want to do-this I keep on doing. Now if I do what I do not want to do, it is no longer I who do it, but it is sin living in me that does it. So I find this law at work: Although I want to do good, evil is right there with me. For in my inner being I delight in God's law; but I see another law at work in me, waging war against the law of my mind and making me a prisoner of the law of sin at work within me. What a wretched man I am! Who will rescue me from this body that is subject to death? Thanks be to God, who delivers me through Jesus Christ our Lord! So then, I myself in my mind am a slave to God's law, but in my sinful nature a slave to the law of sin." [cclxxxvi] (Romans 7, 14:25)

So it seems, "No one does evil but for the sake of a perceived good," but at the same time we tend to do what we hate. What a complicated situation. Are we able, on our own, in a sustainable way, to do at least objectively accepted good? Following lessons from the history of humankind, we can say "not really." We are not strong enough on our own to sustain peace and stay in harmony. Unless we start to believe in something greater than ourselves, something that transcends us – which gives us more clarity on the meaning, reason, and purpose of life, which gives us hope that there is something much better than this. A complicated situation suddenly becomes simple and understandable.

Although most of the world's pain is caused by people, at the same time most (or almost all) of the world's joy is also caused by people. Another incredible paradox.
"God's primary way of working in the world is through people who are empowered and led by God's Spirit." [cclxxxvii] - Adam Hamilton, senior pastor

What about natural disasters and human suffering? Earthquakes or floods are not God.
"We are no longer bound to believe that God sends earthquakes or floods. Likewise we understand why God does not intervene and stop these things from occurring; to do so would be to ensure the destruction of our planet. [...] When human beings get caught in these giant forces of nature, there is death and devastation, but the forces themselves are essential to life on our planet." [cclxxxviii] - Adam Hamilton, senior pastor

What about suffering caused by sickness?
"When we become ill, many of us ask, 'Why me, God?' [...] Sickness is not God's way. When Jesus walked this earth, he devoted much of his time to healing the sick, not to making people sicker." [cclxxxix] - Adam Hamilton, senior pastor

COVID-19

* As of this writing, more than 9,300,000 people have tested positive for COVID-19 in the U.S. and more than 230,000 Americans have died.

* Please follow CDC recommendations and read "How to protect yourself" on www.cdc.gov

I wonder what your reaction would be after reading the following perspective on COVID-19:

"There is so much fear, and perhaps rightfully so, about COVID-19. And, what if... we subscribe to the philosophy that life is always working out for us, that there is an intelligence far greater than humans at work? That all is interconnected? What if... the virus is here to help us? To reset. To remember. What is truly important. Reconnecting with family and community. Reducing travel so that the environment, the skies, the air, our lungs all get a break. Parts of China are seeing blue sky and clouds for the first time in forever with the factories being shut down. Working from home rather than commuting to work means less pollution and more personal time. Reconnecting with family as there is more time at home. An invitation to turn inwards — a deep meditation — rather than the usual extroverted going out to self-soothe. To reconnect with self — what is really important to me? A reset economically. The working poor. The lack of healthcare access for over 30 million in the US. The need for paid sick leave. How hard does one need to work to be able to live, to have a life outside of work? To face our mortality — check back into "living" life rather than simply working, working, working. To reconnect with our elders, who are so susceptible to this virus. And, washing our hands — how did that become a "new" thing that we needed to remember. But, yes, we did. The presence of Grace for all. There is a shift underway in our society — what if it is one that is favorable for us? What if this virus is an ally in our evolution? In our remembrance of what it means to be connected, humane, living a simpler life, to be less impactful / more kind to our environment. An offering from my heart this morning. Offered as another perspective. Another way of relating to this virus, this unfolding, this evolution. It was time for a change, we all knew that. And, change has arrived. What if..."[ccxc] *- by Gurpreet Gill*

I can imagine variety of reactions, but at least these two got my attention recently:

1. "There is so much truth in it. There is a reason, and we will see benefits soon" or
2. "I wonder what the millions infected and the families of those Americans who have died of COVID think? Do they really contemplate the wonder of life?

What is going on here? Is it wonderful, or scary, horrible and dreadful? Why God has allowed those "wonderful" things to happen? Why God has allowed these terrible things to happen?

Is dying part of living?

"Disease and sickness, injury and death are all a part of having flesh-and-blood bodies. [...] Part of the risk of living is that we might get sick and we will die. This is not God's doing, it is simply part of the having bodies like ours in a world like ours." ccxci - Adam Hamilton, senior pastor

Why do we die from viruses?

Because we are vulnerable, chemical and biological living "objects" in this world of "objects," and other chemicals, biological structures, or organisms can destroy us.

Suffering never has the final word in the Christian faith.

"Rejecting God doesn't change the situation that has caused our suffering; it only removes the greatest source of hope, help, comfort, and strength we have. [...] Christianity does not promise that we will not suffer, but it does promise that suffering will never have the final word." ccxcii - Adam Hamilton, senior pastor

What about miracles?

"But if Jesus of Nazareth was more than a man, if in fact God had come to us in him, walking on our planet, would these acts [miracles] not be the very kinds of things we would expect as he encountered suffering, darkness, and death?"[ccxciii] - Adam Hamilton, senior pastor

I believe that God's miracles happen in my life, from the moment I consciously turned to a personal God by kindly asking for support (to be honest, I begged for help) to change my teacher's plans to humiliate me in public before my entire school after my misconduct at the age of 11. The next day, I couldn't recognize my teacher – she transformed from an authoritative, unforgiving, and vindictive person to a friendly, forgiving, and gentle one—a role model. Such metamorphoses do not usually happen overnight. I was not able to ignore what happened. That traumatic and at the same time euphoric experience aroused my curiosity. A visible sign of something unnatural just appeared in my presence. Did Anyone hear me? Was it possible?

Of course, the more I thought about it, the more I tried to explain to myself and rationalize it. I went from a miracle, through my own magical abilities, to just a coincidence. After about thirty-five years of paying attention to those supernatural incidents, I have no doubts – I experience real miracles in my life. Even if I try to classify them as "impossible coincidences," they always fall back into inexplicable, extremely complicated and complex interrelated and interconnected events that bend space-time, orchestrate individual life threads of multiple people, life situations and geographies to ultimately present overwhelming, shocking, indescribable solutions to real-life problems. It lifts my heart to the heights of delight, spiritual pleasure.

Let me give you some examples of my impossible coincidences in life - miracles:

- *My beloved grandfather, who was already an elderly man, was lying unconscious in the emergency room and was qualified for coronary artery bypass surgery - which in his case was assessed as extremely risky.*

I kneeled on my knees for hours asking God for a successful procedure. I wrote down my "pleasures" on a piece of paper and offered to give them up so that I could enjoy the health and life of my grandfather. I really wanted him to take part in my wedding and meet his future grandchildren. He survived. When he looked at me the day after the surgery, he said he was already in Heaven and was ready to go back there at any time. He had a lot of fun at my wedding. He also had a chance to play with his granddaughter. He died many years later. **Miracle or Coincidence?**

- My fiancée and I had a serious problem with our remote relationship, one of us lived in Europe and the other in America.
I was on my knees for many days, asking God for help. This American (Bill), whom I accidentally met at a bus stop in Warsaw, Poland, Europe three years earlier, brought us back together. What really happened? While still a student, I walked around the city of Warsaw coming back from my lectures. A group of American tourists approached me with a request to show them the direction. "Excuse me, how can we get to the old market?" I explained it clearly and we said goodbye. Ten hours later I walked in a completely different place of that big city and like with the touch of a magic wand, the same American tourists came out from around the corner - shock, disbelief and joy. The American (Bill), pulled out his business card and gave it to me, and asked for my e-mail address. After writing it down, we shaken hands, exchanged smiles and said goodbye. Then we kept in touch by e-mail for many years. One day Bill found a 100-year-old envelope in the basement of his house in Chicago and shared it with me. I found, unexpectedly, his European relatives from a barely visible address and a stamp on the envelope. I knocked on the door of a hundred years old apartment and saw a family of three generations waiting to be discovered. After a few years, they all met together. Later I also had the opportunity to visit Bill and his wonderful wife Ann at their lovely home in St. Charles, Illinois. Then, after a few more years, my fiancée worked in the U.S. while I worked in Europe. Then the problem with our remote relationship began. Because she also met the same man I had met many years before, this saved our future marriage. This random American, unknown to us, who took care of her at the right time with great affection and understanding, saved our marriage. The unexpected meeting that took place somewhere in the heart of Europe changed the course of my family life. We have been happily married for 17 years. We love our "random" American women and men and treat them as our American family, our American parents. I have known Bill for 25 years. **Miracle or Coincidence?**

- I was diagnosed as infertile and I have medical records of it.

I ran workshops for missionary organizations that send missionaries and volunteers from Poland to African countries. After successful sessions, I was asked by participants about my deepest dream, because they wanted to pray for it, for me. I told them about my inability to have children. They formed a circle, took their hands and started to pray. At the same time they informed their colleagues from Africa about it and they joined in the prayer. After a month my wife announced to me that we would have a baby. Now we have three beautiful children. **Miracle or Coincidence?**

- Our very close family member, my role model of fatherhood, got into alcoholism and physically, intellectually, emotionally and spiritually "disappeared" from our family life for years.
We all fervently asked God to intervene. In more than human patience, his loving wife prayed on her knees and shed an ocean of tears. Hope once came alive and once died. I spent many hours talking to my God asking: "Please use me as your tool. I want to be your words and your hands. I want to be your helper." Many thoughts and words came straight from my heart during this difficult time when I was sitting with that suffering soul, fighting for a new life. For "he" was born again. He came back as a caring husband, as a wonderful father of three children, as an extremely valuable member of the local community, who serves children and volunteers in crisis situations (now he helps people day and night during the covid pandemic). From non-existence he returned to our life and became our and social hero. **Miracle or Coincidence?**

- Our beloved Ann (an American mother from a previous history) has been lying in a hospital bed in a coma for several days.
My wife and I prayed for her recovery, for relief from her suffering, for strength for her husband Bill, who spent hours at her bedside every day. Many kind people prayed for them during this time. On one Thursday we made a quick decision to take a 9-hour drive from Kansas to St. Charles and visit Ann in her hospital room and spend some time with Bill. To make it more bearable for our children, we made one stop in Des Moines, Iowa and stayed overnight. Finally, with a bouquet of fresh flowers, we arrived around 4 p.m. on Saturday. She was breathing calmly and regularly. We put our hands on her and started praying. I asked God for her recovery, but I also gave it to His decision, saying: "Your will be done on earth as in heaven". My wife was praying: "If this is Your will, please take her home and give her eternal happiness. And before we left, she said to Ann: "Your sons and we will take good care of Bill." Two hours later, when we were having our family dinner with Bill, he got a phone call that his beloved wife and long-time friend died - around 4:40 p.m. (about 20 minutes after our visit). They

had been married for over fifty years. We hugged each other. Was it Ann's decision? Was it a divine decision? Was it just the perfect moment for everyone to synchronize, naturally and spontaneously? I slept at Bill's house that night. The next morning, looking at the Father and Sons sitting together - I realized that what was probably planned had just happened. Ann is now comforted. "I have very good sons," Bill kept saying. "I love them very much." **Miracle or Coincidence?**

- Our dear friend fell unexpectedly and was taken to the hospital by his loving wife. When he woke up, we realized that he had lost his memory and could not recognize anyone or anything.
We prayed for several days for his recovery. Local church leaders, including sophomore guys from the church youth group as well as our relatives in Europe, prayed for him humbly and with hope. He regained his health and is still an excellent husband, an excellent father of his three beautiful children and an excellent friend. **Miracle or Coincidence?**

And another hundred more "completely impossible coincidences" have already happened in my life (impossible job opportunities - given, impossible places - visited, impossible people - met, impossible wisdom – heard). But what is the explanation for all those prayers that were unanswered? Are those miracles as well? Is the lack of a miracle a miracle? After reaching a certain level of extraordinariness, we may be forced to become more honest with ourselves, we may be forced to make a decision: "Do I believe in miracles, or do I believe in coincidences?" If something goes your way, you might call it a miracle, but if something goes wrong, you say 'let's wait and see – that's a miracle delayed in time.'

Am I really being honest here? In the previous paragraph I stated that we must accept life in the chemical, biological, physical world and accept the domination of the law of nature, which simply governs us all, and here I say that when you pray, the law of nature no longer applies. This is the essence of what I decided to believe is true. We can do "nothing" about many things, but with help of the Creator, miracles can happen. And again, it is up to us whether to believe in "coincidences" or in miracles – both are "equally" probable. The former originates from the world of matter as we know it, while the latter relates to the best possible world.

"So, I say to you: Ask and it will be given to you; seek and you will find; knock and the door will be opened to you. For everyone who asks receives; the one who seeks finds; and to the one who knocks, the door will be opened." ccxciv (Luke 11, 9:10)

And what is my best possible answer to the best possible scenario? I am choosing (slightly more probable for me) to believe in superior reality with its superior sense of everything, governed by superior and transcendent intelligence. I am choosing the world of ultimate goodness for you and me, following my and our deepest desires and intuitions to be like that. I am choosing to believe in a personal Being who cares about me, supports me, wants my happiness, and unconditionally loves me. Any unfulfilled wishes go to the basket of "not yet understood and appreciated" future gifts, and my attitude is built on faith and the hope that God's will is the best possible one, according to which my life will move forward in the best possible way.

To believe in miracles or not to believe in them, that is the question. God has been showing us miracles for centuries, and although the Son of God performed miracles when he was among us by feeding thousands of people with loaves and fish, by healing a paralyzed man and a blind one, by raising a widow's son, by forgiving sins, by healing people's souls, and finally, by resurrecting Himself after His own death, that is not how the Son of God usually performs miracles in our everyday lives. What if we do not accept that those historical events really took place?

If we have a problem believing in those historical testimonies, we may try to be receptive to everyday miracles performed by God's followers. According to the design of God's world, we are predestined and called to perform miracles for each other.

Let us be miracles for one another.

How wonderful our world could be is on us.

Be faithful enough to believe in miracles.

Give it time. Be patient. Be hopeful.

Keep on loving.

Why do we believe in God?

There's something in us, this desire for the good, the truth, the just that pushes us beyond this world. You can't desire what you don't know. Therefore, if we're desiring something that transcends anything in this world in some way, we must already know it. Therefore, we do know the truth itself... and that's who God is.

First Argument: Desire

"We human beings desire the truth, our minds seek the truth and we get it sometimes. But no matter how much truth we get out of this world, it's never enough. The mind remains unsatisfied. Our will seeks the good and find[s] it a lot of ways in this world, but no matter how many goods we attain, we're never really satisfied. We seek justice in all kinds of ways, and we achieve it sometimes to a remarkable degree. Think of our own time: the civil rights movement, the end of apartheid, the breakdown of the Soviet Union, all those were wonderful things that were the attainment of justice. But no matter how much justice we attain we never have enough. There's something in us, this desire for the good, the true, the just, that pushes us beyond this world. This approach is called the argument from desire. You can't desire what you don't know. Therefore, if we're desiring something that transcends anything in this world in some way we must already know it. Therefore, we do know the truth itself. We do know the good itself. We do know justice itself and that's who God is. God is not one of the true things in the world, but God is the truth itself which has seized the mind of any scientist, any philosopher, any seeker [of] the truth. God is not one more good thing in the world, but God is goodness itself which has seized anybody when he's living the moral life or seeking the ethically good. God is not one more just thing in the world, but God is justice itself which has seized the will of the lawyer or the judge or anyone seeking justice."[ccxcv] - Bishop Robert Barron

At their depth, religion and science come together. We assume that being is intelligible. That means that the world can be known. The world is filled with reason, which is why, when we understand the truth, we say 'we recognize it.'

Second Argument: Science and Religion

"[There is] the link between religion and science [although] very often those two [are] seen as enemies*. [...] At their depth, religion and science come together, here's why. What does every scientist assume? Whether you're a physicist, a chemist, a biologist, a psychologist, whatever you are, you assume that being is intelligible. That means that the world can be known. Look, even the name psychology designates 'logos' word. The scientist goes out to meet a world that's imbued with meaning. Well, how do you explain that? How do you explain the universality of the meaningfulness of the world? Ratzinger said, 'it's because it's been thought into being.' In other words, the world is not just dumbly there. Rather the world is filled with 'logos.' It's filled with reason with mind, which is why, when we understand the truth, we say 'we recognize it.' He says 'right, you Re-Cognize it.' You think it again because it's already been thought into being by God [...] from the objective intelligibility of the world to the existence of a great intelligence which has thought the world into being." [ccxcvi] - Bishop Robert Barron

Do you also recognize such a desire for the good, the true, and the just? Do you Re-Cognize the Truth? Do you also have a feeling that contemplating it pushes us beyond this world? Do you have such an intuition?

Why do we believe in God? Because faith really works!
"It is very easy to ask an easy [showy, attractive] question - but to answer that question is not so easy. What if we ask a computer scientist: "Could you explain to me how a computer works?" I bet he/she will [take a long time to explain it to me], Some scientists respond: "You have to study it quite a lot to get to know it." Asking God is very easy, but getting answers... Why do I use a computer without knowing how it really works? I also don't know how the Internet really works. But I don't throw the computer away. So many people say, "Because I don't know how God works, I reject religion - this is a suspicious matter. So, I do not use religion [practice religion, engage with religion]. But I use my computer, not because I do understand it, but because it works. Why do I use Christianity [or other religions]? Do I understand the Eucharist? No, I do not understand the Eucharist [says the priest]. Do I fully understand the Bible? I don't. I know one thing—it works. When I step back into silence, when I perform works of love, when I receive acts of love—it works. There are so many tough questions (Why do we have such a history? Why did God do that?, Why didn't God intervene, why did He allow it?) and of course theologians [philosophers, religious scholars] are searching, discovering and studying to understand better and more. But we will never be able to draw God - Jesus into our human concepts [terms or terminologies]. It is not that easy to use "quick" intuition. There are already many thousand-page-PhD-level works about God, theology, or morality. People [who love] live morally, humbly, and honestly - really experience happiness... And pride (lust, gluttony, greed, sloth, wrath, envy) often heralds a fall (suffering, emotional and spiritual unhappiness, and death)."[ccxcvii] – Piotr Pawlukiewicz, priest

Why should we care? To be authentically human, to love, give, serve, and rise above our selfish genes.
"Richard Dawkins once famously wrote, 'We are survival machines— robot vehicles blindly programmed to preserve the selfish molecules known as genes.'* But faith in Jesus says that we were made for more than this. In fact, the pain and brokenness in our world are largely the result of our living as 'robot vehicles' blindly focused on serving the self. Jesus calls us to be authentically human, to love, give, serve, and rise

MY CREATOR

above our selfish genes. As we do so, we not only make the world a more just and compassionate place; we find joy in the process." ccxcviii - Adam Hamilton, senior pastor

Does it all have to be so complicated?

Do we need such complicated philosophies, theologies, or religions to explain all of this? What if someone is not ready and does not want to spend most of his or her life intellectualizing like that? Isn't it all about our death? Isn't it all about our fear of death? Isn't it the most fundamental fear of our lives and the most impactful single factor shaping our thinking patterns, motivations, behaviors, and actions? So, what is a true story? The true story is that "living life" is in fact "dying." Living life means suffering, physically, emotionally, existentially – spiritually. The options are that we die, and we never see ourselves or each other again, or we die and meet again. The first option makes us despair, but the second one gives us hope, relief, and peace. As we are all going to die someday, what do we really want to believe so as to enjoy the moment?

At the end of the day, proof of my faith is defined by answers to these questions:

- **Am I ready to die now?**
- **Am I ready to offer my life for my loved ones?**
- **Am I ready to offer my life for anyone, including my enemies?**
- **Am I ready to handle the death of my loved ones?**

I say "yes" to all of these – only when I stare confidently at Jesus. I hesitate when I lose sight of Him.

""Lord, if it's you," Peter replied, "tell me to come to you on the water." "Come," he said. Then Peter got down out of the boat, walked on the water and came toward Jesus. But when he saw the wind, he was afraid and, beginning to sink, cried out, "Lord, save me!" Immediately Jesus reached out his hand and caught him. "You of little faith," he said, "why did you doubt? ""ccxcix

(Matthew 14, 28:31)

The worst thing for me would be to experience the deaths of my loved ones. So God help me in my hour of trial. Do I really believe?

"Take courage! It is I. Don't be afraid." ccc

(Matthew 14:27)

How do we start believing in God?

We just ask, **"Help me, God,"** and wait.

Start learning more about love. Start opening yourself up to love. Try and let someone love you. Take a risk and start trusting the person who has started loving you. Take even more risks and start loving in return, start doing good for others. Be mindful and intentional. Wait for miracles. Expect miracles. Realize that they have been happening.

Finally, thank God for everyday miracles you notice. Ask God for help, wait, and thank God again. That is how you start talking to God. That is how you pray. "Wait" means, wait one minute, wait one hour, one day, one month, one year, one hundred years – and you will be amazed. Relax, and be patient. Be faithful. Be hopeful. Keep on loving. It's that simple. Enjoy a truly happy life.

One final remark: I made my fundamental decision about the nature of the world and that decision shaped my mindset, worldview, culture, life strategies, and engagement with the visible and invisible world of God through faith. Of course, it was a long process. First, my inherited worldview and what I was given as "initial capital" shaped my initial thinking, but through the systematic elimination of layers of my ego, and by making conscious and informed decisions about my real self, where I wanted to go, and whom to follow, I wrote my own story. Most importantly, my story happened with my full consent. So, whenever you engage in such fundamental decision making, please make sure you do it freely. Your life and your way of life should be the result of your own choices (of course, these aspects can be controlled).

True faith will never be true unless it is born of free choice.

That is why, as a strong believer in our human "free will" that makes us real humans, I encourage you to investigate on your own, with curiosity and courage, your own way of life. Try one thing and reflect. Try a different thing and reflect. Find your best possible role model who represents and will lead you to your best possible reality. Listen and watch carefully, differentiate attractive knowledge from real wisdom, differentiate quick pleasures from long- term happiness, differentiate your current life from the afterlife, and differentiate what's really important and valuable from what's not. Whatever model you choose, you will start acting it out in your thoughts, emotions, behaviors, and actions. You will see results pretty soon, and the world will see them, too. "You will know them by their fruits," and the fruits of our lives will be good or bad. So be careful.

If your life model does not offer you hope, you will feel hopeless. If your life model does not offer you love, you will feel abandoned and lonely. If your life model does not offer you an afterlife, you will be afraid of dying. If your life model offers you the best possible scenario, there is a good chance that you will experience it now.

I chose to follow Jesus (He most probably had chosen me first) and accepted Him as my King and the guarantor of my happy life. So, I'm sharing this with you, and in case you find a similarly beautiful way of life and hope for an afterlife, you can share it with the world as well.

CHAPTER 7

New Independence

Escaping from the American Cage

Regaining Life, Liberty and Happiness

Gaining Truth, Purpose, Dignity, Meaningful Relationships, and Love

How do we regain our independence? How do we live according to the Declaration of Independence? How do we escape from our cages?

What if we first acknowledge that we have a problem?

I hope I have been able to show that the majority of Americans do not experiencing independence as promised by the Declaration.

- **We don't** live as if we were created and endowed by our **Creator.**
- **We don't** live as if we were **all equal.**
- **We don't** live as if we respect our **lives.**
- **We don't** live as if we respect our **liberty.**
- **We don't** live as if we respect our **pursuit of happiness.**

I hope I have been able to show that the majority of Americans do not experience their right to life.

America is a violent country. An unusual number of people die violently here. The rate of murder or manslaughter by firearm in the U.S. is the highest in the developed world. We are used to mass shootings. American citizens still need to protect themselves against themselves. We are the civilian gun capital of the world. There are more than 390 million civilian-owned firearms in the United States. The United States owns close to 50% of the entire global stock of civilian firearms. But interestingly, only 40% of American households report owning guns, implying that those who do own them have on average 8 guns per household. Guns are a big business in America, a $50 billion industry with about 300,000 jobs. We feel unsafe, because we can be killed by anybody, anytime. We don't know how to overcome the implementation problem – to enforce effective gun control or take away guns for good. We do not know how to substitute one harmful industry with a less harmful one. But this we should know as a country of exceptional entrepreneurs, innovators, and inventors.

It seems that we value the right to have a gun more than the right to life. It seems we have forgotten that the most important thing in our life is our life. We have forgotten that our fundamental purpose in life is to survive, to love, to be happy, to have friends and family, and to chase our dreams. We have forgotten that guns were constructed to kill effectively. You cannot defend yourself from today's enemies and from bad government with your personal arsenal of weapons. In case we decide we do want to live and knowing that guns are for killing, the only logical step forward is to reduce the number of guns and ultimately eliminate them entirely from a civilian space.

We live in great fear!

I hope I have been able to show that the majority of Americans do not experience freedom.

We live with the illusion of freedom being quietly steered by "the system," by capitalist magnates and their highly educated heirs, steered by their well-crafted industries such as banking, insurance or real estate. We are imprisoned in the American cage that keeps us busy and makes us mindlessly go round and round. We are caught in the clutches of a captivating economy that forces us to work from morning till night to be able to pay our bills and cover our basic needs. We feel insecure, afraid, lost, and hopeless.

We don't have time. We are always in a hurry. We simply can't afford leisure time, including rest and vacations.

Americans have been robbed. We don't have money. We are poor citizens in the richest country in the universe. The top wealthiest 1% possess close to 50% of the nation's wealth. Almost all wealth is in the hands of less than 20% of the U.S. population. Productivity in our country has improved far more than 70 percent over the last 40 years, but workers' compensation rose only 9 percent over the last 40 years. Money has been transferred to the richest and to corporations, only. 80% of us own only 7% of the country's wealth. More than 40 million Americans living are living below the poverty level. About 80% of American families are living below the "common sense" adjusted poverty level.

The system forces us to value capital and wealth more than human life and personal freedom.

We keep our society uneducated by preventing access to education for all. It is the best possible scenario if you want to steer the masses effectively. The uneducated nation is easily controllable. We don't have enough education. Those who want education are in fact drowning in student debt. The average student loan debt per borrower in 2019 was $32,731. Total student loan debt in 2019 was $1.52 trillion. The number of student loan borrowers in 2019 was 44.7 million. More than 600,000 borrowers in the country are over $200,000 in student debt and that number may continue to increase.[ccci]

We have no idea what the truth is, because we have been brainwashed and manipulated by overinvested media. The cumulative net worth of only 7 individuals who shape the media industry is at the level of $39 billion, which translates to almost 1 million Americans who could have their basic net worth ensured. We don't have access to reality, because we have been brainwashed and manipulated by the film, video game, and social media industries. Billions of dollars go to camouflaged influence practices that use the most advanced digital technologies and modern psychology supported by the brain and by neurosciences. And finally, we are cheated by plaintiffs' lawyers, lead generators, and third-party funders who intentionally create mass tort litigations through misleading and fearmongering ads.

We don't have real freedom of speech anymore. Although there is freedom of speech "on paper," a voice with more capital is a voice that really matters. Someone can always change the socio-economic rules by bringing a sufficiently large bag of money to the table. Most of us are just puppets in the theater of dehumanized capitalism. Although there is freedom of speech "on paper," when you decide to speak up, you will be flooded with hate. There is no longer a culture of substantive, factual debate in our country. You can easily be ostracized, expelled from university, fired from your job, expelled from community or own family.

We are not free anymore!

I hope I have been able to show that the majority of Americans are not experiencing happiness.

The United States of America is performing poorly and substantially below most comparably wealthy nations when it comes to happiness. The United States strongly underperforms in the following dimensions: life expectancy, homicide rate, time devoted to leisure and personal care – locating itself at the very bottom of the rankings. We don't have our American dreams anymore, because we cannot sleep at night.

Health conditions have worsened for much of the population. We don't have enough health coverage. The healthcare system is not accessible to all. It is awfully expensive and complicated. We don't have a healthy lifestyle. Many people are on the edge of obesity or hunger. The U.S. has one of the highest rates of obesity in the world.

We are a mass-addiction society. The U.S. has among the world's highest rates of substance abuse, including antidepressants. Digital addictions are increasing (Internet, social media, gaming, smartphones). We are going through anxiety, stress, and depression. Depression is rising. The "lucky ones" waste their fortunes on socially and morally harmful projects (including drug dealing, recreational drug use, promotion of prostitution, gambling, non-ethical movies, video games, etc.) and cause a regression in the development of society, including its destruction in the worst cases. Although we don't want those demoralizing and destructive markets, they surround us and suck us in using addictive methods.

We are killing ourselves at the highest rates in decades. Major studies have documented rising suicide rates.

Social trust is in decline. We are inundated with lawsuits, as are our businesses. Confidence in the government has fallen.

We don't have meaningful relationships. About 35% of adult Americans are chronically lonely, not to mention the "lonely generation," teenagers. We communicate, but we do not connect.

We are the nation that suffers!

I hope I have been able to show that the majority of Americans do not experience equality.

We experience increasing socioeconomic inequality and income inequality in the United States, which is among the highest of all the richest countries.

We fail to ensure dignity for all. There are no decent living conditions (food, shelter, clothing) for all. There is no early care and early education (pre-schools) for all. There is no safety for all. There is no real equal access to life opportunities – being aware of different starting points (biology, family, community, environment, economic situation).

We experience increasingly senseless acts of violence, racism, and **injustice** that continue to plague our nation. Without sufficient resources you cannot progress, and you cannot defend yourself in our "brutal" country. Many people are extremely vulnerable to unfair treatment and thus become second-class citizens. "Life [in our country] is hard! It's a constant competition with others. No institution or person gives you the basic things that you need to flourish without your fighting to get them." Our system enables disguised racism. How is it possible that such a modern, progressive, "critically and constructively thinking," rational, diverse country has not been able to solve such a "mentally archaic" problem? This is really sad, disappointing, and disheartening. The whole world looks at us in disbelief. We fail to love one another, equally, regardless of our skin color, gender, origin, education, worldviews, and opinions.

We are the nation that is divided.

We are not united!

I also hope that I have been able to show that equality measured by self-earned capital is probably not the best possible way to compare the equality of human beings.

I said that equality could be measured at the highest abstract level of our understanding of life. Shall we take advantage of the best available scientific, philosophical, spiritual, and religious intuitions of what it means to live a peaceful, joyful, harmonious, loving life? What does it mean to live a life that makes sense, that is meaningful to me as an individual, to all of us, to communities of others like me, others like you, others like us, to human beings surrounded by nature? Equality should manifest itself in acts of dignity, respect, deep empathy, and a willingness to satisfy basic human needs in a responsible way. Equality is the quality of life we give and receive. We are all interconnected and should maintain a healthy balance, because if not, we will for sure malfunction, degenerate, and suffer as a whole society and on an individual level. Of course, we are not equal in a biological, situational or economic sense—we are very different. This is why the only reasonable way to compare one person to another could be with regards to the "universal quality of life" level, "universal sense of life" level, or more generally, at the "happiness" level.

And what about capital? Pure capital has to go hand in hand with human capital, social capital and other-capital, and remains an important building block to keep everything rolling, though it is certainly not the only one.

I hope I have been able to show that lack of true happiness may be caused by not living according to the Creator, who created and endowed us.

We have forgotten that we have a Creator. Just think critically for a while about what we really worship. Even if some of us still worship our Creator, we do it mostly at the level of words, with our speech, and we are really very good at it – the best in class. But at the level of the heart, we worship control, power, money, ownership (according to the rule: the more stuff the better), personal prosperity, personal success, and pleasure. Because we have detached ourselves from the Origin, we are lonely and fearful. Because we have detached ourselves from the Origin, we do not know our purpose. Life is meaningless. We prefer to get stuck in a mindless rush so as not to confront the truth. What about creating another irrelevant business (we are indeed good at it – the best in class)? What about creating another irrelevant and usually detrimental and toxic gratifier for our unsatisfied senses and desires? We rush, we act, we never stop so as to avoid thinking about the end. We do it because we are internally motivated by the wrong things. We have forgotten the real reason why we are here.

"It's incredibly easy to get caught up in an activity trap, in the busyness of life, to work harder and harder at climbing the ladder of success only to discover it's leaning against the wrong wall." - Stephen Covey

We have forgotten what real love is. Just think critically about what we really value the most. We say, liberty, self-determination, being self-made (self-made millionaires would be an ideal) and again power and being in control, money and ownership, personal prosperity, personal success, and pleasure. Love may be perceived as weakness. To give someone something without a reason may be perceived as weakness, because it prevents people from becoming self-determined and self-made. We have been trapped in our own thinking. All of the above-mentioned "noble qualities" may still be good (even very good), but the key problem is what the right priorities are. If love is not a priority, whatever comes before love will never bring long-term peace, will never bring satisfaction, will never generate lasting value, will never ensure sustainable growth, will never bring stability because it will not enable trust, will not enable alignment on greater goals, and will not enable inspiration and people's passion for doing their best for themselves and others. We have forgotten that we are called to love. We have forgotten that love is a must-have ingredient of individual and social happiness.

We are afraid, and all it takes is a little provocation and we are ready to explode, showing our hidden frustration and accumulated anger. This is very close to violence.

We are constantly and continually fearful.

"Even when it all feels so overwhelming, working parents are somehow piecing it all together without child care. Teachers are getting creative so that our kids can still learn and grow. Our young people are desperately fighting to pursue their dreams.
And when the horrors of systemic racism shook our country and our consciences, millions of Americans of every age, every background rose up to march for each other, crying out for justice and progress.
This is who we still are: compassionate, resilient, decent people whose fortunes are bound up with one another. And it is well past time for our leaders to once again reflect our truth." [cccii]- Michelle Obama

So, how do we regain our independence? How do we live according to the Declaration? How do we successfully escape from our American cage?

What if we build on our strengths?

I hope I have been able to remind my readers that we admire and are ready to fight for our values: liberty, self-determination, power, being in charge, making our own decisions, entrepreneurship, invention, innovation, diversity, democracy, and free markets—our competitive advantages.

I hope I have been able to remind my readers of our strengths, which are an amazing foundation on which to build. The sky is the limit.

We have a "self-made" mindset. We have a strong work ethic. We have potential and can work harder and longer. We have the American dream. We have a competitive mindset. We have a risk-taking mindset. We have confidence. We have a "work hard, play hard" mentality. We have an incredibly giving mindset.

We are effective and productive human beings.

What if we start with ourselves?

I hope I have been able to show that we can try to escape from our mental cages.

We can do this by desiring **truth, love, and understanding**, by having a clear and open mind, by being **curious, respectful, and compassionate**, and by finding **inconsistencies** in our own motivations, conflicting needs, desires, behaviors, and actions. We can try to escape from our mental prisons by finding **contexts** in which opposite and maybe conflicting ideas can be true, by assuming that the person we are listening to might know something we don't, and by asking control **questions** like: What is truth?, What if the other truth is true?, Who am I?, Who do I want to be?, Why am I here?, Where do I want to be?, What is my purpose?, Why am I thinking like that?, Why am I feeling like that?, What am I doing right now?, Is what I am doing right now consistent with my personal purpose, mission, and values?, What decision should I make?, What are the options, my alternatives?, Am I ready to pay the price for my choices?, What makes me happy?, Why-Why-Why-Why-Why?, Do I love?

"If we want to change a situation, we first have to change ourselves. And to change ourselves effectively, we first have to change our perceptions." - Stephen Covey

I hope I have been able to show the importance of personal responsibility.

I invoked the teachings of Professor Jordan Peterson:

"For people to find meaning in their lives, they have to adopt responsibility and live it.
To be able to take responsibility, a human being needs to have a purpose in life.
Hence, giving purpose to people is of the highest importance."

I said, remind yourself of the purpose of your life and take full responsibility for chasing this purpose. Take full responsibility for your decisions and actions. I said, when you decide something, pay the price upfront, making sure you know risks and benefits. Make sure you love! – I said as well.

I hope I have been able to show how important it is to break with the false self and try to be born again.

The process of breaking with our fake self can be difficult, but it can also be extremely rewarding and beautiful. I said, try to come back to the core of who you are, without any layers, any levels, any labels, any imprinted thinking patterns, or schemas, any fake worldviews, any regrets and any expectations and desires. I suggested that you challenge your motives and truthfulness by observing your thoughts, emotions, decisions, results and overall happiness in your life. After a while you should realize that something is not right, because you have so many untamed internal conflicts, contradictions, and inconsistencies, and so much stress, sadness, anxiety, vanity, uselessness, indifference, self-blame, world-blame, anger, fear, and suffering. The further away from the "inherited false self" you are, the easier it is to get rid of judgements, toxic relationships, and damages that accidentally happened to your "fake life." You move away from "yourself" until you vanish or meet your intellectually and emotionally "naked I." You look into the mirror, and through the eyes of your "soul" you see everything but your old self. To participate in the world you should decide to leave the stillness of consciousness and start moving and interacting with others. Being in a deep state of awareness of your purity, you decide to return on your own terms and conditions, in the best possible way.

Decide to follow the most perfect and practical model of a happy life. Decide to follow the best possible scenario for the best possible life. To take the last step, you need a practical example, a reason to believe that a happy life is possible. You need a life coach, a mentor, or an authority figure to listen to, to talk to, and to follow. I recommended that you better pick the best possible master.

I hope I have been able to show that there is scientific research on happiness worth considering.

I referred to the teachings of Professor Laurie Santos, who runs the very popular course "The Science of Well-Being."[ccciii] I mentioned a few key points on how to improve our well-being, like focusing on your social relationships; staying connected; being other-oriented by paying attention to other people over yourself; having healthy habits, making sure you're getting enough sleep, exercise, the right food; being more present and mindful; being grateful and compassionate; being religious, and taking part in religious practices.

You can take some action and fix this!

But is it enough to leave the cage? Maybe my personal cage, yes. But apart from our own mental prisons, we all sit in our superior American cage. I said that to accomplish so-called "human-oriented capitalism" within our commonly shared cage, America, may require breaking with the conflicting interests of the various mental cages of all citizens. Perhaps the improvement could come from greater awareness, more consciousness, and more transparent motives on the part of all "cage inhabitants." I think we need to go even further and agree on common values and beliefs, one culture, and a single purpose. I also said that our target "human oriented" capitalism may require capitalism and democracy embedded in a superior moral system based on human dignity, responsibility, and love, supported by a wise legal system that works for the people, and not the other way around.

What if we start giving?

I hope I was able to explain that I wish my children to live a happy life. I want to give them **acceptance**, **care and love**, teach them to love, and introduce them to **unconditional love** (God's love). In so doing, I hope to give them **hope, fearlessness,** and **purpose.** I want to give them **food, shelter, clothing, a clean environment, an education, and healthcare.** I want to teach them **responsibility** and **self-control**, so that they are open to living meaningful lives. I will teach them how to create **meaningful relationships.** I want to teach them **critical thinking,** and that **each decision they make shapes their destiny.** I plan to teach them **mindfulness,** and how to **listen and talk to God. I want to** give them **freedom.** I want to show them how to **give** and **thank.**

I hope I have been able to prove that some of us are luckier than others, and that "giving" is the powerful building block of this luck.

I said that those "successful" people we usually admire were given something, by someone – without any exception. Usually they were given care, attention, a good education, initial capital, access to a professional network, access to industry knowledge and practices, personal mentoring, and/or the wisdom of family, of generations, of nations, and/or unconditional love. Thanks to some of these gifts, they were able to overcome the world's adversities.

I asked if we could ensure "dignity for all." Will we be able to ensure equal access to prosperity (not equal prosperity levels) and happiness, equal access to life opportunities – regardless of people's having different starting points? Will we be able to extend this "good" from a few to many, to reinvest that capital in a socially responsible manner? I proposed what if we

- Ensure **human dignity** via **decent living conditions** for all
- Ensure **human dignity** via **early care and education** (starting with pre-school) for all
- Ensure **human dignity** via **safety and basic healthcare** for all

I shared with you what I was given, and the list of gifts was stunning. I was overwhelmed at what I got. I was shocked. I had no words. I said I was the lucky one. I said I was grateful.

"We make a living by what we get, but we make a life by what we give."—Winston Churchill.

What if we shape our new, human-oriented culture?

We should define American culture as one that focuses on **love, personal happiness, trust, integrity, respect, justice, racial justice, and personal and social responsibility.** All this to shape a prosperous and flourishing society. Of course, **liberty, self-determination, diversity, inclusion, power, entrepreneurship, invention and innovation**, as well **democracy,** our competitive advantages, are also key to American culture.

I also advised that we teach such values at the earliest stages of life. Moreover, it is to be expected that American culture is lived by government officials, business owners or investors. Acting according to key behaviors should be weighed at the same level as competency and should be considered when candidates run for office or during recruitment processes. People in charge of others (so-called leaders) – should meet the highest standards and be assessed against these standards.

I said that we will not be able to bring happiness to America unless we balance our ego-driven desire for success with our desire for joy and unity. American culture and social norms have to be rebuilt or reinvented. Because we are not independent, we cannot be happy without one another. We cannot pursue happiness without being connected. We urgently need to regain our social trust, how we look at each other, how we see each other, how we talk to each other, how we understand and appreciate our individual happiness and social happiness, how we agree on and prioritize our new happiness-oriented economy.

What if we define clear problems and work out solutions?

I hope I have offered "spontaneous ideas" for solutions to the most critical problems. I suggested borrowing ideas from model societies and applying them, with some changes, to our specific situation. Among other things, I focused on income inequality trying to find the best balance between both "sufficient" wealth creation coming from economic freedom AND "sufficient" happiness creation coming from well-perceived social justice.

I suggested that we use our strongest intellects that we already have in the country and take advantage of the best science labs, colleges, universities, startups, corporations, individual inventors and innovators.

In addition, I made recommendations for becoming more peaceful, more mindful, more intentional, more responsible for one's own life, more educated on current socio-economic problems, more educated in general, more financially safe, more independent from media, digitalization, games, films, and so on and so forth. All this to become more joyful – happier. I encouraged learning from many sources, especially those you do not agree with, so as to shape your worldview. Those will motivate you to think harder and seek better solutions.

I pointed out that only you can define all possible realistic next steps and execute them effectively. Don't overwhelm yourself but do what is in your sphere of influence. You can always extend your capabilities and sphere of influence but do it in tiny steps so that you stay motivated.

And please, I wrote, let's not forget about the miraculous impact of animals on us!

And please, I beg of all of us, let our children meet and play freely!

What if we write a new Declaration?

Let me try the following wording for a new Declaration:

We hold these truths to be self-evident, that all men are created equal, that they are endowed by their Creator with certain unalienable Rights, that among these are Life, Liberty, the pursuit of Happiness as well as Truth, Dignity, and Love.
We the People of the United States of America, declare that we will respect these Rights.

We hold these truths to be self-evident, that there are certain Qualities of human nature present in every human being that enable all men to flourish and to form a flourishing society, that among these are cooperative, selfless and loving moral instincts, self-consciousness, free will, desire for the good, the true, the just, desire to seek and follow the highest ideal, kindness, humility, integrity, responsibility, purposefulness, need for self-development and wresting order from chaos, discipline, self-determination, self-defense, group defense, courage, mutual trust, diversity, inclusion, social and racial justice, as well as curiosity and entrepreneurship that enable progress and the creation of the greater good.
We the People of the United States of America, declare to live up to these Qualities of human nature.

We declare to protect social justice and stand up to injustice and racism because we recognize the added value of individual differences, life experiences, knowledge, self-expression and the unique capabilities of all of our citizens, and what they collectively bring to our united nation.
We declare to protect everyone's right to practice his or her own religion, or no religion at all – as long as this practice respects the above-mentioned Rights.
We declare to protect our democracy, live in accordance with it, and actively participate in it.
We declare to protect freedom of speech and expression.
We declare to protect our human-centered capitalism based on free-market, human-centered legislation and a universally accepted moral system based on the above-mentioned Rights and live in accordance with them - to create individual and common wealth as well as individual and common happiness.

We declare to eliminate poverty and provide decent living conditions for all.
We declare to provide fair access to good quality early childhood care and education for all.
We declare to provide fair access to good quality healthcare and life-saving interventions for all.
We declare to provide equal access to life opportunities for all.
Fair access must be defined, agreed upon and regularly verified by a democratically elected body representing the entire spectrum of society, and must take into account individual circumstances. The quality of services must be ensured by the forces of the free market.
We declare to ensure safety in our homeland for all.
We declare to protect our country from foreign forces.

Based on the above-mentioned Rights, Qualities & Declarations, we pledge to build a safe, prosperous, united and happy society,
the United Societies of America
- the best human-centered economy and superpower on earth.

In God we trust - to stay fearless and know how to truly love one another and ourselves.
{say people who decide to follow God}
In the highest ideal we trust that we will remain fearless and know how to truly love one another and ourselves.
{say people who decide to follow the highest moral system}

*We understand dignity as "the right of a person to be valued and respected for their own sake, and to be treated ethically."
*We understand happiness as "the experience of joy, contentment, or positive well-being, combined with a sense that one's life is good, meaningful, and worthwhile."
*We understand love as the "act of the will to engage in action for the good of another human being with the support of the highest ideal, our Creator {for the people of faith}."
*We understand freedom of faith and religion as an obvious consequence of free will – "True faith will never be true unless it is born of free choice."

It's time to conclude

In writing this book, my goal was to shed light on how the American cage appears to someone coming from outside the system, coming from another world of values, beliefs, and cultures. This is how I perceived American reality, and I tried to confront it with other possible realities. My motivation was love for people and the world and a deep desire to discover the truth. Let's be honest, the phenomena described in this work are inherently complex, interrelated phenomena. In many cases they are burdened with historical aspects and motives or burdened with present aspects and motives of people in power or those who desire to be in power. These are not one-dimensional matters, these are intricate constructs that require careful study and making wise choices, sometimes choosing the lesser evil. Constant compromises and maintaining balance – that's what this is about. But before agreeing to general compromises, which most of the time lead to lose-lose situations, it is much better to put in additional effort and work out win-win solutions. Whenever there is a chance to see the bigger picture, to think long- term, to spend more time investigating, better outcomes can be expected. Thinking about risks and benefits and anticipating consequences always helps.

As long as we stay loyal to the highest truth, this truth will set us free, and in truth we must build our future. As long as we stay loyal to the highest love, conflicting parties will sooner or later unite.

I hope that I was able to discover at least some truth about America and offer you a fresh perspective, a fresh look at what is happening in your homeland.

But what is the highest truth, what is the highest love?

I encourage you to face your own mental prison with full honesty, humility, courage, curiosity, and the attitude that you can change it. I encourage you to remind yourself who is really thinking your thoughts, who is really experiencing your emotions, who you are, why you are here, what the purpose of your life is, what life mission you recognize for yourself, what responsibility you want and can agree to take. I encourage you to think about what the best possible life for you and the people around you might be. I also encourage you to answer the existential questions, including whether you would like your life and your loved ones to last even after death, whether you would like someone special to always be there for you and with you, who wants your good, who wants your greatest happiness, who made you exist, such an almighty Creator who waits for you somewhere in another dimension of reality. These are life- changing considerations – worldview-shaping forces. Due to the lack of scientific evidence about the existence or non-existence of such a superior reality and such an Ideal, I encourage you to choose the best imaginable scenario – because why choose differently? What is your highest truth? What is your highest love? When you decide, try to follow it and remain faithful and unwavering on this chosen path.

All decisions and awakened free will, will refer to it. All decisions and "liberated" free will, will cooperate with this new moral landscape and this highest authority. Your new North Star. Your Light.

As you have seen, I chose the existence of my God who I tried to describe honestly, as best as I can, but certainly inadequately, I could say, very primitively from the point of view of that God. I chose to follow the existence of the human personification of God, the historical and transcendent Jesus, who is the basis of all my moral choices and a role model for me - my path, my truth, and my life. I chose the reality of eternal life, and I chose to treat life on Earth as only one of the episodes -the practical school of love. I chose love as the most fundamental value and a method of creating a happy life for myself, with others and with my God. In particular, I fell in love with loving kindness. I included the dignity and respect of another person in this love. I chose freedom as the highest right and privilege of existence, as it makes me a true human being, it allows me to be myself, and thanks to it I can decide, I feel empowered, in charge and unique. Free will makes me feel that I am "similar" to the Ideal. I chose responsibility as my power of creation, and thanks to it I become a creator, I become an influencer, shaping my destiny and world around me. Through responsibility I feel that whatever I do matters, I feel the sense of my life mission and that I can carry it out. Taking responsibility makes me grow and develop. I become a more valuable human being, ready to steer my own life and generate good for others.

It is because of love, freedom, and responsibility that I feel inner peace, joy, a sense of meaning, a sense of unity, and ultimate happiness.

We live in an illusion of freedom, prosperity and happiness

I am not saying the American people have given up on the American dream. I am saying that they have been robbed of the critical means to be able to pursue their happiness. How can you really dream when you can't sleep at night? How can you even think "out of the box" when the box is tightly closed and sealed, and it has no windows where you could see the truth of a brighter future and a better life. Don't get me wrong, you continuously try, both consciously and unconsciously, to open those "non-existing" windows because you feel intuitively there is something out there – over the rainbow, beyond the ceiling of your box. How can you really act your dreams out when you can't escape from that box? Even if you realize that the cage is not reality, it is almost too late, and it is extremely hard to leave it. Having no resources, no means to change the situation, we tend to give up, or worse, we shift our thoughts and our dreams into unconsciousness and accept the cage as the norm, as the only possible world. The current implementation of our capitalism obviously works, but only for a small number of us. If that is what the Declaration and the U.S. Constitution meant, it's better for us to start from the very beginning, and learn to read with comprehension.

We worship illusory heroes

Do we still have doubts about what is most important and precious in our lives? Do we still have doubts about how to design our system to properly distribute money to those who care about us? Do we still have doubts who are our real HEROES?

Don't we think that COVID-19 has just shown us the painful truth about our economy and underlying systems?

Don't we think that COVID-19 has just proven to us that we are relatively poor people who live in the richest country on earth? We were unable to stay at home for a couple of months, being in real danger of starvation. We didn't follow the rules of social distancing and we went out into the streets desperate, asking for money, shouting for subsidies, begging to reopen the economy. We were forced to put our lives at stake in exchange for basic food, shelter, and personal protective equipment. Of course, some could say, "this is an extreme situation; you can never be prepared for such an apocalypse." It has been a very unique and extreme situation. But this particular one very quickly revealed our socio-economic reality. There is a huge risk involved in running fast-moving machinery based solely on capital without a fundamental skeleton built on human rights, caring for people, or meeting basic human needs.

Don't we think that COVID-19 has just presented to us what wealth and social inequality really looks like in our country? We can see very clearly who has been put into greater danger – those in poverty. "Disproportionately high mortality is more widespread for Black Americans than any other group. Blacks are dying at elevated rates, relative to their population, overall and in 28 of the 41 jurisdictions we examined. Collectively, they represent 12.9% of the population, but have suffered 25.0% of deaths. In other words, they are dying of the virus at a rate of roughly double their population share, among all American deaths where race and ethnicity is known. [...] The latest [end of May 2020] overall COVID-19 mortality rate for Black Americans is 2.4 times as high as the rate for whites and 2.2 times as high as the rate for Asians and Latinos."[ccciv] Is that a coincidence? Do we really live according to the Declaration?

Don't we think COVID-19 has just reminded us who our real HEROES really are?

We finally found the real heroes

Our essential workers who have been called on to meet our basic needs during the COVID-19 shutdown, "'who conduct a range of operations and services that are typically essential to continued critical infrastructure viability' - the industries they support represent, but are not limited to, medical and healthcare, telecommunications, information technology systems, defense, food and agriculture, transportation and logistics, energy, water and wastewater, law enforcement, and public works." [cccv]

Our first responders: "law enforcement officers, including state troopers, deputies, federal agents, and school resource officers, as well as paramedics, emergency medical technicians, firefighters, rescuers, military personnel, sanitation workers, public works, [emergency department personnel] and other trained members of organizations connected with this type of work."[cccvi]

Our frontline workers (the large majority of workers cannot feasibly work from home): healthcare workers, protective service workers, cashiers in grocery and general merchandise stores, production and food processing workers, janitors and maintenance workers, agricultural workers, truck drivers and more. [...] "'Frontline' workers are also a varied group but receive lower wages on average and come disproportionately from socio-economically disadvantaged groups compared to the overall workforce."[cccvii]

During this tragic time, we saw them giving their own lives for others, for us. They have shown true, selfless, and sacrificial love.

We just learned that everything can be gone within a few weeks, literally everything. We just learned what the most important thing in life is. Will we be able to sustain this knowledge? Will we be able to build a better future on this? Will we turn this into wisdom? Our economy, our culture requires serious revision and our reaction, our intervention. We have to change our system.

Isn't it a good moment to start all over, to start with new hope, with strong motivation, with a newly awakened will to change and with our famous "can-do attitude?" It is a very good moment to open our cage right here, right now. What we need is a new capitalism embedded in our revised human-centric culture, our revised purpose, revised values, and revised beliefs. We need our country back.

Our cage is now wide open

You will not want to fly out towards a different, better, bigger cage unless you have honestly revised your truth, your worldview, your purpose, your values and beliefs, and you have honestly accepted your new mindset, your new behaviors and your adjusted culture.

Even the most powerful bird kept from birth in a locked cage will not think to go free, will not even dare to try. Such a bird has no idea of true freedom – therefore it has no such desires. This is a bird with its wings cut off. It represents a man deprived of love, freedom, and responsibility, a dehumanized, enslaved man with an enslaved mind.

Please be aware that without a clear mind, without honesty, humility, compassion, respect, without curiosity and courage, you will not want to fly towards a different, better, stronger, more united, happier reality.

Please also be aware that without the revision of our systems, without the revision of our economy and the rules that shape it, without new goals, new strategies, and new policies, you will not fly effectively and efficiently. "Physical defects" will sooner or later prevent you from continuing your lofty journey.

Finally, without belief in the existence of the best possible scenario, without belief in the existence of a more superior and broader reality, without trust in something bigger, without faith, hope and love, you will not fly too high and too long because fear will always try to cut off your wings, will try to sow doubts. Without all of these, you will not be able to fly closer to the Sun and draw life-giving energy from it. You will not discover the Truth because you will be too far from the Light.

First, let's overcome fear through faith, hope, and love. Then we can say, what we usually say, the sky is the limit.

Our country calls for revision. Our country needs a new movement, like the **United Societies of America** movement (U*S*A), that promotes our new human-centered capitalism and democracy – our human flourishing economy. If you feel cheated, betrayed and helpless, it's time to do something about it. And based on all our virtues, characters, strengths, and beliefs we have as Americans, let's escape this cage for good.

All this to regain our independence, our right to life, liberty and the pursuit of happiness.

All this to gain truth, purpose, dignity, meaningful relationships, and love.

Never doubted, we the people love our country, but are we ready to love its people too?

Are we ready to write a New Declaration based on Truth, Dignity, and Love?

Are you ready to escape from the American Cage and fly away to your new home, to your new America?

The prize is great and monumental.

Your independence and our independence.

Your happiness and our happiness!

Join the movement

The United Societies of America

U*S*A

www.unitedsocietiesofamerica.org

www.americancage.org

We pledge to build a safe, prosperous, united and happy society,
The United Societies of America
- the best human-centered economy and superpower on earth

THANK YOU

Thank you, Ola!

Thank you, darling, for your love, affection, tenderness, sacrifice, life, time and attention, acceptance and faith. You are the best thing that has happened to me in my life. Everything I do, I do it for you and because of you. I'm still learning how best to show you my love. I love you more than anything else in this world. I wish you true happiness!

Thank you

Paulina, Szymon, and **Kornelia, my beloved children** for your unconditional love, joy, and beautiful smiles. You are giving me the opportunity to experience the miracle of fatherhood. Grow up into fearless, courageous, responsible, loving, happy people who believe in God!

Thank you

My dear parents and **parents-in-law,** for your unconditional love, acceptance, unflagging support, and inspiration. I love you very much.

Thank you

Ann and Bill for your love, lifelong friendship, and incredible wisdom. You are my and my wife's "American father & mother," and in this role you have been shaping us, inspiring us, and helping us for more than two decades. You are one of the main reasons why we decided to move to the United States of America. I wish you good health and a life full of blessings, now and forever!

Thank you

Jennifer and Rolf for your friendship. You have shown a real and practical love towards me and my family. You have offered us unbelievable support, your precious time and attention. I do love our conversations and I am fascinated by your unlimited knowledge and brilliant sense of humor. Thank you for sharing your true American culture with us, for all Easter dinners, Thanksgivings, and gingerbread house building events you have invited us to. We appreciate it very much. I wish you a wonderful life with your fabulous children and amazing parents.

Thank you

Leah and Steve for welcoming us to Kansas with open arms and smiling faces – that was an unforgettable gesture. Thank you for sharing your American culture with us, for our joint Super Bowl evening, all the amazing kids' birthday parties and pumpkin patch adventures you have invited us to. We appreciate it very much. I wish you a wonderful life with your fabulous children.

Thank you

Bethani and Adam for offering us a place in your hearts. Thank you for sharing your American culture with us, for the Thanksgiving dinner, for the kids' birthday parties you have invited us to, and all those frank discussions about what's important in life. We appreciate it very much. I wish you a wonderful life with your fabulous children and friendly parents.

Thank you

Jessica and Valentin, Kelly and Tim, Uzma and Tariq for being exceptional neighbors. Together with my whole family we have received so much warmth, so much good, so much support and attention – it's really hard to put it all into words. You are role model neighbors, citizens and friends. Thank you for your fantastic board game evenings, thank you for your support and valuable advice on lawn, house care and travel, thank you for fresh vegetables and mint straight from your garden and thank you for much more. Indeed, you have enriched our lives. I wish you a wonderful life with your wonderful children and families.

Thank you

Sharon, Bill, and Stefan for your love, joy, healthy distance from the world, and wisdom. You are my only American aunt, uncle, and cousin I have, and it is a blessing to have you around. Your presence gives me peace, self-confidence and at least a small but very important portion of a real family atmosphere, being far from my family home in Europe. Thank you for all those presents, gifts, and greeting cards you sent me throughout my stay. I have to admit, I've never received so many packages from anyone before - unprecedented generosity. I wish you a wonderful life.

Thank you

Iza and Sam for your friendship, kindness, and beautiful hearts. Thank you for such a warm welcome that you gave us when we first landed in America, years ago. Thank you for our joint breakfasts, dinners, and lunches in spectacular places downtown Chicago, thank you for our family-like phone conversations, thank you for your help in organizing a self-development workshop and making sure it was well communicated and enriched by life music performed by you, Sam. Iza, I am fascinated by your determination, perseverance despite life's difficulties, your attitude towards people and your willingness to help. Sam, I am fascinated by your artistic soul and your achievements as a composer and performer. I wish you both success and a wonderful life together. I hope your mom enjoys the beauty of life, too.

Thank you

Rev. Ashley, Taylor, Evan, Alex, Dan, Bill and other leaders I met during our Student Ministry leadership program - for your leadership, testimony of faith, and real-life examples of how to effectively support the proper development of younger generations and serve the community with dedication and love.

Thank you

My American leaders, my peers, and my coworkers for your trust, professionalism, outstanding work ethic and fruitful cooperation. I really enjoy working with you and learning from you. I wish you and your families a happy life.

Thank you

Ola, Jaya, Bill, Rolf, and Kent for being my trustworthy and very constructive critics. Thank you for your brilliant minds and supportive hearts. Thank you for your candid and extremely valuable feedback, suggestions, explanations, and teachings. Thank you for your selflessness and personal effort. Because of you, this book has its final shape and quality.

Thank you

Rev. Adam Hamilton for being the Light.

I wish you a meaningful life, peace, joy, and unity in love.
Especially the love that creates us and gives meaning to our lives.
If we don't have love, we gain nothing, we are nothing, we do not live at all.
I understand love as an act of the will to engage in action for the good of another
human being with the support of our ideal, in my case, Creator.

Konrad Milewski

[i] John Robert Lewis was an American statesman and civil rights leader who served in the United States House of Representatives for Georgia's 5th congressional district from 1987 until his death in 2020.

[ii] "Why are we here? Why are we born? | Ajahn Brahm |" published on Buddhist Society of Western Australia YouTube Channel on Jan 10, 2015.
"This talk by Ajahn Brahm gets to the heart of the existential quest: What are we here? What were we born for?"
https://youtu.be/-RrCjzi74BA

[iii] Which does not exist, but hundreds of similar associations most probably. *Wow, what a joke.*

[iv] "The How of Happiness" book by positive psychology researcher Sonja Lyubomirsky

[v] Happiness, by Psychology Today
https://www.psychologytoday.com/us/basics/happiness
Copyright Sussex Publishers, LLC. Except as otherwise expressly permitted under copyright law, no copying, redistribution, retransmission, publication or commercial exploitation of downloaded material will be permitted without the express written permission of Sussex Publishers, LLC.

[vi] From Wikipedia, the free encyclopedia
https://en.wikipedia.org/wiki/Happiness
From page last edited on 27 June 2019, at 04:15 (UTC).
Note: Text is available under the Creative Commons Attribution-ShareAlike License; additional terms may apply

[vii] "Why Finland And Denmark Are Happier Than The U.S.", published on CNBC Make It. YouTube Channel, on Jan 9, 2020
https://youtu.be/6Pm0Mn0-jYU
Among the speakers: Jeffrey Sachs, a professor at Columbia and the co-editor of the World Happiness Report; Meik Wiking, happiness researcher and CEO of the Happiness Research Institute in Denmark.

[viii] What Is Happiness? Article from Greater Good Magazine, © 2019 The Greater Good Science Center at the University of California, Berkeley
https://greatergood.berkeley.edu/topic/happiness/definition

[ix] The Book of Joy: Lasting Happiness in a Changing World is a book by the Nobel Peace Prize Laureates Tenzin Gyatso, the 14th Dalai Lama, and Archbishop Desmond Tutu published in 2016 by Cornerstone Publishers

[x] World Economic Forum: "These are the happiest countries in the world" Written by Briony Harris, Senior Writer, Formative Content
https://www.weforum.org/agenda/2018/03/these-are-the-happiest-countries-in-the-world/
The views expressed in this article are those of the author alone and not the World Economic Forum.

[xi] World Economic Forum: "These are the happiest countries in the world" Written by Briony Harris, Senior Writer, Formative Content
https://www.weforum.org/agenda/2018/03/these-are-the-happiest-countries-in-the-world/
The views expressed in this article are those of the author alone and not the World Economic Forum.

[xii] World Economic Forum: "These are the happiest countries in the world" Written by Briony Harris, Senior Writer, Formative Content
https://www.weforum.org/agenda/2018/03/these-are-the-happiest-countries-in-the-world/
The views expressed in this article are those of the author alone and not the World Economic Forum.

[xiii] World Economic Forum: "These are the happiest countries in the world" Written by Briony Harris, Senior Writer, Formative Content
https://www.weforum.org/agenda/2018/03/these-are-the-happiest-countries-in-the-world/
The views expressed in this article are those of the author alone and not the World Economic Forum.

[xiv] World Happiness Report 2019, Chapter 7: Addiction and Unhappiness in America
Editor: Jeffrey D. Sachs
https://worldhappiness.report/ed/2019/
https://s3.amazonaws.com/happiness-report/2019/WHR19.pdf

[xv] World Happiness Report 2019, Chapter 7: Addiction and Unhappiness in America
Editor: Jeffrey D. Sachs

https://worldhappiness.report/ed/2019/
https://s3.amazonaws.com/happiness-report/2019/WHR19.pdf

[xvi] Jeffrey Sachs, The renowned economist, one of the World Happiness Report's editors

[xvii] World Economic Forum: "These are the happiest countries in the world" Written by Briony Harris, Senior Writer, Formative Content
https://www.weforum.org/agenda/2018/03/these-are-the-happiest-countries-in-the-world/
The views expressed in this article are those of the author alone and not the World Economic Forum.
[xviii] World Economic Forum: "These are the happiest countries in the world" Written by Briony Harris, Senior Writer, Formative Content
https://www.weforum.org/agenda/2018/03/these-are-the-happiest-countries-in-the-world/
The views expressed in this article are those of the author alone and not the World Economic Forum.

[xix] World Happiness Report 2019, Chapter 7: Addiction and Unhappiness in America
Editor: Jeffrey D. Sachs
https://worldhappiness.report/ed/2019/
https://s3.amazonaws.com/happiness-report/2019/WHR19.pdf
[xx] World Happiness Report 2019, Chapter 7: Addiction and Unhappiness in America
Editor: Jeffrey D. Sachs
https://worldhappiness.report/ed/2019/
https://s3.amazonaws.com/happiness-report/2019/WHR19.pdf
[xxi] World Happiness Report 2019, Chapter 7: Addiction and Unhappiness in America
Editor: Jeffrey D. Sachs
https://worldhappiness.report/ed/2019/
https://s3.amazonaws.com/happiness-report/2019/WHR19.pdf
[xxii] World Happiness Report 2019, Chapter 7: Addiction and Unhappiness in America
Editor: Jeffrey D. Sachs
https://worldhappiness.report/ed/2019/
https://s3.amazonaws.com/happiness-report/2019/WHR19.pdf
[xxiii] World Happiness Report 2019, Chapter 7: Addiction and Unhappiness in America
Editor: Jeffrey D. Sachs
Quote included in the chapter comes from Profs. Richard Wilkinson and Kate Pickett and their book The Inner Level (2019)
https://worldhappiness.report/ed/2019/
https://s3.amazonaws.com/happiness-report/2019/WHR19.pdf
[xxiv] World Happiness Report 2019, Chapter 7: Addiction and Unhappiness in America
Editor: Jeffrey D. Sachs
https://worldhappiness.report/ed/2019/
https://s3.amazonaws.com/happiness-report/2019/WHR19.pdf
[xxv] World Happiness Report 2019, Chapter 7: Addiction and Unhappiness in America
Editor: Jeffrey D. Sachs
https://worldhappiness.report/ed/2019/
https://s3.amazonaws.com/happiness-report/2019/WHR19.pdf

[xxvi] Worlddata.info - a project of eglitis-media, Inh. Lars Eglitis
https://www.worlddata.info/average-income.php
The average income is calculated by gross national income and population. On dividing all annual incomes and profits by the amount of the countries' population, it will show the average income per capita. Included in this amount are all salaries and wages but also other unearned income on investments or capital gain.

Ranking list is calculated according to the Atlas method from the quotient of the gross national income (formerly also called "gross national product") and the population of the country. For both figures, we take the last official numbers, which are usually those of the previous year. For the vast majority of countries, table is based on information from the year 2017. In some countries, however, these starting figures are not regularly collected or published and may be older or official estimates of the institutions mentioned above.

[xxvii] World Happiness Report 2019, Editors: John F. Helliwell, Richard Layard, and Jeffrey D. Sachs, Chapter 2: "Changing World Happiness", Chapter Editors: John F. Helliwell, Haifang Huang and Shun Wang
https://worldhappiness.report/ed/2019/
https://s3.amazonaws.com/happiness-report/2019/WHR19.pdf
Chart prepared by the author based on data from Chapter 2, Figure 2.7: Ranking of Happiness 2016-2018

[xxviii] OECD (2017), How's Life? 2017: Measuring Well-being, OECD Publishing, Paris,
https://doi.org/10.1787/how_life-2017-en.

[xxix] OECD Better Life Index, OECD.Stat
http://www.oecdbetterlifeindex.org/
https://stats.oecd.org/Index.aspx?QueryId=30115#

[xxx] Chart prepared by the author based on OECD.Stat data
https://stats.oecd.org/Index.aspx?QueryId=30115#

[xxxi] OECD Better Life Index, Safety
http://www.oecdbetterlifeindex.org/topics/safety/

[xxxii] Chart prepared by the author based on OECD.Stat data
https://stats.oecd.org/Index.aspx?QueryId=30115#

[xxxiii] OECD Better Life Index, Work-Life Balance
http://www.oecdbetterlifeindex.org/topics/work-life-balance/

[xxxiv] Chart prepared by the author based on OECD.Stat data
https://stats.oecd.org/Index.aspx?QueryId=30115#

[xxxv] World Happiness Report 2019, Editors: John F. Helliwell, Richard Layard, and Jeffrey D. Sachs, Chapter 2: "Changing World Happiness", Chapter Editors: John F. Helliwell, Haifang Huang and Shun Wang
https://worldhappiness.report/ed/2019/
https://s3.amazonaws.com/happiness-report/2019/WHR19.pdf
Chart prepared by the author based on data from Chapter 2, Figure 2.8: Changes in Happiness from 2005-2008 to 2016-2018

[xxxvi] Based on World Happiness Report 2019, Editors: John F. Helliwell, Richard Layard, and Jeffrey D. Sachs, Chapter 5: "The Sad State of Happiness in the United States and the Role of Digital Media", Chapter editor: Jean M. Twenge
https://worldhappiness.report/ed/2019/
https://s3.amazonaws.com/happiness-report/2019/WHR19.pdf
Chart re-created by the author based on data from Chapter 5, Figure 5.1: General happiness, U.S. adults, General Social Survey, 1973-2016

[xxxvii] World Happiness Report 2019, Chapter 7: Addiction and Unhappiness in America
Editor: Jeffrey D. Sachs, Director, SDSN, and Director, Center for Sustainable Development, Columbia University
https://worldhappiness.report/ed/2019/
https://s3.amazonaws.com/happiness-report/2019/WHR19.pdf

[xxxviii] Mikołaj Jan Piskorski, currently Dean of IMD South East Asia and Professor of Strategy and Innovation at IMD Business School, before professor of Stanford's Graduate School of Business and Harvard, author of "A Social Strategy: How We Profit from Social Media". Mikołaj Piskorski has taught classes such as Competing with Social Networks and Building and Sustaining Competitive Advantage. He graduated from University of Cambridge and Harvard University.
https://www.linkedin.com/in/mpiskorski/

[xxxix] "The Shallows: What the Internet Is Doing to Our Brains", book by Nicholas Carr, which was a finalist for the 2011 Pulitzer Prize in General Nonfiction

[xl] Facebook is a "social networking website where users can post comments, share photographs and post links to news or other interesting content on the web, chat live, and watch short-form video" as explained on https://www.lifewire.com/what-is-facebook-3486391. Facebook service is owned by Facebook, Inc.
Facebook, Inc. is an American online social media and social networking service company.
https://www.facebook.com
https://en.wikipedia.org/wiki/Facebook

[xli] Twitter is a microblogging and social networking service on which users post and interact with messages known as "tweets", owned by Twitter, Inc.
www.twitter.com
https://en.wikipedia.org/wiki/Twitter

[xlii] Instagram is a photo and video-sharing social networking service owned by Facebook
https://www.instagram.com
https://en.wikipedia.org/wiki/Instagram

[xliii] Snapchat is a multimedia messaging app developed by Snap Inc., originally Snapchat Inc.
https://www.snapchat.com

[xliv] "Screens, Social Media and Mental Health" transcript from Susan Dunaway presentation at Church of the Resurrection, Leawood, Kansas. Published on "rezlife leawood" YouTube channel, Feb 20, 2020.
https://youtu.be/3dSCthmbaFI
Susan Dunaway is licensed and certified counselor, specializes in children adolescents and parents plus digital and screen based challenges when kids struggle academically behaviorally and socially, owns her own neural counseling business.
Rezlife staff partnered with Susan Dunaway, MC LCPC BCN, from Amend Neurocounseling, to lead an informative night for parents about screens, social media and mental health. Susan shares information and tools to help you navigate your conversations at home.
https://cor.org/leawood/
https://cor.org/leawood/students

[xlv] Nihil, latin word, (indefinite) the absence of anything; nothing.

[xlvi] "Gaming the System: How Lawsuit Advertising Drives the Litigation Lifecycle" by U.S. Chamber Institute for Legal Reform, April 13, 2020.
https://www.instituteforlegalreform.com/research/gaming-the-system-how-lawsuit-advertising-drives-the-litigation-lifecycle
https://www.instituteforlegalreform.com/uploads/sites/1/Gaming_the_System_How_Lawsuit_Advertising_Drives_Litigation_Lifecycle_2020April.pdf

[xlvii] "Gaming the System: How Lawsuit Advertising Drives the Litigation Lifecycle" by U.S. Chamber Institute for Legal Reform, April 13, 2020.
https://www.instituteforlegalreform.com/research/gaming-the-system-how-lawsuit-advertising-drives-the-litigation-lifecycle
https://www.instituteforlegalreform.com/uploads/sites/1/Gaming_the_System_How_Lawsuit_Advertising_Drives_Litigation_Lifecycle_2020April.pdf

[xlviii] "Gaming the System: How Lawsuit Advertising Drives the Litigation Lifecycle" by U.S. Chamber Institute for Legal Reform, April 13, 2020.
https://www.instituteforlegalreform.com/research/gaming-the-system-how-lawsuit-advertising-drives-the-litigation-lifecycle
https://www.instituteforlegalreform.com/uploads/sites/1/Gaming_the_System_How_Lawsuit_Advertising_Drives_Litigation_Lifecycle_2020April.pdf

[xlix] "Gaming the System: How Lawsuit Advertising Drives the Litigation Lifecycle" by U.S. Chamber Institute for Legal Reform, April 13, 2020.
https://www.instituteforlegalreform.com/research/gaming-the-system-how-lawsuit-advertising-drives-the-litigation-lifecycle
https://www.instituteforlegalreform.com/uploads/sites/1/Gaming_the_System_How_Lawsuit_Advertising_Drives_Litigation_Lifecycle_2020April.pdf

[l] "Gaming the System: How Lawsuit Advertising Drives the Litigation Lifecycle" by U.S. Chamber Institute for Legal Reform, April 13, 2020.
https://www.instituteforlegalreform.com/research/gaming-the-system-how-lawsuit-advertising-drives-the-litigation-lifecycle
https://www.instituteforlegalreform.com/uploads/sites/1/Gaming_the_System_How_Lawsuit_Advertising_Drives_Litigation_Lifecycle_2020April.pdf

[li] "Gaming the System: How Lawsuit Advertising Drives the Litigation Lifecycle" by U.S. Chamber Institute for Legal Reform, April 13, 2020.
https://www.instituteforlegalreform.com/research/gaming-the-system-how-lawsuit-advertising-drives-the-litigation-lifecycle
https://www.instituteforlegalreform.com/uploads/sites/1/Gaming_the_System_How_Lawsuit_Advertising_Drives_Litigation_Lifecycle_2020April.pdf

[lii] "International Comparisons of Litigation Costs: Canada, Europe, Japan, and the United States" by U.S. Chamber Institute for Legal Reform, June 2013

https://www.instituteforlegalreform.com/research/international-comparisons-of-litigation-costs-europe-the-united-states-and-canada

liii "International Comparisons of Litigation Costs: Canada, Europe, Japan, and the United States" by U.S. Chamber Institute for Legal Reform, June 2013
https://www.instituteforlegalreform.com/research/international-comparisons-of-litigation-costs-europe-the-united-states-and-canada

liv HARVARD, JOHN M. OLIN CENTER FOR LAW, ECONOMICS, AND BUSINESS COMPARATIVE LITIGATION RATES, J. Mark Ramseyer & Eric B. Rasmusen, Discussion Paper No. 681, 11/2010, Harvard Law School, Cambridge, MA 02138

lv World Happiness Report 2019, Chapter 7: Addiction and Unhappiness in America
Editor: Jeffrey D. Sachs, Director, SDSN, and Director, Center for Sustainable Development, Columbia University
https://worldhappiness.report/ed/2019/
https://s3.amazonaws.com/happiness-report/2019/WHR19.pdf
DALYs, Disability-Adjusted Life Years per 100,000 (100K) population, measure.

lvi Opioid epidemic in the United States, From Wikipedia, the free encyclopedia
https://en.wikipedia.org/wiki/Opioid_epidemic_in_the_United_States
Text is available under the Creative Commons Attribution-ShareAlike License; additional terms may apply. Wikipedia® is a registered trademark of the Wikimedia Foundation, Inc., a non-profit organization.

lvii News from September 11th, 2019

lviii Quote from "Hustlers", a 2019 American crime drama film written and directed by Lorene Scafaria, based on New York magazine's 2015 article "The Hustlers at Scores" by Jessica Pressler.
https://en.wikipedia.org/wiki/Hustlers_(2019_film)
Text is available under the Creative Commons Attribution-ShareAlike License.
Wikipedia® is a registered trademark of the Wikimedia Foundation, Inc., a non-profit organization.

"Hustlers" film is about a band of strippers who drugged their Wall Street clients to steal their money.
https://www.imdb.com/title/tt5503686/
https://www.facebook.com/HustlersMovie/

lix From "Bishop Robert Barron" YouTube channel, video: "Karl Marx and Millennials", discussion with Bishop Robert Barron, Published on Aug 12, 2019
https://www.youtube.com/watch?v=Eexugi6umeY
"Bishop Robert Barron" channel: brief and insightful commentaries on faith and culture by Catholic theologian and author Bishop Robert Barron

lx John Paul II, Polish pope
C entesimus Annus, Pope John Paul II's social encyclical, with his thoughts about freedom

lxi From "Bishop Robert Barron" YouTube channel, video: "Karl Marx and Millennials", discussion with Bishop Robert Barron, Published on Aug 12, 2019
https://www.youtube.com/watch?v=Eexugi6umeY
"Bishop Robert Barron" channel: brief and insightful commentaries on faith and culture by Catholic theologian and author Bishop Robert Barron

lxii Data can be found on National Center for Injury Prevention and Control website; Fatal Injury Data, Content source: Centers for Disease Control and Prevention, National Center for Injury Prevention and Control
https://www.cdc.gov/injury/wisqars/fatal.html
https://wisqars-viz.cdc.gov:8006/

lxiii Latest data on suicide can be found in the Centers for Disease Control and Prevention (CDC) Data & Statistics Fatal Injury Report for 2017 or other suicide prevention sources, incl. websites (e.g. https://afsp.org/about-suicide/suicide-statistics/)

lxiv Examples of Risk and Protective Factors can be found on Centers for Disease Control and Prevention (CDC) website:
https://www.cdc.gov/violenceprevention/suicide/riskprotectivefactors.html
lxv Examples of Risk and Protective Factors can be found on Centers for Disease Control and Prevention (CDC) website:
https://www.cdc.gov/violenceprevention/suicide/riskprotectivefactors.html
lxvi Examples of Risk and Protective Factors can be found on Centers for Disease Control and Prevention (CDC) website:

https://www.cdc.gov/violenceprevention/suicide/riskprotectivefactors.html

lxvii World Happiness Report 2019, Chapter 1: Happiness and Community: An Overview
Editors: John F. Helliwell, Richard Layard, and Jeffrey D. Sachs
https://worldhappiness.report/ed/2019/
https://s3.amazonaws.com/happiness-report/2019/WHR19.pdf

lxviii "Why Finland And Denmark Are Happier Than The U.S.", published on CNBC Make It. Youtube Channel, on Jan 9, 2020
https://youtu.be/6Pm0Mn0-jYU

Among the speakers: Jeffrey Sachs, a professor at Columbia and the co-editor of the World Happiness Report; Meik Wiking, happiness researcher and CEO of the Happiness Research Institute in Denmark.

lxix Viktor Emil Frankl was an Austrian neurologist and psychiatrist as well as a Holocaust survivor.
"Man's Search for Meaning" is a 1946 book by Viktor Frankl chronicling his experiences as a prisoner in Nazi concentration camps during World War II, and describing his psychotherapeutic method, which involved identifying a purpose in life to feel positively about, and then immersively imagining that outcome
https://en.wikipedia.org/wiki/Man%27s_Search_for_Meaning
Text is available under the Creative Commons Attribution-ShareAlike License; additional terms may apply; Wikipedia® is a registered trademark of the Wikimedia Foundation, Inc., a non-profit organization.

lxx Jordan Bernt Peterson (born June 12, 1962) is a Canadian clinical psychologist and a professor of psychology at the University of Toronto. His main areas of study are in abnormal, social, and personality psychology,[1] with a particular interest in the psychology of religious and ideological belief[2] and the assessment and improvement of personality and performance.[3]
https://en.wikipedia.org/wiki/Jordan_Peterson
Text is available under the Creative Commons Attribution-ShareAlike License; additional terms may apply. Wikipedia® is a registered trademark of the Wikimedia Foundation, Inc., a non-profit organization.

lxxi From video posted on YouTube: "TRANSCEND YOUR SUFFERING - Powerful Motivational Video | Jordan Peterson"
https://www.youtube.com/watch?v=5PdoU4vPTqk
lxxii From video posted on YouTube: "TRANSCEND YOUR SUFFERING - Powerful Motivational Video | Jordan Peterson"
https://www.youtube.com/watch?v=5PdoU4vPTqk
lxxiii From video posted on YouTube: "TRANSCEND YOUR SUFFERING - Powerful Motivational Video | Jordan Peterson"
https://www.youtube.com/watch?v=5PdoU4vPTqk

lxxiv Jordan Bernt Peterson (born June 12, 1962) is a Canadian clinical psychologist and a professor of psychology at the University of Toronto. His main areas of study are in abnormal, social, and personality psychology,[1] with a particular interest in the psychology of religious and ideological belief[2] and the assessment and improvement of personality and performance.
https://en.wikipedia.org/wiki/Jordan_Peterson
Text is available under the Creative Commons Attribution-ShareAlike License; Wikipedia® is a registered trademark of the Wikimedia Foundation, Inc., a non-profit organization.

lxxv "Jordan Peterson on Universal Basic Income.. 'Money ISN'T the Problem!'" – transcript of an interview published on "Enlightainment", YouTube channel, on Sep 11, 2018
https://youtu.be/DR2rYCxT0lg

lxxvi From a teachings of Jordan Peterson

lxxvii As Posted on Twitter by Donald J. Trump, verified account @realDonaldTrump, 45th President of the United States of America
https://twitter.com/realdonaldtrump/status/1151103647637487616
also can be watched on YouTube:
https://www.youtube.com/watch?v=dpJE5qd9CRM

lxxviii Transcript from the video published on "The Daily Wire" YouTube channel: "FULL VIDEO: Hurricane Shapiro Takes Berkeley By Storm", lecture given by Ben Shapiro
https://youtu.be/aP_9cRUzqMw
The Daily Wire is a politically conservative news and opinion website featuring daily podcasts by Matt Andrew Klavan, Michael Knowles, Matt Walsh, and Editor-In-Chief Ben Shapiro. The Daily Wire YouTube channel live streams all episodes of each podcast every weekday

[lxxix] As per Wikipedia: "Hakuna-matata" is a Swahili language phrase from East Africa, meaning "no trouble" or "no problems". The phrase was used in Disney animated film The Lion King (which features a song named after the phrase), in which it is translated as "no worries"....
The Lion King song, In 1994 the Walt Disney Animation Studios animated movie The Lion King brought the phrase international recognition, featuring it prominently in the plot and devoting a song to it. A meerkat and a warthog, Timon and Pumbaa, teach Simba that he should forget his troubled past and live in the present. The song was written by Elton John (music) and Tim Rice (lyrics), who found the term in a Swahili phrasebook.
HAKUNA MATATA Trademark of Walt Disney Company, The - Registration Number 2700605 - Serial Number 74558335 :: Justia Trademarks". trademarks.justia.com. Retrieved 19 December 2018.

https://en.wikipedia.org/wiki/Hakuna_matata
Note: Text is available under the Creative Commons Attribution-ShareAlike License; additional terms may apply.

[lxxx] Said by Denzel Washington during his commencement speech at Dillard University:
"Put God First - Denzel Washington Motivational & Inspiring Commencement Speech"
https://www.youtube.com/watch?v=BxY_eJLBflk

[lxxxi] There is a book under the same title: "Economics of Good and Evil" by Tomas Sedlacek.

[lxxxii] "Why Finland And Denmark Are Happier Than The U.S.", published on CNBC Make It. YouTube Channel, on Jan 9, 2020
https://youtu.be/6Pm0Mn0-jYU
Among the speakers: Jeffrey Sachs, a professor at Columbia and the co-editor of the World Happiness Report; Meik Wiking, happiness researcher and CEO of the Happiness Research Institute in Denmark.

[lxxxiii] The transcript of Michelle Obama's speech at the Democratic National Convention.
* Sentence order adjusted; Original sentence: "That is the truest form of empathy — not just feeling, but doing;"
"Michelle Obama delivers keynote speech from first night of the Democratic National Convention", published on CNBC Television YouTube channel, Aug 17, 2020.
https://youtu.be/CznOnxFNy0Q

[lxxxiv] „5 Whys" as per wikipedia
https://en.wikipedia.org/wiki/5_Whys
The technique was originally developed by Sakichi Toyoda and was used within the Toyota Motor Corporation during the evolution of its manufacturing methodologies. It is a critical component of problem-solving training, delivered as part of the induction into the Toyota Production System.
Note: Text is available under the Creative Commons Attribution-ShareAlike License; additional terms may apply.
[lxxxv] Sam Harris, "Making Sense with Sam Harris #196 - The Science of Happiness (with Laurie Santos)", Sam Harris YouTube Channel, published on Apr 10, 2020
https://youtu.be/p1UxKD8C_GA
https://samharris.org/

Laurie Santos is an Associate Professor in the Department of Psychology at Yale University. She hosts the popular podcast The Happiness Lab and she teaches the most popular course offered at Yale to date, titled The Science of Well-Being. Laurie is also the director of the Comparative Cognition Laboratory and the Canine Cognition Center at Yale. She received her A.B. in Psychology and Biology from Harvard University in 1997 and her Ph.D. in Psychology from Harvard in 2003.
Twitter:@lauriesantos
https://caplab.yale.edu/

[lxxxvi] "Deep Connections: The Power of the Human-Animal Bond" by the Lone Tree Veterinary Medical Team, on December 30, 2016, published on Lone Tree Veterinary Medical Center website:
https://www.lonetreevet.com/blog/human-animal-bond/

[lxxxvii] Jeff Simmons, President and CEO at Elanco, is a purpose-driven leader with nearly 30 years of experience focused on delivering business results while engaging employees and developing the next generation of leaders.
Elanco is a global animal health company.
Elanco's Healthy Purpose™ (CSR framework), was established to embody that belief through programs that advance the well-being of animals, people and the planet while empowering our people to make a difference to society.
https://www.elanco.com/healthy-purpose#animal-rediscovered
https://assets.ctfassets.net/f77lgyyxjmq2/2HI9yV7YdsepVgZjb7ZPsA/09fc8413f6f74e7679c18ebb5901b030/Rediscovering_the_Power_of_Healthy_Animals_Fact_Sheet.pdf

[lxxxviii] Elanco's Healthy Purpose ™
https://www.elanco.com/healthy-purpose#animal-rediscovered

https://assets.ctfassets.net/f77lgyyxjmq2/2HI9yV7YdsepVgZjb7ZPsA/09fc8413f6f74e7679c18ebb5901b030/Redisc
overing_the_Power_of_Healthy_Animals_Fact_Sheet.pdf

[lxxxix] HABRI, Survey: Pet Owners and the Human-Animal Bond.
https://habri.org/2016-pet-owners-survey

[xc] Science Direct, Social capital and pet ownership – A tale of four cities.
https://www.sciencedirect.com/science/article/pii/S2352827317300344

[xci] Medical News Today, Cat lovers, this is how a feline friend can boost your health.
https://www.medicalnewstoday.com/articles/322716.php

[xcii] Nature, Scientific Reports, Dog ownership and the risk of cardiovascular disease and death – a nationwide cohort
study.
https://www.nature.com/articles/s41598-017-16118-6.pdf

[xciii] Angela L Curl, Jessica Bibbo, Rebecca A Jonson, Dog Walking, the Human–Animal Bond and Older
Adults' Physical Health, The Gerontologist, Volume 57, Issue 5, October 2017, Pages 930–939. https://doi.
org/10.1093/geront/gnw051.
https://academic.oup.com/gerontologist/article/57/5/930/2632039

[xciv] "New Research Reveals Powerful Health Benefits of Dog Companionship", Post by: Tina Gaines, on 7-Feb-2017.
https://www.elanco.com/news/press-releases/elanco-purdue-release
Elanco Animal Health in collaboration with Purdue University's College of Veterinary Medicine, released preliminary
research findings that support the power of the human-animal bond, GREENFIELD, Ind. Feb. 7, 2017.

[xcv] Human Animal Bond Research Institute
https://habri.org/the-pet-effect/
https://habri.org/research/

[xcvi] Search engine results on the "Snapchat" keyword.
Snapchat is a multimedia messaging app developed by Snap Inc., originally Snapchat Inc.
https://www.snapchat.com

[xcvii] John Richard Kasich Jr. is an American politician, author, and television news host who served as the 69th
Governor of Ohio from 2011 to 2019. Elected in 2010 and re-elected in 2014, He failed to secure the republican
nomination for president in 2016. Kasich is a Republican.
https://en.wikipedia.org/wiki/John_Kasich
Text is available under the Creative Commons Attribution-ShareAlike License;
Wikipedia® is a registered trademark of the Wikimedia Foundation, Inc., a non-profit organization.

[xcviii] "Governor John Kasich on Trump Impeachment, Climate Change & Unifying America", transcript of John Kasich's
statement from interview published Jimmy Kimmel Live! YouTube Channel, on Dec 20, 2019
https://youtu.be/UpawU5i_zlk

[xcixxcix] The United Societies of America, the social movement created by the author, Konrad Milewski

[c] Vernā Myers Online Diversity and Inclusion Courses
https://learning.vernamyers.com/

[ci] Boundary Spanning Leadership, product of Center for Creative Leadership;
Also Book: "BOUNDARY SPANNING LEADERSHIP: SIX PRACTICES FOR SOLVING PROBLEMS, DRIVING INNOVATION,
AND TRANSFORMING ORGANIZATIONS" by Chris Ernst, Donna Chrobot-Mason, Publisher: McGraw-Hill Publishers.
Powered by a decade of global research and practice by the top-ranked Center for Creative Leadership (CCL), this
book will introduce you to practical tools and tactics to apply the six boundary spanning practices that occur at the
nexus where groups collide, intersect, and link.
https://www.ccl.org/leadership-solutions/request-a-speaker/speakers-bureau-boundary-spanning-leadership/

[cii] "Diversity is being invited to the party. Inclusion is being asked to dance." said by Verna Myers, diversity and
inclusion expert, founder and president of Verna Myers Consulting Group and star of a TED Talk on overcoming bias.
https://learning.vernamyers.com/

[ciii] "Profit and Purpose" by Adi Ignatius, from the March–April 2019 Issue, published on hbr.org (Harvard Business
Review)
https://hbr.org/2019/03/profit-and-purpose

also
"The Dual-Purpose Playbook" by Julie Battilana, Anne-Claire Pache, Metin Sengul, Marissa Kimsey, from the March–April 2019 Issue, published on hbr.org (Harvard Business Review)
https://hbr.org/2019/03/the-dual-purpose-playbook

civ Transcript from the speech of Senator Mike Lee, Chairman of the Joint Economic Committee, on Social Capital Project.
https://youtu.be/JMJYbcPPs4E
https://www.jec.senate.gov/public/index.cfm/republicans/socialcapitalproject

cvcv The first 20 hours -- how to learn anything | Josh Kaufman | TEDxCSU
https://youtu.be/5MgBikgcWnY

cvi The Science of Well-Being taught by Professor Laurie Santos, Yale University.
Course can be found at Coursera:
https://www.coursera.org/learn/the-science-of-well-being?utm_source=gg&utm_medium=sem&utm_content=09-ScienceofWellBeing-US&campaignid=9728548210&adgroupid=99699672436&device=c&keyword=science%20of%20well%20being%20yale&matchtype=b&network=g&devicemodel=&adpostion=&creativeid=428321686708&hide_mobile_promo&gclid=Cj0KCQjw_ez2BRCyARIsAJfg-kuAftjzxzPQ-Ea_DNQYf_poUBcDSKxzC_LkovKV4re6Zk4drR4Dr8oaAl5UEALw_wcB

cvii Search Inside Yourself Leadership Institute
https://siyli.org/programs/search-inside-yourself

cviii USAFacts is a not-for-profit, nonpartisan civic initiative.
„OUR NATION, IN NUMBERS, Government data to drive fact-based discussion"
https://usafacts.org/

cix 17 Goals to Transform Our World by the United Nations
https://www.un.org/sustainabledevelopment/
cx #Envision2030: 17 goals to transform the world for persons with disabilities, by the United Nations
https://www.un.org/development/desa/disabilities/envision2030.html
https://www.un.org/sustainabledevelopment/be-the-change/

cxi "Why Finland And Denmark Are Happier Than The U.S.", published on CNBC Make It. YouTube Channel, on Jan 9, 2020
https://youtu.be/6Pm0Mn0-jYU
Among the speakers: Jeffrey Sachs, a professor at Columbia and the co-editor of the World Happiness Report;
Meik Wiking, happiness researcher and CEO of the Happiness Research Institute in Denmark.

cxii "Why Finland And Denmark Are Happier Than The U.S.", published on CNBC Make It. YouTube Channel, on Jan 9, 2020
https://youtu.be/6Pm0Mn0-jYU
Among the speakers: Jeffrey Sachs, a professor at Columbia and the co-editor of the World Happiness Report;
Meik Wiking, happiness researcher and CEO of the Happiness Research Institute in Denmark.

cxiii "Why Finland And Denmark Are Happier Than The U.S.", published on CNBC Make It. YouTube Channel, on Jan 9, 2020
https://youtu.be/6Pm0Mn0-jYU
Among the speakers: Jeffrey Sachs, a professor at Columbia and the co-editor of the World Happiness Report;
Meik Wiking, happiness researcher and CEO of the Happiness Research Institute in Denmark.

cxiv * This article uses material from the Wikipedia article: Poverty in the United States:
https://en.wikipedia.org/wiki/Poverty_in_the_United_States
which is released under the Creative Commons Attribution-ShareAlike License;
https://creativecommons.org/licenses/by-sa/3.0/

cxv 2018 Poverty Guidelines can be reviewed at: https://aspe.hhs.gov/poverty-guidelines

cxvi * Article: How much of my income should I save every month? Authored by Paula Pant published within Teachers Insurance and Annuity Association of America
https://www.tiaa.org/public/offer/insights/starting-out/how-much-of-my-income-should-i-save-every-month

cxvii One of the sources:
https://www.statista.com/statistics/203183/percentage-distribution-of-household-income-in-the-us/

cxviii Source: "Minimum wage"
https://en.wikipedia.org/wiki/Minimum_wage

cxix *Source: "Economic Policy Institute"
https://www.epi.org/
also "Family Budget Calculator"
https://www.epi.org/resources/budget/

cxx Transcription fragment of Dan Gilbert speech: "Dan Gilbert: Happiness: What Your Mother Didn't Tell You (2018 WORLD.MINDS Annual Symposium)", published on WORLD.MINDS YouTube Channel, on Dec 13, 2018.
https://youtu.be/b1Y2Z1BGwno

cxxi Source: "The NFL's Highest-Paid Players 2018: Aaron Rodgers Leads With $76 Million"
https://www.forbes.com/sites/kurtbadenhausen/2018/09/20/the-nfls-highest-paid-players-2018-aaron-rodgers-leads-with-76-million/#e34cca4117bd

cxxii Source: "The 20 highest-paid actors in the world include 2 Ryans, 2 Toms and only 3 women"
https://www.cnbc.com/2018/03/02/the-worlds-highest-paid-actors-include-2-ryans-2-toms-and-3-women.html

cxxiii Source: "The 20 highest-paid actors in the world include 2 Ryans, 2 Toms and only 3 women"
https://www.cnbc.com/2018/03/02/the-worlds-highest-paid-actors-include-2-ryans-2-toms-and-3-women.html

cxxiv Source: "Highest paid CEOs at America's 100 largest companies"
https://www.usatoday.com/story/money/business/2018/04/05/highest-paid-ceos-americas-100-largest-companies/488630002/

cxxv Published on LinkedIn profile of my friend Remigiusz :-)

cxxvi By Ruth Marcus, Deputy editorial page editor, Overseeing Washington Post signed opinion content and writing on domestic politics and policy.
March 27, 2020 at 5:11 p.m. CDT
https://www.washingtonpost.com/opinions/2020/03/27/nurses-doctors-are-heroes-this-moment/

cxxvii Example ranking can be found online, "The Forbes 400: The Definitive Ranking Of The Wealthiest Americans " as part of article edited by Luisa Kroll and Kerry A. Dolan:
https://www.forbes.com/forbes-400/#52c9c90f7e2f

cxxviii Source: U.S. Census Bureau, Current Population Survey, 2018 and 2019 Annual Social and Economic Supplements (CPS ASEC).
"Income and Poverty in the United States: 2018"
Table: "People in Poverty by Selected Characteristics: 2017 and 2018"
https://www.census.gov/data/tables/2019/demo/income-poverty/p60-266.html

cxxix Amount of Americans was calculated using the following basic formula: {total cumulated net worth of top 400 which is ca. $3 trillion in 2019}, divided by {the median net worth of the average U.S. household which was $97,300 in 2018}, which (=) gives number of all households that could be theoretically covered by the total net worth of top 400 and then divided by {the average number of household' members (which is 2.58)}.
Example source of average household's net worth: https://www.marketwatch.com/story/whats-your-net-worth-and-how-do-you-compare-to-others-2018-09-24

cxxx "Giving USA 2018: Americans Gave $410.02 Billion to Charity in 2017, Crossing the $400 Billion Mark for the First Time", Posted on June 13, 2018 at 1:19 am., Written by Giving USA
https://givingusa.org/giving-usa-2018-americans-gave-410-02-billion-to-charity-in-2017-crossing-the-400-billion-mark-for-the-first-time/

cxxxi "America's Top 50 Givers MEET THE PHILANTHROPISTS WHO GAVE AWAY THE MOST MONEY IN 2018" Edited By Jennifer Wang, published on November 20, 2019
https://www.forbes.com/top-givers/#713b11fb66ff

cxxxii The Giving Pledge
https://givingpledge.org/
https://en.wikipedia.org/wiki/The_Giving_Pledge
Text is available under the Creative Commons Attribution-ShareAlike License; additional terms may apply

cxxxiii Bill Ackman's letter to Warren, April 17, 2012 on joining the Giving Pledge
https://givingpledge.org/Pledger.aspx?id=157

cxxxiv Bill Ackman's letter to Warren, April 17, 2012 on joining the Giving Pledge
https://givingpledge.org/Pledger.aspx?id=157

cxxxv Tegan and Brian Acton's letter to The Giving Pledge, May 2019 on joining the Giving Pledge
https://givingpledge.org/Pledger.aspx?id=391

cxxxvi "Why Finland And Denmark Are Happier Than The U.S.", published on CNBC Make It. YouTube Channel, on Jan 9, 2020
https://youtu.be/6Pm0Mn0-jYU
Among the speakers: Jeffrey Sachs, a professor at Columbia and the co-editor of the World Happiness Report; Meik Wiking, happiness researcher and CEO of the Happiness Research Institute in Denmark.

cxxxvii SMART is a well-established tool that you can use to plan and achieve your goals. According to most common definition, goals should be Specific, Measurable, Achievable, Relevant, and Time-bound.

cxxxviii "The Case Against Socialism" by Rand Paul, Broadside, 2019

cxxxix Capitalism
https://en.wikipedia.org/wiki/Capitalism
Text is available under the Creative Commons Attribution-ShareAlike License
Wikipedia® is a registered trademark of the Wikimedia Foundation, Inc., a non-profit organization.
cxl Capitalism
https://en.wikipedia.org/wiki/Capitalism
Text is available under the Creative Commons Attribution-ShareAlike License
Wikipedia® is a registered trademark of the Wikimedia Foundation, Inc., a non-profit organization.
cxli Capitalism
https://en.wikipedia.org/wiki/Capitalism
Text is available under the Creative Commons Attribution-ShareAlike License
Wikipedia® is a registered trademark of the Wikimedia Foundation, Inc., a non-profit organization.
cxlii Capitalism
https://en.wikipedia.org/wiki/Capitalism
Text is available under the Creative Commons Attribution-ShareAlike License
Wikipedia® is a registered trademark of the Wikimedia Foundation, Inc., a non-profit organization.
cxliii Capitalism
https://en.wikipedia.org/wiki/Capitalism
Text is available under the Creative Commons Attribution-ShareAlike License
Wikipedia® is a registered trademark of the Wikimedia Foundation, Inc., a non-profit organization.
cxliv Capitalism
https://en.wikipedia.org/wiki/Capitalism
Text is available under the Creative Commons Attribution-ShareAlike License
Wikipedia® is a registered trademark of the Wikimedia Foundation, Inc., a non-profit organization.

cxlv Capitalism
https://en.wikipedia.org/wiki/Capitalism
Text is available under the Creative Commons Attribution-ShareAlike License
Wikipedia® is a registered trademark of the Wikimedia Foundation, Inc., a non-profit organization.
cxlvi Capitalism
https://en.wikipedia.org/wiki/Capitalism
Text is available under the Creative Commons Attribution-ShareAlike License
Wikipedia® is a registered trademark of the Wikimedia Foundation, Inc., a non-profit organization.

cxlvii "Alexandria Ocasio-Cortez calls out Trump in five-minute corruption game", fragment of hearing published on CNN, YouTube channel, Feb 8, 2019

https://youtu.be/TJlpS4vhKP0
CNN operates as a division of Turner Broadcasting System, which is a subsidiary of Warner Media. CNN identifies itself as -- and is widely known to be - the most trusted source for news and information. The CNN umbrella includes nine cable and satellite television networks, two radio networks, the CNN Digital Network, which is the top network of news Web sites in the United States, and CNN Newsource, the world's most extensively syndicated news service. CNN is proud of our ability to bring you up-to-the-minute news from around the world, as a result of our many extensions.

cxlviii Karen Hobert Flynn, a democracy reform activist and leader for more than three decades, including 25-plus years on staff and in state and national leadership positions with Common Cause, is the organization's ninth president.
https://www.commoncause.org/people/karen-hobert-flynn/

cxlix Karen Hobert Flynn, a democracy reform activist and leader for more than three decades, including 25-plus years on staff and in state and national leadership positions with Common Cause, is the organization's ninth president.
https://www.commoncause.org/people/karen-hobert-flynn/

cl Rudy Mehrbani is a fellow and senior counsel at the Brennan Center. He leads the Center's work on the bipartisan National Task Force on Rule of Law and Democracy. He previously served as an assistant to President Obama and director of the Presidential Personnel Office at the White House, where he advised the president, cabinet members, and other senior government officials on human capital issues arising across the executive branch of the federal government.
https://www.brennancenter.org/experts/rudy-mehrbani

cli "President Obama: FULL INTERVIEW | Real Time with Bill Maher (HBO)", published on "Real Time with Bill Maher" YouTube Channel, on Nov 4, 2016
https://youtu.be/xXH5agV7skw

William Maher is an American comedian, political commentator, and television host. He is known for the HBO political talk show Real Time with Bill Maher (2003–present) and the similar late-night show called Politically Incorrect (1993–2002), originally on Comedy Central and later on ABC. Maher is known for his political satire and sociopolitical commentary.
https://en.wikipedia.org/wiki/Bill_Maher
Barack Hussein Obama is an American attorney and politician who served as the 44th president of the United States from 2009 to 2017. A member of the Democratic Party, he was the first African American president of the United States. He previously served as a U.S. senator from Illinois from 2005 to 2008 and an Illinois state senator from 1997 to 2004.
https://en.wikipedia.org/wiki/Barack_Obama
Text is available under the Creative Commons Attribution-ShareAlike License
Wikipedia® is a registered trademark of the Wikimedia Foundation, Inc., a non-profit organization.

clii Nick Hanauer, "The dirty secret of capitalism -- and a new way forward | Nick Hanauer" speech published on TED's YouTube channel, October 2019
https://youtu.be/th3KE_H27bs
The TED Talks channel features the best talks and performances from the TED Conference, where the world's leading thinkers and doers give the talk of their lives in 18 minutes (or less).

cliii World Population Review, World Countries by GDP
http://worldpopulationreview.com/countries/countries-by-gdp/
http://worldpopulationreview.com/countries/countries-by-gdp/#worldCountries

cliv The Inclusive Development Index 2018
https://www.weforum.org/reports/the-inclusive-development-index-2018

clv Individual income tax rates table by KPMG
https://home.kpmg/xx/en/home/services/tax/tax-tools-and-resources/tax-rates-online/individual-income-tax-rates-table.html

clvi Corporate tax rates table by KPMG
https://home.kpmg/xx/en/home/services/tax/tax-tools-and-resources/tax-rates-online/corporate-tax-rates-table.html

clvii 2019 Worldwide VAT, GST and Sales Tax Guide by EY
https://www.ey.com/gl/en/services/tax/worldwide-vat--gst-and-sales-tax-guide---xmlqs?preview&XmlUrl=/ec1mages/taxguides/VAT-2019/VAT-US.xml
EY refers to the global organization, and may refer to one or more, of the member firms of Ernst & Young Global Limited, each of which is a separate legal entity.

clviii Taxation in Sweden
https://en.wikipedia.org/wiki/Taxation_in_Sweden
Text is available under the Creative Commons Attribution-ShareAlike License; additional terms may apply
Wikipedia® is a registered trademark of the Wikimedia Foundation, Inc., a non-profit organization.

clix Taxation in Sweden

https://en.wikipedia.org/wiki/Taxation_in_Sweden
Text is available under the Creative Commons Attribution-ShareAlike License; additional terms may apply
Wikipedia® is a registered trademark of the Wikimedia Foundation, Inc., a non-profit organization.

clix "HOW SWEDEN CREATED A MORE STABLE ECONOMY" published on the official site of Sweden
https://sweden.se/business/how-sweden-created-a-more-stable-economy/

clxi "Why Sweden beats other countries at just about everything" published at World Economic Forum's
website
https://www.weforum.org/agenda/2017/01/why-sweden-beats-most-other-countries-at-just-about-everything/
© 2019 World Economic Forum

clxii Maternity leave in the United States
https://en.wikipedia.org/wiki/Maternity_leave_in_the_United_States
Text is available under the Creative Commons Attribution-ShareAlike License; additional terms may apply
Wikipedia® is a registered trademark of the Wikimedia Foundation, Inc., a non-profit organization.

clxiii "Why Sweden beats other countries at just about everything" published at World Economic Forum's
website
https://www.weforum.org/agenda/2017/01/why-sweden-beats-most-other-countries-at-just-about-everything/
© 2019 World Economic Forum

clxiv FREE EDUCATION FROM AGE 6 TO 19, published on Sweden.se, from: 21 June 2016
https://sweden.se/society/free-education-from-age-6-to-19/

clxv HEALTHCARE IN SWEDEN, published on Sweden.se, from: 30 October 2019
https://sweden.se/society/health-care-in-sweden/

clxvi "Why Sweden beats other countries at just about everything" published at World Economic Forum's
website
https://www.weforum.org/agenda/2017/01/why-sweden-beats-most-other-countries-at-just-about-everything/
© 2019 World Economic Forum

clxvii Intentional homicides (per 100,000 people)
https://data.worldbank.org/indicator/VC.IHR.PSRC.P5
UN Office on Drugs and Crime's International Homicide Statistics database.
License : CC BY-4.0

clxviii Gun Laws in Sweden 2015 By Anastacia Sampson
https://www.sweden.org.za/gun-laws-in-sweden.html

clxix "Why Sweden beats other countries at just about everything" published at World Economic Forum's
website
https://www.weforum.org/agenda/2017/01/why-sweden-beats-most-other-countries-at-just-about-everything/
© 2019 World Economic Forum

clxx Religion in Sweden
https://en.wikipedia.org/wiki/Religion_in_Sweden
Text is available under the Creative Commons Attribution-ShareAlike License; additional terms may apply
Wikipedia® is a registered trademark of the Wikimedia Foundation, Inc., a non-profit organization.

clxxi Text published on www.quora.com on Nov 16, 2019 by Chris Ebbert, who lives in Sweden
https://www.quora.com/Why-are-Swedes-so-successful
Chris Ebbert, Innovation Advisor and Industrial Designer
"Industrial- and Transportation Designer, innovation professional, lecturer, researcher; lived here and there and
done this and that. Harmless, unless there is food involved. I appear to have what I call chronic innovation disorder;
show me what you will, I will have a better idea."

clxxii "Why Finland And Denmark Are Happier Than The U.S.", published on CNBC Make It. YouTube Channel, on Jan
9, 2020
https://youtu.be/6Pm0Mn0-jYU
Among the speakers: Jeffrey Sachs, a professor at Columbia and the co-editor of the World Happiness Report;
Meik Wiking, happiness researcher and CEO of the Happiness Research Institute in Denmark.

clxxiii "The Rich Really Do Pay Lower Taxes Than You", By David Leonhardt, OCT. 6, 2019

https://www.nytimes.com/interactive/2019/10/06/opinion/income-tax-rate-wealthy.html

clxxiv "Capital in the Twenty-First Century", book by French economist Thomas Piketty
https://en.wikipedia.org/wiki/Capital_in_the_Twenty-First_Century

clxxv The World Inequality Report 2018 produced by the World Inequality Lab, a research center based at the Paris School of Economics, coordinated by Facundo Alvaredo, Lucas Chancel, Thomas Piketty, Emmanuel Saez, Gabriel Zucman
https://wir2018.wid.world/files/download/wir2018-full-report-english.pdf
https://www.gfmag.com/global-data/economic-data/wealth-distribution-income-inequality

clxxvi Chapter: 2.4 "Income inequality in the United States"
Remark: Information in that chapter is based on the article "Distributional National Accounts: Methods and Estimates for the United States." by Thomas Piketty, Emmanuel Saez, and Gabriel Zucman, forthcoming in the Quarterly Journal of Economics (2018).
https://wir2018.wid.world/files/download/wir2018-full-report-english.pdf

clxxvii The World Inequality Report, box 2.4.1: "Measuring pre-tax and post-tax income inequality":
"In this chapter, we present estimates of pre- and post-tax income inequality for the USA, which are two complementary concepts for the analysis of inequality. Comparing pre- and post-tax income inequality allows to better assessing the impact of personal taxes and in-kind transfers on the dynamics of income inequality. In the WID.world database, pre-tax income refers to incomes measured before personal income and wealth taxes and in-kind transfers (typically health transfers) but after the operation of the pension and employment insurance systems (as well as after Social security and disability transfers in the case of the United States). In contrast, post-tax income refers to incomes measured after all taxes (in particular, after direct personal and wealth taxes) and after all government transfers (cash and in-kind). It is important to note that pensions and unemployment insurance represent the vast majority of cash transfers in the United States and more generally in rich countries. Therefore our notion of pre-tax income inequality (which we used in previous chapters to make international comparisons) already includes most cash redistribution."
https://wir2018.wid.world/files/download/wir2018-full-report-english.pdf

clxxviii „Inequality for All" is a 2013 documentary film directed by Jacob Kornbluth. The film examines widening income inequality in the United States. The film is presented by American economist, author and professor Robert Reich and is based on his 2010 book Aftershock: The Next Economy and America's Future.
https://en.wikipedia.org/wiki/Inequality_for_All
http://inequalityforall.com/

clxxix Former U.S. Labor Secretary Robert Reich commentary made in the movie "Inequality for all".
https://www.netflix.com/title/70267834

clxxx "Global poverty: Facts, FAQs, and how to help"
Graph: "Share of the World Population living in Absolute Poverty, 1820-2015", based on the image from Our World in Data.
https://www.worldvision.org/sponsorship-news-stories/global-poverty-facts#:~:text=How%20many%20people%20live%20in%20poverty%20in%20the%20world%3F,according%20to%20the%20World%20Bank

Our World in Data (OWID) is a scientific online publication that focuses on large global problems such as poverty, disease, hunger, climate change, war, existential risks, and inequality.
https://ourworldindata.org/

clxxxi "The ONLY Reason Marxism Will ALWAYS FAIL - Jordan Peterson", transcript from an interview published on WisdomTalks YouTube Channel, on Sep 14, 2018
https://youtu.be/1lTGu35BpZs
https://youtu.be/Jpru53j6qNU

clxxxii "Bill Maher | Full Q&A | Oxford Union" transcript from interview published on OxfordUnion YouTube Channel, on May 31, 2015.
https://youtu.be/MPb1VNt2EOo
The Oxford Union is the home of talks and debates by intriguing and influential people who shape our world.
It has been established for 190 years, aiming to promote debate and discussion not just in Oxford University, but across the globe. All Rights Reserved by the Oxford Union.

clxxxiii Transcript of an interview with Daniel Markovits published on the YouTube Channel of Sam Harris, Episode #205: "Making Sense with Sam Harris #205 - The Failure of Meritocracy (with Daniel Markovits)".

https://youtu.be/UOuRYsAP5Lo

Daniel Markovits is Guido Calabresi Professor of Law at Yale Law School and Founding Director of the Center for the Study of Private Law. Markovits works in the philosophical foundations of private law, moral and political philosophy, and behavioral economics.
His writing has appeared in a number of notable publications including The New York Times, The Atlantic, Science, The American Economic Review, and The Yale Law Journal. His latest book, The Meritocracy Trap: How America's Foundational Myth Feeds Inequality, Dismantles The Middle Class, and Devours The Elite, places meritocracy at the center of rising economic inequality and social and political dysfunction. The book takes up the law, economics, and politics of human capital to identify the mechanisms through which meritocracy breeds inequality and to expose the burdens that meritocratic inequality imposes on all who fall within meritocracy's orbit.
Website: https://law.yale.edu/daniel-markovits

[clxxxiv] "Why Finland And Denmark Are Happier Than The U.S.", published on CNBC Make It. YouTube Channel, on Jan 9, 2020
https://youtu.be/6Pm0Mn0-jYU
Among the speakers: Jeffrey Sachs, a professor at Columbia and the co-editor of the World Happiness Report; Meik Wiking, happiness researcher and CEO of the Happiness Research Institute in Denmark.
[clxxxv] "The Prosperity Paradox: How Innovation Can Lift Nations Out of Poverty" By: Clayton Christensen, Efosa Ojomo and Karen Dillon, November 29, 2018
https://www.christenseninstitute.org/books/the-prosperity-paradox-how-innovation-can-lift-nations-out-of-poverty/

[clxxxvi] LOL is an internet slang term that means "laugh out loud". LOL is often used in messages meaning "That is really funny."

[clxxxvii] Policy Analysis MONEY AND SCHOOL PERFORMANCE Lessons from the Kansas City Desegregation Experiment by Paul Ciotti, March 16, 1998, No. 298

[clxxxviii] Closing the GAP, Vision 2030 by © Church of the Resurrection
https://cor.org
https://build.cor.org/

[clxxxix] The World Inequality Report 2018 produced by the World Inequality Lab, a research center based at the Paris School of Economics, coordinated by Facundo Alvaredo, Lucas Chancel, Thomas Piketty, Emmanuel Saez, Gabriel Zucman
https://wir2018.wid.world/files/download/wir2018-full-report-english.pdf
https://www.gfmag.com/global-data/economic-data/wealth-distribution-income-inequality

[cxc] The Clash
[cxci] Daniel Markovits is the Guido Calabresi Professor of Law at the Yale Law School, and the Founding Director of the Yale Centre for the Study of Private Law.

[cxcii] "Second Amendment to the United States Constitution":
https://en.wikipedia.org/wiki/Second_Amendment_to_the_United_States_Constitution
Text is available under the Creative Commons Attribution-ShareAlike License.

[cxciii] "America is a violent country" - Kieran Healy is a professor of sociology at Duke University, Originally posted on October 2, 2017. https://www.washingtonpost.com/news/monkey-cage/wp/2017/10/03/america-is-a-violent-country/?utm_term=.aebd8bddc024

[cxciv] "Key takeaways on Americans' views of guns and gun ownership" BY RUTH IGIELNIK AND ANNA BROWN (Ruth Igielnik is a senior researcher at Pew Research Center; Anna Brown is a research analyst focusing on social and demographic trends at Pew Research Center)
Published on JUNE 22, 2017
https://www.pewresearch.org/fact-tank/2017/06/22/key-takeaways-on-americans-views-of-guns-and-gun-ownership/

[cxcv] BBC "America's gun culture in 10 charts"
https://www.bbc.com/news/world-us-canada-41488081
Published: 27 October 2018

[cxcvi] Guns, by Gallup
https://news.gallup.com/poll/1645/guns.aspx

cxcvii MSN.com article: "Gun industry contributes $51.3B to US economy, research shows"
By Andrew Lisa, published on 4/24/2018
https://www.msn.com/en-us/news/other/gun-industry-contributes-dollar513b-to-us-economy-research-shows/ar-AAvuCzz
All of the data for this article was sourced from the NSSF's 2017 Firearms and Ammunition Industry Economic Impact Report:
https://d3aya7xwz8momx.cloudfront.net/wp-content/uploads/2017/07/EconomicImpactofIndustry2017.pdf

cxcviii ProCon.org, "History of Violent Video Games", Last updated on: 6/3/2016 11:27:13 AM PST, https://videogames.procon.org/view.resource.php?resourceID=006520
Craig A. Anderson and Wayne A. Warburton, "The Impact of Violent Video Games: An Overview," Growing Up Fast and Furious, 2012
Craig A. Anderson and Brad J. Bushman, "Effects of Violent Video Games on Aggressive Behavior, Aggressive Cognition, Aggressive Affect, Physiological Arousal, and Prosocial Behavior: A Meta-Analytic Review of the Scientific Literature," Psychological Science, Sep. 2001
Douglas A. Gentile, "The Multiple Dimensions of Video Game Effects," Child Development Perspectives, June 2011
Mike Jaccarino, "'Training Simulation:' Mass Killers Often Share Obsession with Violent Video Games," foxnews.com, Sep. 12, 2013

cxcix ProCon.org, "History of Violent Video Games", Last updated on: 6/3/2016 11:27:13 AM PST, https://videogames.procon.org/view.resource.php?resourceID=006520
Karen Sternheimer, "Do Video Games Kill?," Contexts, Feb. 2007

cc ProCon.org, "History of Violent Video Games", Last updated on: 6/3/2016 11:27:13 AM PST, https://videogames.procon.org/view.resource.php?resourceID=006520
Dmitri Williams and Marko Skoric, "Internet Fantasy Violence: A Test of Aggression in an Online Game," Communication Monographs, June 2005
Cheryl Olson, Lawrence Kutner, and Dorothy Warner, "The Role of Violent Video Game Content in Adolescent Development: Boys' Perspectives," Journal of Adolescent Research, Jan. 2008
Cheryl Olson, Lawrence Kutner, Dorothy Warner, Jason Almerigi, Lee Baer, Armand Nicholi, and Eugene Beresin, "Factors Correlated with Violent Video Game Use by Adolescent Boys and Girls," Journal of Adolescent Health, July 2007

cci ProCon.org, "History of Violent Video Games", Last updated on: 6/3/2016 11:27:13 AM PST, https://videogames.procon.org/view.resource.php?resourceID=006520
"Crime in the United States, 2008," FBI website, Sep. 2009
"Essential Facts about the Computer and Video Game Industry," Entertainment Software Association website, May 2009
National Center for Juvenile Justice, "Juvenile Offenders and Victims: 2014 National Report," ojjdp.gov, Dec. 2014
Ronald Bailey, "Kill Pixels, Not People," reason.com, Feb. 2015

ccii Commentary given by Sean Patrick Hannity to the Fox News after El Paso, TX shooting, summer 2019. Sean Patrick Hannity is an American talk show host and conservative political commentator. He hosts a cable news show as well as The Sean Hannity Show, a nationally syndicated talk radio show.
https://en.wikipedia.org/wiki/Sean_Hannity
https://hannity.com/

cciii Fragment of lyrics of "When You Believe" song from the 1998 DreamWorks musical animated feature The Prince of Egypt. It was written and composed by Stephen Schwartz. A pop single version of "When You Believe", with additional music and lyrics by writer-producer Babyface, was also recorded for the film by American singers Mariah Carey and Whitney Houston for the film's end credits and its soundtrack album.
https://en.wikipedia.org/wiki/When_You_Believe
Text is available under the Creative Commons Attribution-ShareAlike License; Wikipedia® is a registered trademark of the Wikimedia Foundation, Inc., a non-profit organization.

cciv The right to life – as per Wikipedia:
https://en.wikipedia.org/wiki/Right_to_life
Text is available under the Creative Commons Attribution-ShareAlike License; Wikipedia® is a registered trademark of the Wikimedia Foundation, Inc., a non-profit organization.

ccv Fragment of an interview given by Michael Dale Huckabee to Fox News an American conservative pay television news channel in Aug 2019.

Michael Dale Huckabee (born August 24, 1955) is an American politician and Christian minister who served as the 44th governor of Arkansas from 1996 to 2007. He was a candidate in the United States Republican presidential primaries in both 2008 and 2016.
https://en.wikipedia.org/wiki/Mike_Huckabee
Text is available under the Creative Commons Attribution-ShareAlike License; Wikipedia® is a registered trademark of the Wikimedia Foundation, Inc., a non-profit organization.

ccvi Result of Google Search on „post traumatic stress disorder"

ccvii Fragment of an interview "Reflections with General James Mattis - Conversations with History" given by James Norman Mattis, published on University of California Television (UCTV) YouTube channel:
https://youtu.be/HOc38ZwEO8s
James Norman Mattis is an American veteran and former government official who served as the 26th United States Secretary of Defense from January 2017 through December 2018. A retired United States Marine Corps general.
https://en.wikipedia.org/wiki/Jim_Mattis
Text is available under the Creative Commons Attribution-ShareAlike License; Wikipedia® is a registered trademark of the Wikimedia Foundation, Inc., a non-profit organization.

ccviii Fragment of an interview "Jim Mattis, "Call Sign Chaos" (with David Brooks)" given by James Norman Mattis, published on "Politics and Prose" YouTube channel:
https://youtu.be/EVw_d69C8UY
James Norman Mattis is an American veteran and former government official who served as the 26th United States Secretary of Defense from January 2017 through December 2018. A retired United States Marine Corps general.
https://en.wikipedia.org/wiki/Jim_Mattis
Text is available under the Creative Commons Attribution-ShareAlike License; Wikipedia® is a registered trademark of the Wikimedia Foundation, Inc., a non-profit organization.

Interview worth watching: "Jim Mattis on Call Sign Chaos: Learning to Lead" published on "HooverInstitution" YouTube channel:
https://youtu.be/zlOWx7Ft3SQ
Book worth reading: "Call Sign Chaos: Learning to Lead" by Jim Mattis and Bing West

ccix Fragment of an interview "Jim Mattis, "Call Sign Chaos" (with David Brooks)" given by James Norman Mattis, published on "Politics and Prose" YouTube channel:
https://youtu.be/EVw_d69C8UY

ccx Tgun Wikipedia: "Tranquillizer gun"
https://en.wikipedia.org/wiki/Tranquillizer_gun
Text is available under the Creative Commons Attribution-ShareAlike License; Wikipedia® is a registered trademark of the Wikimedia Foundation, Inc., a non-profit organization.

ccxi Winston Churchill

ccxii Rezlife Student Ministries, Church of the Resurrection, LEAWOOD.
https://cor.org/leawood/students
ccxiii Rezlife Student Ministries, Church of the Resurrection, LEAWOOD.
https://cor.org/leawood/students

ccxiv "To love is to will the good of the other", by Saint Thomas Aquinas, Summa Theologica (1265–1274), II-II, q. 26, art. 6

ccxv Winston Churchill

ccxvi Louis Pasteur (27 December 1822 – 28 September 1895) French microbiologist, chemist, pioneer of the "Germ theory of disease", discoverer of molecular asymmetry and stereo-chemistry, and inventor of the process of Pasteurization.
https://en.wikiquote.org/wiki/Louis_Pasteur
Text is available under the Creative Commons Attribution-ShareAlike License; Wikipedia® is a registered trademark of the Wikimedia Foundation, Inc., a non-profit organization.

ccxvii Quote from "What is a Leader?" the seventh episode of the Toy Story mini-series "Forky Asks a Question" on Disney +. It premiered December 20, 2019.

ccxviii Sam Harris, "Making Sense with Sam Harris #196 - The Science of Happiness (with Laurie Santos)", Sam Harris YouTube Channel, published on Apr 10, 2020

https://youtu.be/p1UxKD8C_GA
https://samharris.org/
Laurie Santos is an Associate Professor in the Department of Psychology at Yale University. She hosts the popular podcast The Happiness Lab and she teaches the most popular course offered at Yale to date, titled The Science of Well-Being. Laurie is also the director of the Comparative Cognition Laboratory and the Canine Cognition Center at Yale. She received her A.B. in Psychology and Biology from Harvard University in 1997 and her Ph.D. in Psychology from Harvard in 2003.
Twitter:@lauriesantos
https://caplab.yale.edu/
ccxix Sam Harris, "Making Sense with Sam Harris #196 - The Science of Happiness (with Laurie Santos)", Sam Harris YouTube Channel, published on Apr 10, 2020
https://youtu.be/p1UxKD8C_GA
https://samharris.org/
Laurie Santos is an Associate Professor in the Department of Psychology at Yale University. She hosts the popular podcast The Happiness Lab and she teaches the most popular course offered at Yale to date, titled The Science of Well-Being. Laurie is also the director of the Comparative Cognition Laboratory and the Canine Cognition Center at Yale. She received her A.B. in Psychology and Biology from Harvard University in 1997 and her Ph.D. in Psychology from Harvard in 2003.
Twitter:@lauriesantos
https://caplab.yale.edu/

ccxx "Why are we here? Why are we born? | Ajahn Brahm |" published on Buddhist Society of Western Australia YouTube Channel on Jan 10, 2015.
"This talk by Ajahn Brahm gets to the heart of the existential quest: What are we here? What were we born for?"
https://youtu.be/-RrCjzi74BA

ccxxi "Sam Harris on the Illusion of Free Will" published on EAE YouTube Channel, Jan 28, 2017
https://youtu.be/7t_Uyi9bNS4
Other original sources:
"Making Sense with Sam Harris #39 - Free Will Revisited (with Daniel Dennett)" https://youtu.be/t7Yst8l51GY
"Sam Harris - Free Will" https://youtu.be/_FanhvXO9Pk

ccxxii Sam Harris
https://en.wikipedia.org/wiki/Sam_Harris
Text is available under the Creative Commons Attribution-ShareAlike License. Wikipedia® is a registered trademark of the Wikimedia Foundation, Inc., a non-profit organization.

ccxxiii Khan Academy
https://www.khanacademy.org/
ccxxiv The Bible, Revelation, Chapter 22.

Source:
https://www.christianity.com/bible/bible.php?q=Revelation+22&ver=niv
Other online sources:
https://biblehub.com/bsb/revelation/22.htm

ccxxv Bishop Robert Barron, transcript from "Bishop Barron on Who God Is & Who God Isn't", published on Bishop Robert Barron YouTube Channel, on Oct 31, 2013
https://youtu.be/1zMf_8hkCdc

ccxxvi Thomas Aquinas ('Thomas of Aquino') (1225 – 7 March 1274) was an Italian Dominican friar, philosopher, Catholic priest, and Doctor of the Church. An immensely influential philosopher, theologian, and jurist in the tradition of scholasticism.
https://en.wikipedia.org/wiki/Thomas_Aquinas
Text is available under the Creative Commons Attribution-ShareAlike License. Wikipedia® is a registered trademark of the Wikimedia Foundation, Inc., a non-profit organization.
ccxxvii Thomas Aquinas ('Thomas of Aquino') (1225 – 7 March 1274) was an Italian Dominican friar, philosopher, Catholic priest, and Doctor of the Church. An immensely influential philosopher, theologian, and jurist in the tradition of scholasticism.
https://en.wikipedia.org/wiki/Thomas_Aquinas
Text is available under the Creative Commons Attribution-ShareAlike License. Wikipedia® is a registered trademark of the Wikimedia Foundation, Inc., a non-profit organization.

ccxxviii Five Ways (Aquinas)
https://en.wikipedia.org/wiki/Five_Ways_(Aquinas)

ccxxix Thomas Aquinas ('Thomas of Aquino') (1225 – 7 March 1274) was an Italian Dominican friar, philosopher, Catholic priest, and Doctor of the Church. An immensely influential philosopher, theologian, and jurist in the tradition of scholasticism.
https://en.wikipedia.org/wiki/Thomas_Aquinas
Text is available under the Creative Commons Attribution-ShareAlike License. Wikipedia® is a registered trademark of the Wikimedia Foundation, Inc., a non-profit organization.

ccxxx Thomas Aquinas ('Thomas of Aquino') (1225 – 7 March 1274) was an Italian Dominican friar, philosopher, Catholic priest, and Doctor of the Church. An immensely influential philosopher, theologian, and jurist in the tradition of scholasticism.
https://en.wikipedia.org/wiki/Thomas_Aquinas
Text is available under the Creative Commons Attribution-ShareAlike License. Wikipedia® is a registered trademark of the Wikimedia Foundation, Inc., a non-profit organization.

ccxxxi Bishop Robert Barron, transcript from "Bishop Barron on Who God Is & Who God Isn't", published on Bishop Robert Barron YouTube Channel, on Oct 31, 2013
https://youtu.be/1zMf_8hkCdc
ccxxxii Adam Hamilton, "CREED WHAT CHRISTIANS BELIEVE AND WHY", "EXPLORING THE APOSTOLES' CREED", 2016 Abingdon Press / Nashville. Chapter 1. God. PAGE 18-19

(*Quote from Einstein from George Sylvester Viereck, "What Life Means to Einstein: An interview by George Sylvester Viereck,"The Saturday Evening Post (Indianapolis:IN), October 6, 1929, 117.
http://www.saturdayeveningpost.com/wp-content/uploads/satevepost/what_life_means_to_einstein.pdf)

ccxxxiii Adam Hamilton is the founding pastor of the United Methodist Church of the Resurrection in Leawood, Kansas. He grew up in the Kansas City area, earned a B.A. degree in Pastoral Ministry from Oral Roberts and a Master of Divinity Degree from Southern Methodist University, where he was awarded the B'nai B'rith Award in Social Ethics. He was named one of the "Ten people to watch in America's spiritual landscape" by Religion and Ethics Newsweekly. For his work in racial reconciliation Adam was awarded the Martin Luther King, Jr. Legacy Award. Named United Methodist Person of the Year for 2012 by the United Methodist Reporter for his leadership within the United Methodist Church. He's received numerous other awards for community service.
Hamilton launched Church of the Resurrection with his wife and two children in 1990. It has since grown to over 20,000 adults and children in 2018 under his leadership. Today the church is the largest United Methodist Church in the United States with an average weekend attendance of over 12,000.
The congregation has a three-fold focus: Connecting with thinking people and inviting them to become followers of Jesus Christ, engaging in acts of justice and mercy in the community, and working to renew the United Methodist Church.
Adam has written over 25 books, published by Abingdon Press and Harper Collins, and Convergent.
https://cor.org/leawood/staff#d/person/2323/cor_l

ccxxxiv Thomas Aquinas ('Thomas of Aquino') (1225 – 7 March 1274) was an Italian Dominican friar, philosopher, Catholic priest, and Doctor of the Church. An immensely influential philosopher, theologian, and jurist in the tradition of scholasticism.
https://en.wikipedia.org/wiki/Thomas_Aquinas
Text is available under the Creative Commons Attribution-ShareAlike License. Wikipedia® is a registered trademark of the Wikimedia Foundation, Inc., a non-profit organization.

ccxxxv Bishop Robert Barron, transcript from "Bishop Barron on Who God Is & Who God Isn't", published on Bishop Robert Barron YouTube Channel, on Oct 31, 2013
https://youtu.be/1zMf_8hkCdc
(*Bishop Barron makes reference to the book 'The Experience of God: Being, Consciousness, Bliss' by David Bentley Hart.)

ccxxxvi Thomas Aquinas ('Thomas of Aquino') (1225 – 7 March 1274) was an Italian Dominican friar, philosopher, Catholic priest, and Doctor of the Church. An immensely influential philosopher, theologian, and jurist in the tradition of scholasticism.
https://en.wikipedia.org/wiki/Thomas_Aquinas
Text is available under the Creative Commons Attribution-ShareAlike License. Wikipedia® is a registered trademark of the Wikimedia Foundation, Inc., a non-profit organization.

ccxxxvii Thomas Aquinas ('Thomas of Aquino') (1225 – 7 March 1274) was an Italian Dominican friar, philosopher, Catholic priest, and Doctor of the Church. An immensely influential philosopher, theologian, and jurist in the tradition of scholasticism.
https://en.wikipedia.org/wiki/Thomas_Aquinas
Text is available under the Creative Commons Attribution-ShareAlike License. Wikipedia® is a registered trademark of the Wikimedia Foundation, Inc., a non-profit organization.

ccxxxviii TOP 10 ALTERNATIVE RELIGIONS
http://www.thinkhouse.ie/features/top-10-alternative-religions
ccxxxix "Economics of Good and Evil: The Quest for Economic Meaning from Gilgamesh to Wall Street" Book by Tomáš Sedláček

ccxl Transcript from „Bishop Robert Barron | The Ben Shapiro Show Sunday Special Ep. 31", published on The Daily Wire YouTube Channel, on Dec 16, 2018
https://youtu.be/OoDt8wWQsiA

ccxli Transcript from „Bishop Barron on Having a 'Personal Relationship' with Jesus", published on Bishop Robert Barron YouTube Channel, on Dec 8, 2016
https://youtu.be/w2KZDQSxwF4

ccxlii Comment made by Bishop Robert Barron on a YouTube chat: "Bishop Barron on Hitchens' 'God Is Not Great' (Part 3 of 3)", published on Bishop Robert Barron YouTube Channel, on Dec 6, 2007
https://youtu.be/Ev8EhqVbJaY

ccxliii "WHO WE ARE", Historic Teaching, published on Website of St. Mark's Church (Geneva, Illinois)
https://stmarks-geneva.org/about/who-we-are/

ccxliv Story of Jesus can be found in The Bible, The New Testament.
"The New Testament is the second part of the Christian biblical canon, the first being the Old Testament. The New Testament discusses the teachings and person of Jesus, as well as events in first-century Christianity. Christians regard both the Old and New Testaments together as sacred scripture." as per Wikipedia, https://en.wikipedia.org/wiki/New_Testament

A simplified and unauthorized portrait of Jesus can also be found on Wikipedia ☺ and thousands of other works
https://en.wikipedia.org/wiki/Jesus

ccxlv Transcript from „Bishop Robert Barron | The Ben Shapiro Show Sunday Special Ep. 31", published on The Daily Wire YouTube Channel, on Dec 16, 2018
https://youtu.be/OoDt8wWQsiA

ccxlvi Transcript from Bishop Robert Barron, "Who is Jesus?", published on Bishop Robert Barron YouTube Channel
https://youtu.be/4Y4xacvLUXo

ccxlvii The Bible, John, Chapter 14.
Source: New International Version (NIV):
https://www.christianity.com/bible/bible.php?q=John+14&ver=niv
Other online sources:
https://www.catholic.org/bible/book.php?id=50&bible_chapter=14
https://biblehub.com/bsb/john/14.htm
https://www.bible.com/bible/1/JHN.14.KJV

ccxlviii Bart Ehrman, "Did Jesus Exist?" (New York: HarperCollins, 2012), 339.

ccxlix Adam Hamilton, "CREED WHAT CHRISTIANS BELIEVE AND WHY", "EXPLORING THE APOSTOLES' CREED", 2016 Abingdon Press / Nashville, Chapter 2. Jesus Christ. Page 38-39.

ccl Adam Hamilton, "CREED WHAT CHRISTIANS BELIEVE AND WHY", "EXPLORING THE APOSTOLES' CREED", 2016 Abingdon Press / Nashville, Chapter 2. Jesus Christ. Page 69.

ccli Adam Hamilton, "CREED WHAT CHRISTIANS BELIEVE AND WHY", "EXPLORING THE APOSTOLES' CREED", 2016 Abingdon Press / Nashville, Chapter 2. Jesus Christ. Page 75.
cclii Transcript from „Bishop Robert Barron | The Ben Shapiro Show Sunday Special Ep. 31", published on The Daily Wire YouTube Channel, on Dec 16, 2018
https://youtu.be/OoDt8wWQsiA

cclii The Bible, 2 Timothy, Chapter 4.
Online source:
https://www.christianity.com/bible/bible.php?q=2+Timothy+4&ver=niv

ccliv The Bible, Matthew, Chapter 15.
Source:
https://www.catholic.org/bible/book.php?id=47&bible_chapter=22
Other online sources:
https://biblehub.com/bsb/matthew/22.htm
https://www.bible.com/bible/1/MAT.22.KJV

cclv Saint Thomas Aquinas, Summa Theologica (1265–1274), II-II, q. 26, art. 6

cclvi The Bible, Matthew, Chapter 15.
Source:
https://www.catholic.org/bible/book.php?id=47&bible_chapter=22
Other online sources:
https://biblehub.com/bsb/matthew/22.htm
https://www.bible.com/bible/1/MAT.22.KJV

cclvii The Bible, Luke, Chapter 10
Source:
https://www.catholic.org/bible/book.php?id=49&bible_chapter=10
Other online sources:
https://biblehub.com/bsb/luke/10.htm
https://www.bible.com/bible/1/LUK.10.KJV

cclviii The Bible, 1 John, Chapter 3.
Online source:
https://www.christianity.com/bible/bible.php?q=1+John+3&ver=niv

cclix Transcript from "Bishop Robert Barron | The Ben Shapiro Show Sunday Special Ep. 31", published on The Daily Wire YouTube Channel, on Dec 16, 2018
https://youtu.be/OoDt8wWQsiA

cclx The Bible, Matthew, Chapter 5. Jesus said:
Source:
https://www.catholic.org/bible/book.php?id=47&bible_chapter=5
Other online sources:
https://biblehub.com/bsb/matthew/5.htm
https://www.bible.com/bible/1/MAT.5.KJV

cclxi Transcript from „Bishop Robert Barron | The Ben Shapiro Show Sunday Special Ep. 31", published on The Daily Wire YouTube Channel, on Dec 16, 2018
https://youtu.be/OoDt8wWQsiA

cclxii The Bible, John, Chapter 13. Jesus said:
Source:
https://www.christianity.com/bible/bible.php?q=john+13&ver=niv

cclxiii The Bible, Luke, Chapter 9. Jesus said:
Source:
https://www.catholic.org/bible/book.php?id=49&bible_chapter=9
Other online sources:
https://biblehub.com/bsb/luke/9.htm
https://www.bible.com/bible/1/LUK.9.KJV

cclxiv The Bible, John, Chapter 15. Jesus said:
Source:
https://www.catholic.org/bible/book.php?bible_chapter=15&id=50
Other online sources:
https://biblehub.com/bsb/john/15.htm
https://www.bible.com/bible/1/JHN.15.KJV

cclxv Transcript from „Bishop Robert Barron | The Ben Shapiro Show Sunday Special Ep. 31", published on The Daily Wire YouTube Channel, on Dec 16, 2018
https://youtu.be/0oDt8wWQsiA

cclxvi Transcript from "Bishop Robert Barron | The Ben Shapiro Show Sunday Special Ep. 31", published on The Daily Wire YouTube Channel, on Dec 16, 2018
https://youtu.be/0oDt8wWQsiA

cclxvii The Bible, 1 Corinthians, Chapter 13. Love
Online source:
https://www.christianity.com/bible/bible.php?q=1+Cor+13&ver=niv

cclxviii Own summary and translation of the lecture by Polish priest Marek Dziewiecki: "ks. Marek Dziewiecki - O miłości w małżeństwie i rodzinie - Konferencja w Białystoku", published on „Dobre Media Nowej Ewangelizacji" YouTube Channel, Oct 31, 2017
https://youtu.be/FgPgHhwGbLg

cclxix "Why are we here? Why are we born? | Ajahn Brahm |" published on Buddhist Society of Western Australia YouTube Channel on Jan 10, 2015.
"This talk by Ajahn Brahm gets to the heart of the existential quest: What are we here? What were we born for?"
https://youtu.be/-RrCjzi74BA

cclxx Transcript from „Bishop Barron on Having a 'Personal Relationship' with Jesus", published on Bishop Robert Barron YouTube Channel, on Dec 8, 2016
https://youtu.be/w2KZDQSxwF4

cclxxi "Cheek to Cheek" is a song written by Irving Berlin in 1935, for the Fred Astaire/Ginger Rogers movie Top Hat (1935).

cclxxii "Meet Joe Black" is a 1998 American romantic fantasy film directed and produced by Martin Brest, and starring Brad Pitt, Anthony Hopkins, and Claire Forlani.
Quoted fragment taken from "Meet Joe Black (1998) - Lightning Could Strike Scene (1/10) | Movieclips" published on Movieclips YouTube Channel.
https://youtu.be/9EV3DKPo-4U

cclxxiii The Bible, Matthew, Chapter 25.
Online source:
https://www.christianity.com/bible/bible.php?q=Mathew+25&ver=niv

cclxxiv The Bible, John, Chapter 18.
Online source:
https://www.christianity.com/bible/bible.php?q=john+18&ver=niv

cclxxv "What causes ocean waves?"
https://oceanexplorer.noaa.gov/facts/waves.html

cclxxvi "Oceans in Motion: Waves and Tides"
https://ci.coastal.edu/~sgilman/770Oceansinmotion.htm

cclxxvii Anna Maria Jopek „A Niebo, wieczne Niebo Jeśli jest sumą naszych dusz, To blisko nam do niego. Tuż tuż." (My translation from Polish: "If Heaven, eternal Heaven is the sum of our souls, we are almost there, so close to it, so close")

Anna Maria Jopek (born 14 December 1970) is a Polish vocalist, songwriter, and improviser. She records and tours all over the world with the most outstanding artists of our times. In Poland she had the honor of singing with Marek Grechuta, Jeremi Przybora or Wojciech Młynarski. Abroad she shared the stage with Pat Metheny, Youssu'n Dour, Bobby McFerrin, Ivan Linz, Branford Marsalis, Nigel Kennedy, Richard Bona, Oscar Castro-Neves, Makoto Ozone and Gonzalo Rubalcaba among others. In 2017 Anna also spontaneously sung a duet with Sting at a New Year's TV program. Anna Maria Jopek has performed at the world's most renowned concert halls such as: Carnegie Hall, Hollywood Bowl, Royal Festival Hall, Tokyo Opera City Concert Hall, Blue Note Tokyo, The Israeli Opera in Tel Aviv or Hamer Hall in Melbourne. She recorded at Peter Gabriel's Real World studio, Abbey Road in London and Power Station in New York. She has received numerous awards for her music.
https://youtu.be/7XVyQsRJygs
http://annamariajopek.pl/en/
https://en.wikipedia.org/wiki/Anna_Maria_Jopek

cclxxviii The Bible. Colossians, Chapter 1.
Online source:
https://www.christianity.com/bible/bible.php?q=Colossians+1&ver=niv

cclxxix Adam Hamilton, "WHY? MAKING SENSE OF GOD's WILL", Abington Press / Nashville, 2011. Page 1-2.

cclxxx Adam Hamilton, "WHY? MAKING SENSE OF GOD's WILL", Abington Press / Nashville, 2011. Page 8-9.

cclxxxi Adam Hamilton, "WHY? MAKING SENSE OF GOD's WILL", Abington Press / Nashville, 2011. Page 4-5.

cclxxxii "Free will in theology" as per Wikipedia
https://en.wikipedia.org/wiki/Free_will_in_theology

cclxxxiii Adam Hamilton, "WHY? MAKING SENSE OF GOD's WILL", Abington Press / Nashville, 2011. Page 20-23.

cclxxxiv Adam Hamilton, "CREED WHAT CHRISTIANS BELIEVE AND WHY", "EXPLORING THE APOSTOLES' CREED", 2016 Abingdon Press / Nashville. Chapter 2. Jesus Christ. PAGE 52.

cclxxxv "A Socratic Perspective on the Nature of Human Evil" by Max Maxwell and Melete, Essay Version 2.0
http://www.socraticmethod.net/socratic_essay_nature_of_human_evil.htm

cclxxxvi The Bible, Romans, Chapter 7.
Online source:
https://www.christianity.com/bible/bible.php?q=roman+7&ver=niv

cclxxxvii Adam Hamilton, "WHY? MAKING SENSE OF GOD's WILL", Abington Press / Nashville, 2011. Page 12.

cclxxxviii Adam Hamilton, "WHY? MAKING SENSE OF GOD's WILL", Abington Press / Nashville, 2011. Page 17.

cclxxxix Adam Hamilton, "WHY? MAKING SENSE OF GOD's WILL", Abington Press / Nashville, 2011. Page 25.

ccxc http://gurpreetkgill.com/what-if/

ccxci Adam Hamilton, "WHY? MAKING SENSE OF GOD's WILL", Abington Press / Nashville, 2011. Page 26.

ccxcii Adam Hamilton, "WHY? MAKING SENSE OF GOD's WILL", Abington Press / Nashville, 2011. Page 28-29.

ccxciii Adam Hamilton, "CREED WHAT CHRISTIANS BELIEVE AND WHY", "EXPLORING THE APOSTOLES' CREED", 2016 Abingdon Press / Nashville, Chapter 2. Jesus Christ. Page 61-63.

ccxciv The Bible, Luke, Chapter 11.
Online source:
https://www.christianity.com/bible/bible.php?q=Luke+11&ver=niv

ccxcv "Bishop Barron on Why Do We Believe in God?" - published on Bishop Robert Barron YouTube Channel, Jul 11, 2007
https://youtu.be/qP2rLgrBtTI

ccxcvi "Bishop Barron on Why Do We Believe in God?" - published on Bishop Robert Barron YouTube Channel, Jul 11, 2007
https://youtu.be/qP2rLgrBtTI
(* reference to the book 'Introduction to Christianity' written by Joseph Ratzinger, Pope Emeritus Benedict XVI)

ccxcvii Piotr Pawlukiewicz, „Faith – it works" [original title in Polish: "Wiara - to działa | ks. Piotr Pawlukiewicz"] by Polish priest Piotr Pawlukiewicz, published on „Kazania inne niż wszystkie" YouTube Channel, on May 17, 2016
https://youtu.be/iGOTlrcAxD4
https://pl.wikipedia.org/wiki/Piotr_Pawlukiewicz

ccxcviii Adam Hamilton, "CREED WHAT CHRISTIANS BELIEVE AND WHY", "EXPLORING THE APOSTOLES' CREED", 2016 Abingdon Press / Nashville, Chapter 2. Jesus Christ. Page 76.
*Richard Dawkins, The Selfish Gene 30th Anniversary Edition (New York: Oxford University Press Inc., 2006), xxi.

ccxcix The Bible. Matthew. Chapter 14.
Online source:

https://www.christianity.com/bible/bible.php?q=Mathew+14&ver=niv
ccc The Bible. Matthew. Chapter 14.
Online source:
https://www.christianity.com/bible/bible.php?q=Mathew+14&ver=niv
ccci "Average Student Loan Debt in America: 2019 Facts & Figures"
https://www.valuepenguin.com/average-student-loan-debt
Copyright © 2020 ValuePenguin

cccii The transcript of Michelle Obama's speech at the Democratic National Convention.
"Michelle Obama delivers keynote speech from first night of the Democratic National Convention", published on CNBC Television YouTube channel, Aug 17, 2020.
https://youtu.be/Czn0nxFNy0Q

ccciii Laurie Santos is an Associate Professor in the Department of Psychology at Yale University. She hosts the popular podcast The Happiness Lab and she teaches the most popular course offered at Yale to date, titled The Science of Well-Being. Laurie is also the director of the Comparative Cognition Laboratory and the Canine Cognition Center at Yale. She received her A.B. in Psychology and Biology from Harvard University in 1997 and her Ph.D. in Psychology from Harvard in 2003.
Twitter:@lauriesantos
https://caplab.yale.edu/
https://coursera.org/share/703ac204d3ca55e126d3c76100b9c638

ccciv THE COLOR OF CORONAVIRUS: COVID-19 DEATHS BY RACE AND ETHNICITY IN THE U.S. by APM Research Lab.
https://www.apmresearchlab.org/covid/deaths-by-race

cccv "Essential and Frontline Workers in the COVID-19 Crisis" by Francine D. Blau, Josefine Koebe and Pamela A. Meyerhofer·April 30, 2020, Cornell University and DIW Berlin / Universität Hamburg
https://econofact.org/essential-and-frontline-workers-in-the-covid-19-crisis

cccvi First responder
https://en.wikipedia.org/wiki/First_responder
Text is available under the Creative Commons Attribution-ShareAlike License.
Wikipedia® is a registered trademark of the Wikimedia Foundation, Inc., a non-profit organization.

cccvii "Essential and Frontline Workers in the COVID-19 Crisis" by Francine D. Blau, Josefine Koebe and Pamela A. Meyerhofer·April 30, 2020, Cornell University and DIW Berlin / Universität Hamburg
https://econofact.org/essential-and-frontline-workers-in-the-covid-19-crisis

Made in the USA
Columbia, SC
11 November 2020